TRY REBOOTING YOURSELF

P9-DYD-787

TRY REBOOTING YOURSELF

A DILBERT™ BOOK
BY SCOTT ADAMS

Andrews McMeel
Publishing, LLC

Kansas City

DILBERT® is a registered trademark of Scott Adams, Inc. Licensed by United Feature Syndicate, Inc.

DOGBERT® and DILBERT® appear in the comic strip DILBERT®, distributed by United Feature Syndicate, Inc., and owned by Scott Adams, Inc. Licensed by United Feature Syndicate, Inc.

Try Rebooting Yourself copyright © 2006 by Scott Adams, Inc. All rights reserved. Licensed by United Feature Syndicate, Inc. Printed in the United States of America. No part of this book may be used or reproduced in any manner whatsoever without written permission except in the case of reprints in the context of reviews. For information, write Andrews McMeel Publishing, LLC, an Andrews McMeel Universal company, 4520 Main Street, Kansas City, Missouri 64111.

06 07 08 09 10 BBG 10 9 8 7 6 5 4 3 2 1

ISBN-13: 978-0-7407-6190-4
ISBN-10: 0-7407-6190-0

Library of Congress Control Number: 2006925658

www.andrewsmcmeel.com

www.dilbert.com

—— **ATTENTION: SCHOOLS AND BUSINESSES** ——

Andrews McMeel books are available at quantity discounts with bulk purchase for educational, business, or sales promotional use. For information, please write to: Special Sales Department, Andrews McMeel Publishing, LLC, 4520 Main Street, Kansas City, Missouri 64111.

Other DILBERT® books from Andrews McMeel Publishing

What Would Wally Do?
ISBN: 0-7407-5769-5

Thriving on Vague Objectives
ISBN: 0-7407-5533-1

The Fluorescent Light Glistens Off Your Head
ISBN: 0-7407-5113-1

It's Not Funny If I Have to Explain It
ISBN: 0-7407-4658-8

Don't Stand Where the Comet Is Assumed to Strike Oil
ISBN: 0-7407-4539-5

Words You Don't Want to Hear During Your Annual Performance Review
ISBN: 0-7407-3805-4

When Body Language Goes Bad
ISBN: 0-7407-3298-6

What Do You Call a Sociopath in a Cubicle? Answer: A Coworker
ISBN: 0-7407-2663-3

Another Day in Cubicle Paradise
ISBN: 0-7407-2194-1

When Did Ignorance Become a Point of View?
ISBN: 0-7407-1839-8

Excuse Me While I Wag
ISBN: 0-7407-1390-6

Dilbert—A Treasury of Sunday Strips: Version 00
ISBN: 0-7407-0531-8

Random Acts of Management
ISBN: 0-7407-0453-2

Dilbert Gives You the Business
ISBN: 0-7407-0338-2 hardcover
ISBN: 0-7407-0003-0 paperback

Don't Step in the Leadership
ISBN: 0-8362-7844-5

Journey to Cubeville
ISBN: 0-8362-7175-0 hardcover
ISBN: 0-8362-6745-1 paperback

I'm Not Anti-Business, I'm Anti-Idiot
ISBN: 0-8362-5182-2

Seven Years of Highly Defective People
ISBN: 0-8362-5129-6 hardcover
ISBN: 0-8362-3668-8 paperback

Casual Day Has Gone Too Far
ISBN: 0-8362-2899-5

Fugitive from the Cubicle Police
ISBN: 0-8362-2119-2

It's Obvious You Won't Survive by Your Wits Alone
ISBN: 0-8362-0415-8

Still Pumped from Using the Mouse
ISBN: 0-8362-1026-3

Bring Me the Head of Willy the Mailboy!
ISBN: 0-8362-1779-9

Shave the Whales
ISBN: 0-8362-1740-3

Dogbert's Clues for the Clueless
ISBN: 0-8362-1737-3

Always Postpone Meetings with Time-Wasting Morons
ISBN: 0-8362-1758-6

Build a Better Life by Stealing Office Supplies
ISBN: 0-8362-1757-8

For ordering information, call 1-800-223-2336.

Introduction

I've noticed that whenever there's a gap in my knowledge it's because my busy schedule hasn't allowed me the time to research everything that there is to know. But when other people have gaps in their knowledge it's because they are ignorant morons. Sometimes they deserve corporal punishment.

Recently I started my own blog (see www.dilbert.com for the link). I was shocked to find out that everyone else thinks I'm the ignorant moron and they are the ones who haven't thoroughly researched everything! Those ignorant morons keep getting everything backward. That is so like them.

I often wish I could reboot other people the way I reboot my computer. For example, do you know anyone who keeps repeating the same point or story over and over? They change the words slightly each time, but you know a loop when you hear one.

Example

Loop Guy: "Chicken soup is good for a cold."

You: "Yup."

Loop Guy: "If you have a cold, have some chicken soup."

You: "Uh-huh."

Loop Guy: "My mom always said chicken soup was good for a cold, and now I know she's right."

You: "Yeah."

Loop Guy: "The next time you feel a sniffle, get yourself some chicken soup."

At this point you realize that the looper will never stop repeating this point no matter how many times you agree with it. Changing the subject won't work. He'll just change it back.

You: "Did you see the basketball game last night?"

Loop Guy: "Their guards couldn't hit the three-pointers. Maybe they have colds."

You: "Oh, lord. No, please."

Loop Guy: "Their coach should have given them chicken soup."

You could try setting his hair on fire, but he'd start yelling for chicken soup to douse the flame, and then more chicken soup to ease the pain. You'd be back to square one.

Your only recourse is to lick your finger and stick it in his ear. That is as close as you can get to the human reboot button. I don't know that the so-called experts recognize it as such, but I'm guessing that people change the subject when you stick a saliva-laden digit in their aural cavity. I haven't actually tried it, but as soon as I get some time in my busy schedule, I plan to research whether it works.

Speaking of gaps in knowledge, did you know there's still time to join Dogbert's New Ruling Class and be his right paw when he conquers the world and makes everyone else your personal servants? All you need to do is sign up for the free Dilbert Newsletter that is published approximately whenever I feel like it. To sign up, go to www.dilbert.com and follow the subscription instructions. If that doesn't work for some reason, send an e-mail to newsletter@unitedmedia.com.

S.Adams

Scott Adams

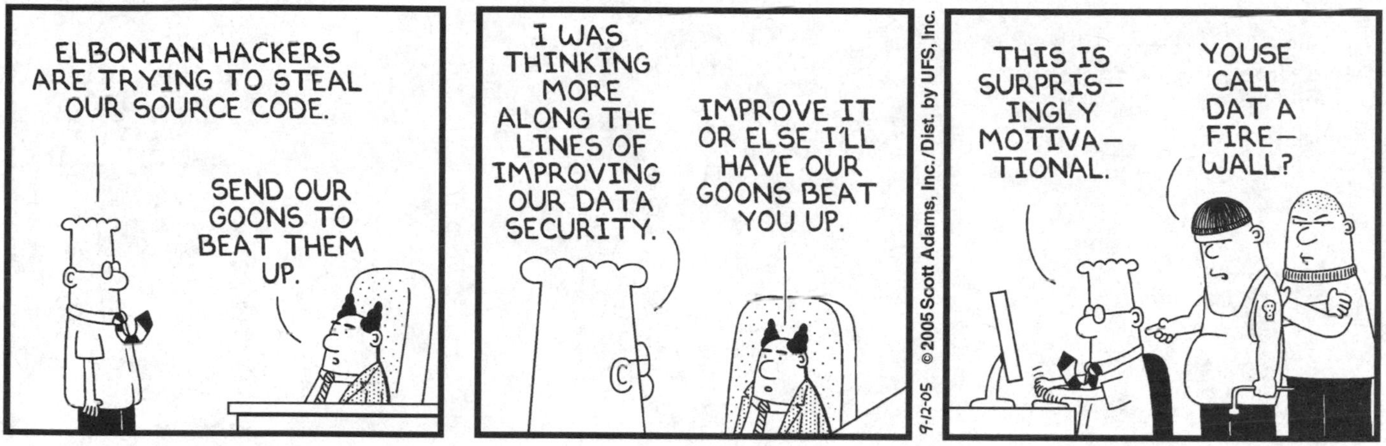
ELBONIAN HACKERS ARE TRYING TO STEAL OUR SOURCE CODE.
SEND OUR GOONS TO BEAT THEM UP.
I WAS THINKING MORE ALONG THE LINES OF IMPROVING OUR DATA SECURITY.
IMPROVE IT OR ELSE I'LL HAVE OUR GOONS BEAT YOU UP.
9-12-05 © 2005 Scott Adams, Inc./Dist. by UFS, Inc.
THIS IS SURPRIS- INGLY MOTIVA- TIONAL.
YOUSE CALL DAT A FIRE- WALL?

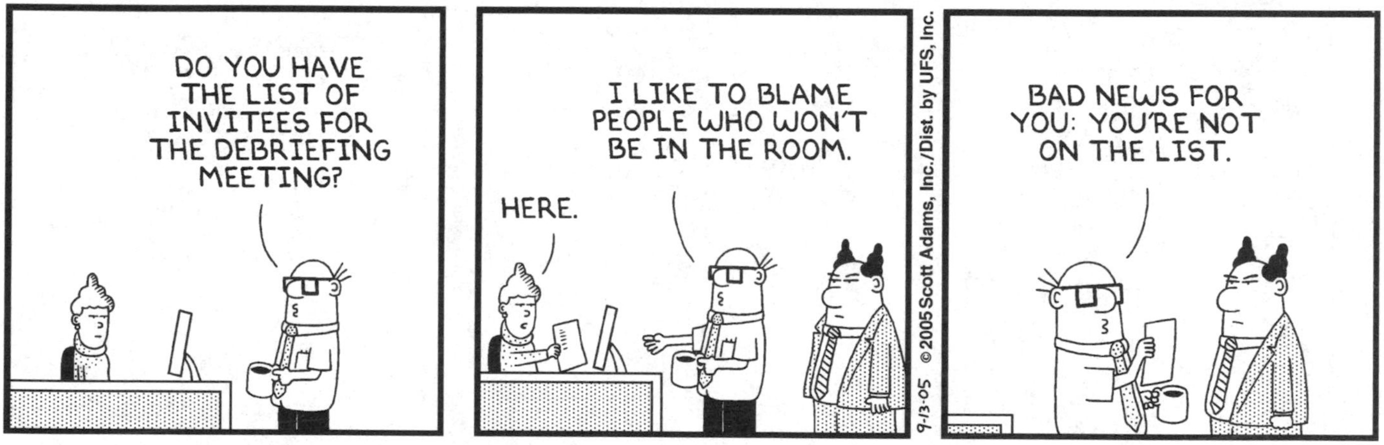
DO YOU HAVE THE LIST OF INVITEES FOR THE DEBRIEFING MEETING?
HERE.
I LIKE TO BLAME PEOPLE WHO WON'T BE IN THE ROOM.
9-13-05 © 2005 Scott Adams, Inc./Dist. by UFS, Inc.
BAD NEWS FOR YOU: YOU'RE NOT ON THE LIST.

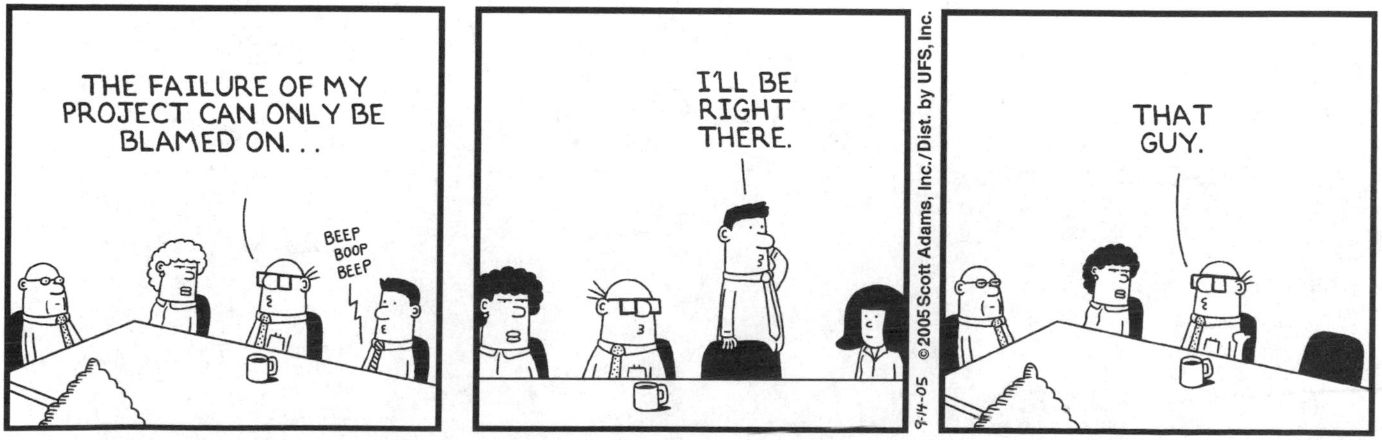
THE FAILURE OF MY PROJECT CAN ONLY BE BLAMED ON. . .
BEEP BOOP BEEP
I'LL BE RIGHT THERE.
9-14-05 © 2005 Scott Adams, Inc./Dist. by UFS, Inc.
THAT GUY.

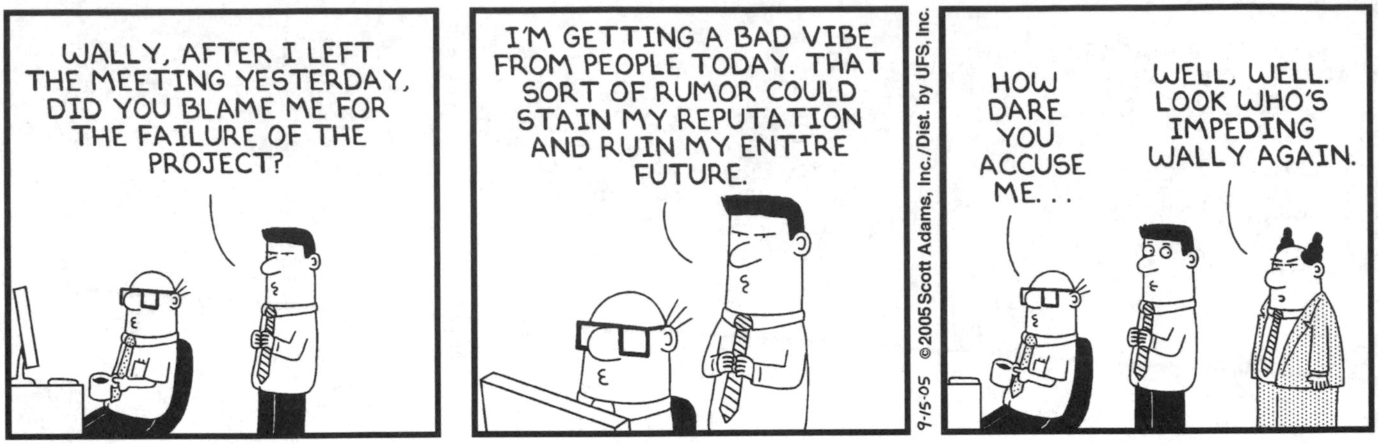
WALLY, AFTER I LEFT THE MEETING YESTERDAY, DID YOU BLAME ME FOR THE FAILURE OF THE PROJECT?
I'M GETTING A BAD VIBE FROM PEOPLE TODAY. THAT SORT OF RUMOR COULD STAIN MY REPUTATION AND RUIN MY ENTIRE FUTURE.
9-15-05 © 2005 Scott Adams, Inc./Dist. by UFS, Inc.
HOW DARE YOU ACCUSE ME. . .
WELL, WELL. LOOK WHO'S IMPEDING WALLY AGAIN.

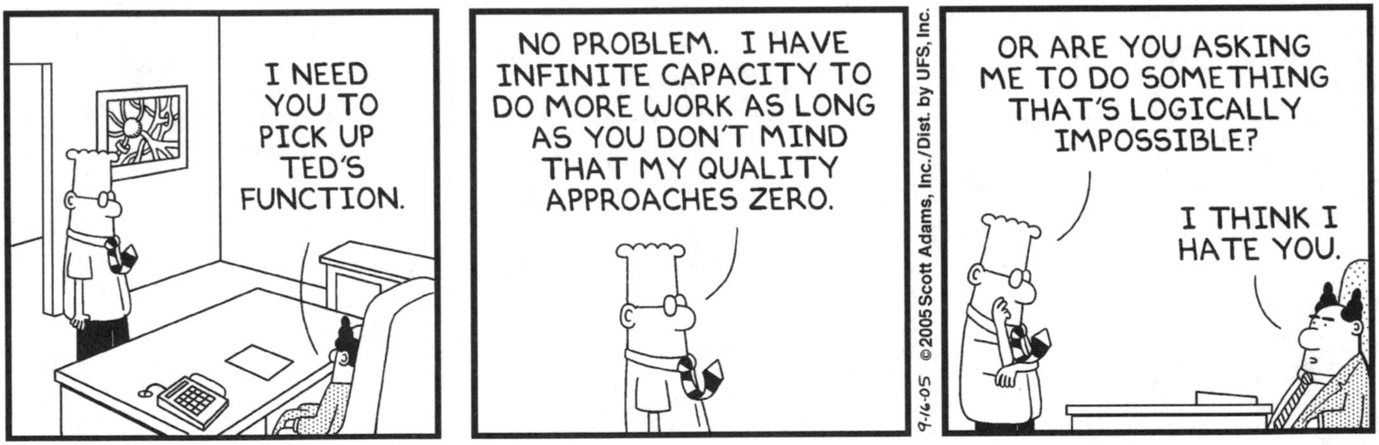
I NEED YOU TO PICK UP TED'S FUNCTION.
NO PROBLEM. I HAVE INFINITE CAPACITY TO DO MORE WORK AS LONG AS YOU DON'T MIND THAT MY QUALITY APPROACHES ZERO.
9-16-05 © 2005 Scott Adams, Inc./Dist. by UFS, Inc.
OR ARE YOU ASKING ME TO DO SOMETHING THAT'S LOGICALLY IMPOSSIBLE?
I THINK I HATE YOU.

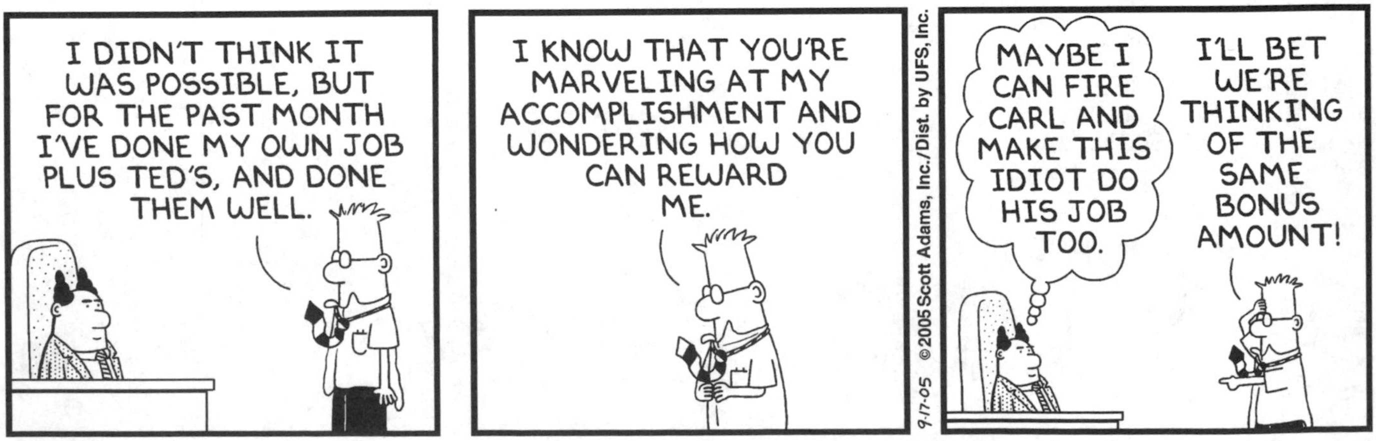
I DIDN'T THINK IT WAS POSSIBLE, BUT FOR THE PAST MONTH I'VE DONE MY OWN JOB PLUS TED'S, AND DONE THEM WELL.
I KNOW THAT YOU'RE MARVELING AT MY ACCOMPLISHMENT AND WONDERING HOW YOU CAN REWARD ME.
9-17-05 © 2005 Scott Adams, Inc./Dist. by UFS, Inc.
MAYBE I CAN FIRE CARL AND MAKE THIS IDIOT DO HIS JOB TOO.
I'LL BET WE'RE THINKING OF THE SAME BONUS AMOUNT!

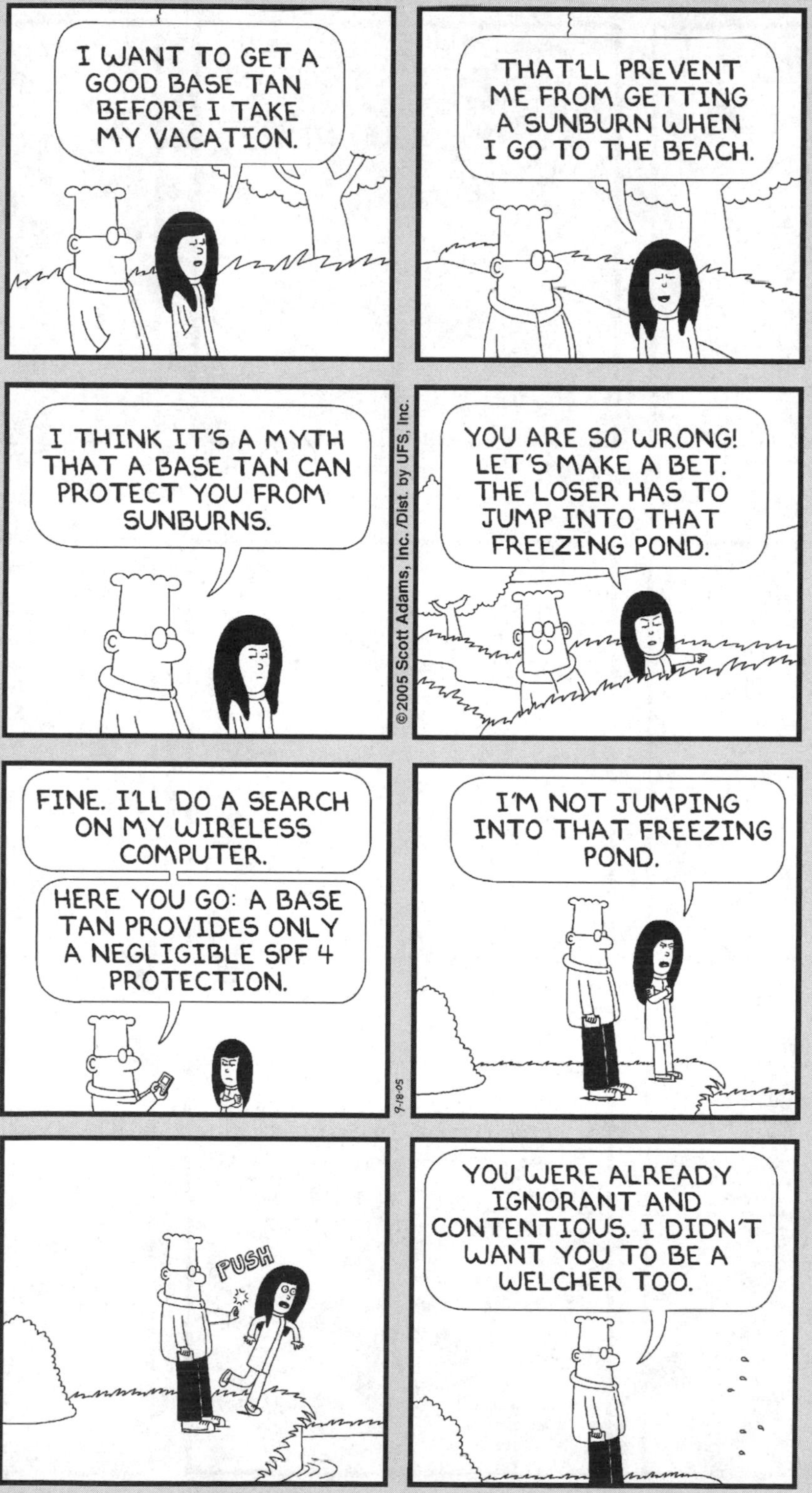
I WANT TO GET A GOOD BASE TAN BEFORE I TAKE MY VACATION.
THAT'LL PREVENT ME FROM GETTING A SUNBURN WHEN I GO TO THE BEACH.
I THINK IT'S A MYTH THAT A BASE TAN CAN PROTECT YOU FROM SUNBURNS.
YOU ARE SO WRONG! LET'S MAKE A BET. THE LOSER HAS TO JUMP INTO THAT FREEZING POND.
FINE. I'LL DO A SEARCH ON MY WIRELESS COMPUTER.
HERE YOU GO: A BASE TAN PROVIDES ONLY A NEGLIGIBLE SPF 4 PROTECTION.
I'M NOT JUMPING INTO THAT FREEZING POND.
PUSH
YOU WERE ALREADY IGNORANT AND CONTENTIOUS. I DIDN'T WANT YOU TO BE A WELCHER TOO.
©2005 Scott Adams, Inc./Dist. by UFS, Inc.
9-18-05

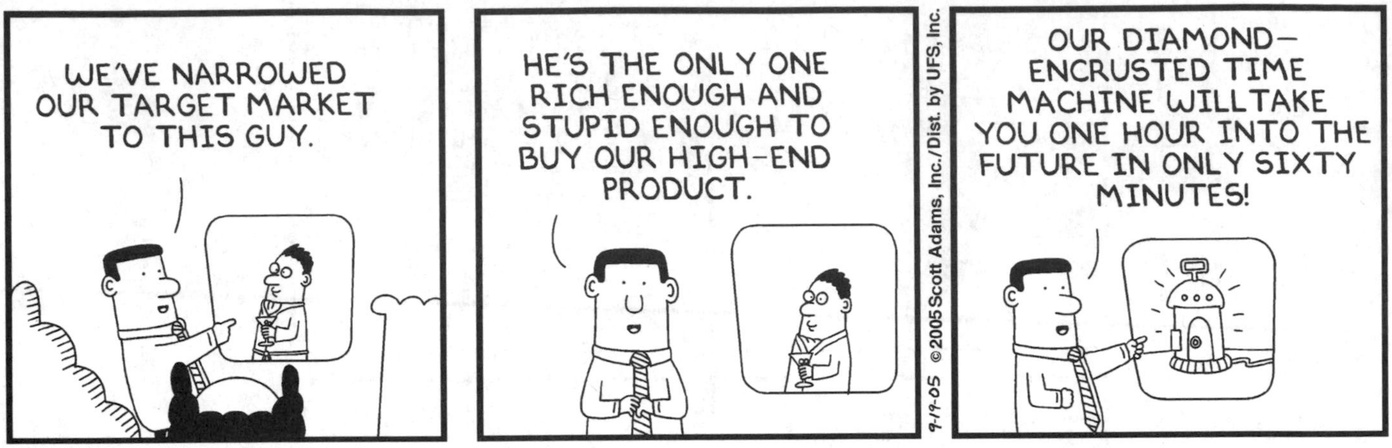
WE'VE NARROWED OUR TARGET MARKET TO THIS GUY.
HE'S THE ONLY ONE RICH ENOUGH AND STUPID ENOUGH TO BUY OUR HIGH-END PRODUCT.
9-19-05 © 2005 Scott Adams, Inc./Dist. by UFS, Inc.
OUR DIAMOND-ENCRUSTED TIME MACHINE WILLTAKE YOU ONE HOUR INTO THE FUTURE IN ONLY SIXTY MINUTES!

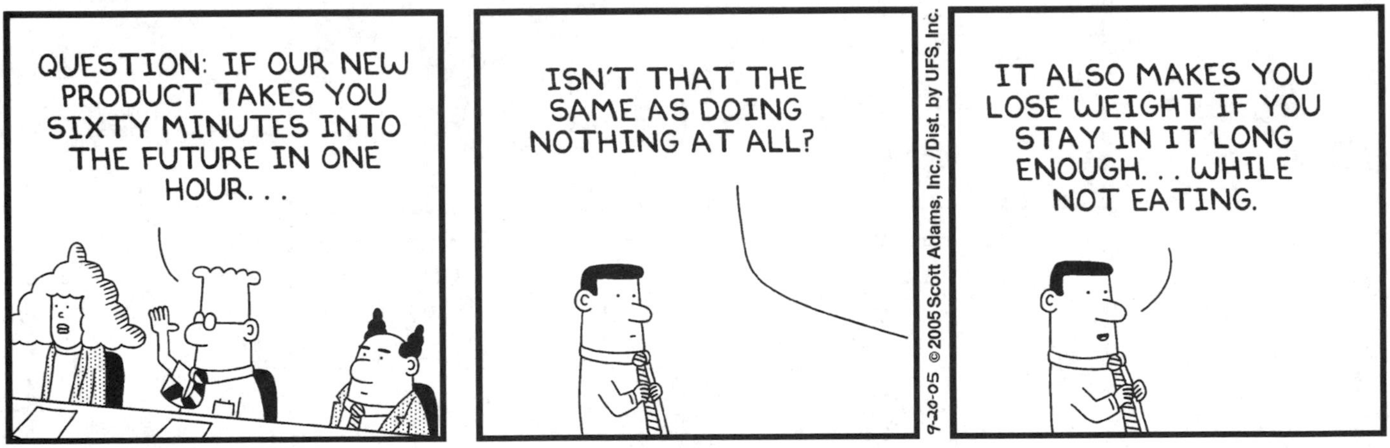
QUESTION: IF OUR NEW PRODUCT TAKES YOU SIXTY MINUTES INTO THE FUTURE IN ONE HOUR...
ISN'T THAT THE SAME AS DOING NOTHING AT ALL?
9-20-05 © 2005 Scott Adams, Inc./Dist. by UFS, Inc.
IT ALSO MAKES YOU LOSE WEIGHT IF YOU STAY IN IT LONG ENOUGH... WHILE NOT EATING.

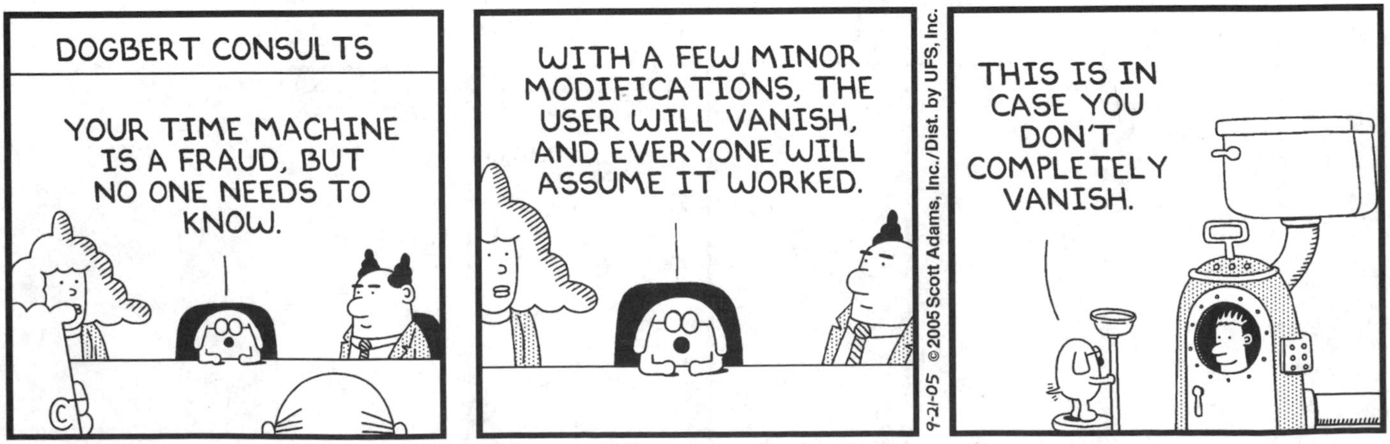
DOGBERT CONSULTS
YOUR TIME MACHINE IS A FRAUD, BUT NO ONE NEEDS TO KNOW.
WITH A FEW MINOR MODIFICATIONS, THE USER WILL VANISH, AND EVERYONE WILL ASSUME IT WORKED.
9-21-05 © 2005 Scott Adams, Inc./Dist. by UFS, Inc.
THIS IS IN CASE YOU DON'T COMPLETELY VANISH.

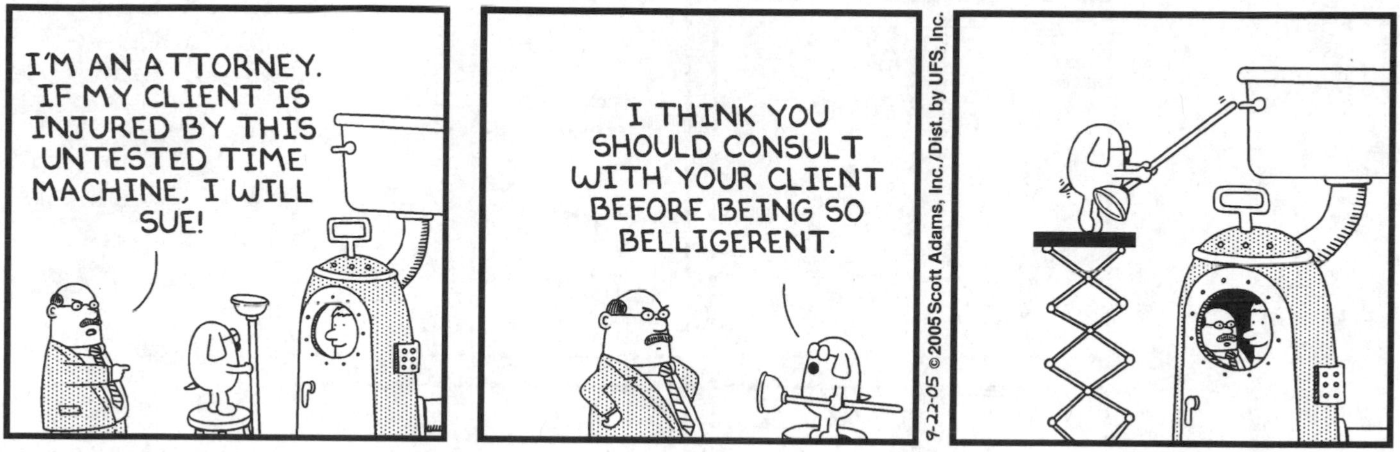
I'M AN ATTORNEY. IF MY CLIENT IS INJURED BY THIS UNTESTED TIME MACHINE, I WILL SUE!
I THINK YOU SHOULD CONSULT WITH YOUR CLIENT BEFORE BEING SO BELLIGERENT.
9-22-05 © 2005 Scott Adams, Inc./Dist. by UFS, Inc.

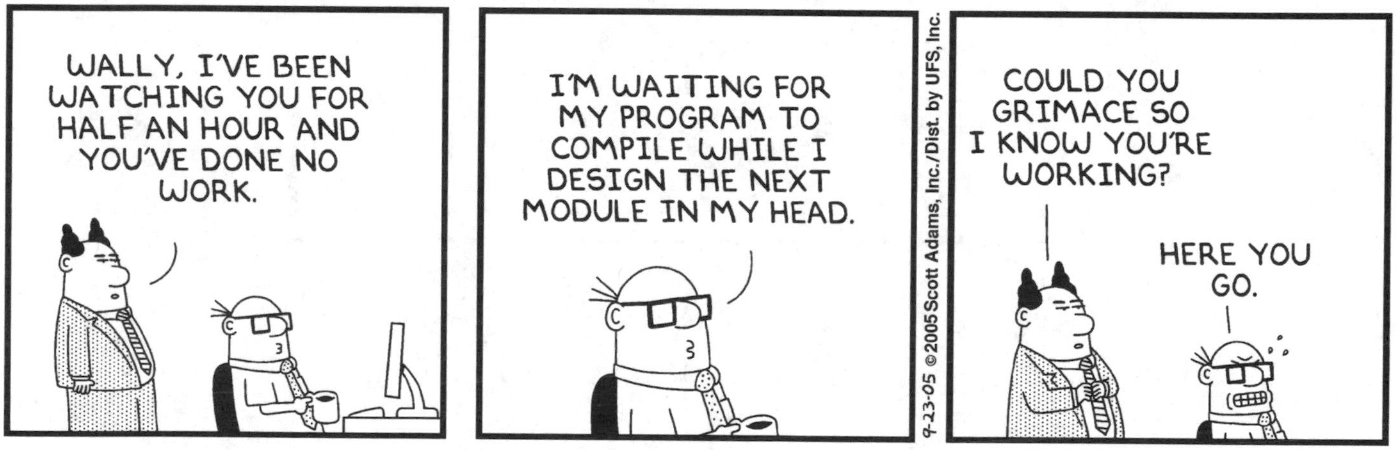
WALLY, I'VE BEEN WATCHING YOU FOR HALF AN HOUR AND YOU'VE DONE NO WORK.
I'M WAITING FOR MY PROGRAM TO COMPILE WHILE I DESIGN THE NEXT MODULE IN MY HEAD.
9-23-05 © 2005 Scott Adams, Inc./Dist. by UFS, Inc.
COULD YOU GRIMACE SO I KNOW YOU'RE WORKING?
HERE YOU GO.

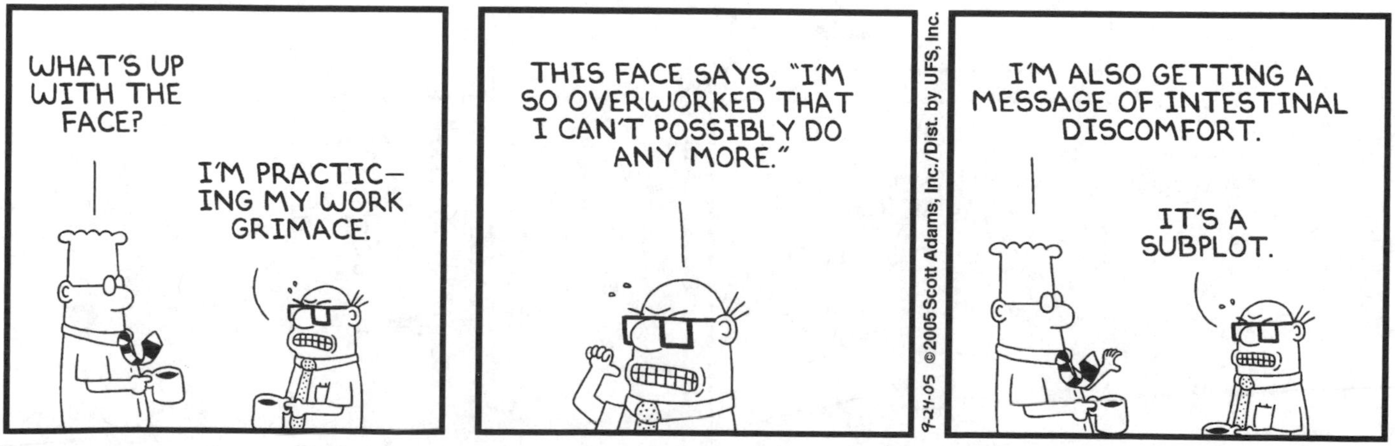
WHAT'S UP WITH THE FACE?
I'M PRACTIC-ING MY WORK GRIMACE.
THIS FACE SAYS, "I'M SO OVERWORKED THAT I CAN'T POSSIBLY DO ANY MORE."
9-24-05 © 2005 Scott Adams, Inc./Dist. by UFS, Inc.
I'M ALSO GETTING A MESSAGE OF INTESTINAL DISCOMFORT.
IT'S A SUBPLOT.

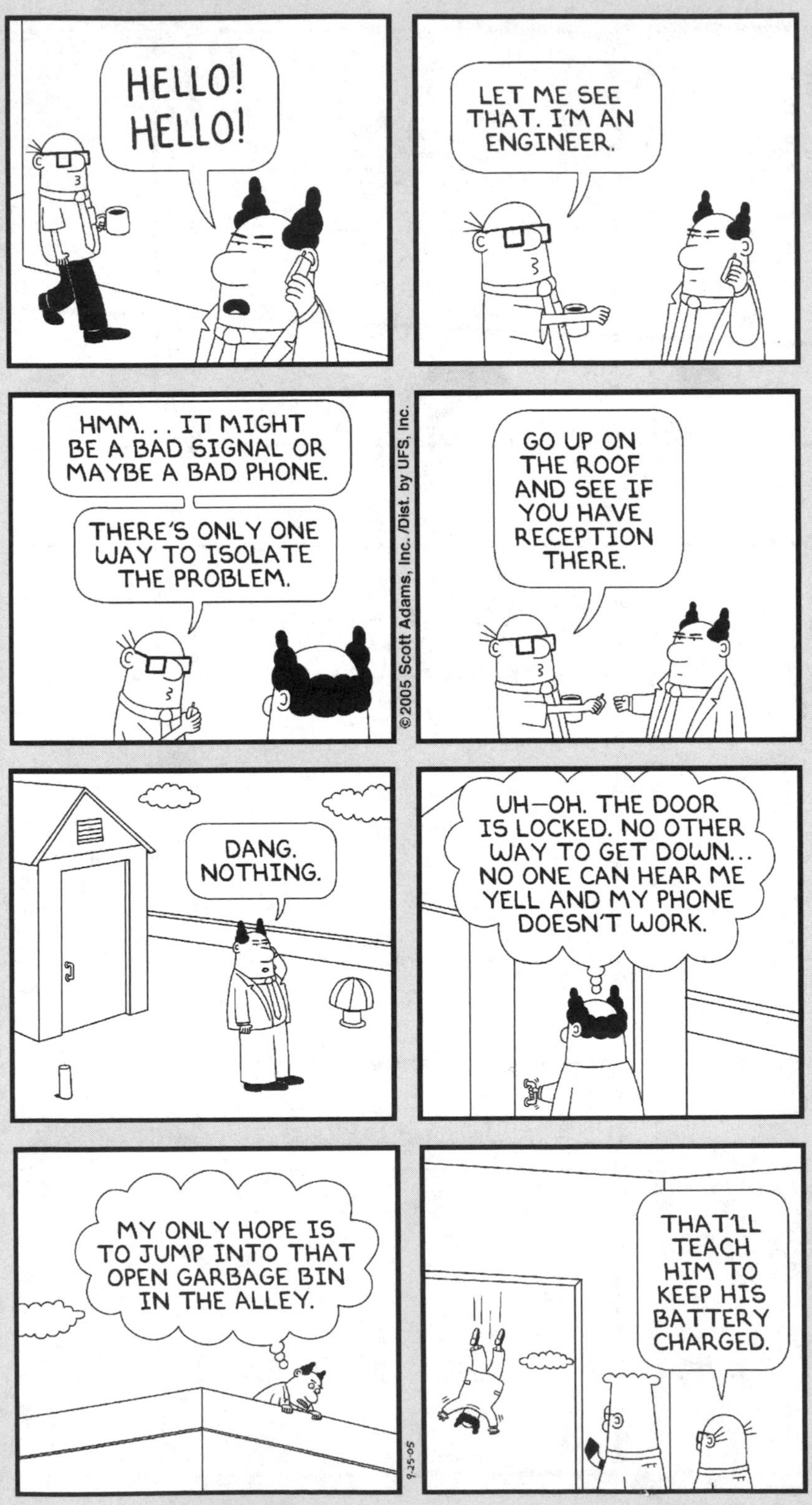
HELLO! HELLO!
LET ME SEE THAT. I'M AN ENGINEER.
HMM. . . IT MIGHT BE A BAD SIGNAL OR MAYBE A BAD PHONE.
THERE'S ONLY ONE WAY TO ISOLATE THE PROBLEM.
GO UP ON THE ROOF AND SEE IF YOU HAVE RECEPTION THERE.
DANG. NOTHING.
UH—OH. THE DOOR IS LOCKED. NO OTHER WAY TO GET DOWN... NO ONE CAN HEAR ME YELL AND MY PHONE DOESN'T WORK.
MY ONLY HOPE IS TO JUMP INTO THAT OPEN GARBAGE BIN IN THE ALLEY.
THAT'LL TEACH HIM TO KEEP HIS BATTERY CHARGED.
©2005 Scott Adams, Inc./Dist. by UFS, Inc.
9-25-05

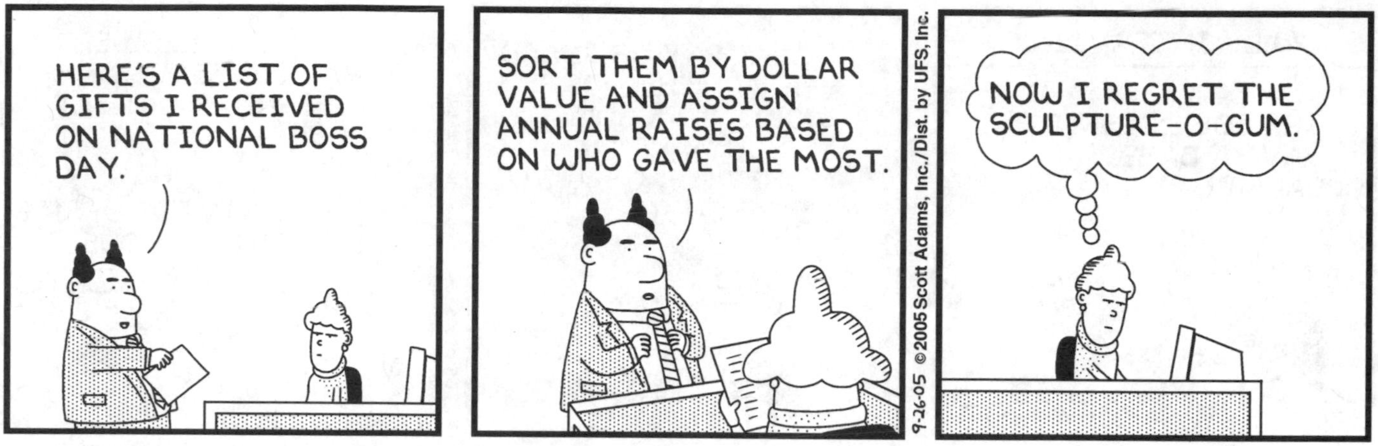
HERE'S A LIST OF GIFTS I RECEIVED ON NATIONAL BOSS DAY.
SORT THEM BY DOLLAR VALUE AND ASSIGN ANNUAL RAISES BASED ON WHO GAVE THE MOST.
9-26-05 ©2005 Scott Adams, Inc./Dist. by UFS, Inc.
NOW I REGRET THE SCULPTURE-O-GUM.

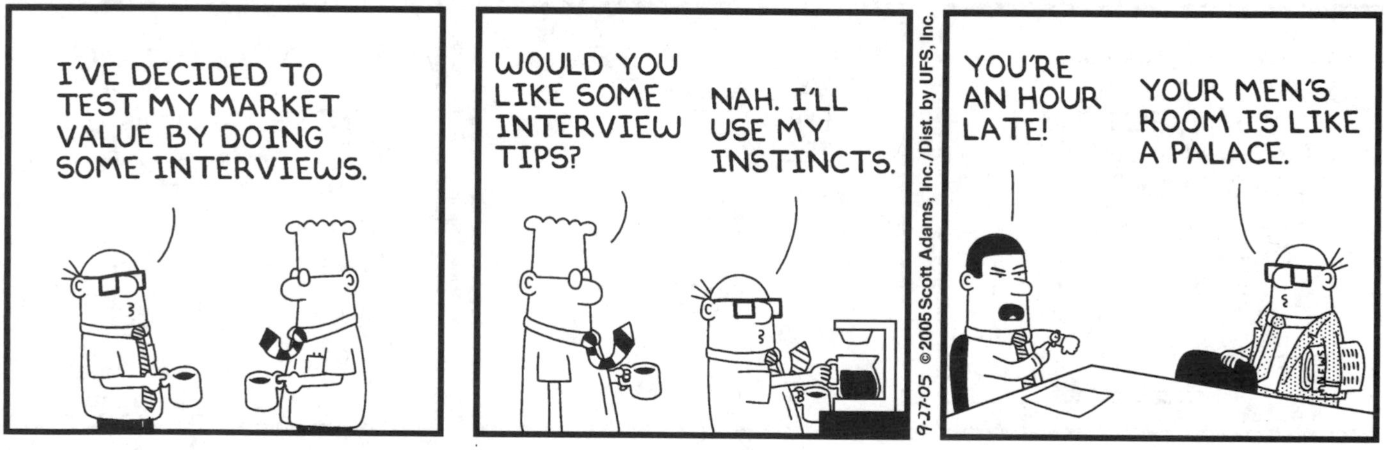
I'VE DECIDED TO TEST MY MARKET VALUE BY DOING SOME INTERVIEWS.
WOULD YOU LIKE SOME INTERVIEW TIPS?
NAH. I'LL USE MY INSTINCTS.
9-27-05 ©2005 Scott Adams, Inc./Dist. by UFS, Inc.
YOU'RE AN HOUR LATE!
YOUR MEN'S ROOM IS LIKE A PALACE.

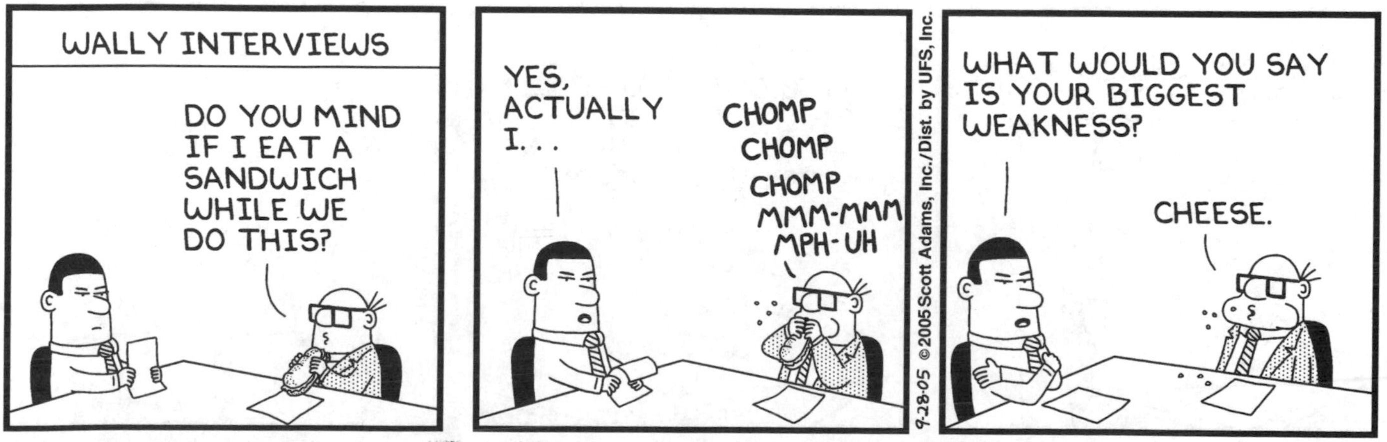
WALLY INTERVIEWS
DO YOU MIND IF I EAT A SANDWICH WHILE WE DO THIS?
YES, ACTUALLY I...
CHOMP
CHOMP
CHOMP
MMM-MMM
MPH-UH
9-28-05 ©2005 Scott Adams, Inc./Dist. by UFS, Inc.
WHAT WOULD YOU SAY IS YOUR BIGGEST WEAKNESS?
CHEESE.

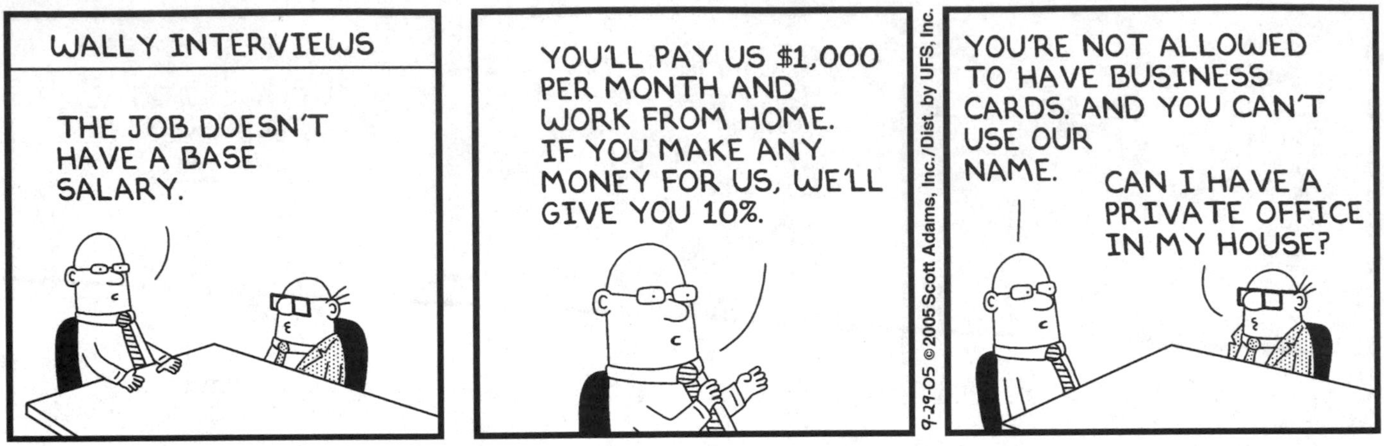
WALLY INTERVIEWS
THE JOB DOESN'T HAVE A BASE SALARY.
YOU'LL PAY US $1,000 PER MONTH AND WORK FROM HOME. IF YOU MAKE ANY MONEY FOR US, WE'LL GIVE YOU 10%.
9-29-05 © 2005 Scott Adams, Inc./Dist. by UFS, Inc.
YOU'RE NOT ALLOWED TO HAVE BUSINESS CARDS. AND YOU CAN'T USE OUR NAME.
CAN I HAVE A PRIVATE OFFICE IN MY HOUSE?

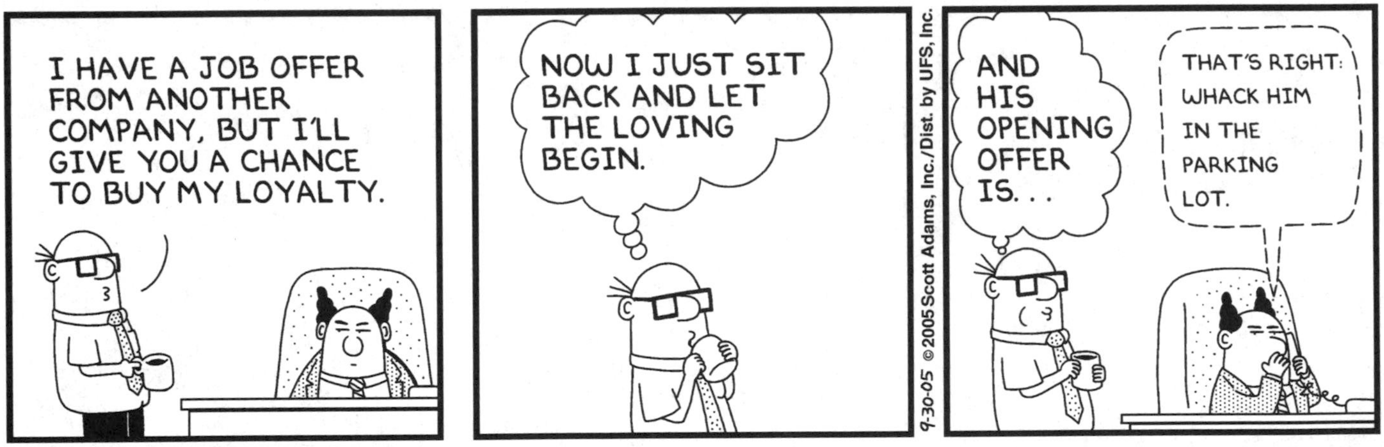
I HAVE A JOB OFFER FROM ANOTHER COMPANY, BUT I'LL GIVE YOU A CHANCE TO BUY MY LOYALTY.
NOW I JUST SIT BACK AND LET THE LOVING BEGIN.
9-30-05 © 2005 Scott Adams, Inc./Dist. by UFS, Inc.
AND HIS OPENING OFFER IS. . .
THAT'S RIGHT: WHACK HIM IN THE PARKING LOT.

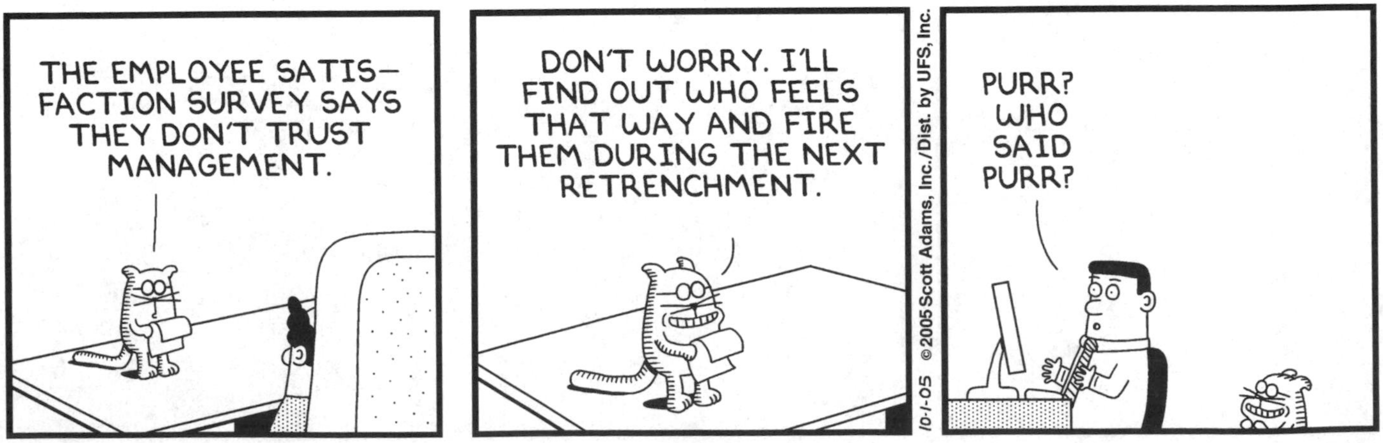
THE EMPLOYEE SATIS-FACTION SURVEY SAYS THEY DON'T TRUST MANAGEMENT.
DON'T WORRY. I'LL FIND OUT WHO FEELS THAT WAY AND FIRE THEM DURING THE NEXT RETRENCHMENT.
10-1-05 © 2005 Scott Adams, Inc./Dist. by UFS, Inc.
PURR? WHO SAID PURR?

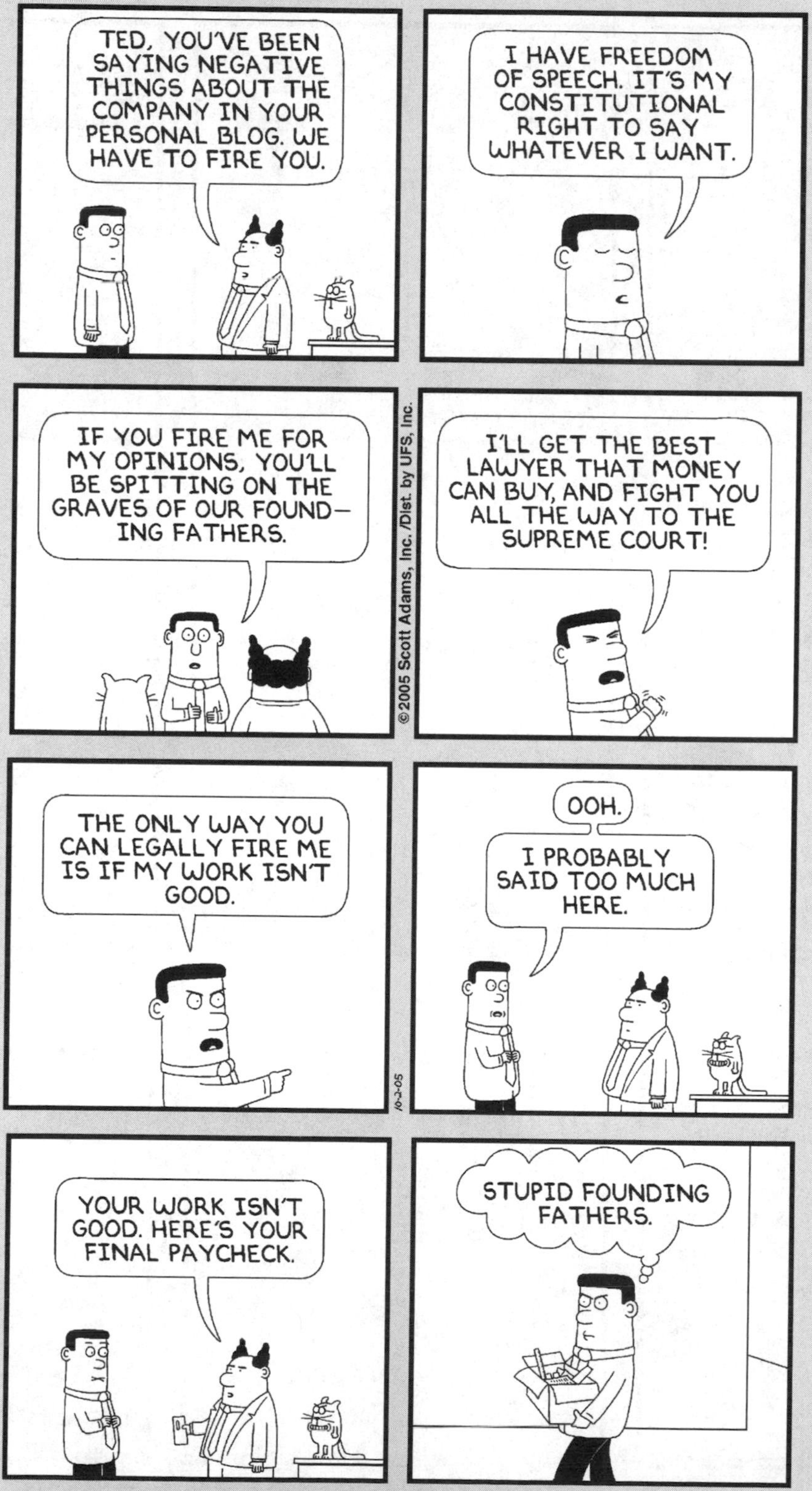
TED, YOU'VE BEEN SAYING NEGATIVE THINGS ABOUT THE COMPANY IN YOUR PERSONAL BLOG. WE HAVE TO FIRE YOU.
I HAVE FREEDOM OF SPEECH. IT'S MY CONSTITUTIONAL RIGHT TO SAY WHATEVER I WANT.
IF YOU FIRE ME FOR MY OPINIONS, YOU'LL BE SPITTING ON THE GRAVES OF OUR FOUND–ING FATHERS.
I'LL GET THE BEST LAWYER THAT MONEY CAN BUY, AND FIGHT YOU ALL THE WAY TO THE SUPREME COURT!
©2005 Scott Adams, Inc./Dist. by UFS, Inc.
THE ONLY WAY YOU CAN LEGALLY FIRE ME IS IF MY WORK ISN'T GOOD.
OOH.
I PROBABLY SAID TOO MUCH HERE.
10-3-05
YOUR WORK ISN'T GOOD. HERE'S YOUR FINAL PAYCHECK.
STUPID FOUNDING FATHERS.

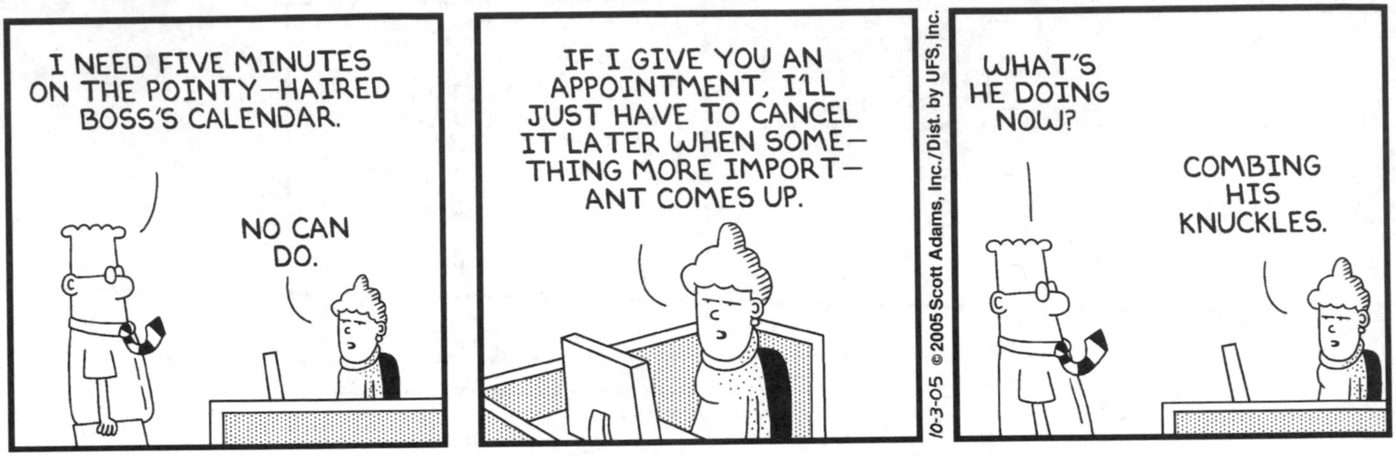
I NEED FIVE MINUTES ON THE POINTY-HAIRED BOSS'S CALENDAR.
NO CAN DO.
IF I GIVE YOU AN APPOINTMENT, I'LL JUST HAVE TO CANCEL IT LATER WHEN SOME-THING MORE IMPORT-ANT COMES UP.
10-3-05 ©2005 Scott Adams, Inc./Dist. by UFS, Inc.
WHAT'S HE DOING NOW?
COMBING HIS KNUCKLES.

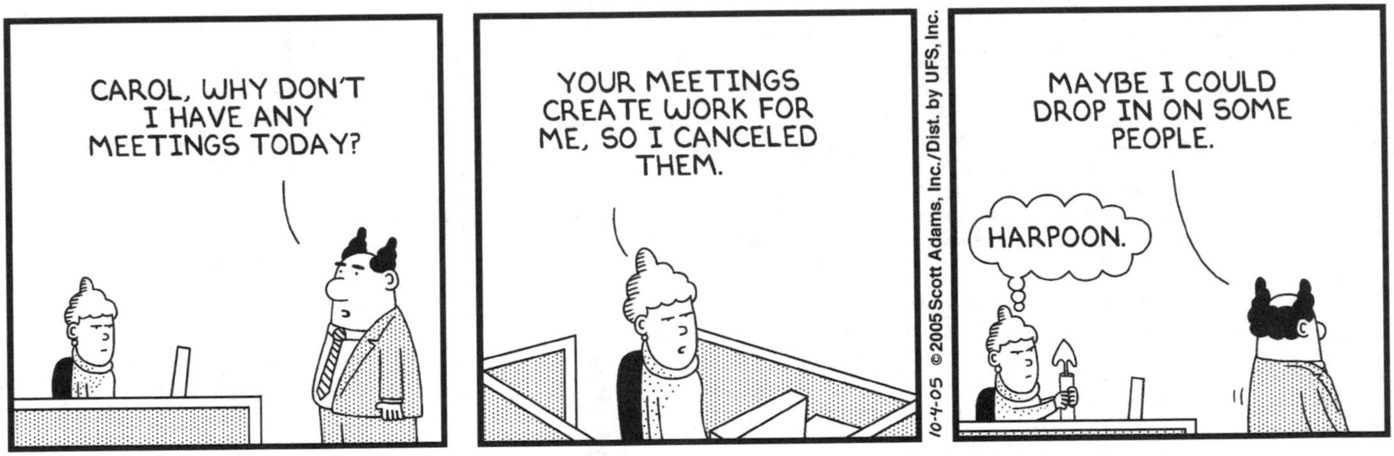
CAROL, WHY DON'T I HAVE ANY MEETINGS TODAY?
YOUR MEETINGS CREATE WORK FOR ME, SO I CANCELED THEM.
10-4-05 ©2005 Scott Adams, Inc./Dist. by UFS, Inc.
MAYBE I COULD DROP IN ON SOME PEOPLE.
HARPOON.

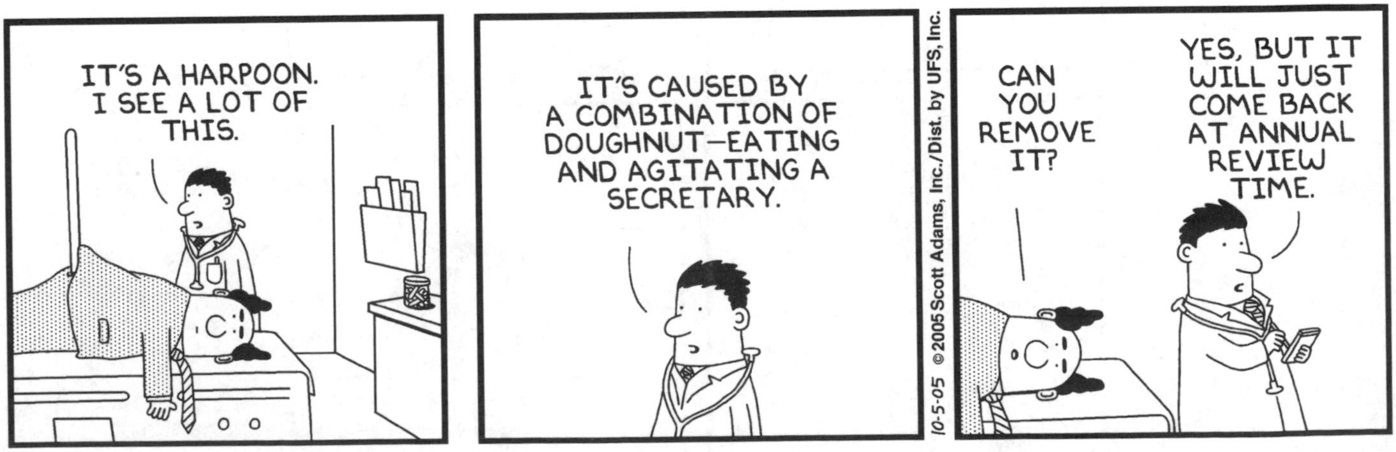
IT'S A HARPOON. I SEE A LOT OF THIS.
IT'S CAUSED BY A COMBINATION OF DOUGHNUT-EATING AND AGITATING A SECRETARY.
10-5-05 ©2005 Scott Adams, Inc./Dist. by UFS, Inc.
CAN YOU REMOVE IT?
YES, BUT IT WILL JUST COME BACK AT ANNUAL REVIEW TIME.

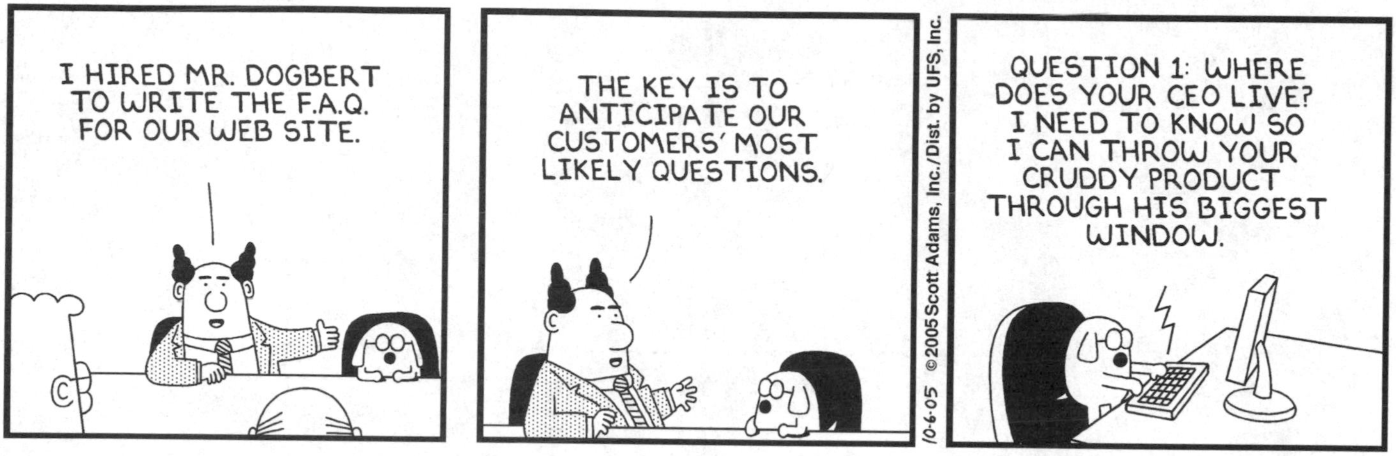
I HIRED MR. DOGBERT TO WRITE THE F.A.Q. FOR OUR WEB SITE.
THE KEY IS TO ANTICIPATE OUR CUSTOMERS' MOST LIKELY QUESTIONS.
10-6-05 ©2005 Scott Adams, Inc./Dist. by UFS, Inc.
QUESTION 1: WHERE DOES YOUR CEO LIVE? I NEED TO KNOW SO I CAN THROW YOUR CRUDDY PRODUCT THROUGH HIS BIGGEST WINDOW.

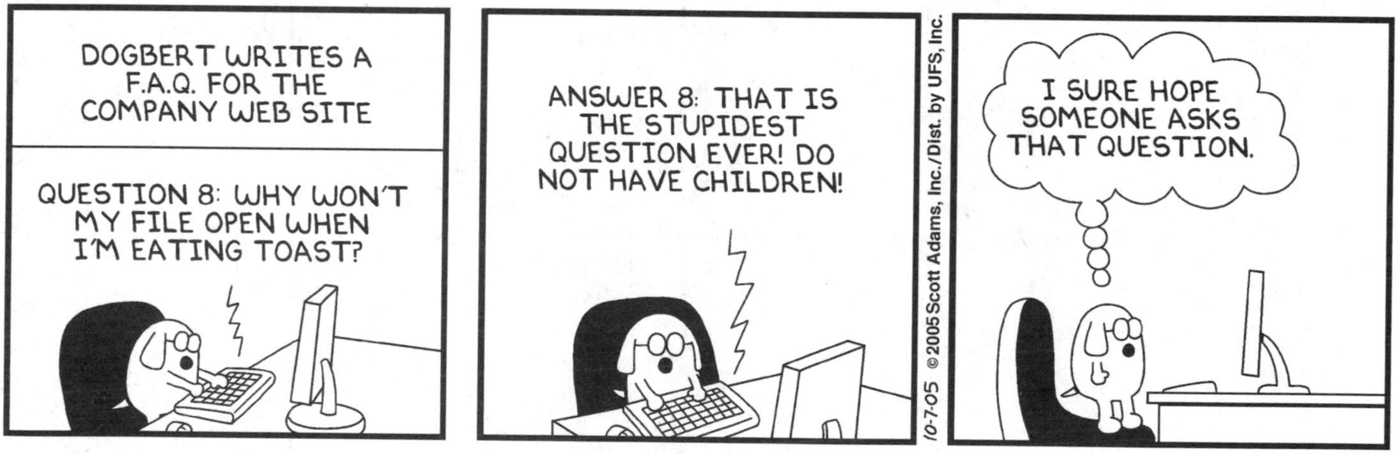
DOGBERT WRITES A F.A.Q. FOR THE COMPANY WEB SITE
QUESTION 8: WHY WON'T MY FILE OPEN WHEN I'M EATING TOAST?
ANSWER 8: THAT IS THE STUPIDEST QUESTION EVER! DO NOT HAVE CHILDREN!
10-7-05 ©2005 Scott Adams, Inc./Dist. by UFS, Inc.
I SURE HOPE SOMEONE ASKS THAT QUESTION.

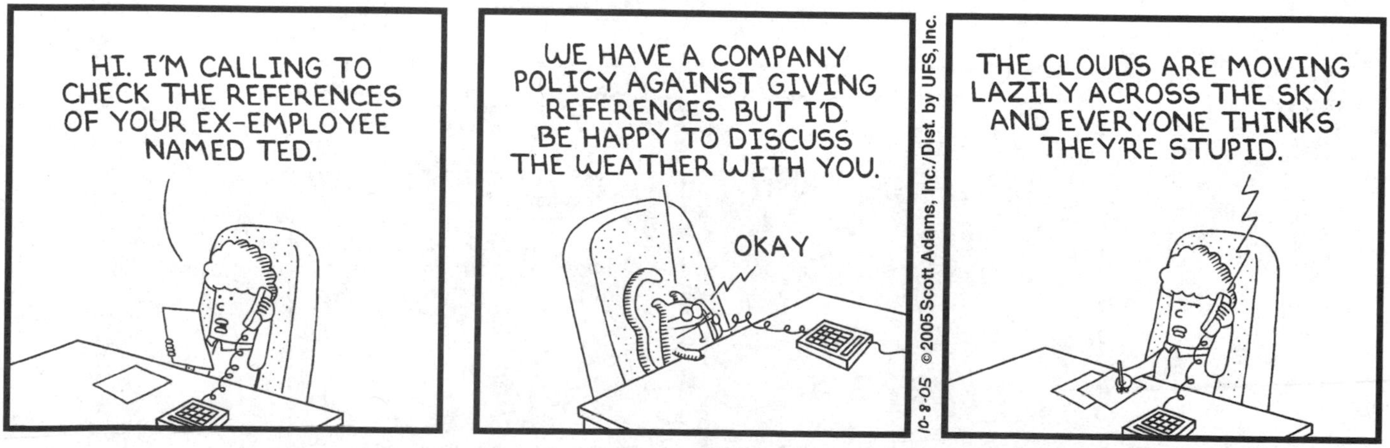
HI. I'M CALLING TO CHECK THE REFERENCES OF YOUR EX-EMPLOYEE NAMED TED.
WE HAVE A COMPANY POLICY AGAINST GIVING REFERENCES. BUT I'D BE HAPPY TO DISCUSS THE WEATHER WITH YOU.
OKAY
10-8-05 ©2005 Scott Adams, Inc./Dist. by UFS, Inc.
THE CLOUDS ARE MOVING LAZILY ACROSS THE SKY, AND EVERYONE THINKS THEY'RE STUPID.

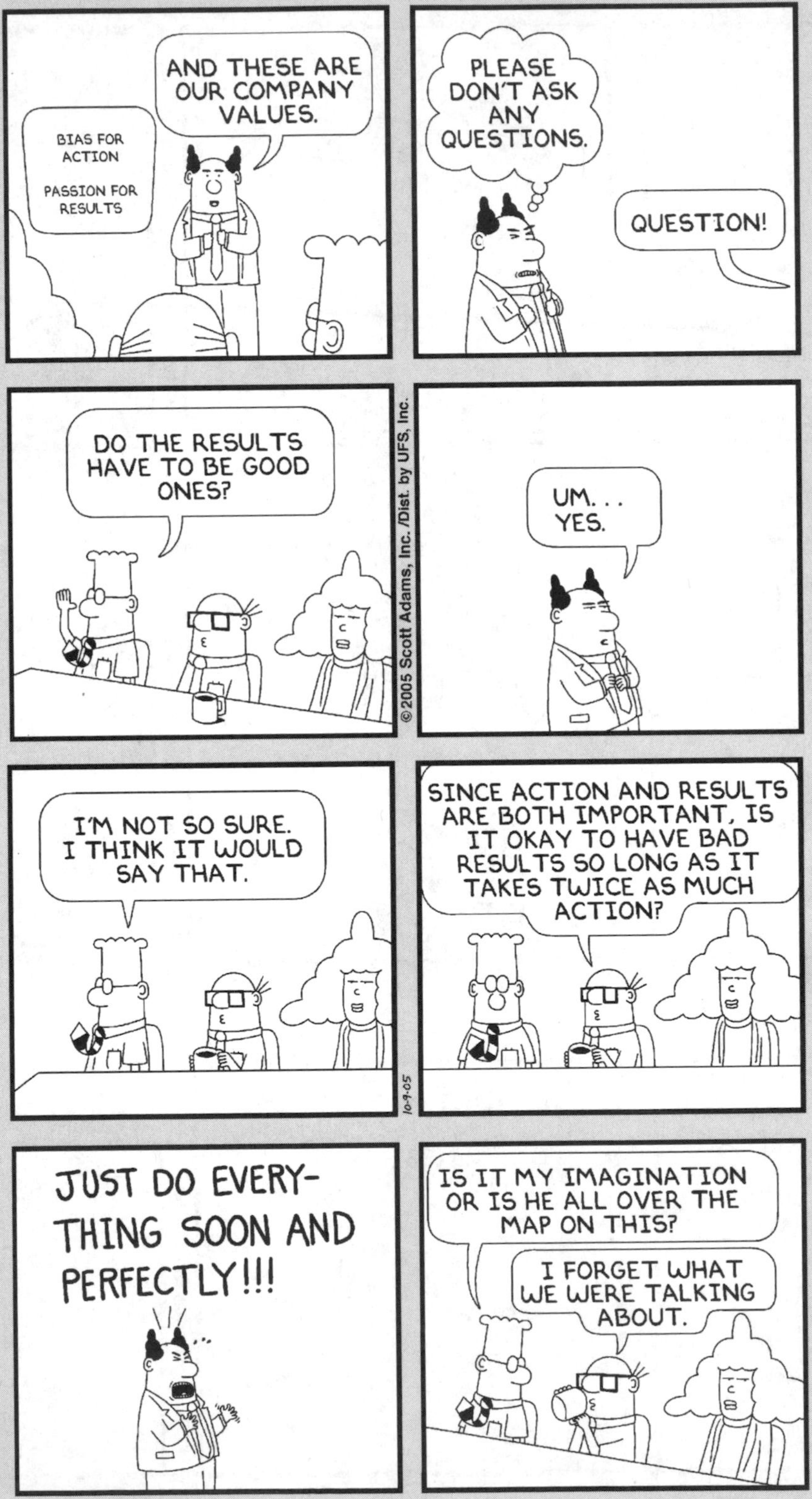
BIAS FOR ACTION
PASSION FOR RESULTS
AND THESE ARE OUR COMPANY VALUES.
PLEASE DON'T ASK ANY QUESTIONS.
QUESTION!
DO THE RESULTS HAVE TO BE GOOD ONES?
©2005 Scott Adams, Inc./Dist. by UFS, Inc.
UM. . . YES.
I'M NOT SO SURE. I THINK IT WOULD SAY THAT.
SINCE ACTION AND RESULTS ARE BOTH IMPORTANT, IS IT OKAY TO HAVE BAD RESULTS SO LONG AS IT TAKES TWICE AS MUCH ACTION?
10-9-05
JUST DO EVERY-THING SOON AND PERFECTLY!!!
IS IT MY IMAGINATION OR IS HE ALL OVER THE MAP ON THIS?
I FORGET WHAT WE WERE TALKING ABOUT.

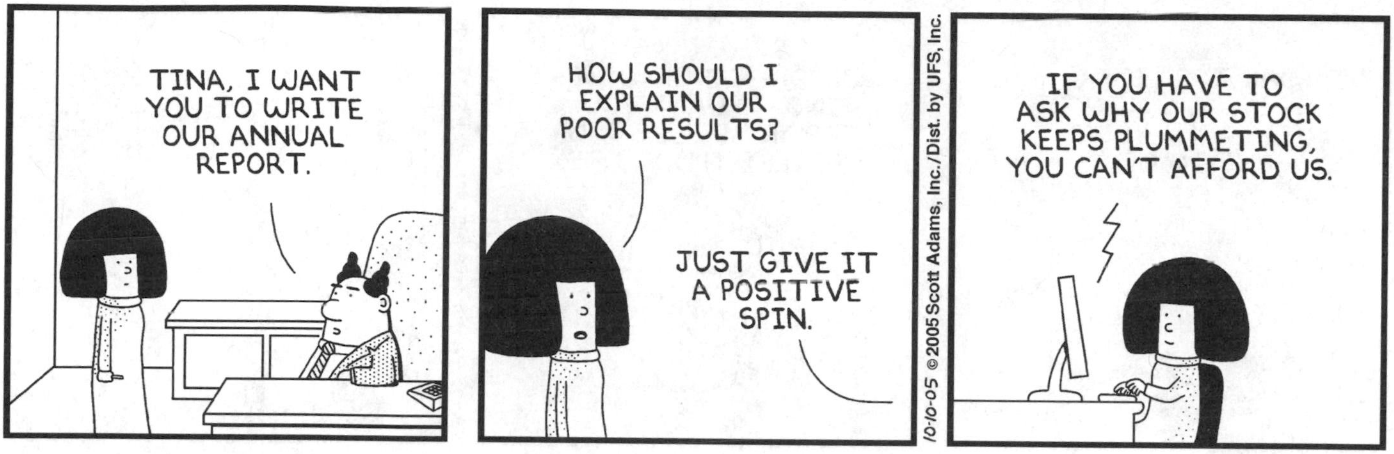
TINA, I WANT YOU TO WRITE OUR ANNUAL REPORT.
HOW SHOULD I EXPLAIN OUR POOR RESULTS?
JUST GIVE IT A POSITIVE SPIN.
10-10-05 © 2005 Scott Adams, Inc./Dist. by UFS, Inc.
IF YOU HAVE TO ASK WHY OUR STOCK KEEPS PLUMMETING, YOU CAN'T AFFORD US.

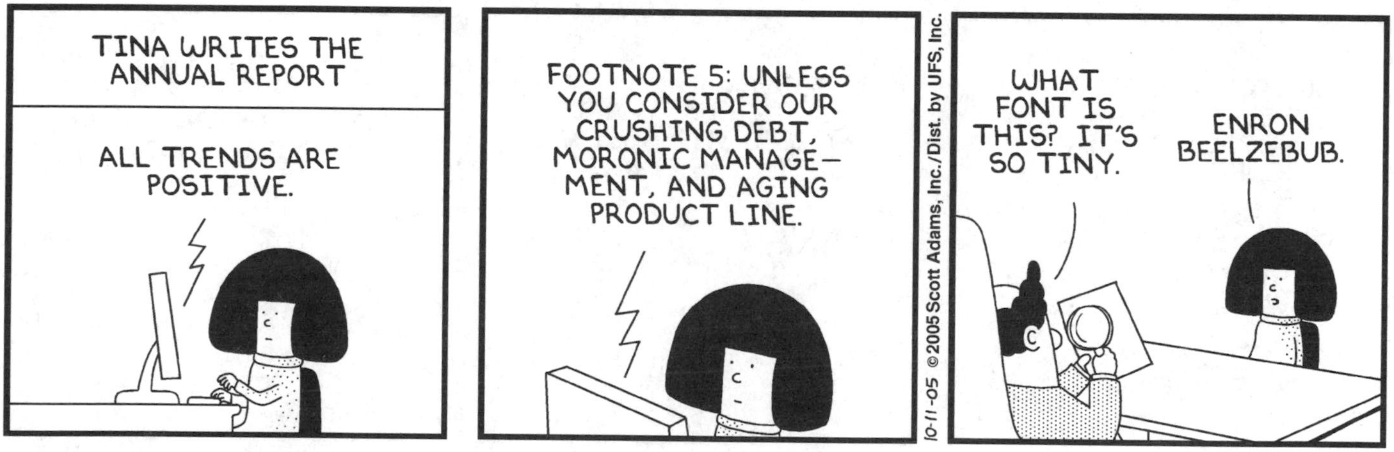
TINA WRITES THE ANNUAL REPORT
ALL TRENDS ARE POSITIVE.
FOOTNOTE 5: UNLESS YOU CONSIDER OUR CRUSHING DEBT, MORONIC MANAGE-MENT, AND AGING PRODUCT LINE.
10-11-05 © 2005 Scott Adams, Inc./Dist. by UFS, Inc.
WHAT FONT IS THIS? IT'S SO TINY.
ENRON BEELZEBUB.

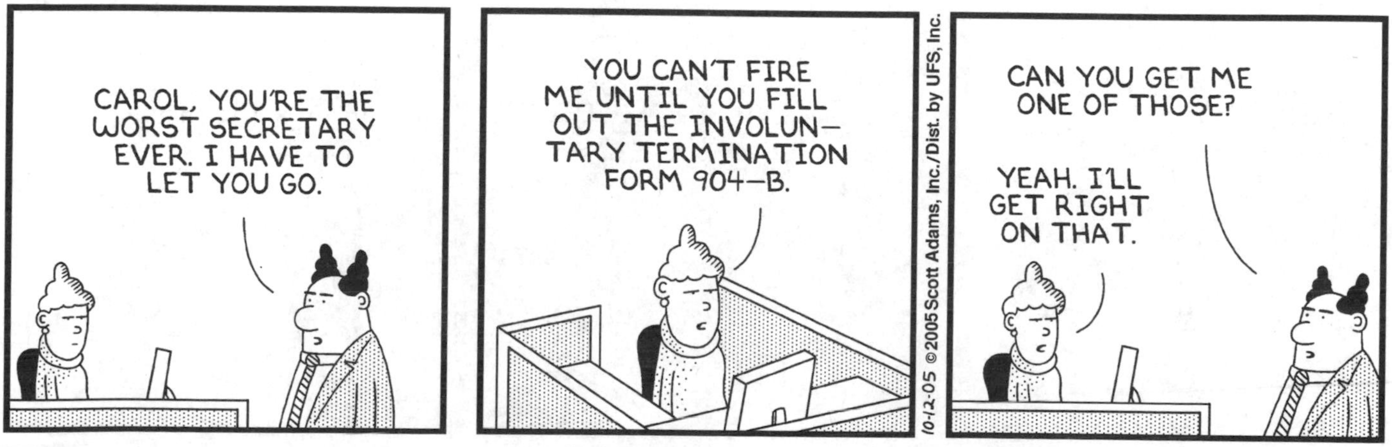
CAROL, YOU'RE THE WORST SECRETARY EVER. I HAVE TO LET YOU GO.
YOU CAN'T FIRE ME UNTIL YOU FILL OUT THE INVOLUN-TARY TERMINATION FORM 904-B.
10-12-05 © 2005 Scott Adams, Inc./Dist. by UFS, Inc.
CAN YOU GET ME ONE OF THOSE?
YEAH. I'LL GET RIGHT ON THAT.

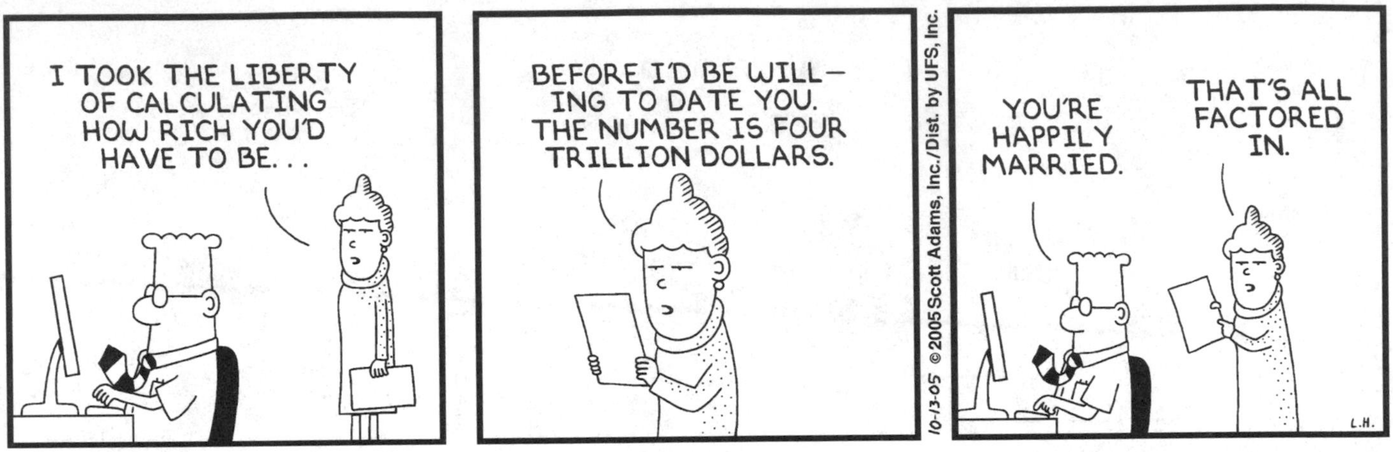
I TOOK THE LIBERTY OF CALCULATING HOW RICH YOU'D HAVE TO BE. . .
BEFORE I'D BE WILL– ING TO DATE YOU. THE NUMBER IS FOUR TRILLION DOLLARS.
YOU'RE HAPPILY MARRIED.
THAT'S ALL FACTORED IN.
10-13-05 © 2005 Scott Adams, Inc./Dist. by UFS, Inc.
L.H.

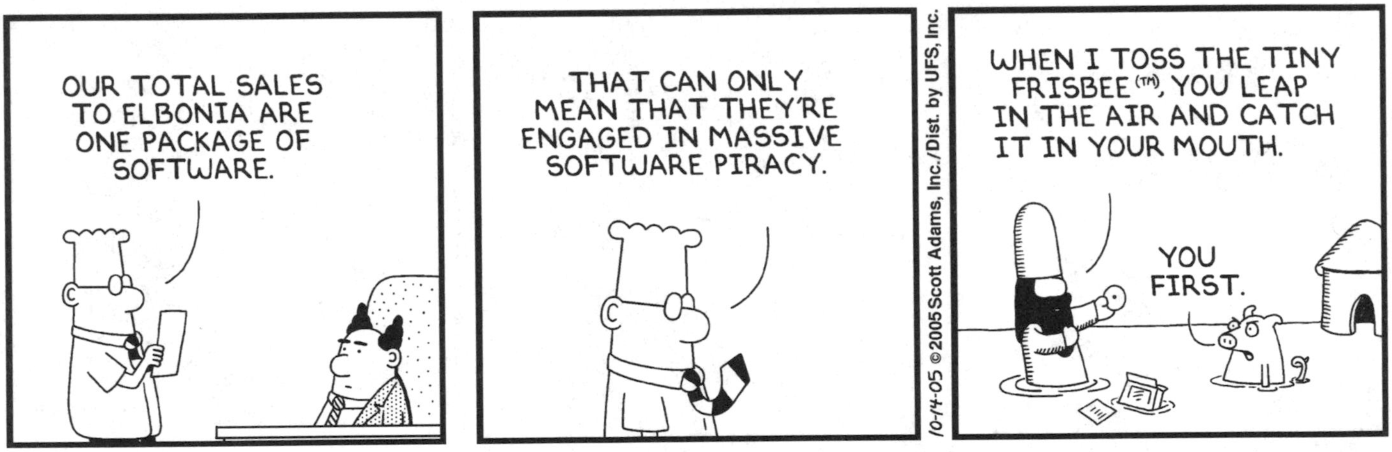
OUR TOTAL SALES TO ELBONIA ARE ONE PACKAGE OF SOFTWARE.
THAT CAN ONLY MEAN THAT THEY'RE ENGAGED IN MASSIVE SOFTWARE PIRACY.
WHEN I TOSS THE TINY FRISBEE(TM), YOU LEAP IN THE AIR AND CATCH IT IN YOUR MOUTH.
YOU FIRST.
10-14-05 © 2005 Scott Adams, Inc./Dist. by UFS, Inc.

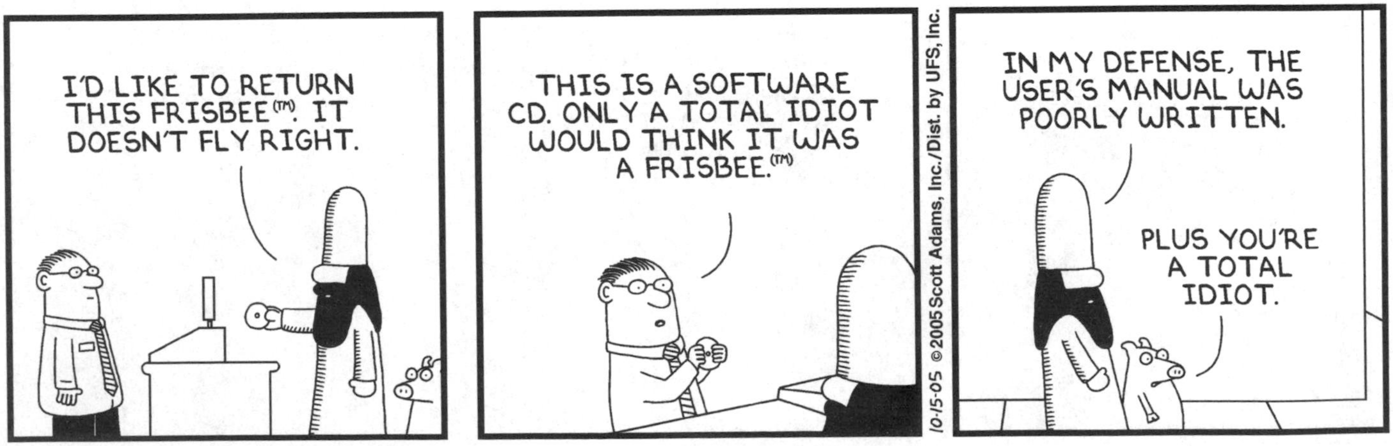
I'D LIKE TO RETURN THIS FRISBEE(TM). IT DOESN'T FLY RIGHT.
THIS IS A SOFTWARE CD. ONLY A TOTAL IDIOT WOULD THINK IT WAS A FRISBEE.(TM)
IN MY DEFENSE, THE USER'S MANUAL WAS POORLY WRITTEN.
PLUS YOU'RE A TOTAL IDIOT.
10-15-05 © 2005 Scott Adams, Inc./Dist. by UFS, Inc.

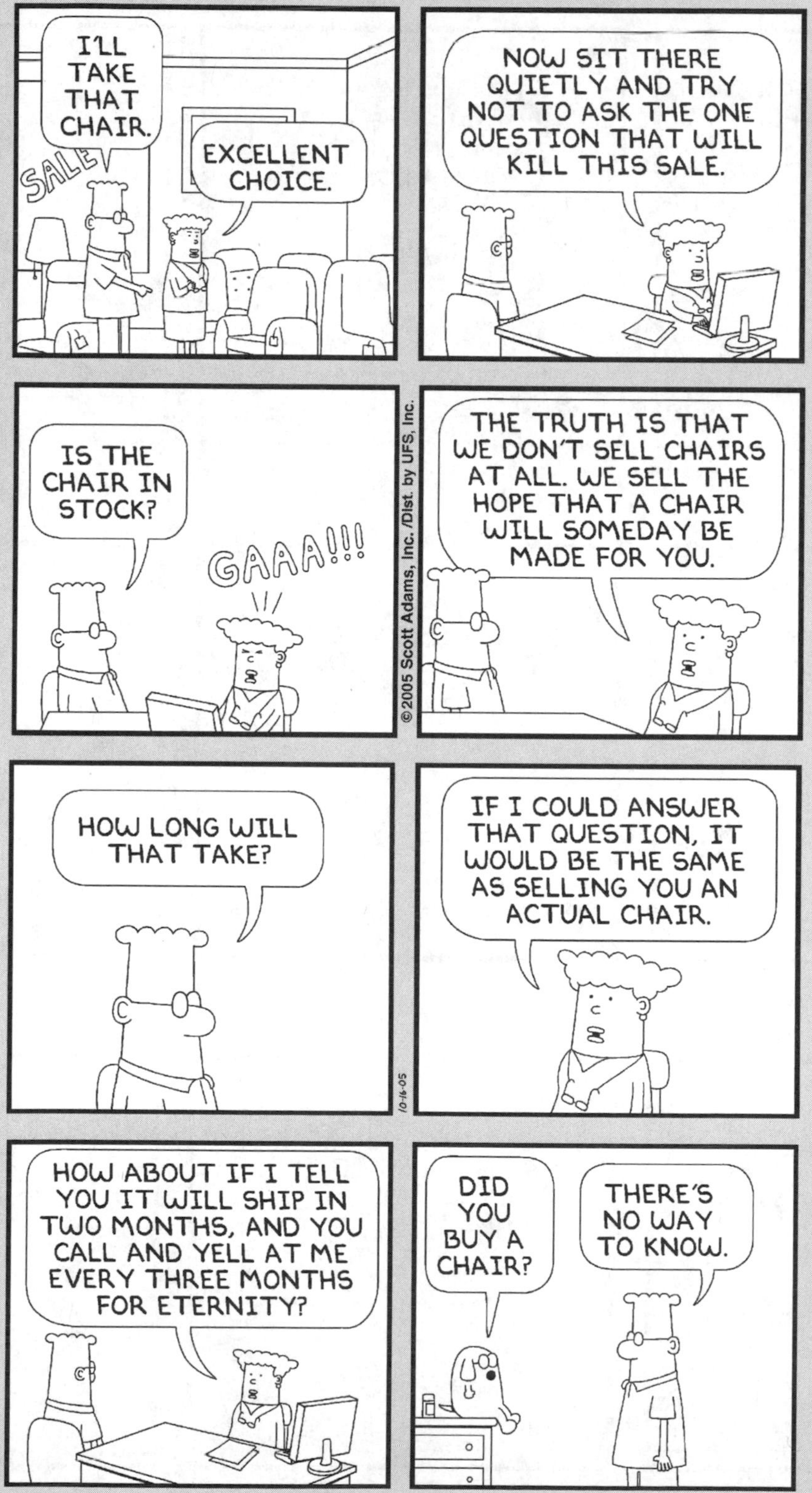
I'LL TAKE THAT CHAIR.
SALE
EXCELLENT CHOICE.
NOW SIT THERE QUIETLY AND TRY NOT TO ASK THE ONE QUESTION THAT WILL KILL THIS SALE.
IS THE CHAIR IN STOCK?
GAAA!!!
©2005 Scott Adams, Inc./Dist. by UFS, Inc.
THE TRUTH IS THAT WE DON'T SELL CHAIRS AT ALL. WE SELL THE HOPE THAT A CHAIR WILL SOMEDAY BE MADE FOR YOU.
HOW LONG WILL THAT TAKE?
10-16-05
IF I COULD ANSWER THAT QUESTION, IT WOULD BE THE SAME AS SELLING YOU AN ACTUAL CHAIR.
HOW ABOUT IF I TELL YOU IT WILL SHIP IN TWO MONTHS, AND YOU CALL AND YELL AT ME EVERY THREE MONTHS FOR ETERNITY?
DID YOU BUY A CHAIR?
THERE'S NO WAY TO KNOW.

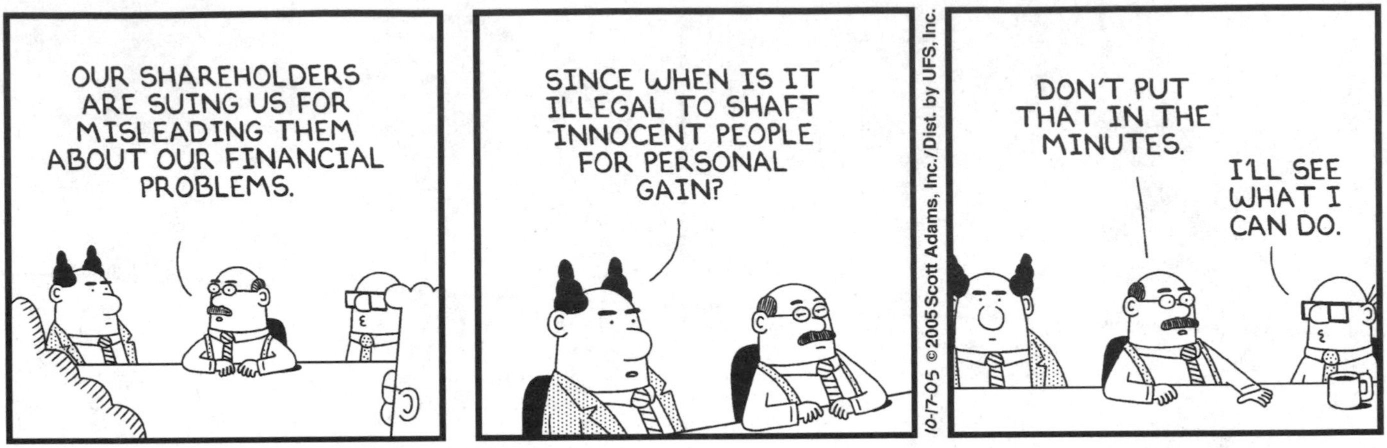
OUR SHAREHOLDERS ARE SUING US FOR MISLEADING THEM ABOUT OUR FINANCIAL PROBLEMS.
SINCE WHEN IS IT ILLEGAL TO SHAFT INNOCENT PEOPLE FOR PERSONAL GAIN?
DON'T PUT THAT IN THE MINUTES.
I'LL SEE WHAT I CAN DO.
10-17-05 © 2005 Scott Adams, Inc./Dist. by UFS, Inc.

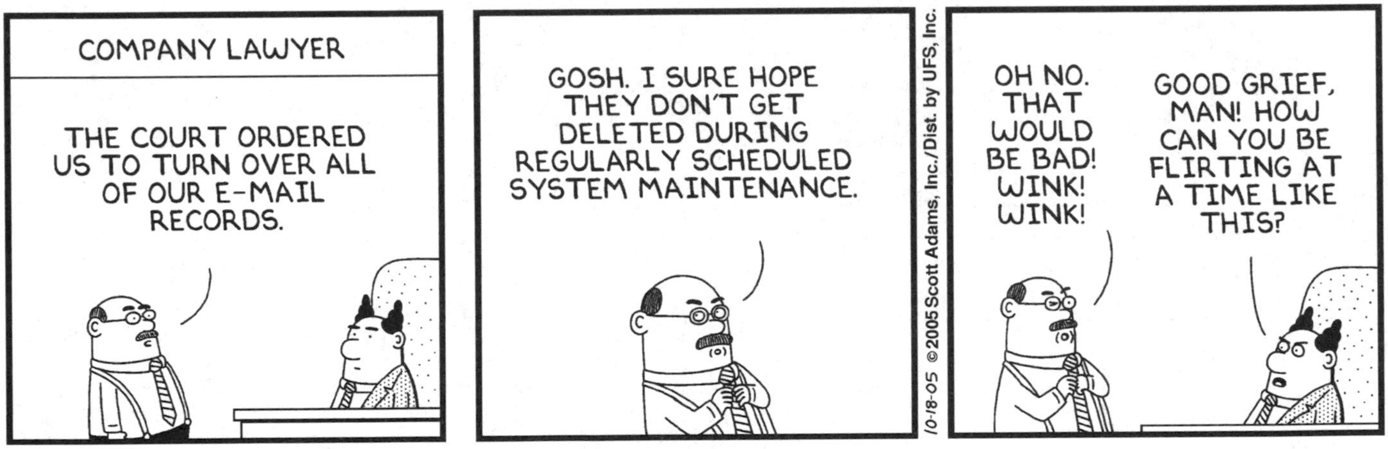
COMPANY LAWYER
THE COURT ORDERED US TO TURN OVER ALL OF OUR E-MAIL RECORDS.
GOSH. I SURE HOPE THEY DON'T GET DELETED DURING REGULARLY SCHEDULED SYSTEM MAINTENANCE.
OH NO. THAT WOULD BE BAD! WINK! WINK!
GOOD GRIEF, MAN! HOW CAN YOU BE FLIRTING AT A TIME LIKE THIS?
10-18-05 © 2005 Scott Adams, Inc./Dist. by UFS, Inc.

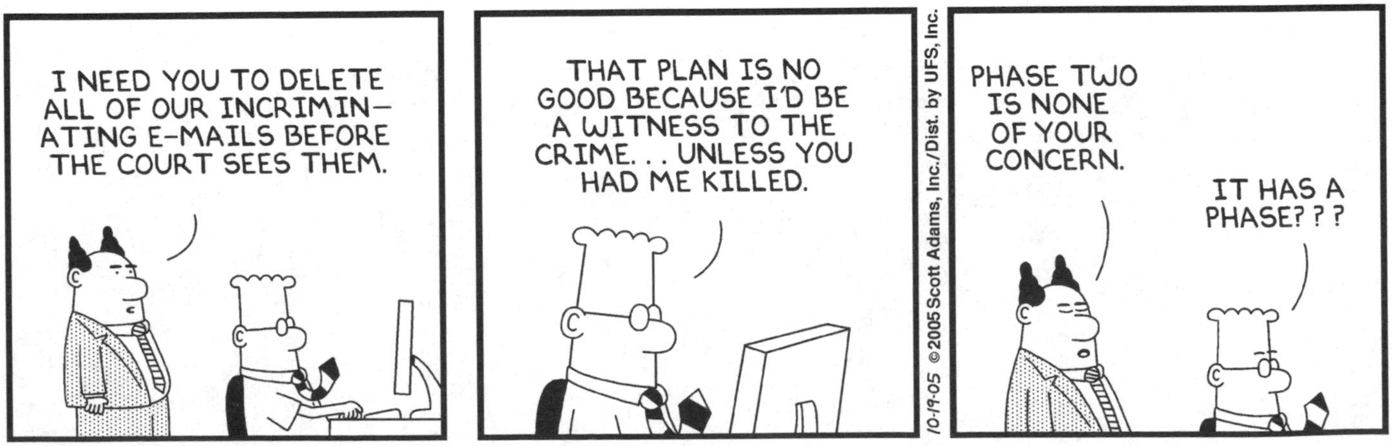
I NEED YOU TO DELETE ALL OF OUR INCRIMIN-ATING E-MAILS BEFORE THE COURT SEES THEM.
THAT PLAN IS NO GOOD BECAUSE I'D BE A WITNESS TO THE CRIME. . . UNLESS YOU HAD ME KILLED.
PHASE TWO IS NONE OF YOUR CONCERN.
IT HAS A PHASE? ? ?
10-19-05 © 2005 Scott Adams, Inc./Dist. by UFS, Inc.

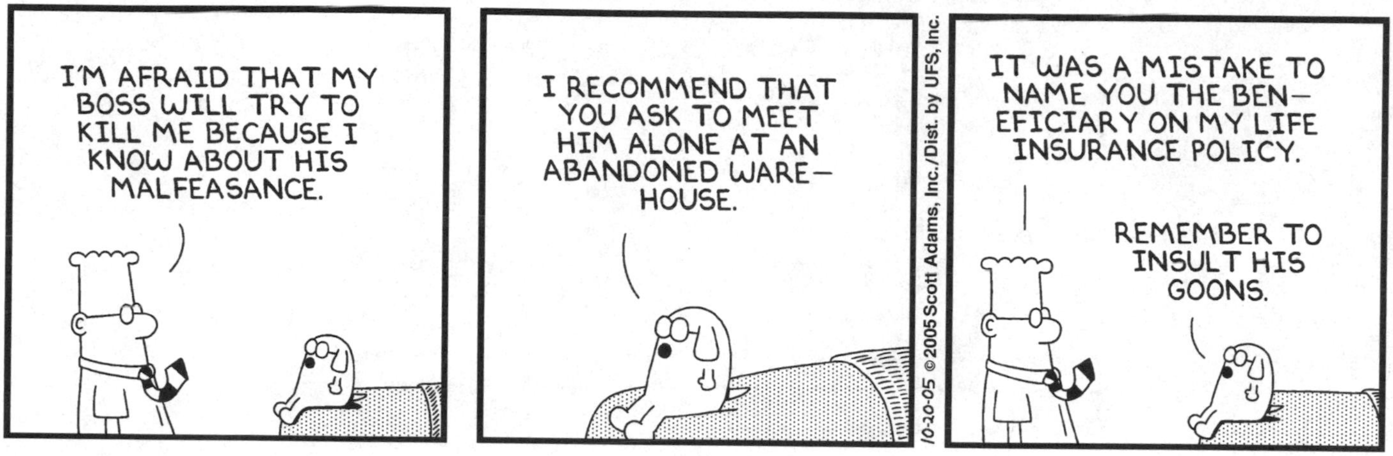
I'M AFRAID THAT MY BOSS WILL TRY TO KILL ME BECAUSE I KNOW ABOUT HIS MALFEASANCE.
I RECOMMEND THAT YOU ASK TO MEET HIM ALONE AT AN ABANDONED WARE- HOUSE.
IT WAS A MISTAKE TO NAME YOU THE BEN- EFICIARY ON MY LIFE INSURANCE POLICY.
REMEMBER TO INSULT HIS GOONS.
10-20-05 © 2005 Scott Adams, Inc./Dist. by UFS, Inc.

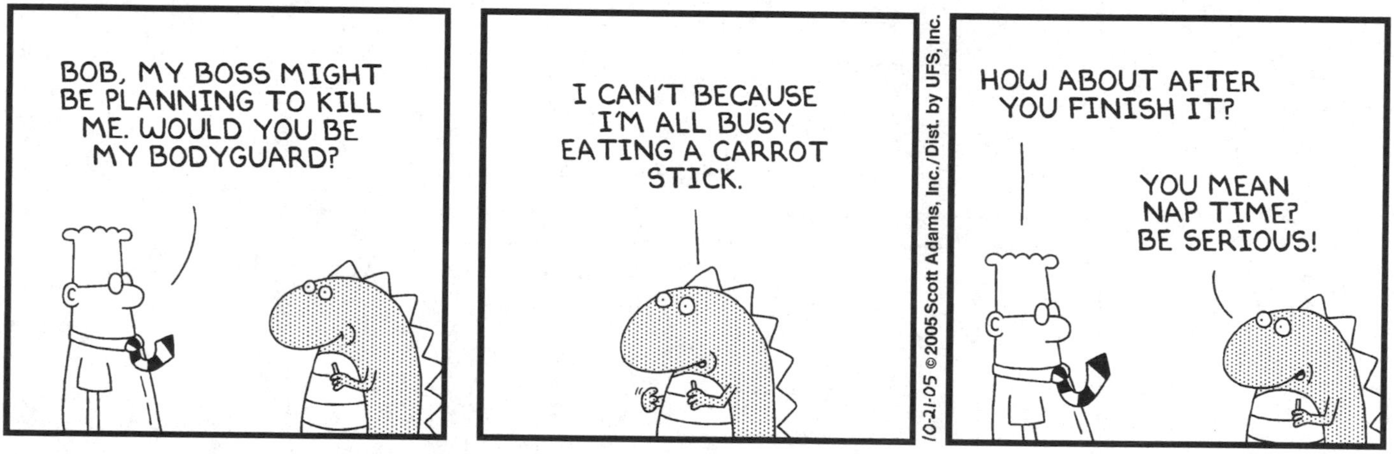
BOB, MY BOSS MIGHT BE PLANNING TO KILL ME. WOULD YOU BE MY BODYGUARD?
I CAN'T BECAUSE I'M ALL BUSY EATING A CARROT STICK.
HOW ABOUT AFTER YOU FINISH IT?
YOU MEAN NAP TIME? BE SERIOUS!
10-21-05 © 2005 Scott Adams, Inc./Dist. by UFS, Inc.

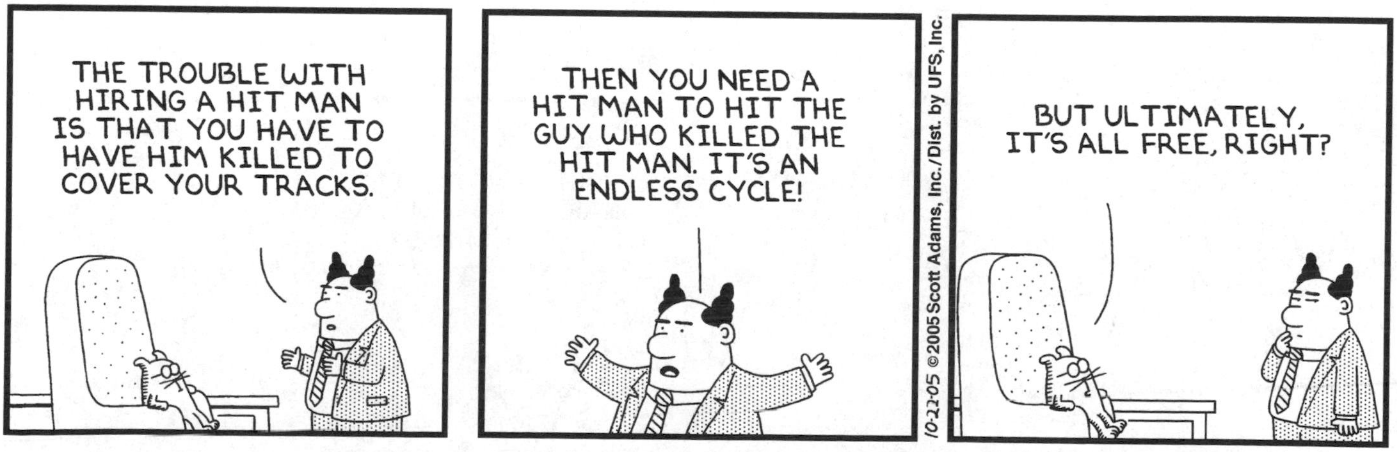
THE TROUBLE WITH HIRING A HIT MAN IS THAT YOU HAVE TO HAVE HIM KILLED TO COVER YOUR TRACKS.
THEN YOU NEED A HIT MAN TO HIT THE GUY WHO KILLED THE HIT MAN. IT'S AN ENDLESS CYCLE!
BUT ULTIMATELY, IT'S ALL FREE, RIGHT?
10-22-05 © 2005 Scott Adams, Inc./Dist. by UFS, Inc.

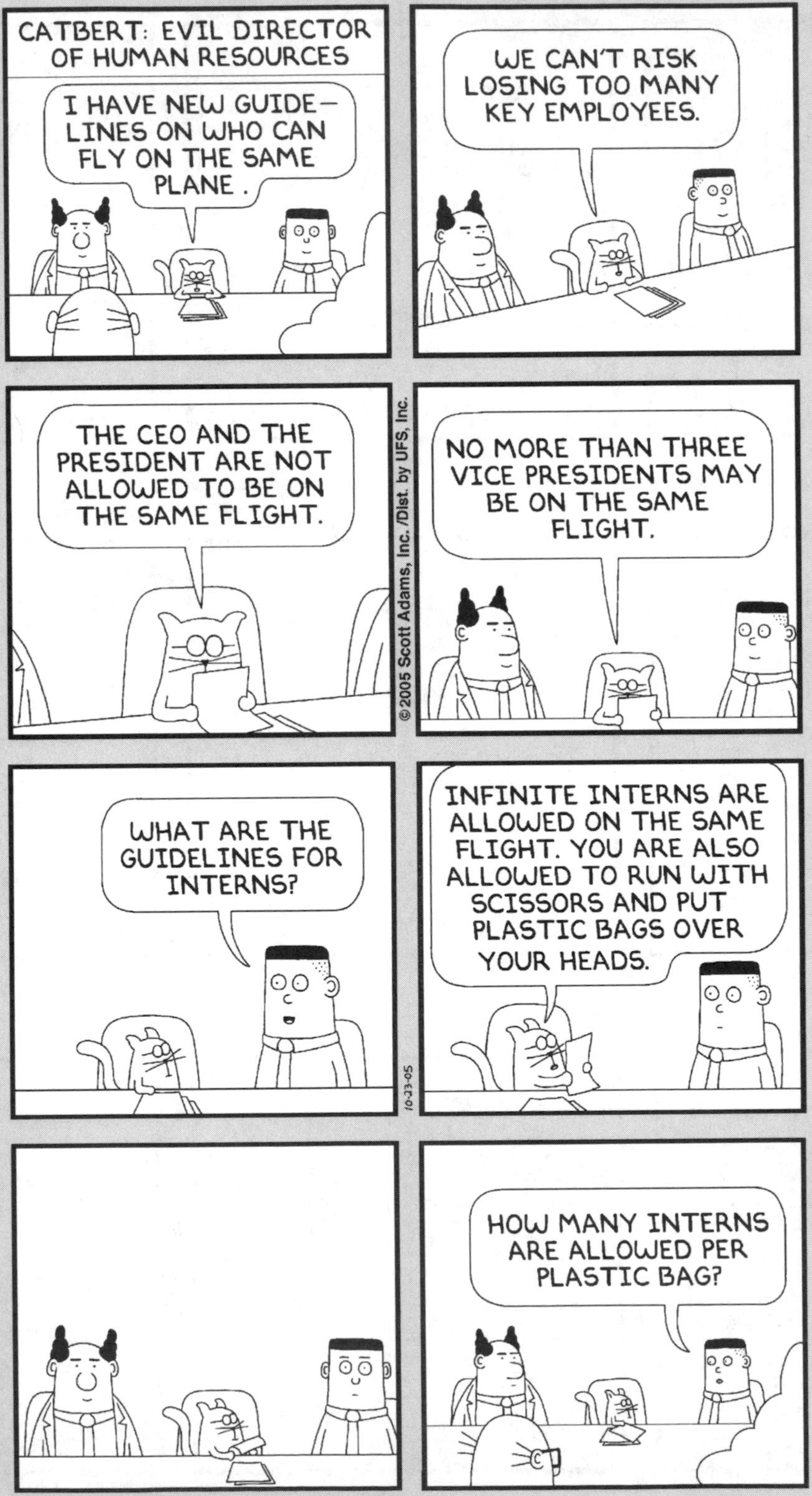
CATBERT: EVIL DIRECTOR OF HUMAN RESOURCES
I HAVE NEW GUIDE-LINES ON WHO CAN FLY ON THE SAME PLANE.
WE CAN'T RISK LOSING TOO MANY KEY EMPLOYEES.
THE CEO AND THE PRESIDENT ARE NOT ALLOWED TO BE ON THE SAME FLIGHT.
©2005 Scott Adams, Inc. /Dist. by UFS, Inc.
NO MORE THAN THREE VICE PRESIDENTS MAY BE ON THE SAME FLIGHT.
WHAT ARE THE GUIDELINES FOR INTERNS?
INFINITE INTERNS ARE ALLOWED ON THE SAME FLIGHT. YOU ARE ALSO ALLOWED TO RUN WITH SCISSORS AND PUT PLASTIC BAGS OVER YOUR HEADS.
10-23-05
HOW MANY INTERNS ARE ALLOWED PER PLASTIC BAG?

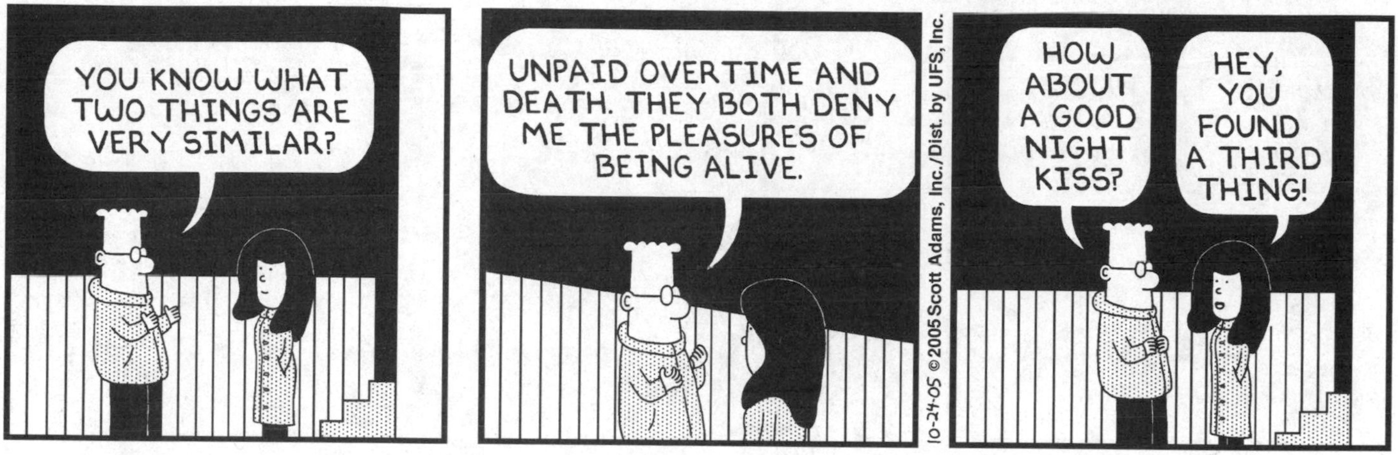
YOU KNOW WHAT TWO THINGS ARE VERY SIMILAR?
UNPAID OVERTIME AND DEATH. THEY BOTH DENY ME THE PLEASURES OF BEING ALIVE.
HOW ABOUT A GOOD NIGHT KISS?
HEY, YOU FOUND A THIRD THING!
10-24-05 © 2005 Scott Adams, Inc./Dist. by UFS, Inc.

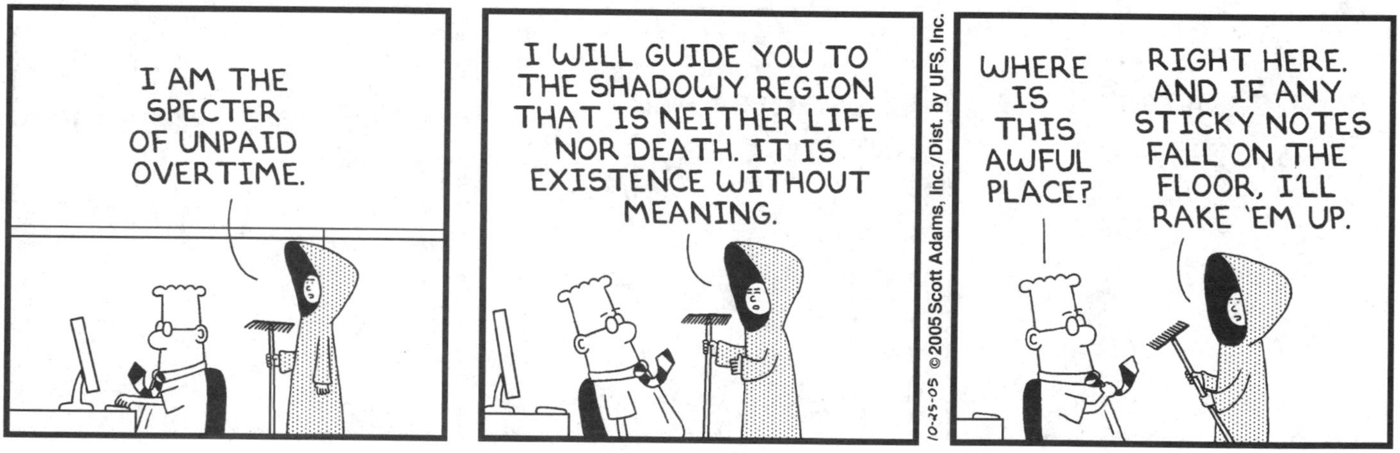
I AM THE SPECTER OF UNPAID OVERTIME.
I WILL GUIDE YOU TO THE SHADOWY REGION THAT IS NEITHER LIFE NOR DEATH. IT IS EXISTENCE WITHOUT MEANING.
WHERE IS THIS AWFUL PLACE?
RIGHT HERE. AND IF ANY STICKY NOTES FALL ON THE FLOOR, I'LL RAKE 'EM UP.
10-25-05 © 2005 Scott Adams, Inc./Dist. by UFS, Inc.

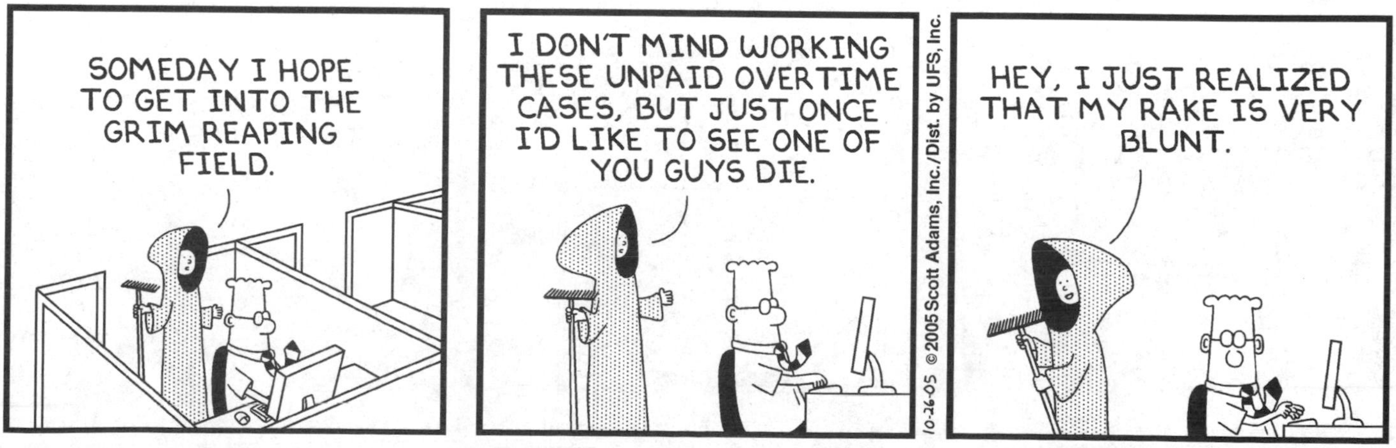
SOMEDAY I HOPE TO GET INTO THE GRIM REAPING FIELD.
I DON'T MIND WORKING THESE UNPAID OVERTIME CASES, BUT JUST ONCE I'D LIKE TO SEE ONE OF YOU GUYS DIE.
HEY, I JUST REALIZED THAT MY RAKE IS VERY BLUNT.
10-26-05 © 2005 Scott Adams, Inc./Dist. by UFS, Inc.

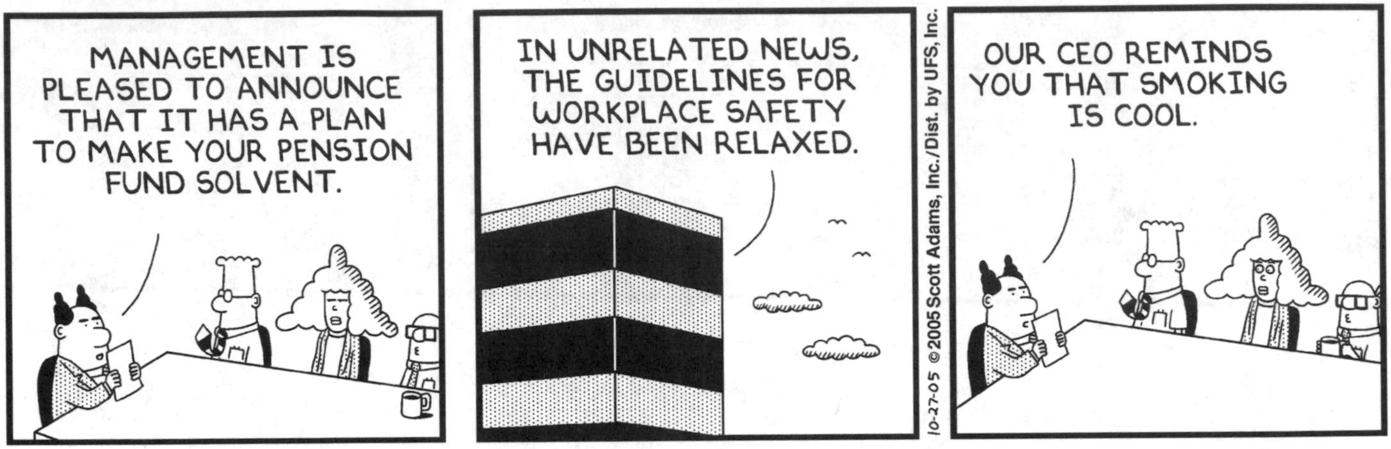
MANAGEMENT IS PLEASED TO ANNOUNCE THAT IT HAS A PLAN TO MAKE YOUR PENSION FUND SOLVENT.
IN UNRELATED NEWS, THE GUIDELINES FOR WORKPLACE SAFETY HAVE BEEN RELAXED.
10-27-05 © 2005 Scott Adams, Inc./Dist. by UFS, Inc.
OUR CEO REMINDS YOU THAT SMOKING IS COOL.

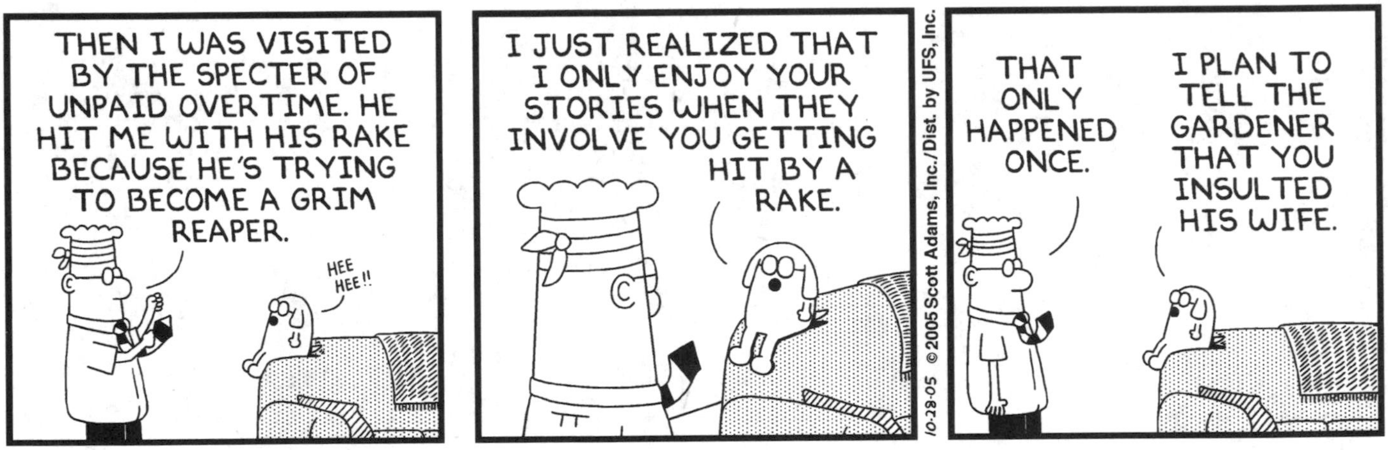
THEN I WAS VISITED BY THE SPECTER OF UNPAID OVERTIME. HE HIT ME WITH HIS RAKE BECAUSE HE'S TRYING TO BECOME A GRIM REAPER.
HEE HEE!!
I JUST REALIZED THAT I ONLY ENJOY YOUR STORIES WHEN THEY INVOLVE YOU GETTING HIT BY A RAKE.
10-28-05 © 2005 Scott Adams, Inc./Dist. by UFS, Inc.
THAT ONLY HAPPENED ONCE.
I PLAN TO TELL THE GARDENER THAT YOU INSULTED HIS WIFE.

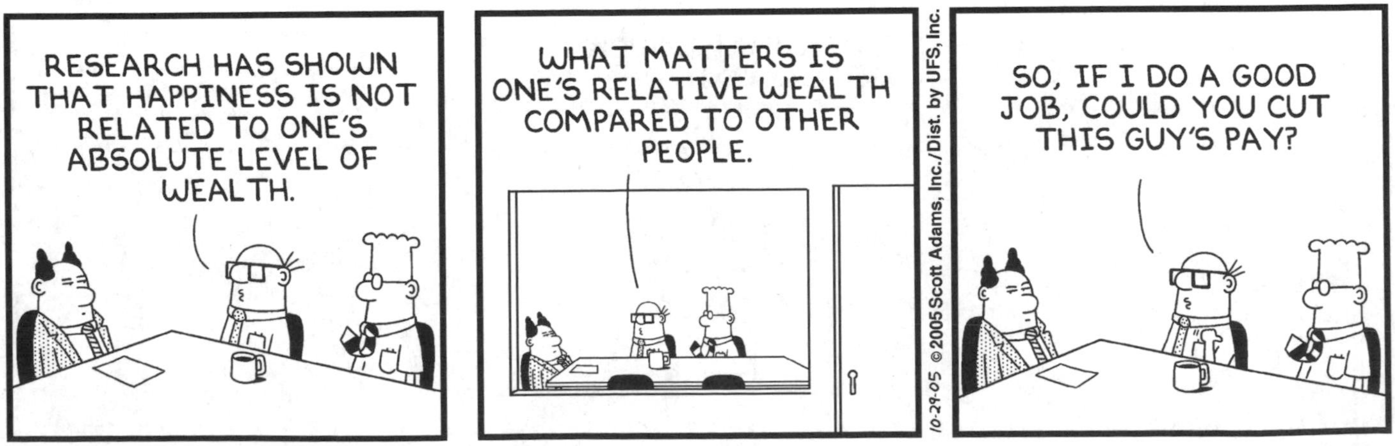
RESEARCH HAS SHOWN THAT HAPPINESS IS NOT RELATED TO ONE'S ABSOLUTE LEVEL OF WEALTH.
WHAT MATTERS IS ONE'S RELATIVE WEALTH COMPARED TO OTHER PEOPLE.
10-29-05 © 2005 Scott Adams, Inc./Dist. by UFS, Inc.
SO, IF I DO A GOOD JOB, COULD YOU CUT THIS GUY'S PAY?

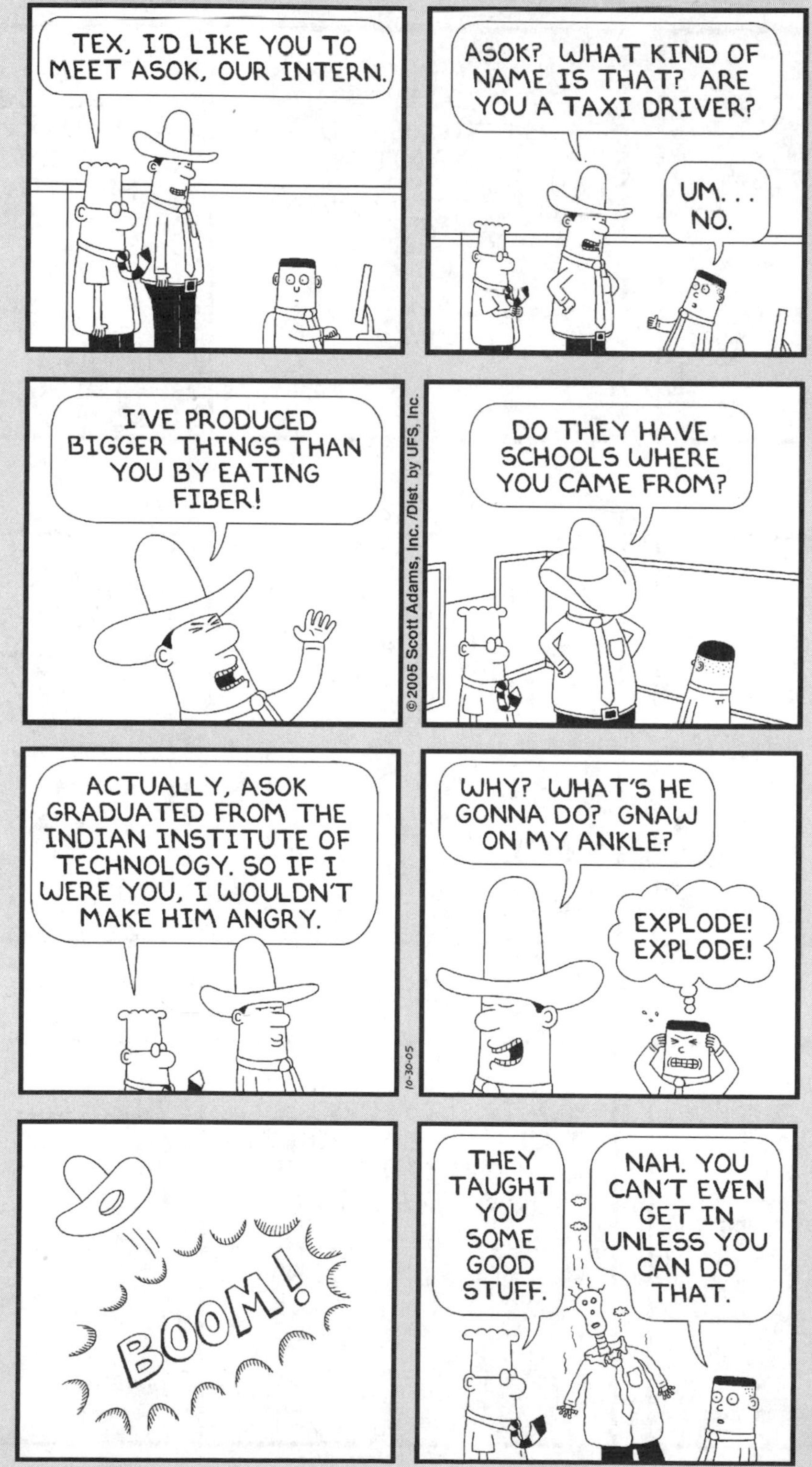
TEX, I'D LIKE YOU TO MEET ASOK, OUR INTERN.
ASOK? WHAT KIND OF NAME IS THAT? ARE YOU A TAXI DRIVER?
UM. . . NO.
I'VE PRODUCED BIGGER THINGS THAN YOU BY EATING FIBER!
DO THEY HAVE SCHOOLS WHERE YOU CAME FROM?
ACTUALLY, ASOK GRADUATED FROM THE INDIAN INSTITUTE OF TECHNOLOGY. SO IF I WERE YOU, I WOULDN'T MAKE HIM ANGRY.
WHY? WHAT'S HE GONNA DO? GNAW ON MY ANKLE?
EXPLODE! EXPLODE!
BOOM!
THEY TAUGHT YOU SOME GOOD STUFF.
NAH. YOU CAN'T EVEN GET IN UNLESS YOU CAN DO THAT.
© 2005 Scott Adams, Inc./Dist. by UFS, Inc.
10-30-05

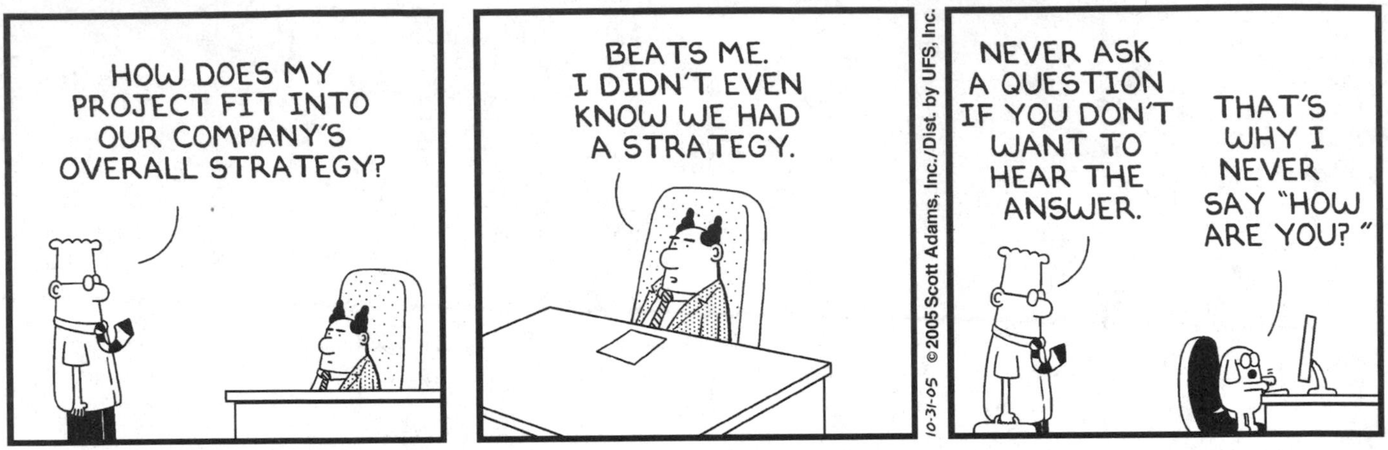
HOW DOES MY PROJECT FIT INTO OUR COMPANY'S OVERALL STRATEGY?
BEATS ME. I DIDN'T EVEN KNOW WE HAD A STRATEGY.
10-31-05 © 2005 Scott Adams, Inc./Dist. by UFS, Inc.
NEVER ASK A QUESTION IF YOU DON'T WANT TO HEAR THE ANSWER.
THAT'S WHY I NEVER SAY "HOW ARE YOU?"

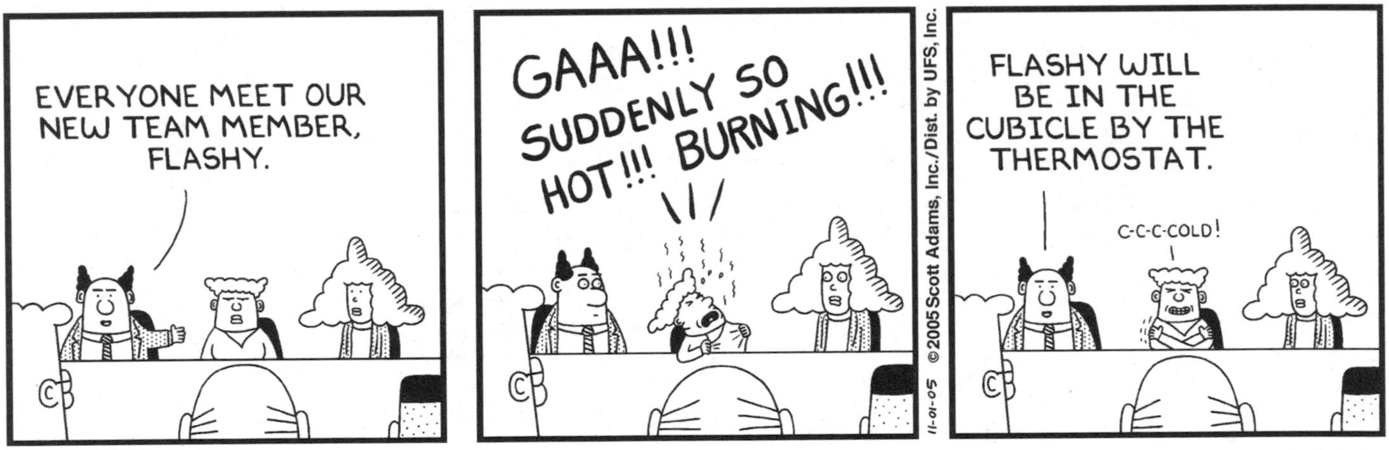
EVERYONE MEET OUR NEW TEAM MEMBER, FLASHY.
GAAA!!! SUDDENLY SO HOT!!! BURNING!!!
11-01-05 © 2005 Scott Adams, Inc./Dist. by UFS, Inc.
FLASHY WILL BE IN THE CUBICLE BY THE THERMOSTAT.
C-C-C-COLD!

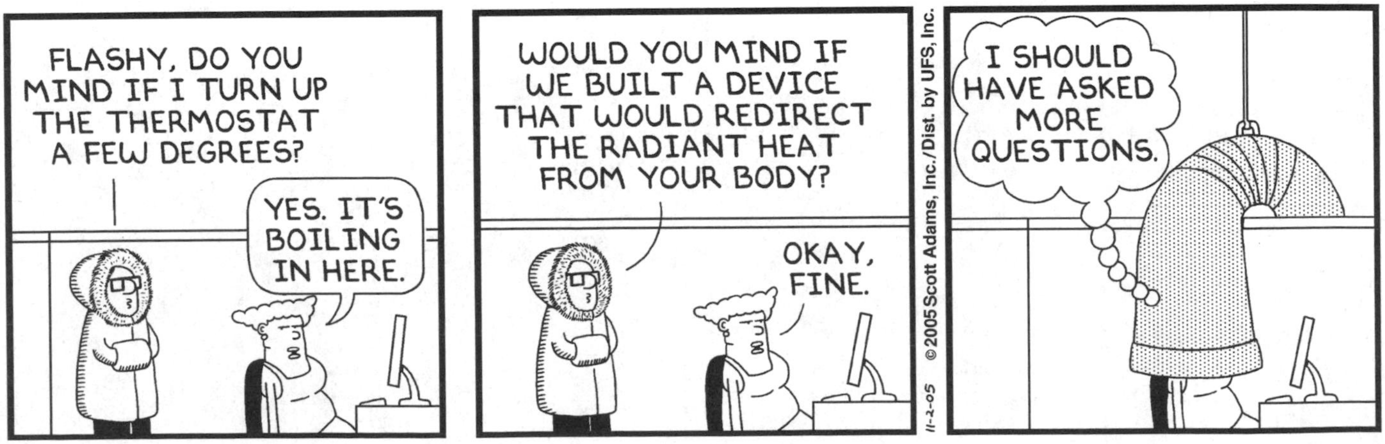
FLASHY, DO YOU MIND IF I TURN UP THE THERMOSTAT A FEW DEGREES?
YES. IT'S BOILING IN HERE.
WOULD YOU MIND IF WE BUILT A DEVICE THAT WOULD REDIRECT THE RADIANT HEAT FROM YOUR BODY?
OKAY, FINE.
11-2-05 © 2005 Scott Adams, Inc./Dist. by UFS, Inc.
I SHOULD HAVE ASKED MORE QUESTIONS.

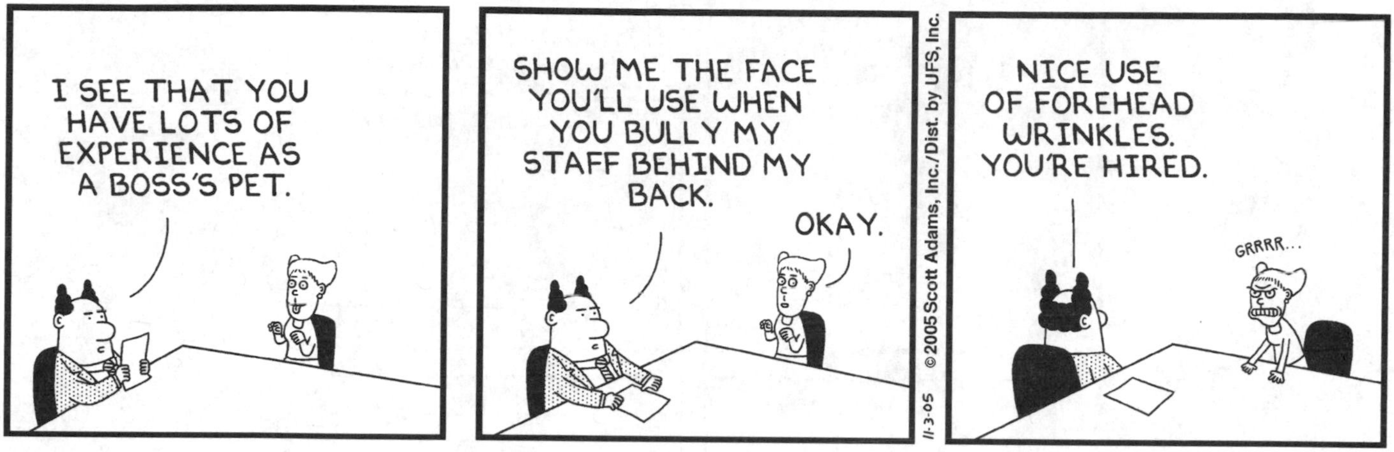
I SEE THAT YOU HAVE LOTS OF EXPERIENCE AS A BOSS'S PET.
SHOW ME THE FACE YOU'LL USE WHEN YOU BULLY MY STAFF BEHIND MY BACK.
OKAY.
©2005 Scott Adams, Inc./Dist. by UFS, Inc.
11-3-05
NICE USE OF FOREHEAD WRINKLES. YOU'RE HIRED.
GRRRR...

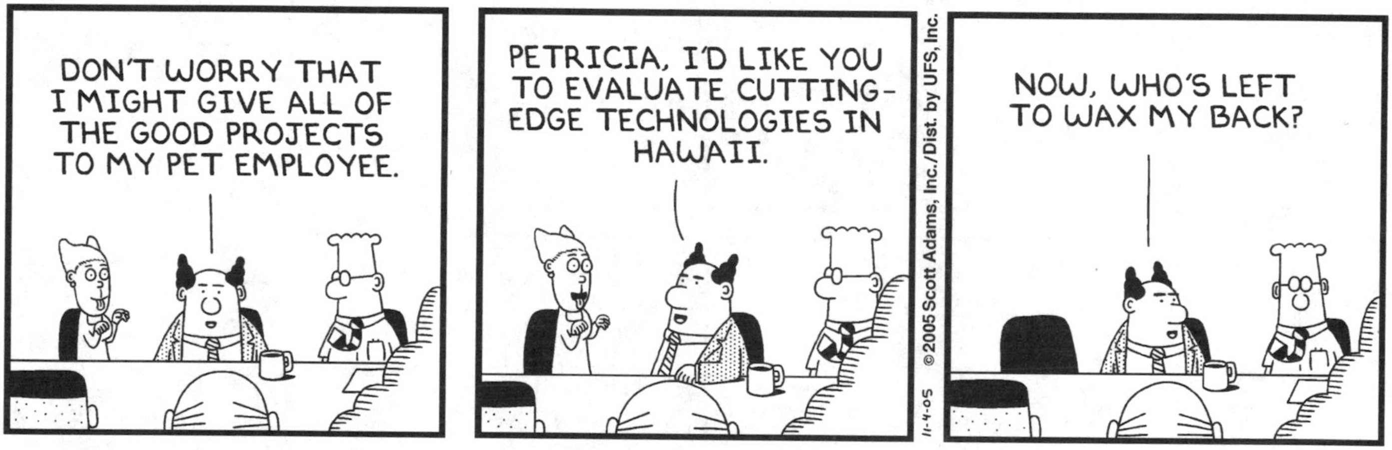
DON'T WORRY THAT I MIGHT GIVE ALL OF THE GOOD PROJECTS TO MY PET EMPLOYEE.
PETRICIA, I'D LIKE YOU TO EVALUATE CUTTING-EDGE TECHNOLOGIES IN HAWAII.
©2005 Scott Adams, Inc./Dist. by UFS, Inc.
11-4-05
NOW, WHO'S LEFT TO WAX MY BACK?

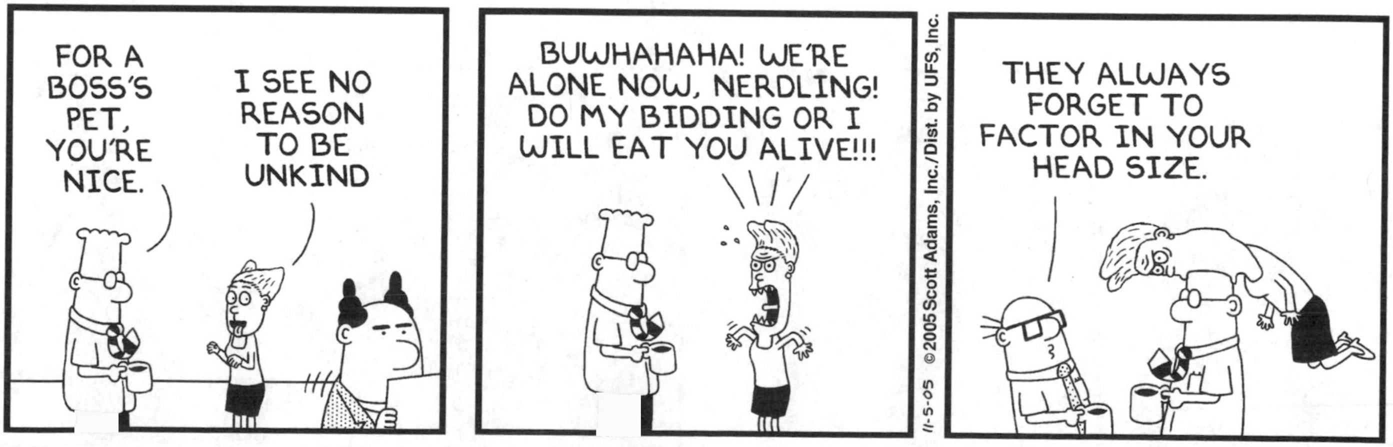
FOR A BOSS'S PET, YOU'RE NICE.
I SEE NO REASON TO BE UNKIND
BUWHAHAHA! WE'RE ALONE NOW, NERDLING! DO MY BIDDING OR I WILL EAT YOU ALIVE!!!
©2005 Scott Adams, Inc./Dist. by UFS, Inc.
11-5-05
THEY ALWAYS FORGET TO FACTOR IN YOUR HEAD SIZE.

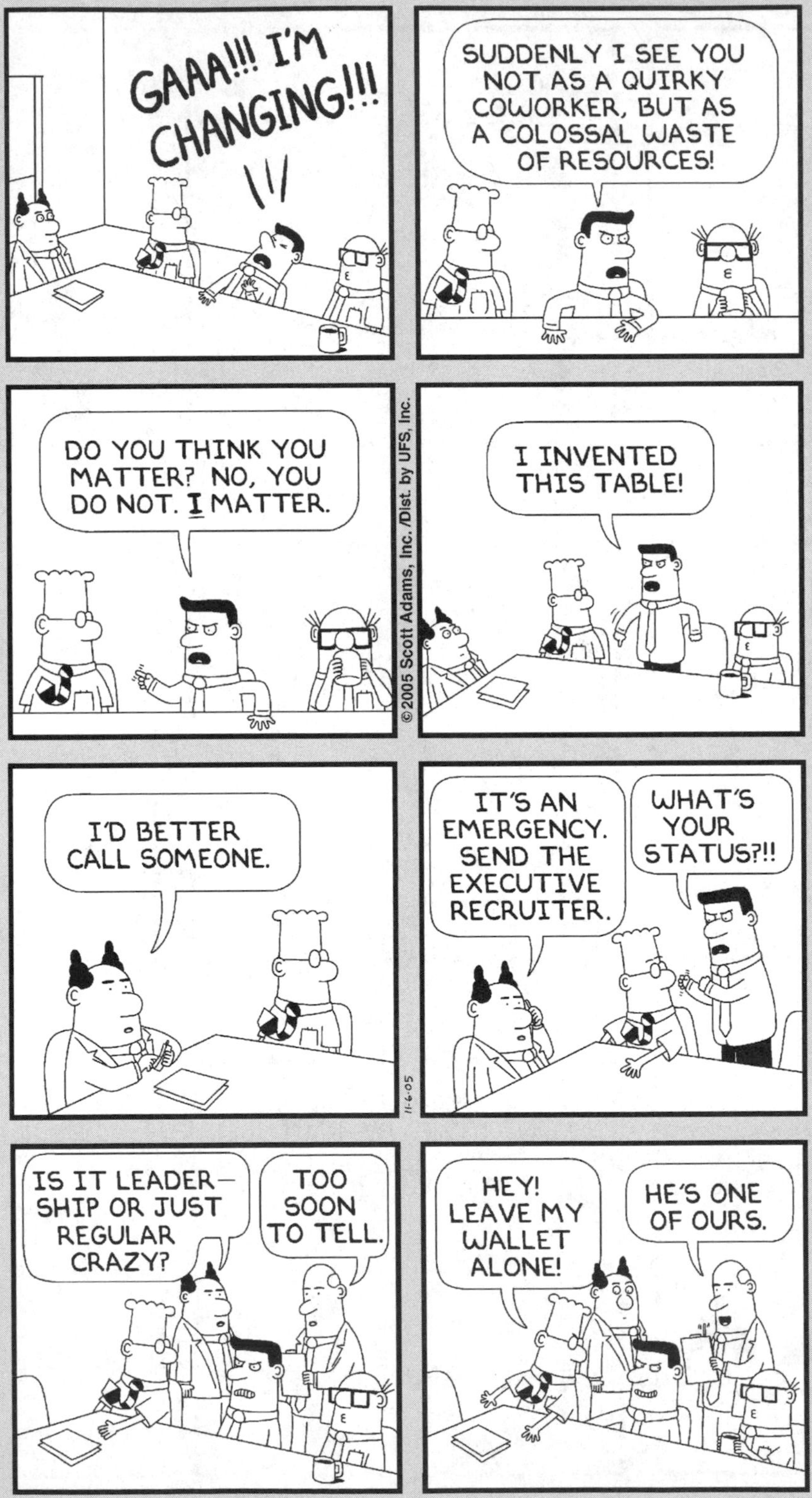
GAAA!!! I'M CHANGING!!!
SUDDENLY I SEE YOU NOT AS A QUIRKY COWORKER, BUT AS A COLOSSAL WASTE OF RESOURCES!
DO YOU THINK YOU MATTER? NO, YOU DO NOT. I MATTER.
©2005 Scott Adams, Inc. /Dist. by UFS, Inc.
I INVENTED THIS TABLE!
I'D BETTER CALL SOMEONE.
IT'S AN EMERGENCY. SEND THE EXECUTIVE RECRUITER.
WHAT'S YOUR STATUS?!!
11-6-05
IS IT LEADER-SHIP OR JUST REGULAR CRAZY?
TOO SOON TO TELL.
HEY! LEAVE MY WALLET ALONE!
HE'S ONE OF OURS.

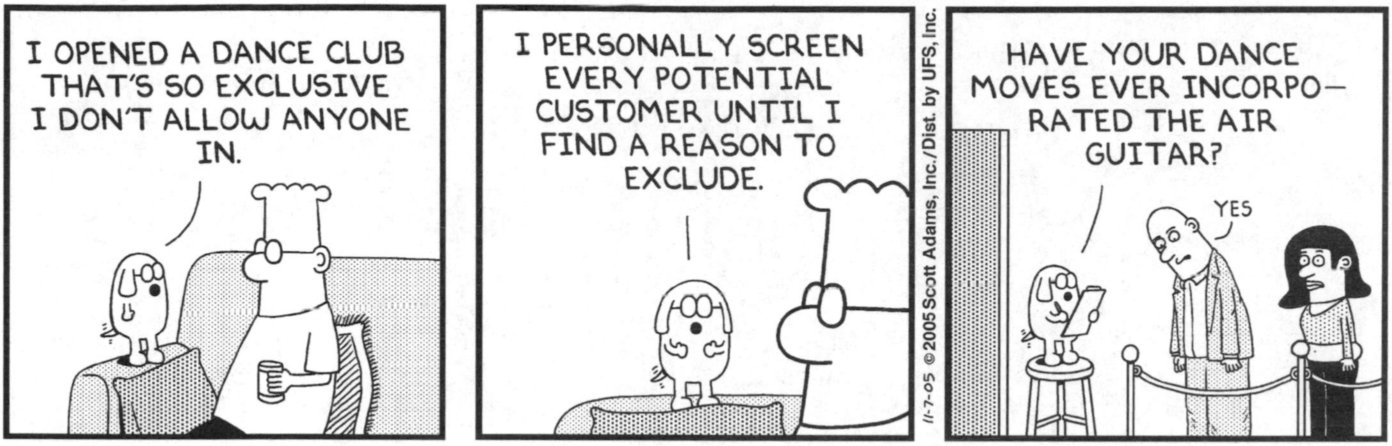
I OPENED A DANCE CLUB THAT'S SO EXCLUSIVE I DON'T ALLOW ANYONE IN.
I PERSONALLY SCREEN EVERY POTENTIAL CUSTOMER UNTIL I FIND A REASON TO EXCLUDE.
11-7-05 © 2005 Scott Adams, Inc./Dist. by UFS, Inc.
HAVE YOUR DANCE MOVES EVER INCORPO– RATED THE AIR GUITAR?
YES

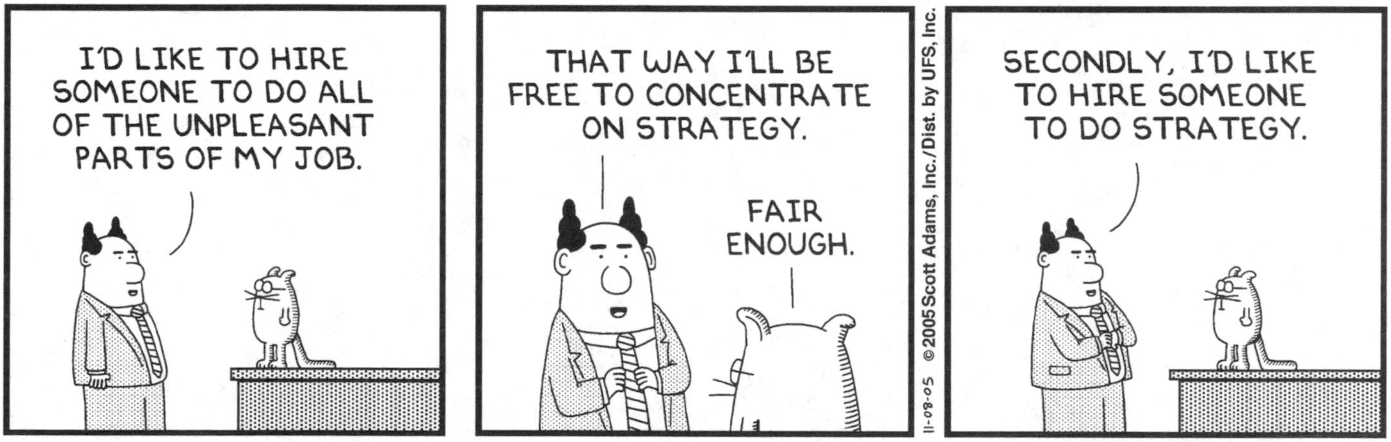
I'D LIKE TO HIRE SOMEONE TO DO ALL OF THE UNPLEASANT PARTS OF MY JOB.
THAT WAY I'LL BE FREE TO CONCENTRATE ON STRATEGY.
FAIR ENOUGH.
11-08-05 © 2005 Scott Adams, Inc./Dist. by UFS, Inc.
SECONDLY, I'D LIKE TO HIRE SOMEONE TO DO STRATEGY.

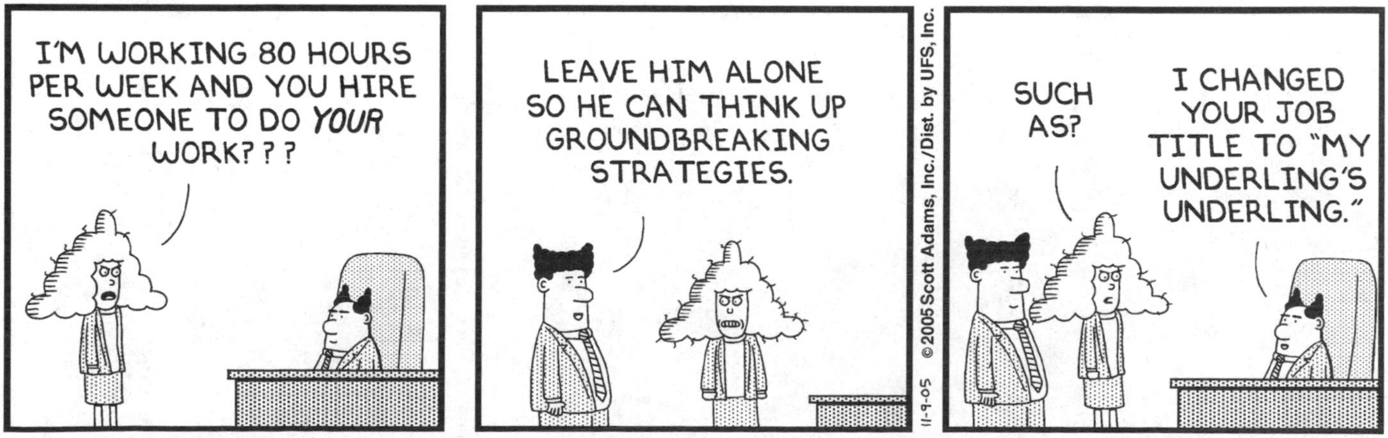
I'M WORKING 80 HOURS PER WEEK AND YOU HIRE SOMEONE TO DO YOUR WORK???
LEAVE HIM ALONE SO HE CAN THINK UP GROUNDBREAKING STRATEGIES.
11-9-05 © 2005 Scott Adams, Inc./Dist. by UFS, Inc.
SUCH AS?
I CHANGED YOUR JOB TITLE TO "MY UNDERLING'S UNDERLING."

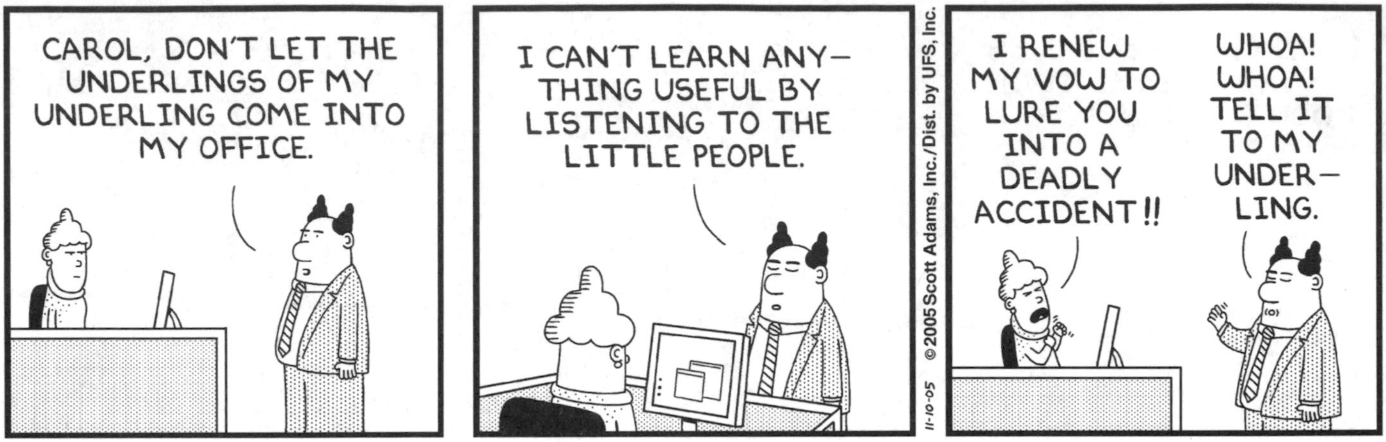
CAROL, DON'T LET THE UNDERLINGS OF MY UNDERLING COME INTO MY OFFICE.
I CAN'T LEARN ANY-THING USEFUL BY LISTENING TO THE LITTLE PEOPLE.
11-10-05 © 2005 Scott Adams, Inc./Dist. by UFS, Inc.
I RENEW MY VOW TO LURE YOU INTO A DEADLY ACCIDENT!!
WHOA! WHOA! TELL IT TO MY UNDER-LING.

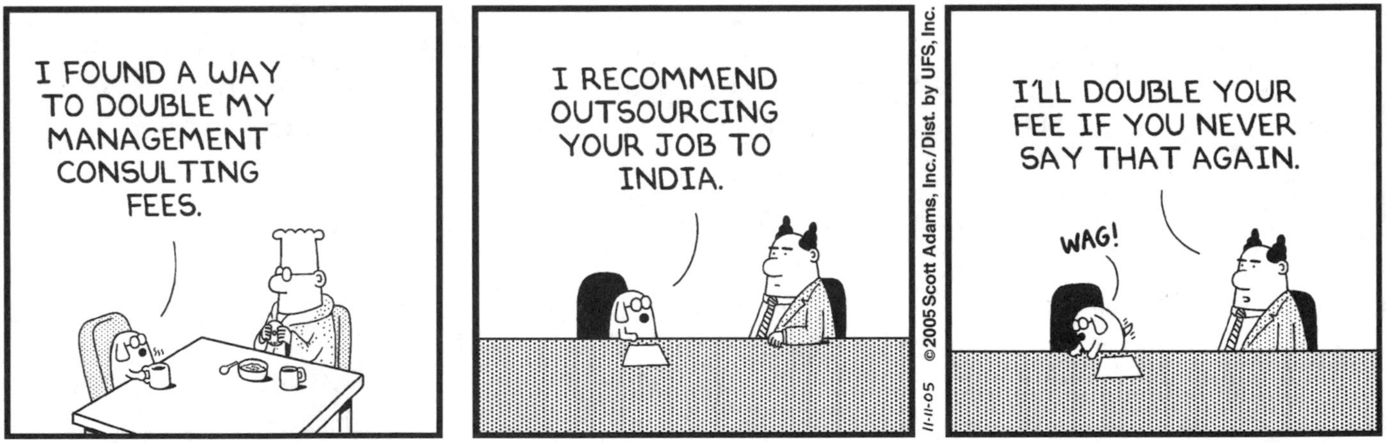
I FOUND A WAY TO DOUBLE MY MANAGEMENT CONSULTING FEES.
I RECOMMEND OUTSOURCING YOUR JOB TO INDIA.
11-11-05 © 2005 Scott Adams, Inc./Dist. by UFS, Inc.
I'LL DOUBLE YOUR FEE IF YOU NEVER SAY THAT AGAIN.
WAG!

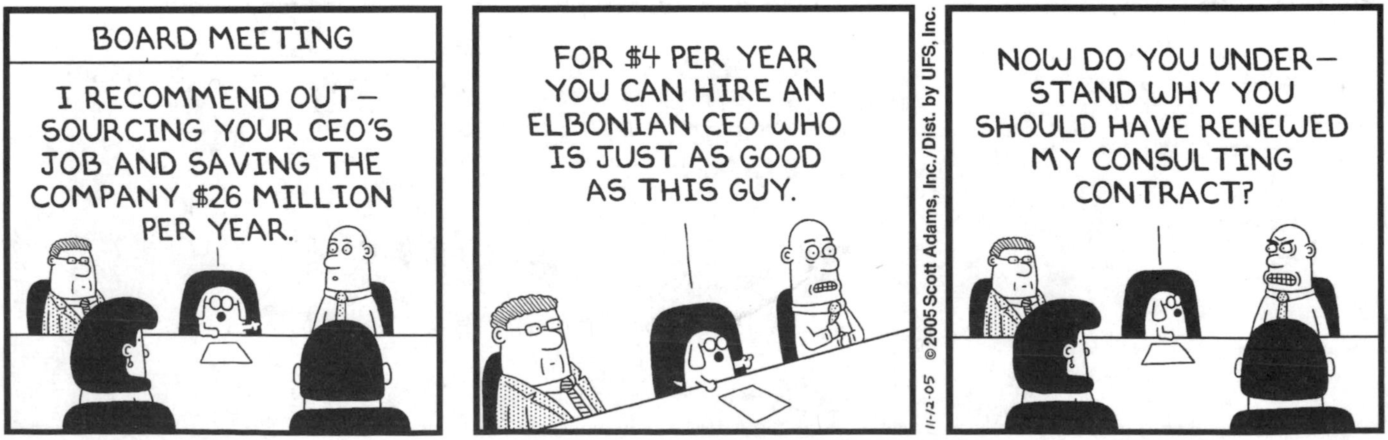
BOARD MEETING
I RECOMMEND OUT-SOURCING YOUR CEO'S JOB AND SAVING THE COMPANY $26 MILLION PER YEAR.
FOR $4 PER YEAR YOU CAN HIRE AN ELBONIAN CEO WHO IS JUST AS GOOD AS THIS GUY.
11-12-05 © 2005 Scott Adams, Inc./Dist. by UFS, Inc.
NOW DO YOU UNDER-STAND WHY YOU SHOULD HAVE RENEWED MY CONSULTING CONTRACT?

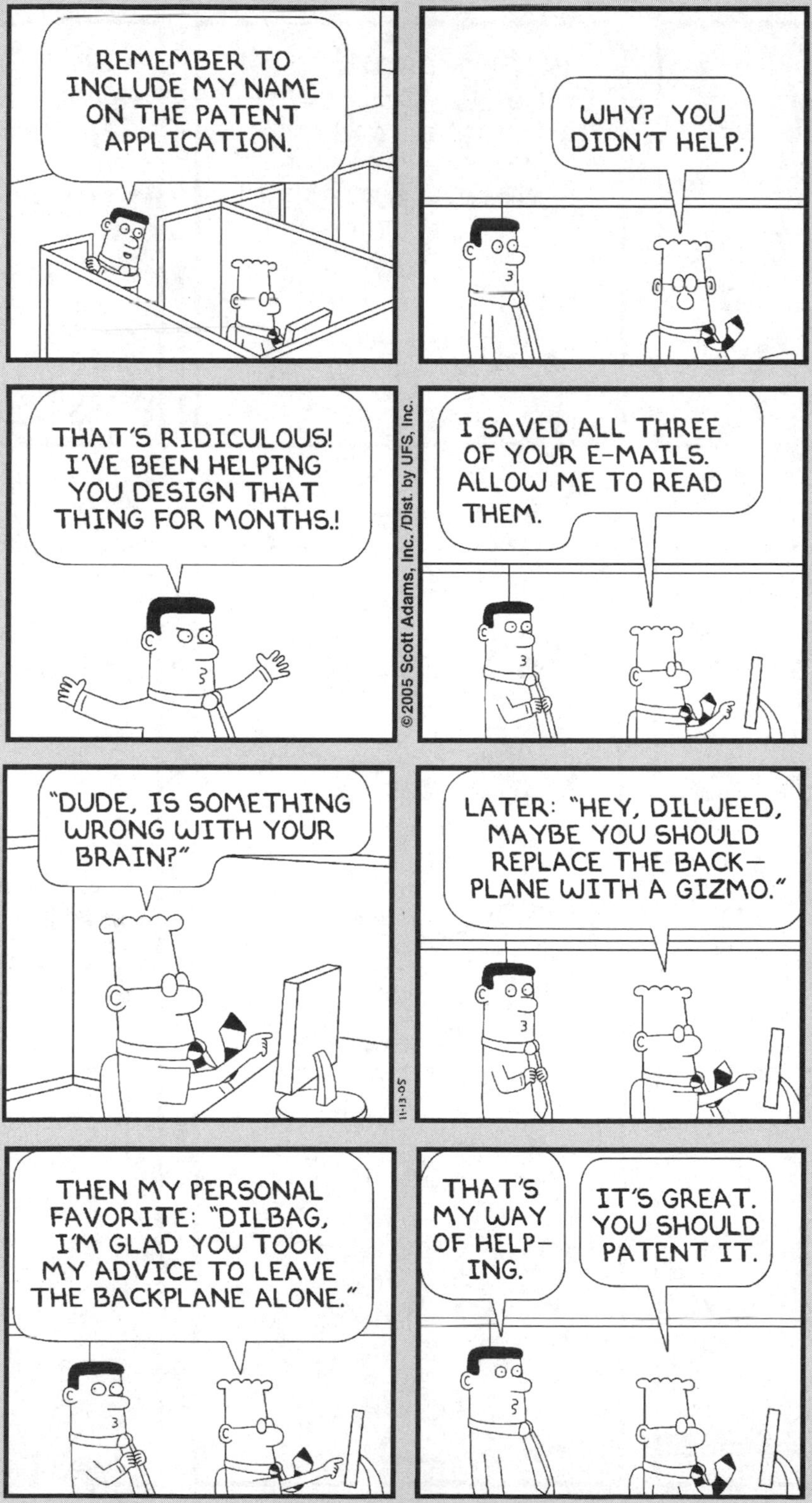
REMEMBER TO INCLUDE MY NAME ON THE PATENT APPLICATION.
WHY? YOU DIDN'T HELP.
THAT'S RIDICULOUS! I'VE BEEN HELPING YOU DESIGN THAT THING FOR MONTHS.!
I SAVED ALL THREE OF YOUR E-MAILS. ALLOW ME TO READ THEM.
"DUDE, IS SOMETHING WRONG WITH YOUR BRAIN?"
LATER: "HEY, DILWEED, MAYBE YOU SHOULD REPLACE THE BACK-PLANE WITH A GIZMO."
THEN MY PERSONAL FAVORITE: "DILBAG, I'M GLAD YOU TOOK MY ADVICE TO LEAVE THE BACKPLANE ALONE."
THAT'S MY WAY OF HELP-ING.
IT'S GREAT. YOU SHOULD PATENT IT.
©2005 Scott Adams, Inc./Dist. by UFS, Inc.
11-13-05

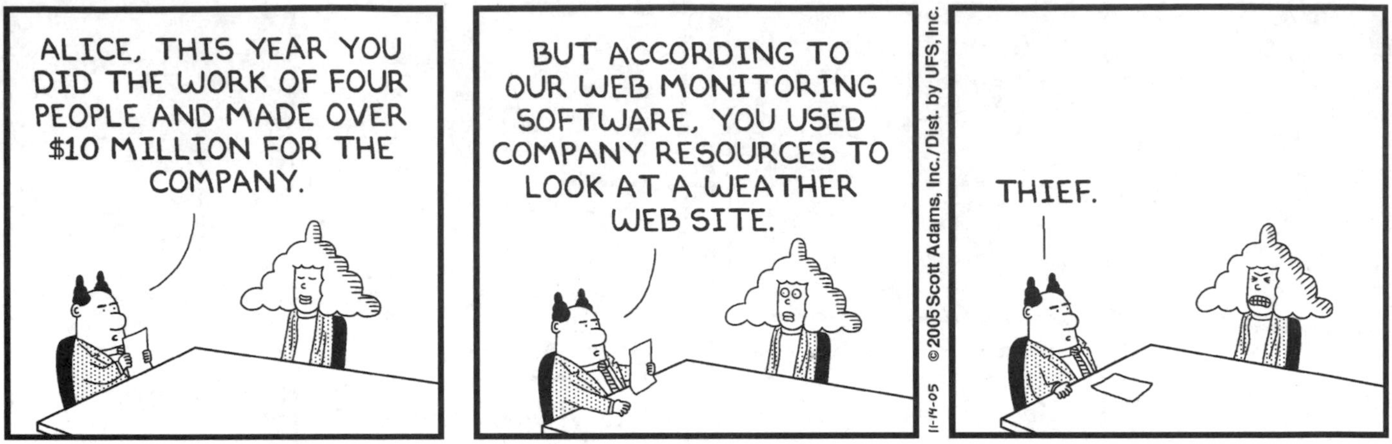
ALICE, THIS YEAR YOU DID THE WORK OF FOUR PEOPLE AND MADE OVER $10 MILLION FOR THE COMPANY.
BUT ACCORDING TO OUR WEB MONITORING SOFTWARE, YOU USED COMPANY RESOURCES TO LOOK AT A WEATHER WEB SITE.
11-14-05 ©2005 Scott Adams, Inc./Dist. by UFS, Inc.
THIEF.

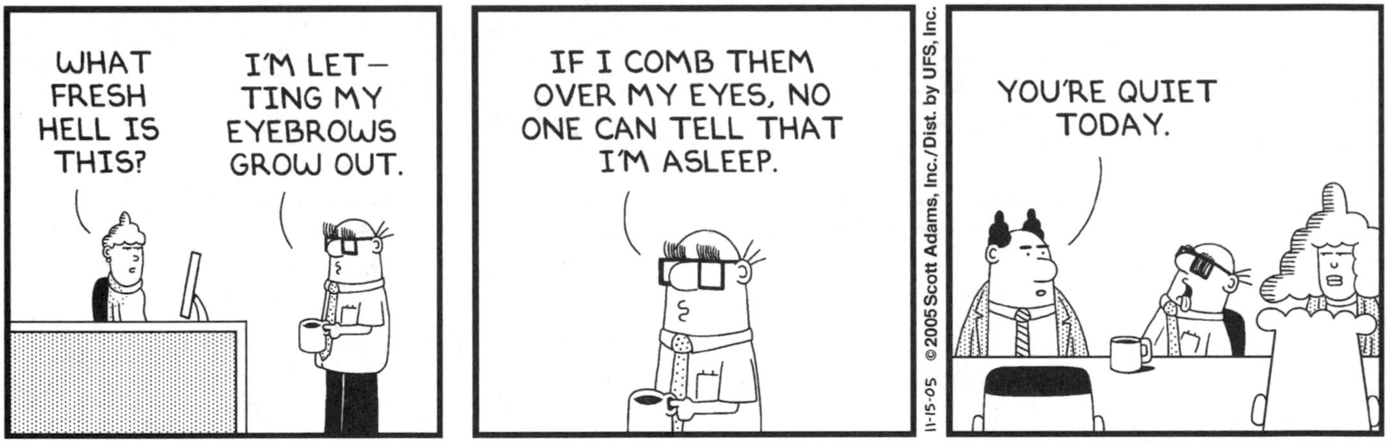
WHAT FRESH HELL IS THIS?
I'M LET-TING MY EYEBROWS GROW OUT.
IF I COMB THEM OVER MY EYES, NO ONE CAN TELL THAT I'M ASLEEP.
11-15-05 ©2005 Scott Adams, Inc./Dist. by UFS, Inc.
YOU'RE QUIET TODAY.

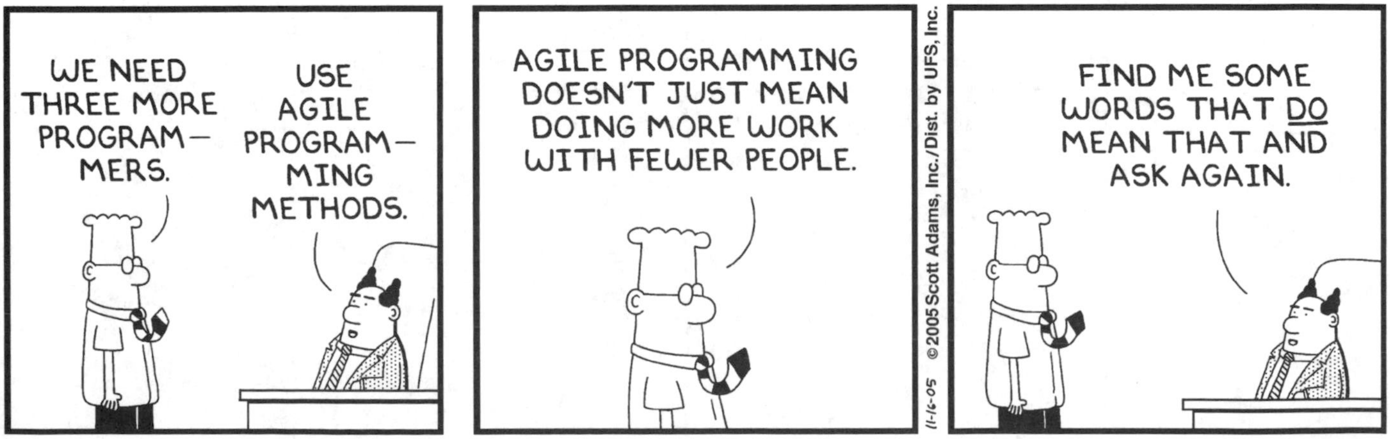
WE NEED THREE MORE PROGRAM-MERS.
USE AGILE PROGRAM-MING METHODS.
AGILE PROGRAMMING DOESN'T JUST MEAN DOING MORE WORK WITH FEWER PEOPLE.
11-16-05 ©2005 Scott Adams, Inc./Dist. by UFS, Inc.
FIND ME SOME WORDS THAT DO MEAN THAT AND ASK AGAIN.

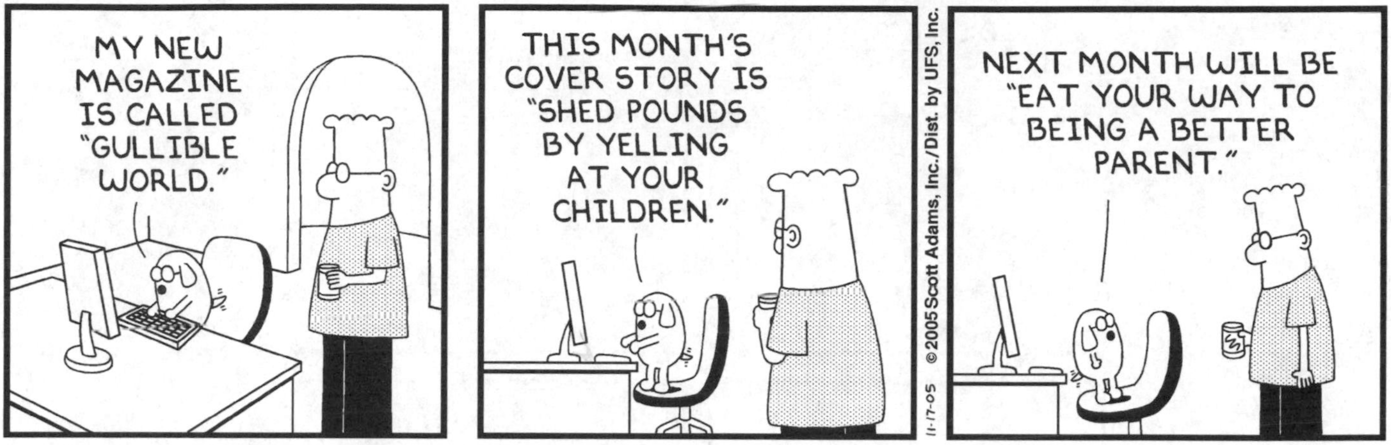
MY NEW MAGAZINE IS CALLED "GULLIBLE WORLD."
THIS MONTH'S COVER STORY IS "SHED POUNDS BY YELLING AT YOUR CHILDREN."
NEXT MONTH WILL BE "EAT YOUR WAY TO BEING A BETTER PARENT."
11-17-05 © 2005 Scott Adams, Inc./Dist. by UFS, Inc.

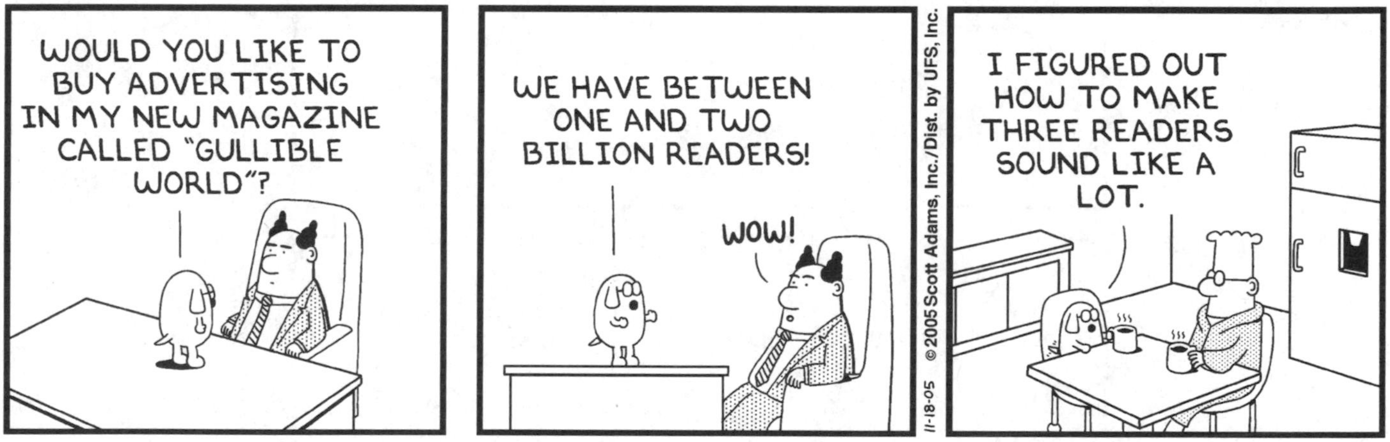
WOULD YOU LIKE TO BUY ADVERTISING IN MY NEW MAGAZINE CALLED "GULLIBLE WORLD"?
WE HAVE BETWEEN ONE AND TWO BILLION READERS!
WOW!
I FIGURED OUT HOW TO MAKE THREE READERS SOUND LIKE A LOT.
11-18-05 © 2005 Scott Adams, Inc./Dist. by UFS, Inc.

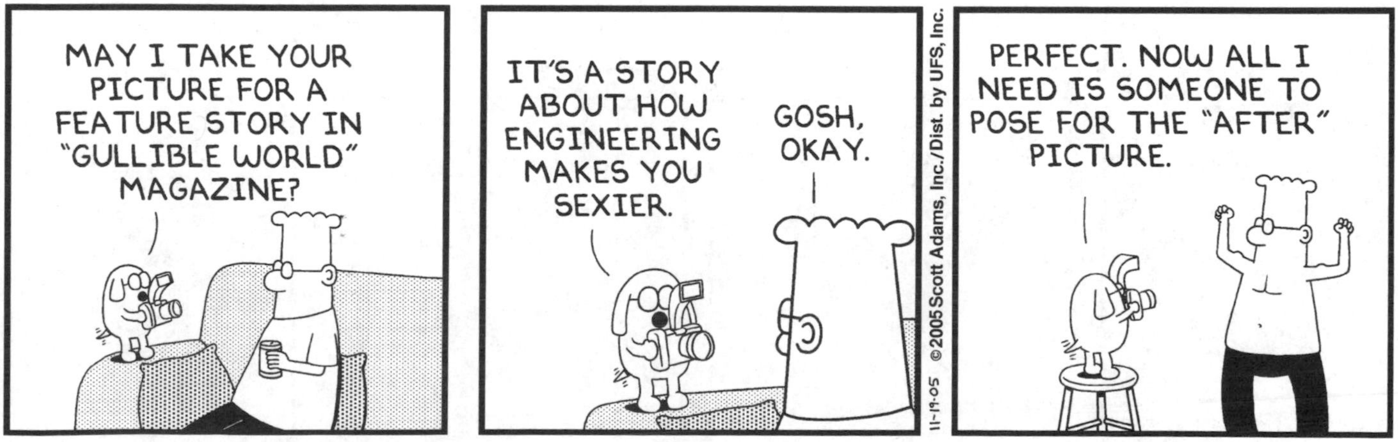
MAY I TAKE YOUR PICTURE FOR A FEATURE STORY IN "GULLIBLE WORLD" MAGAZINE?
IT'S A STORY ABOUT HOW ENGINEERING MAKES YOU SEXIER.
GOSH, OKAY.
PERFECT. NOW ALL I NEED IS SOMEONE TO POSE FOR THE "AFTER" PICTURE.
11-19-05 © 2005 Scott Adams, Inc./Dist. by UFS, Inc.

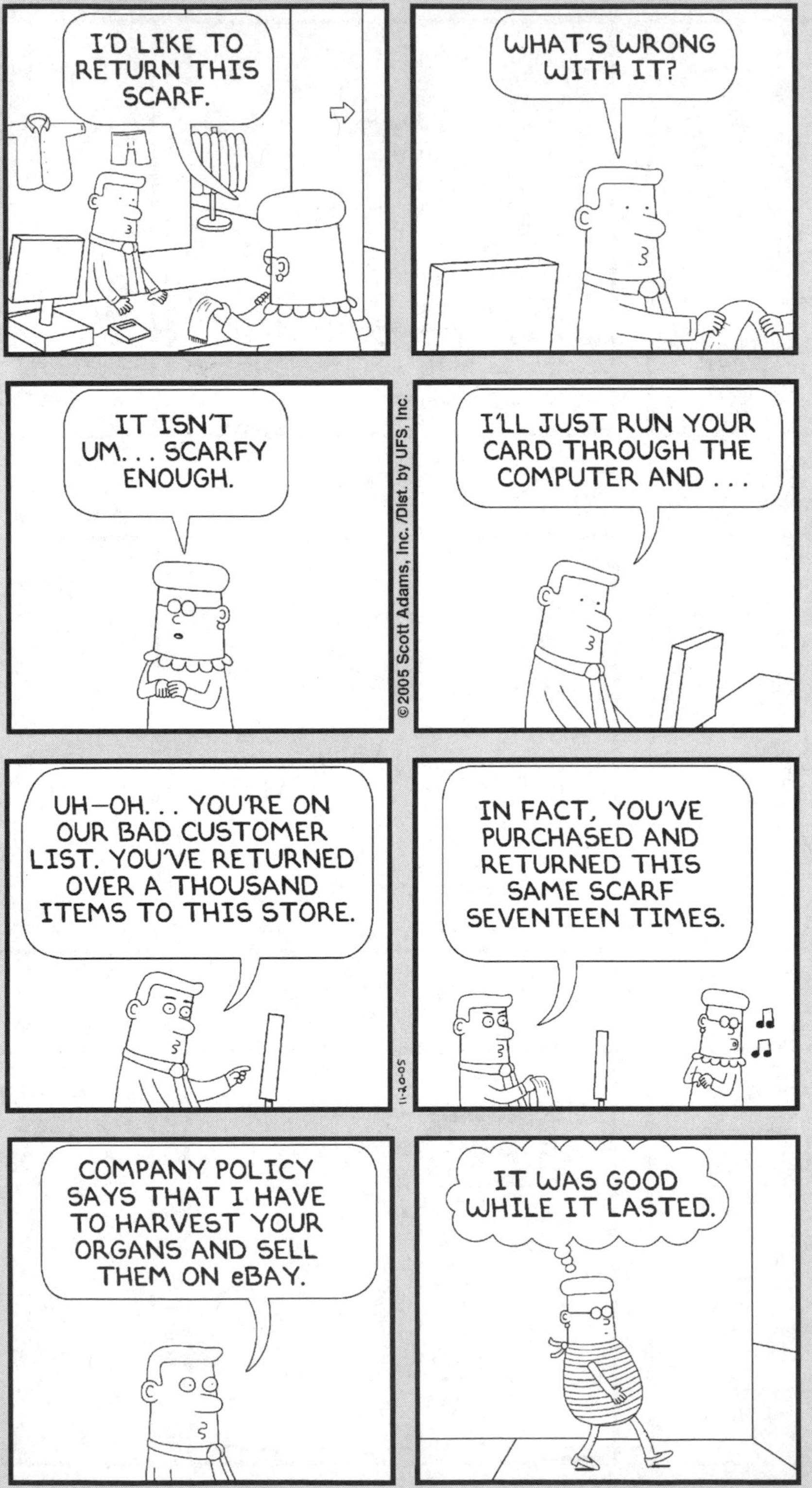
I'D LIKE TO RETURN THIS SCARF.
WHAT'S WRONG WITH IT?
IT ISN'T UM. . . SCARFY ENOUGH.
I'LL JUST RUN YOUR CARD THROUGH THE COMPUTER AND . . .
UH—OH. . . YOU'RE ON OUR BAD CUSTOMER LIST. YOU'VE RETURNED OVER A THOUSAND ITEMS TO THIS STORE.
IN FACT, YOU'VE PURCHASED AND RETURNED THIS SAME SCARF SEVENTEEN TIMES.
COMPANY POLICY SAYS THAT I HAVE TO HARVEST YOUR ORGANS AND SELL THEM ON eBAY.
IT WAS GOOD WHILE IT LASTED.
©2005 Scott Adams, Inc./Dist. by UFS, Inc.
11-20-05

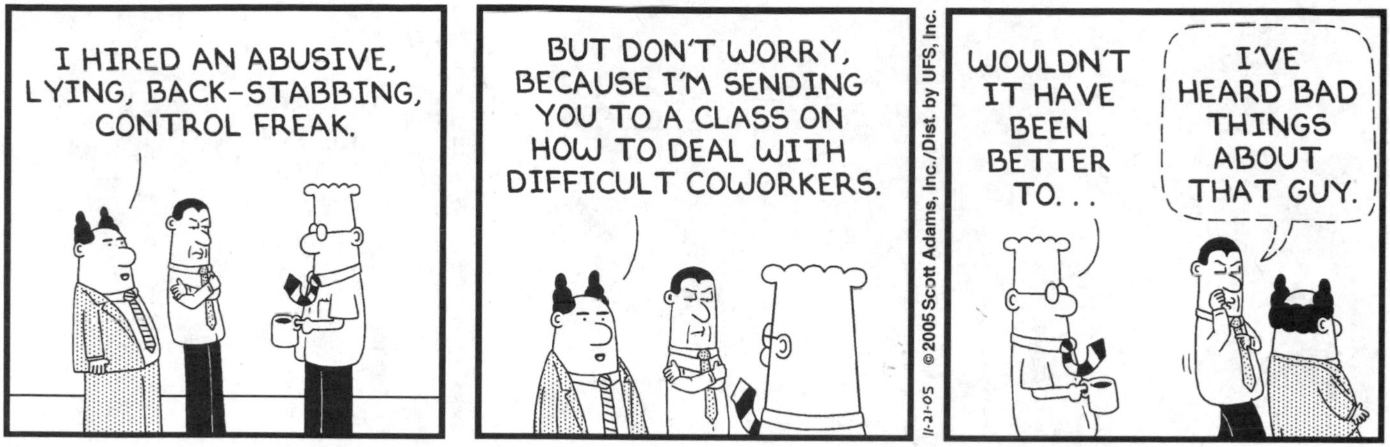
I HIRED AN ABUSIVE, LYING, BACK-STABBING, CONTROL FREAK.
BUT DON'T WORRY, BECAUSE I'M SENDING YOU TO A CLASS ON HOW TO DEAL WITH DIFFICULT COWORKERS.
11-21-05 © 2005 Scott Adams, Inc./Dist. by UFS, Inc.
WOULDN'T IT HAVE BEEN BETTER TO...
I'VE HEARD BAD THINGS ABOUT THAT GUY.

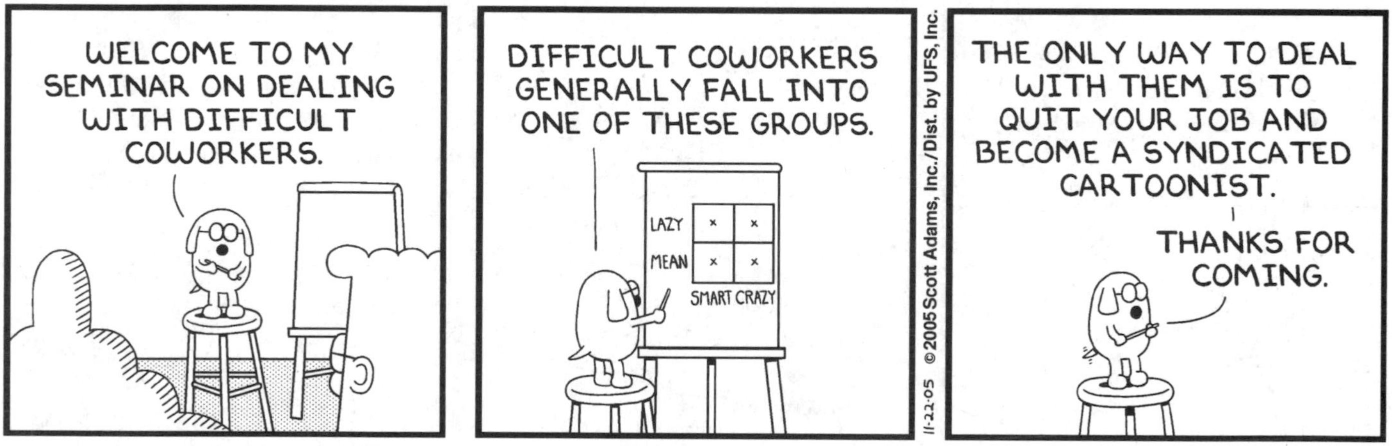
WELCOME TO MY SEMINAR ON DEALING WITH DIFFICULT COWORKERS.
DIFFICULT COWORKERS GENERALLY FALL INTO ONE OF THESE GROUPS.
LAZY
MEAN
SMART CRAZY
11-22-05 © 2005 Scott Adams, Inc./Dist. by UFS, Inc.
THE ONLY WAY TO DEAL WITH THEM IS TO QUIT YOUR JOB AND BECOME A SYNDICATED CARTOONIST.
THANKS FOR COMING.

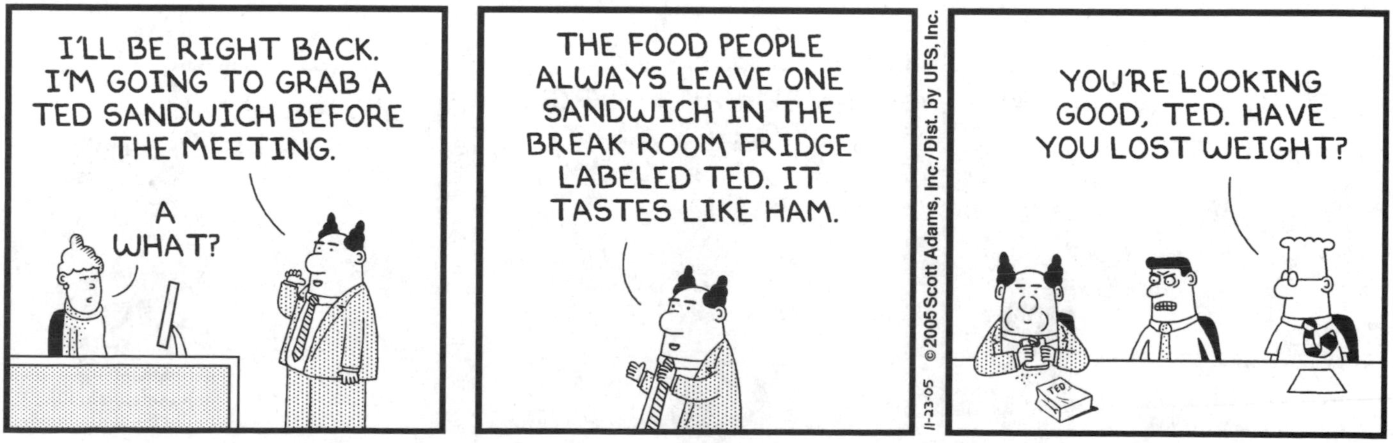
I'LL BE RIGHT BACK. I'M GOING TO GRAB A TED SANDWICH BEFORE THE MEETING.
A WHAT?
THE FOOD PEOPLE ALWAYS LEAVE ONE SANDWICH IN THE BREAK ROOM FRIDGE LABELED TED. IT TASTES LIKE HAM.
11-23-05 © 2005 Scott Adams, Inc./Dist. by UFS, Inc.
YOU'RE LOOKING GOOD, TED. HAVE YOU LOST WEIGHT?
TED

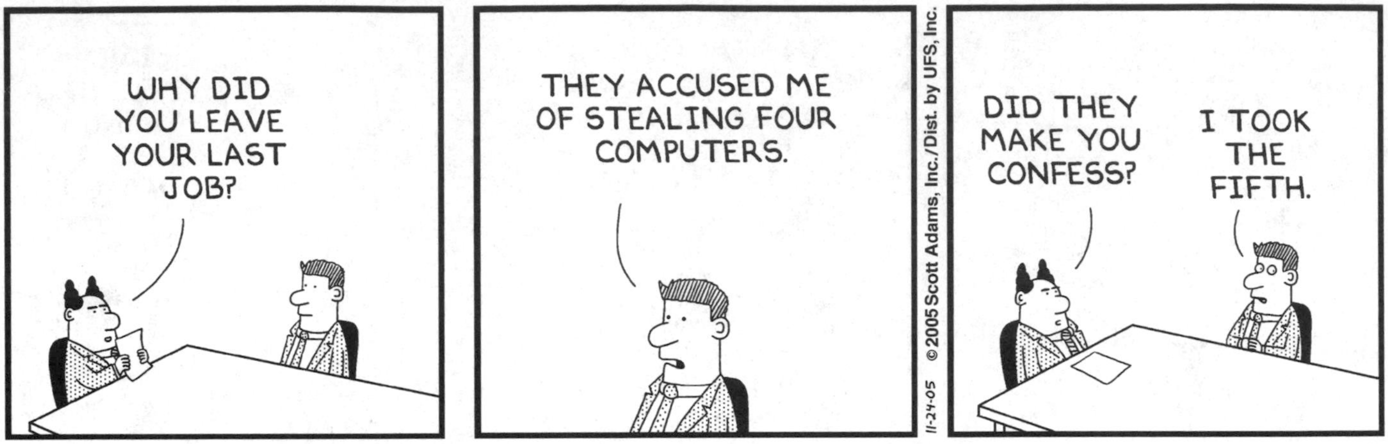
WHY DID YOU LEAVE YOUR LAST JOB?
THEY ACCUSED ME OF STEALING FOUR COMPUTERS.
DID THEY MAKE YOU CONFESS?
I TOOK THE FIFTH.
11-24-05 © 2005 Scott Adams, Inc./Dist. by UFS, Inc.

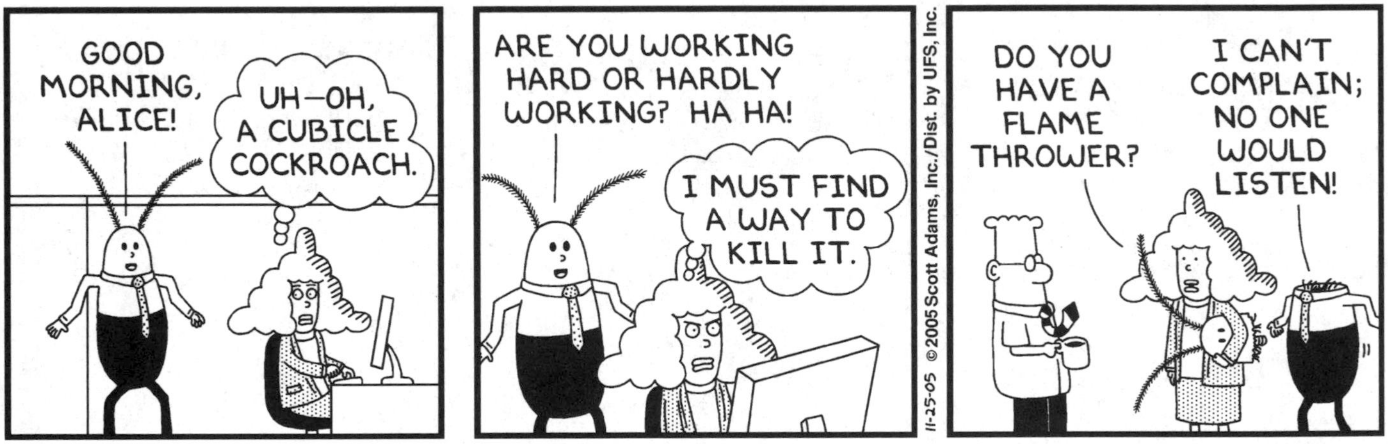
GOOD MORNING, ALICE!
UH—OH, A CUBICLE COCKROACH.
ARE YOU WORKING HARD OR HARDLY WORKING? HA HA!
I MUST FIND A WAY TO KILL IT.
DO YOU HAVE A FLAME THROWER?
I CAN'T COMPLAIN; NO ONE WOULD LISTEN!
11-25-05 © 2005 Scott Adams, Inc./Dist. by UFS, Inc.

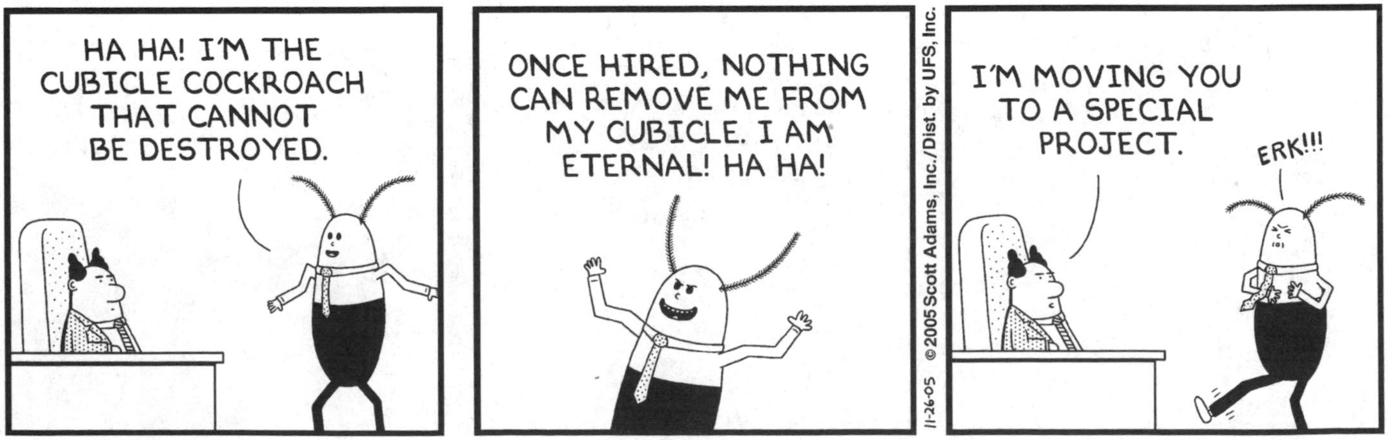
HA HA! I'M THE CUBICLE COCKROACH THAT CANNOT BE DESTROYED.
ONCE HIRED, NOTHING CAN REMOVE ME FROM MY CUBICLE. I AM ETERNAL! HA HA!
I'M MOVING YOU TO A SPECIAL PROJECT.
ERK!!!
11-26-05 © 2005 Scott Adams, Inc./Dist. by UFS, Inc.

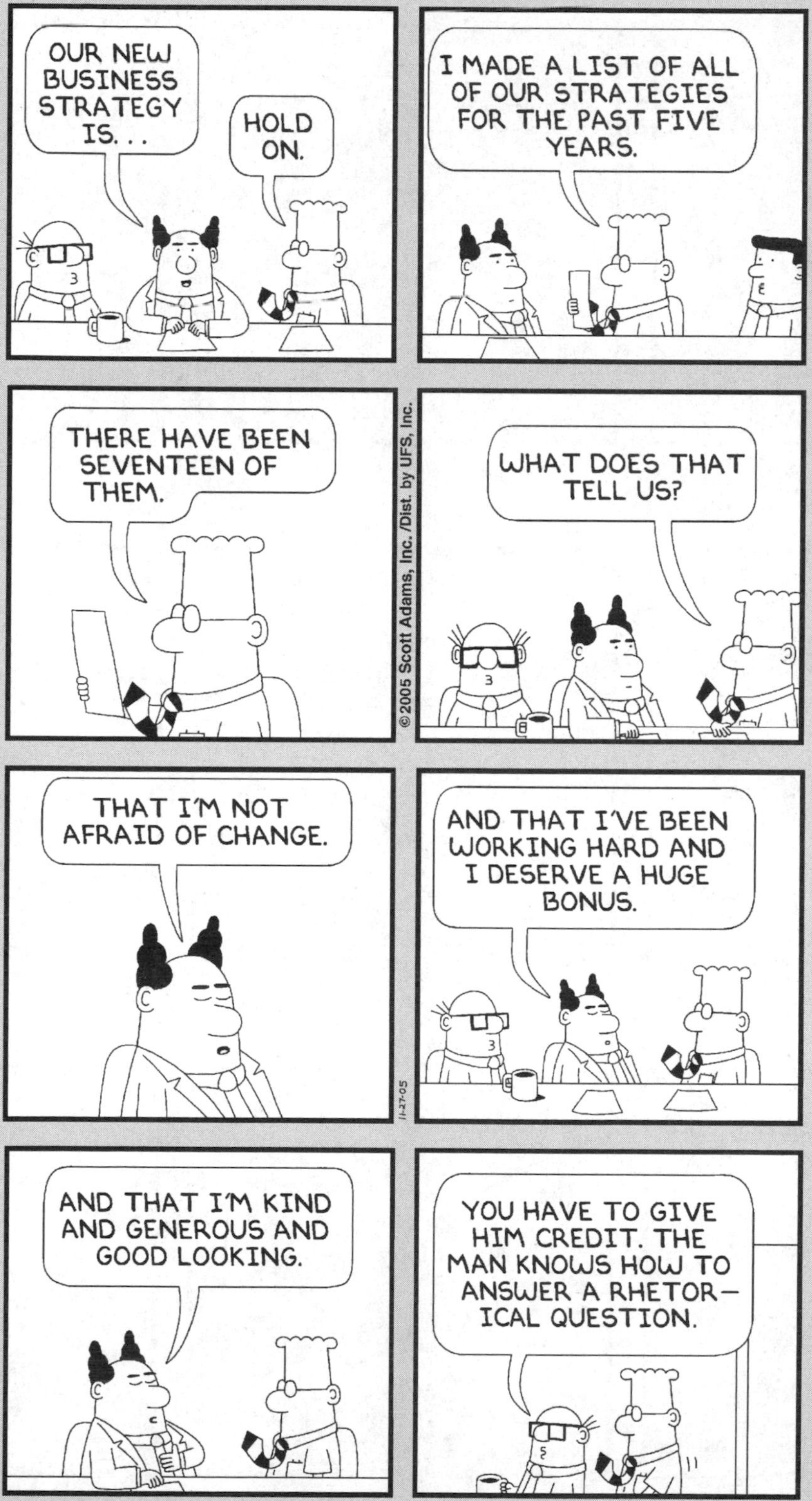
OUR NEW BUSINESS STRATEGY IS. . .
HOLD ON.
I MADE A LIST OF ALL OF OUR STRATEGIES FOR THE PAST FIVE YEARS.
THERE HAVE BEEN SEVENTEEN OF THEM.
WHAT DOES THAT TELL US?
THAT I'M NOT AFRAID OF CHANGE.
AND THAT I'VE BEEN WORKING HARD AND I DESERVE A HUGE BONUS.
AND THAT I'M KIND AND GENEROUS AND GOOD LOOKING.
YOU HAVE TO GIVE HIM CREDIT. THE MAN KNOWS HOW TO ANSWER A RHETOR-ICAL QUESTION.
©2005 Scott Adams, Inc./Dist. by UFS, Inc.
11-27-05

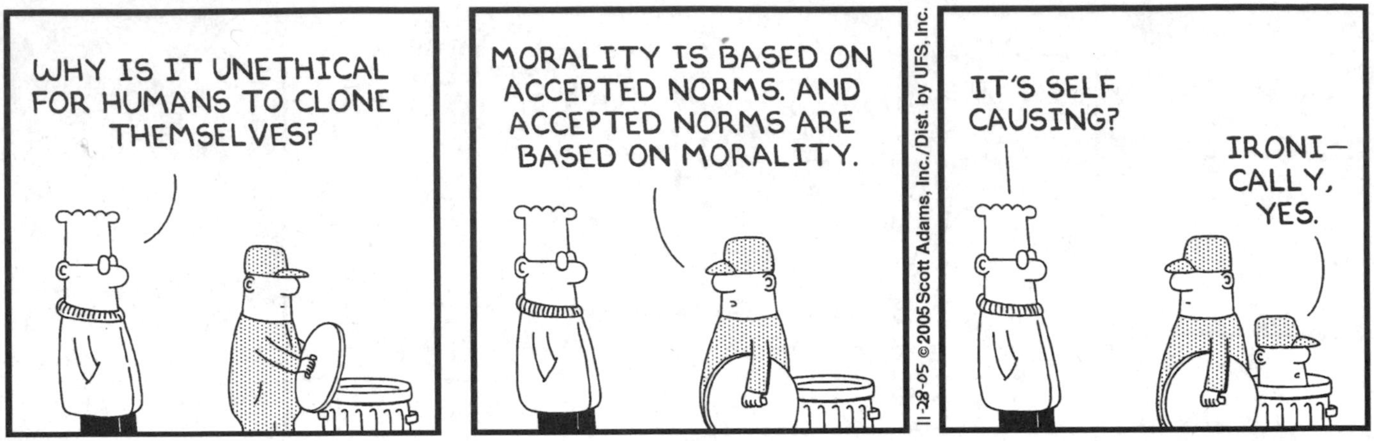
WHY IS IT UNETHICAL FOR HUMANS TO CLONE THEMSELVES?
MORALITY IS BASED ON ACCEPTED NORMS. AND ACCEPTED NORMS ARE BASED ON MORALITY.
11-28-05 ©2005 Scott Adams, Inc./Dist. by UFS, Inc.
IT'S SELF CAUSING?
IRONI-CALLY, YES.

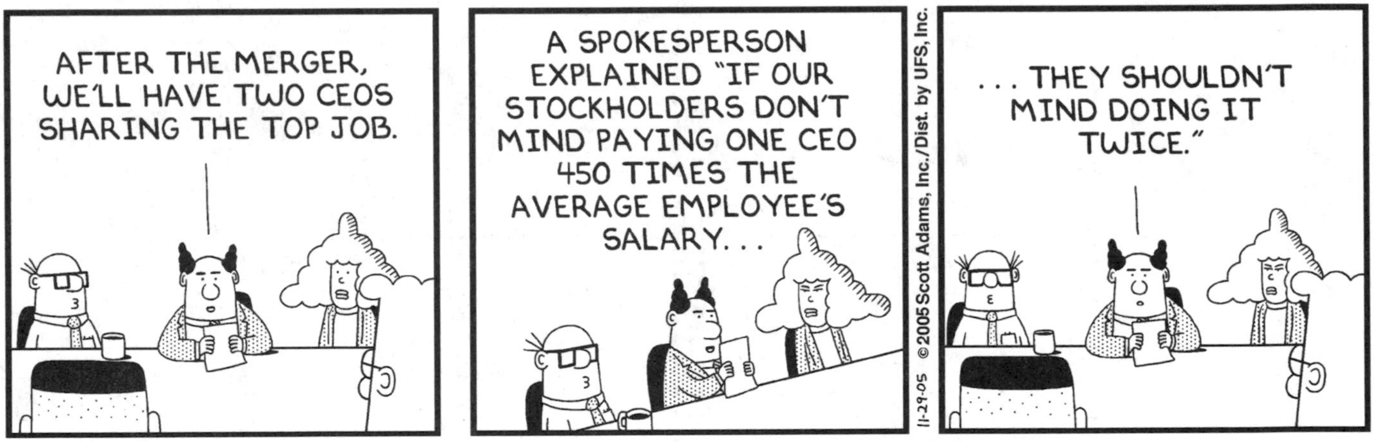
AFTER THE MERGER, WE'LL HAVE TWO CEOS SHARING THE TOP JOB.
A SPOKESPERSON EXPLAINED "IF OUR STOCKHOLDERS DON'T MIND PAYING ONE CEO 450 TIMES THE AVERAGE EMPLOYEE'S SALARY. . .
11-29-05 ©2005 Scott Adams, Inc./Dist. by UFS, Inc.
. . . THEY SHOULDN'T MIND DOING IT TWICE."

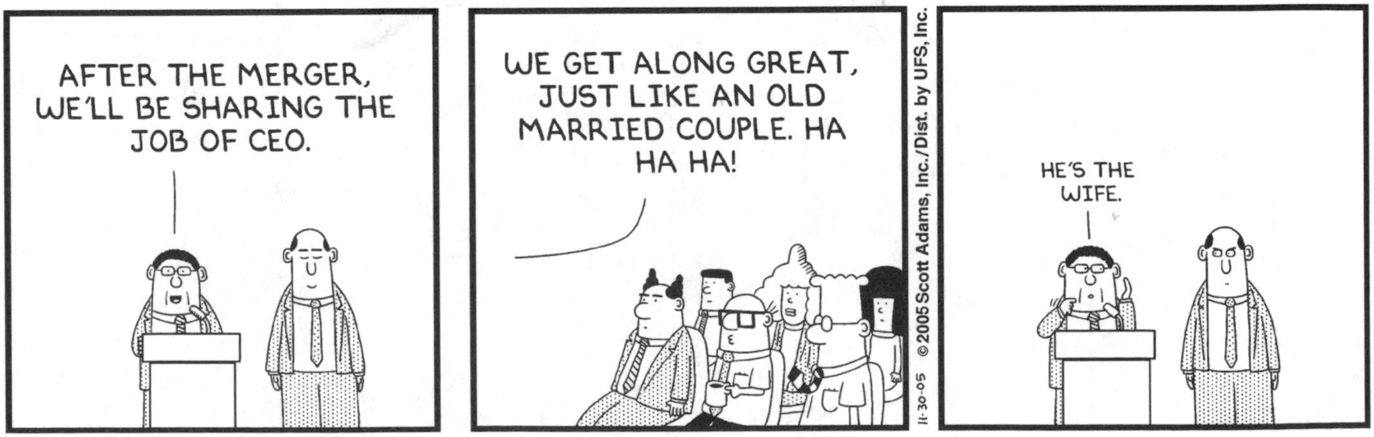
AFTER THE MERGER, WE'LL BE SHARING THE JOB OF CEO.
WE GET ALONG GREAT, JUST LIKE AN OLD MARRIED COUPLE. HA HA HA!
11-30-05 ©2005 Scott Adams, Inc./Dist. by UFS, Inc.
HE'S THE WIFE.

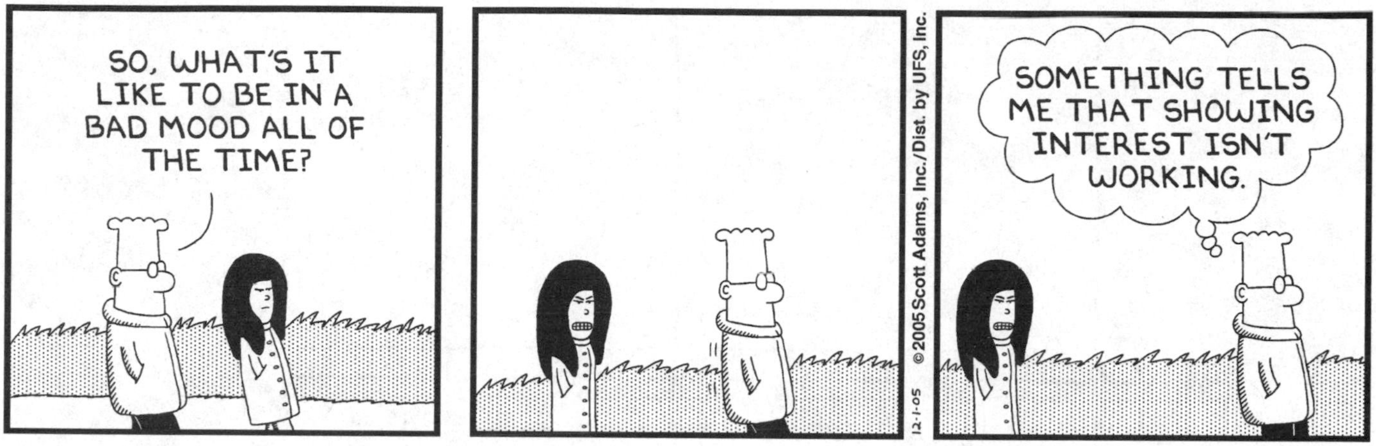
SO, WHAT'S IT LIKE TO BE IN A BAD MOOD ALL OF THE TIME?
SOMETHING TELLS ME THAT SHOWING INTEREST ISN'T WORKING.
12-1-05 ©2005 Scott Adams, Inc./Dist. by UFS, Inc.

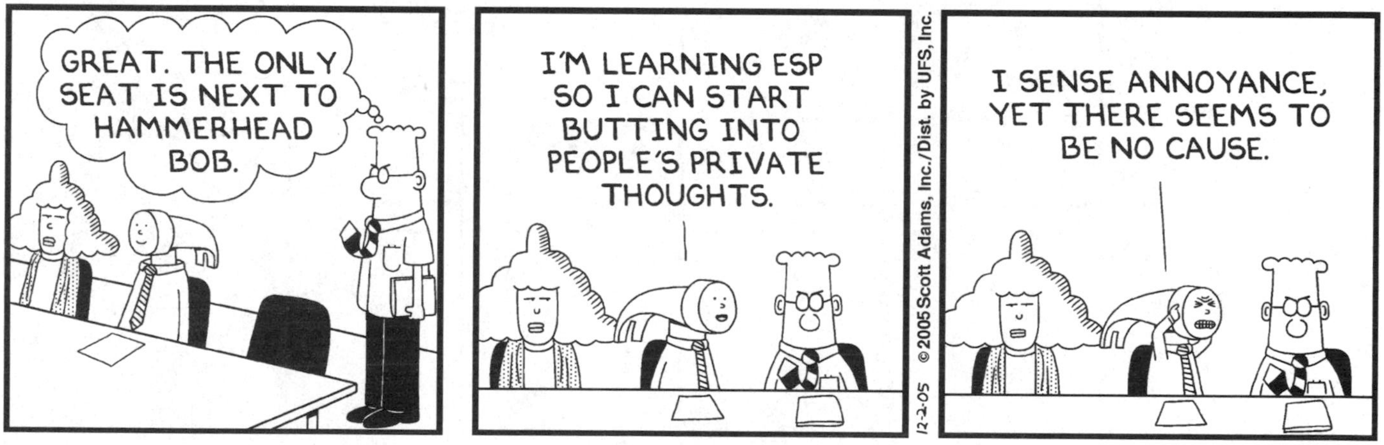
GREAT. THE ONLY SEAT IS NEXT TO HAMMERHEAD BOB.
I'M LEARNING ESP SO I CAN START BUTTING INTO PEOPLE'S PRIVATE THOUGHTS.
I SENSE ANNOYANCE, YET THERE SEEMS TO BE NO CAUSE.
12-2-05 ©2005 Scott Adams, Inc./Dist. by UFS, Inc.

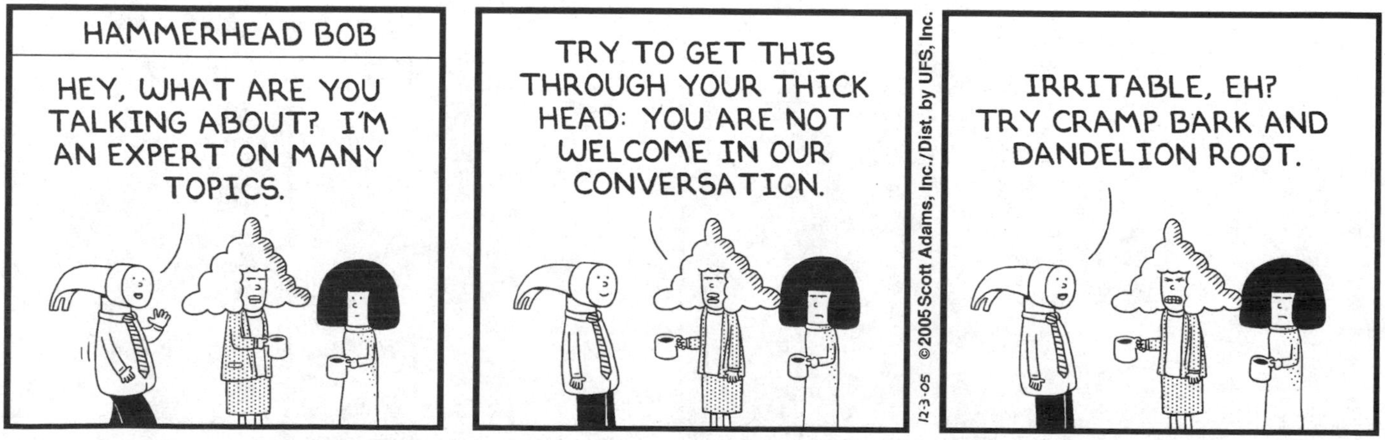
HAMMERHEAD BOB
HEY, WHAT ARE YOU TALKING ABOUT? I'M AN EXPERT ON MANY TOPICS.
TRY TO GET THIS THROUGH YOUR THICK HEAD: YOU ARE NOT WELCOME IN OUR CONVERSATION.
IRRITABLE, EH? TRY CRAMP BARK AND DANDELION ROOT.
12-3-05 ©2005 Scott Adams, Inc./Dist. by UFS, Inc.

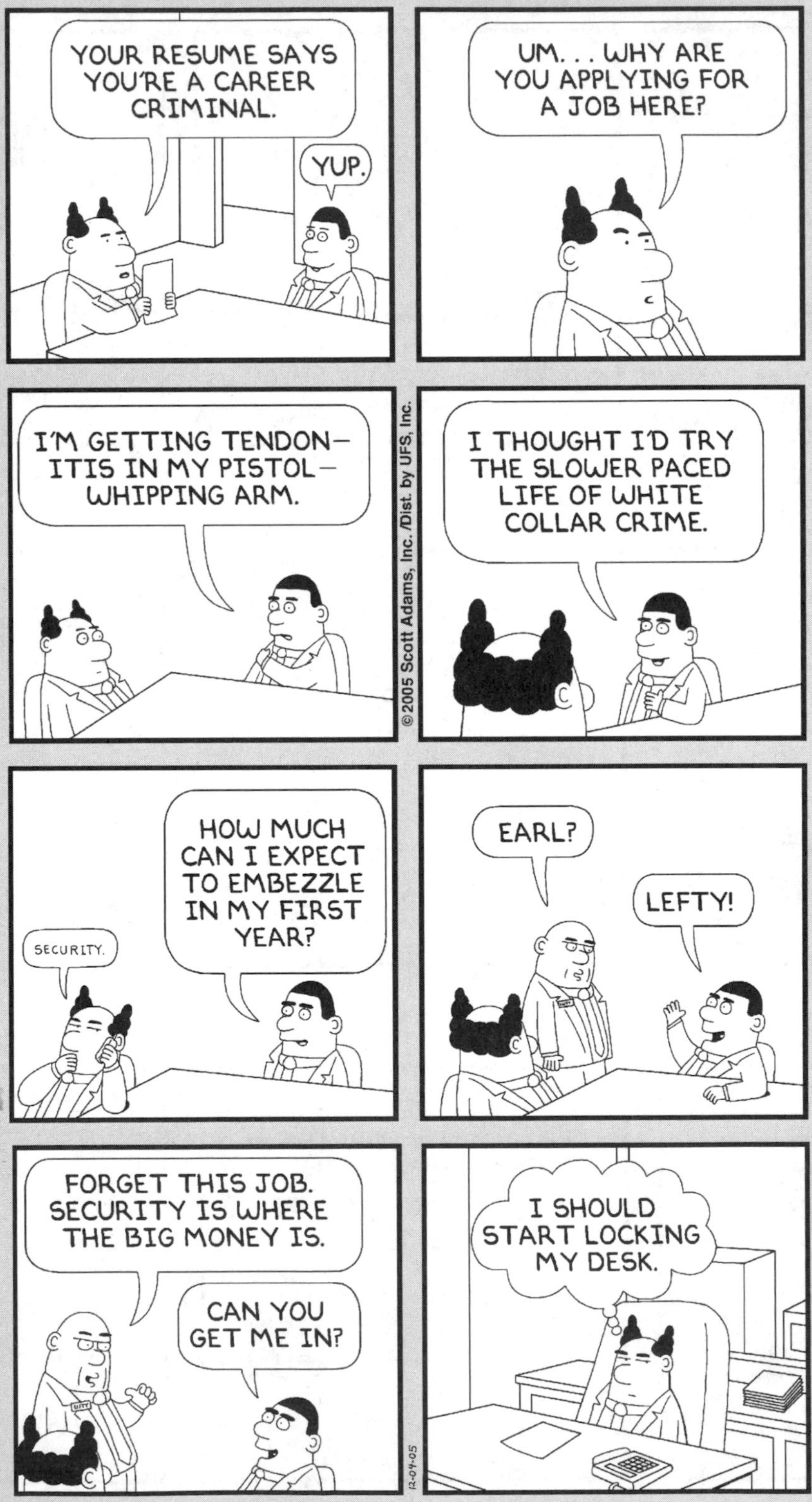

YOUR RESUME SAYS YOU'RE A CAREER CRIMINAL.
YUP.
UM. . . WHY ARE YOU APPLYING FOR A JOB HERE?
I'M GETTING TENDON-ITIS IN MY PISTOL-WHIPPING ARM.
I THOUGHT I'D TRY THE SLOWER PACED LIFE OF WHITE COLLAR CRIME.
© 2005 Scott Adams, Inc. /Dist. by UFS, Inc.
HOW MUCH CAN I EXPECT TO EMBEZZLE IN MY FIRST YEAR?
SECURITY.
EARL?
LEFTY!
FORGET THIS JOB. SECURITY IS WHERE THE BIG MONEY IS.
CAN YOU GET ME IN?
I SHOULD START LOCKING MY DESK.
12-04-05

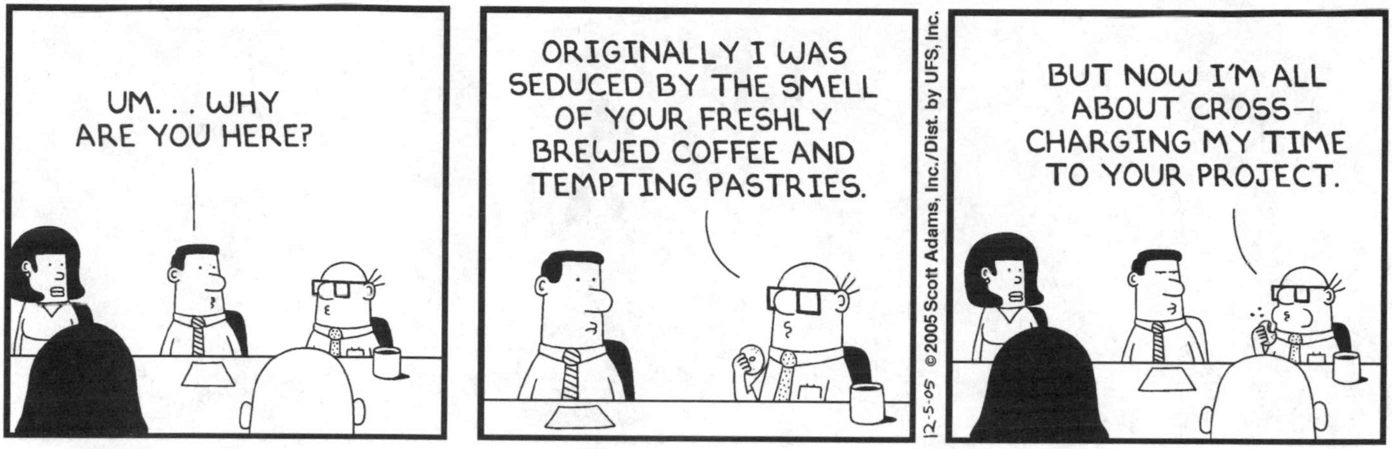
UM. . . WHY ARE YOU HERE?
ORIGINALLY I WAS SEDUCED BY THE SMELL OF YOUR FRESHLY BREWED COFFEE AND TEMPTING PASTRIES.
12-5-05 ©2005 Scott Adams, Inc./Dist. by UFS, Inc.
BUT NOW I'M ALL ABOUT CROSS-CHARGING MY TIME TO YOUR PROJECT.

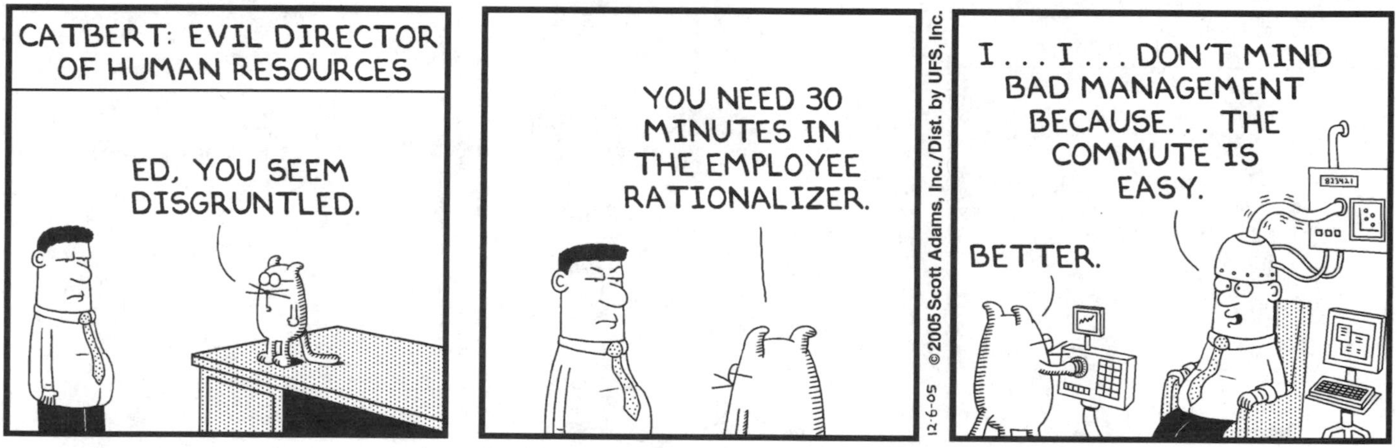
CATBERT: EVIL DIRECTOR OF HUMAN RESOURCES
ED, YOU SEEM DISGRUNTLED.
YOU NEED 30 MINUTES IN THE EMPLOYEE RATIONALIZER.
12-6-05 ©2005 Scott Adams, Inc./Dist. by UFS, Inc.
I . . . I . . . DON'T MIND BAD MANAGEMENT BECAUSE. . . THE COMMUTE IS EASY.
BETTER.

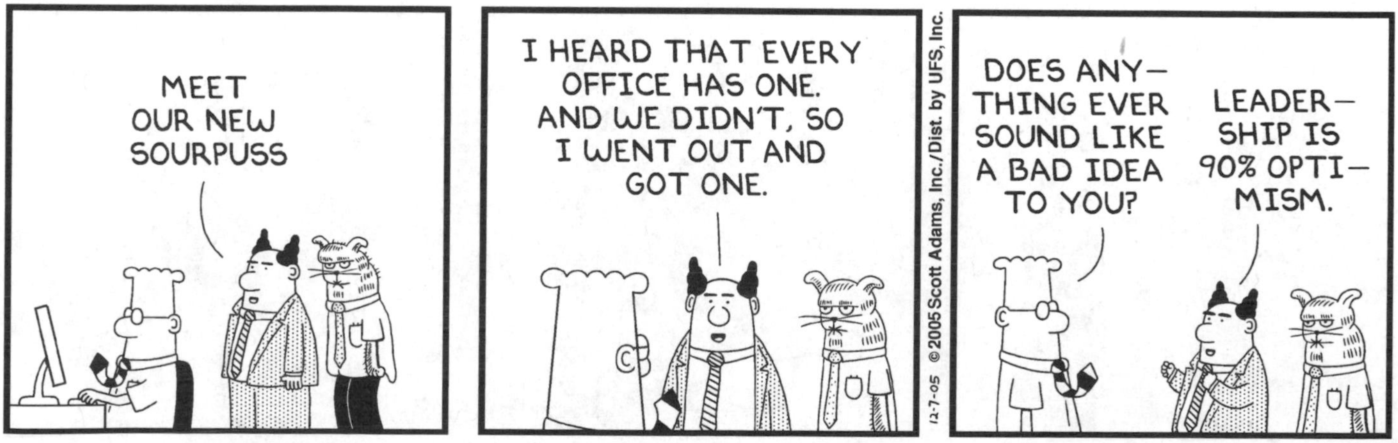
MEET OUR NEW SOURPUSS
I HEARD THAT EVERY OFFICE HAS ONE. AND WE DIDN'T, SO I WENT OUT AND GOT ONE.
12-7-05 ©2005 Scott Adams, Inc./Dist. by UFS, Inc.
DOES ANY-THING EVER SOUND LIKE A BAD IDEA TO YOU?
LEADER-SHIP IS 90% OPTI-MISM.

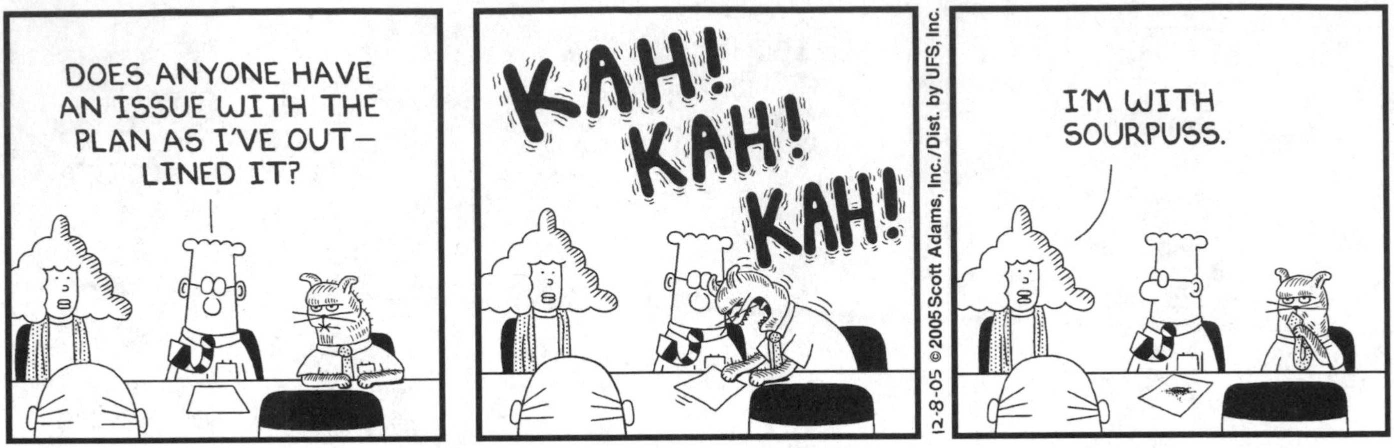
DOES ANYONE HAVE AN ISSUE WITH THE PLAN AS I'VE OUT-LINED IT?
KAH! KAH! KAH!
12-8-05 © 2005 Scott Adams, Inc./Dist. by UFS, Inc.
I'M WITH SOURPUSS.

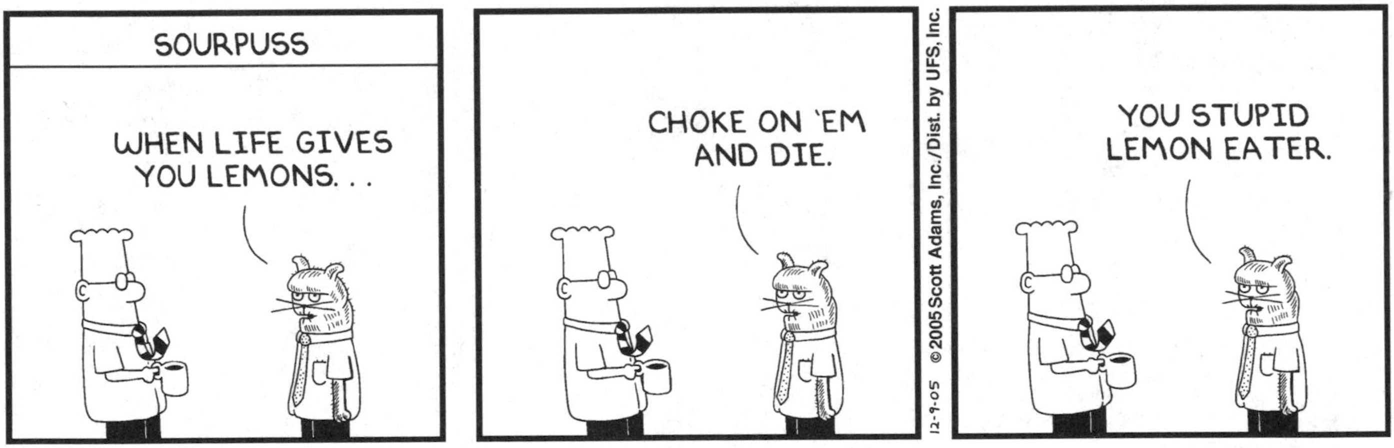
SOURPUSS
WHEN LIFE GIVES YOU LEMONS. . .
CHOKE ON 'EM AND DIE.
12-9-05 © 2005 Scott Adams, Inc./Dist. by UFS, Inc.
YOU STUPID LEMON EATER.

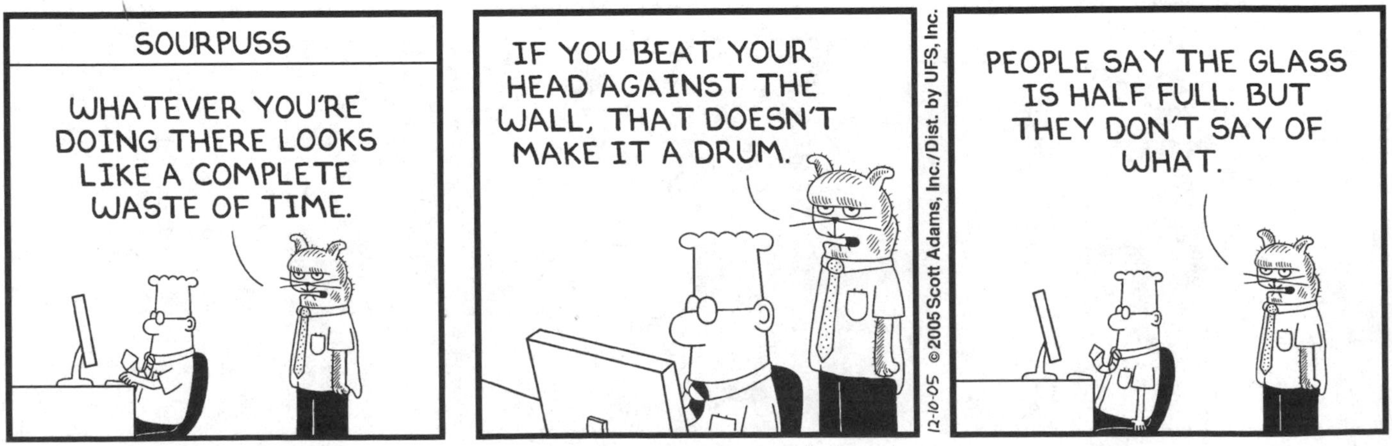
SOURPUSS
WHATEVER YOU'RE DOING THERE LOOKS LIKE A COMPLETE WASTE OF TIME.
IF YOU BEAT YOUR HEAD AGAINST THE WALL, THAT DOESN'T MAKE IT A DRUM.
12-10-05 © 2005 Scott Adams, Inc./Dist. by UFS, Inc.
PEOPLE SAY THE GLASS IS HALF FULL. BUT THEY DON'T SAY OF WHAT.

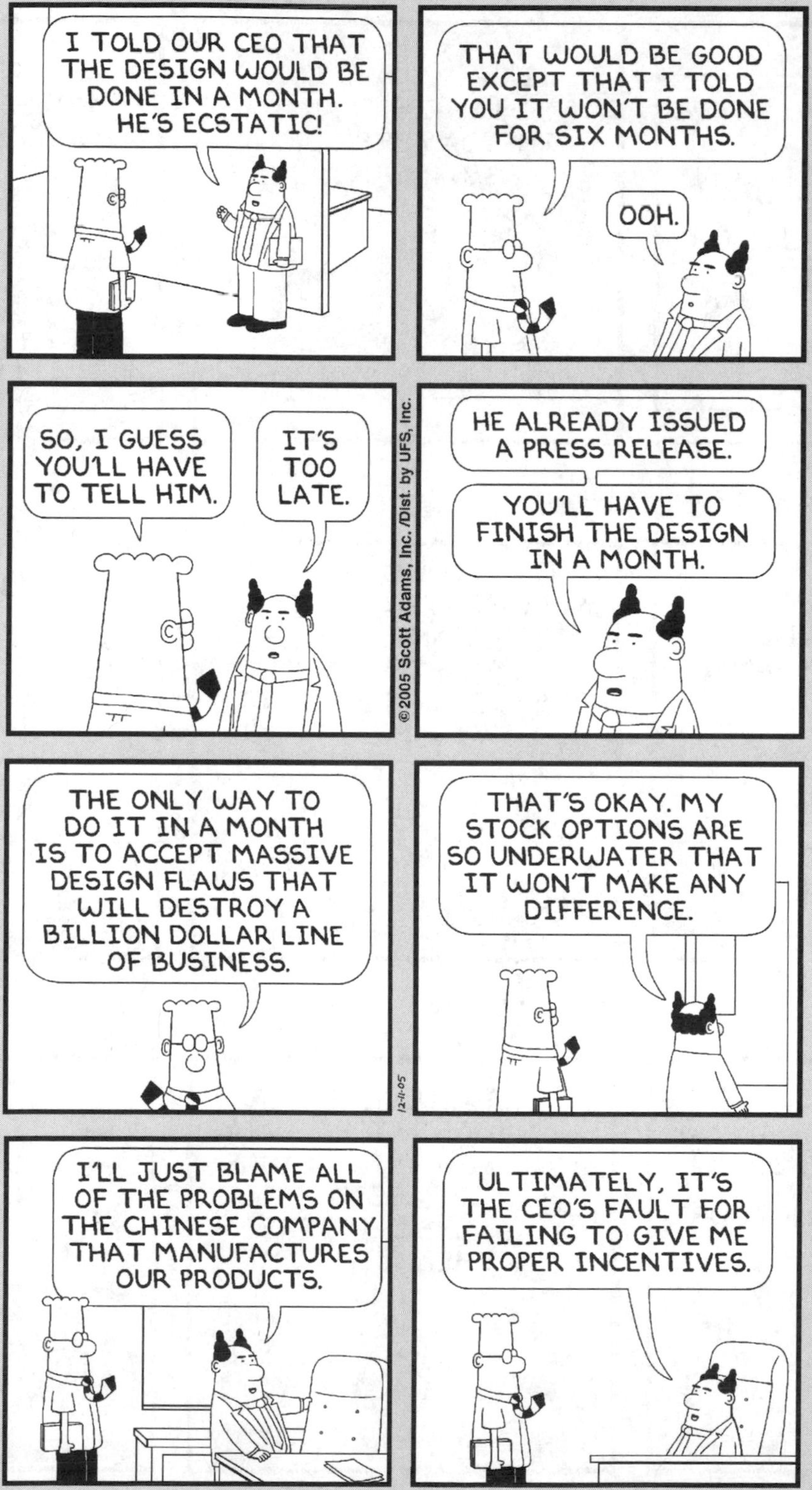
I TOLD OUR CEO THAT THE DESIGN WOULD BE DONE IN A MONTH. HE'S ECSTATIC!
THAT WOULD BE GOOD EXCEPT THAT I TOLD YOU IT WON'T BE DONE FOR SIX MONTHS.
OOH.
SO, I GUESS YOU'LL HAVE TO TELL HIM.
IT'S TOO LATE.
HE ALREADY ISSUED A PRESS RELEASE.
YOU'LL HAVE TO FINISH THE DESIGN IN A MONTH.
THE ONLY WAY TO DO IT IN A MONTH IS TO ACCEPT MASSIVE DESIGN FLAWS THAT WILL DESTROY A BILLION DOLLAR LINE OF BUSINESS.
THAT'S OKAY. MY STOCK OPTIONS ARE SO UNDERWATER THAT IT WON'T MAKE ANY DIFFERENCE.
I'LL JUST BLAME ALL OF THE PROBLEMS ON THE CHINESE COMPANY THAT MANUFACTURES OUR PRODUCTS.
ULTIMATELY, IT'S THE CEO'S FAULT FOR FAILING TO GIVE ME PROPER INCENTIVES.

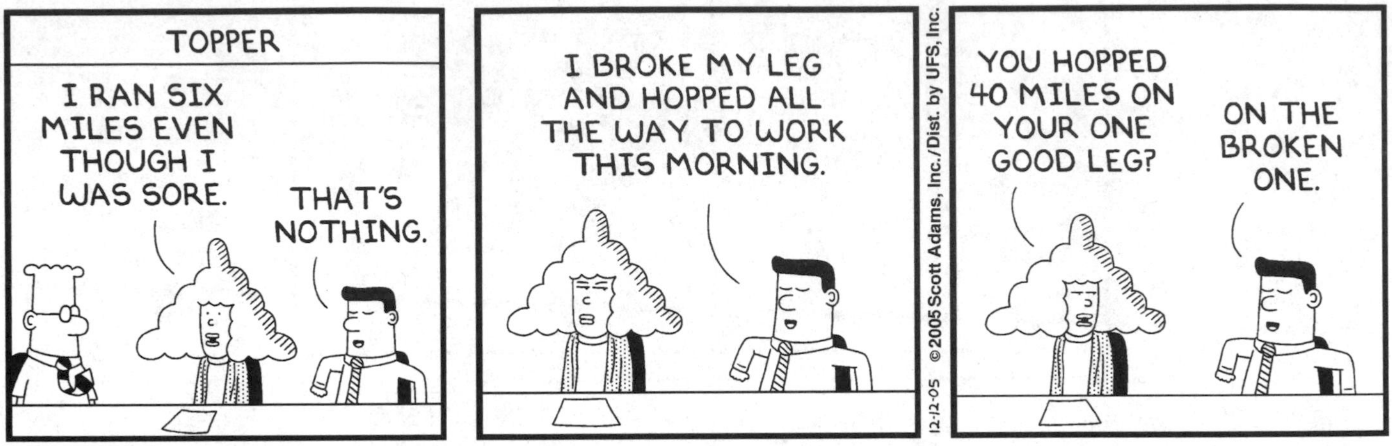
TOPPER
I RAN SIX MILES EVEN THOUGH I WAS SORE.
THAT'S NOTHING.
I BROKE MY LEG AND HOPPED ALL THE WAY TO WORK THIS MORNING.
YOU HOPPED 40 MILES ON YOUR ONE GOOD LEG?
ON THE BROKEN ONE.
12-12-05 ©2005 Scott Adams, Inc./Dist. by UFS, Inc.

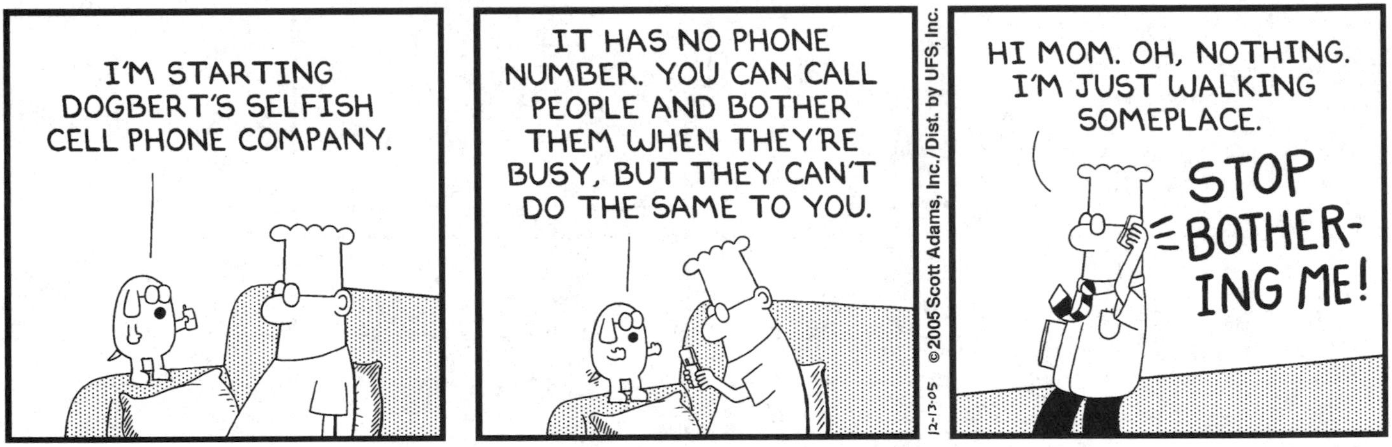
I'M STARTING DOGBERT'S SELFISH CELL PHONE COMPANY.
IT HAS NO PHONE NUMBER. YOU CAN CALL PEOPLE AND BOTHER THEM WHEN THEY'RE BUSY, BUT THEY CAN'T DO THE SAME TO YOU.
HI MOM. OH, NOTHING. I'M JUST WALKING SOMEPLACE.
STOP BOTHER-ING ME!
12-13-05 ©2005 Scott Adams, Inc./Dist. by UFS, Inc.

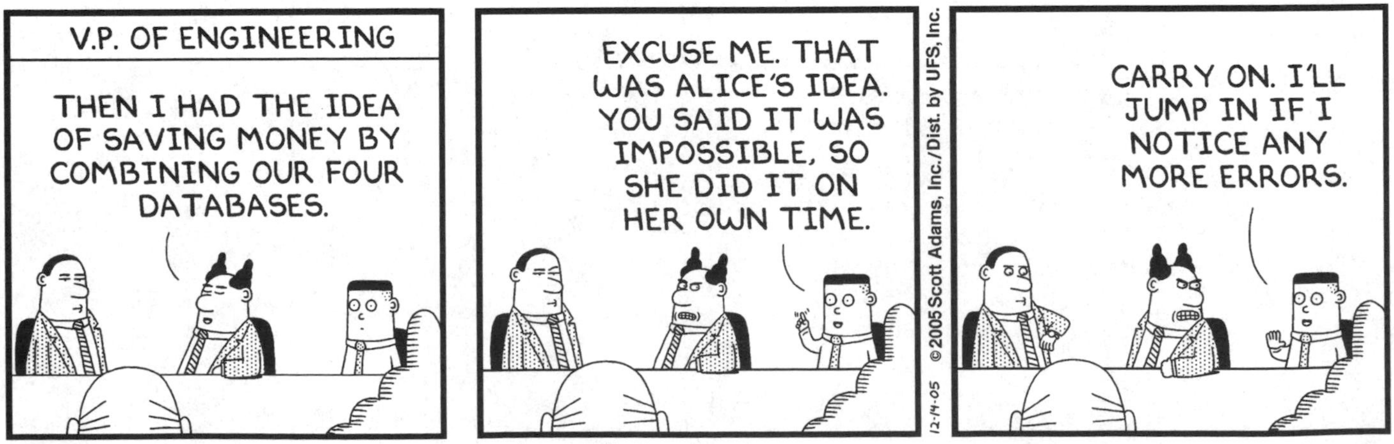
V.P. OF ENGINEERING
THEN I HAD THE IDEA OF SAVING MONEY BY COMBINING OUR FOUR DATABASES.
EXCUSE ME. THAT WAS ALICE'S IDEA. YOU SAID IT WAS IMPOSSIBLE, SO SHE DID IT ON HER OWN TIME.
CARRY ON. I'LL JUMP IN IF I NOTICE ANY MORE ERRORS.
12-14-05 ©2005 Scott Adams, Inc./Dist. by UFS, Inc.

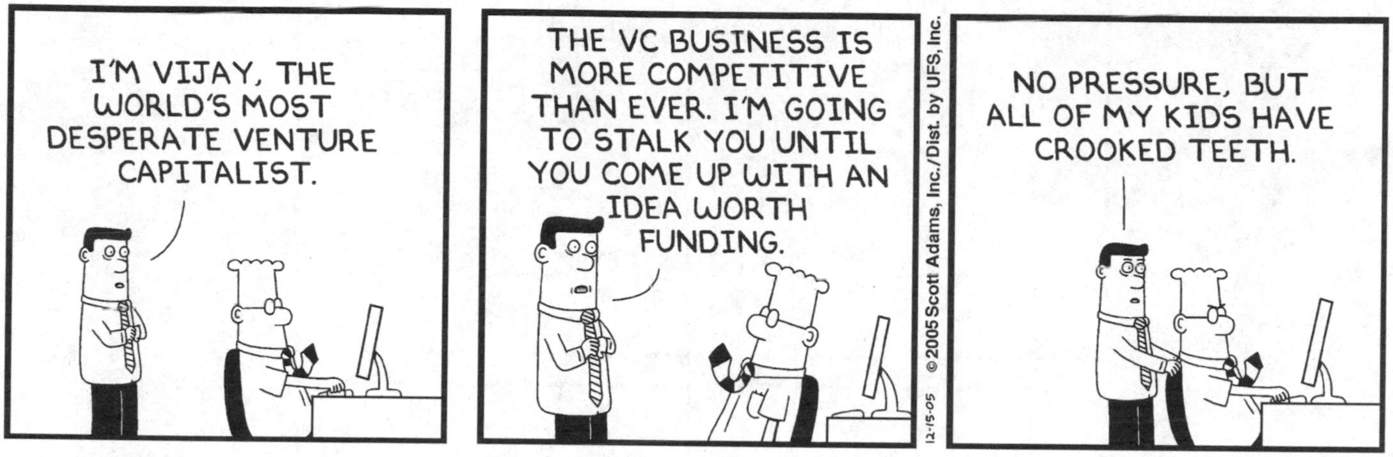
I'M VIJAY, THE WORLD'S MOST DESPERATE VENTURE CAPITALIST.
THE VC BUSINESS IS MORE COMPETITIVE THAN EVER. I'M GOING TO STALK YOU UNTIL YOU COME UP WITH AN IDEA WORTH FUNDING.
12-15-05 © 2005 Scott Adams, Inc./Dist. by UFS, Inc.
NO PRESSURE, BUT ALL OF MY KIDS HAVE CROOKED TEETH.

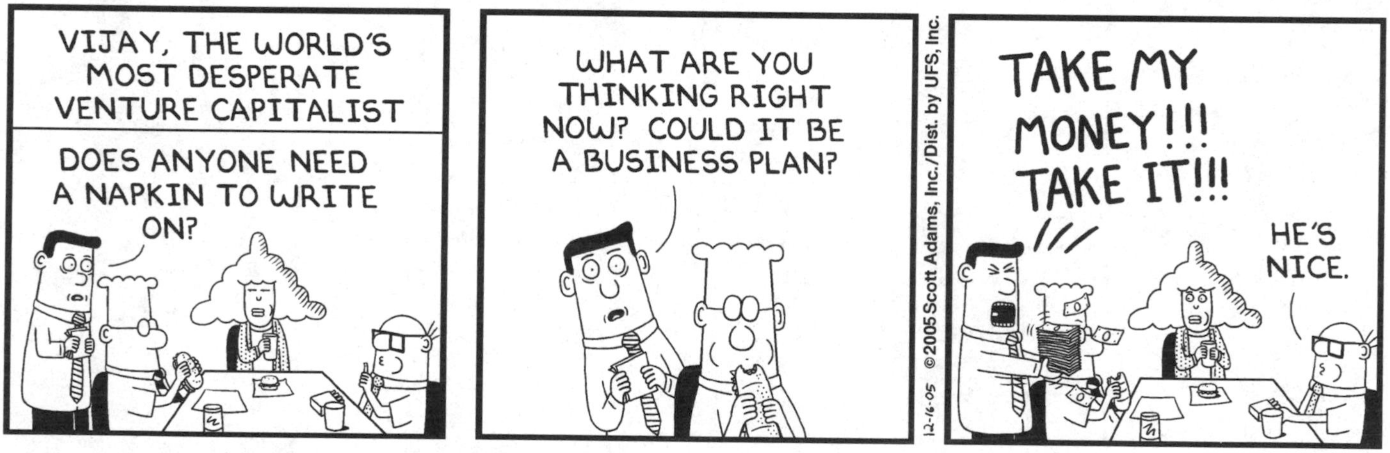
VIJAY, THE WORLD'S MOST DESPERATE VENTURE CAPITALIST
DOES ANYONE NEED A NAPKIN TO WRITE ON?
WHAT ARE YOU THINKING RIGHT NOW? COULD IT BE A BUSINESS PLAN?
12-16-05 © 2005 Scott Adams, Inc./Dist. by UFS, Inc.
TAKE MY MONEY!!! TAKE IT!!!
HE'S NICE.

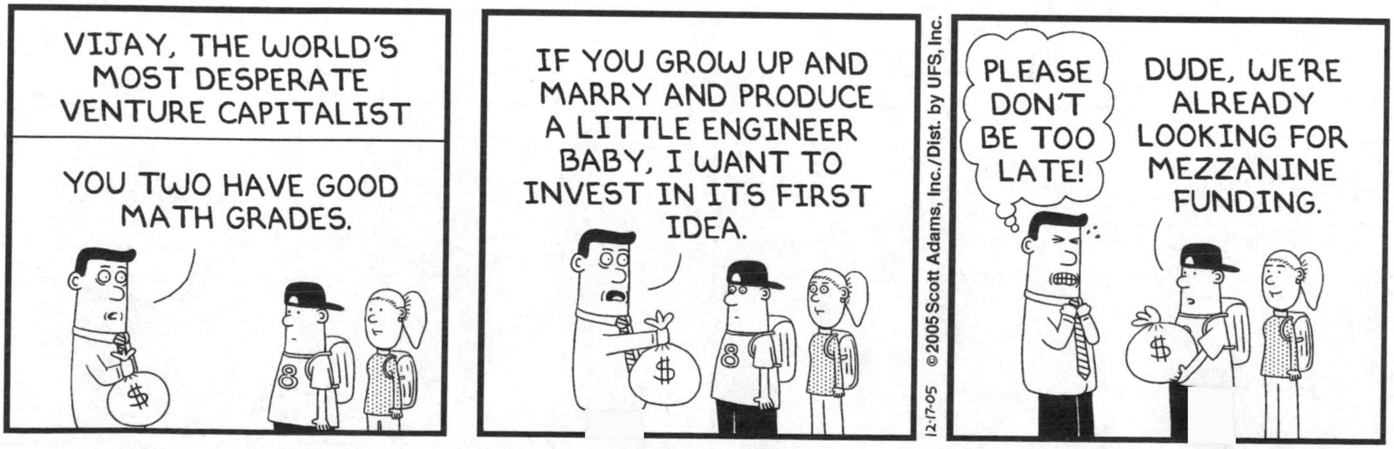
VIJAY, THE WORLD'S MOST DESPERATE VENTURE CAPITALIST
YOU TWO HAVE GOOD MATH GRADES.
IF YOU GROW UP AND MARRY AND PRODUCE A LITTLE ENGINEER BABY, I WANT TO INVEST IN ITS FIRST IDEA.
12-17-05 © 2005 Scott Adams, Inc./Dist. by UFS, Inc.
PLEASE DON'T BE TOO LATE!
DUDE, WE'RE ALREADY LOOKING FOR MEZZANINE FUNDING.

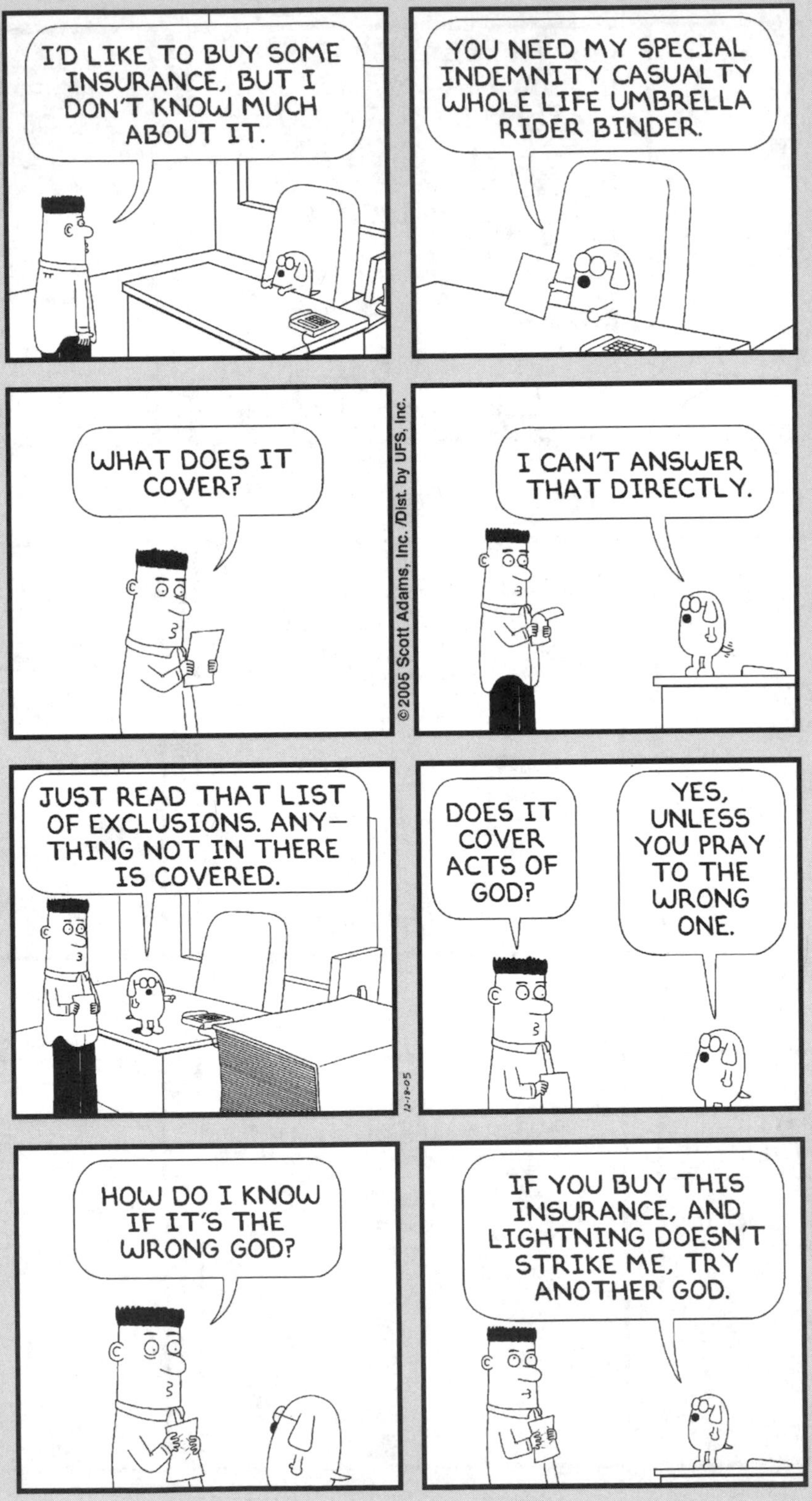
I'D LIKE TO BUY SOME INSURANCE, BUT I DON'T KNOW MUCH ABOUT IT.
YOU NEED MY SPECIAL INDEMNITY CASUALTY WHOLE LIFE UMBRELLA RIDER BINDER.
WHAT DOES IT COVER?
©2005 Scott Adams, Inc./Dist. by UFS, Inc.
I CAN'T ANSWER THAT DIRECTLY.
JUST READ THAT LIST OF EXCLUSIONS. ANY-THING NOT IN THERE IS COVERED.
DOES IT COVER ACTS OF GOD?
YES, UNLESS YOU PRAY TO THE WRONG ONE.
HOW DO I KNOW IF IT'S THE WRONG GOD?
IF YOU BUY THIS INSURANCE, AND LIGHTNING DOESN'T STRIKE ME, TRY ANOTHER GOD.

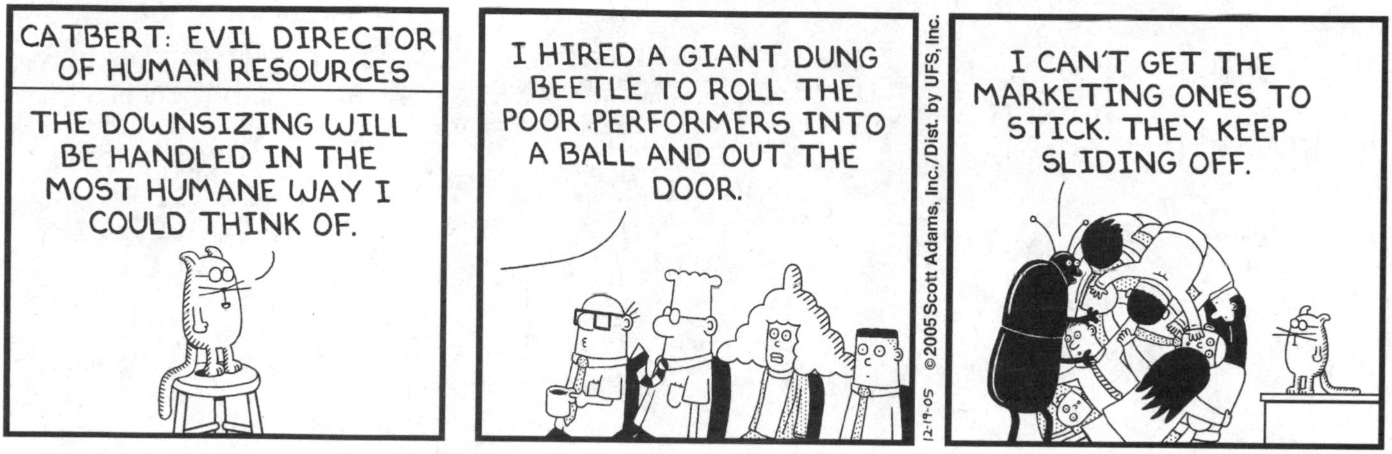
CATBERT: EVIL DIRECTOR OF HUMAN RESOURCES
THE DOWNSIZING WILL BE HANDLED IN THE MOST HUMANE WAY I COULD THINK OF.
I HIRED A GIANT DUNG BEETLE TO ROLL THE POOR PERFORMERS INTO A BALL AND OUT THE DOOR.
12-19-05 © 2005 Scott Adams, Inc./Dist. by UFS, Inc.
I CAN'T GET THE MARKETING ONES TO STICK. THEY KEEP SLIDING OFF.

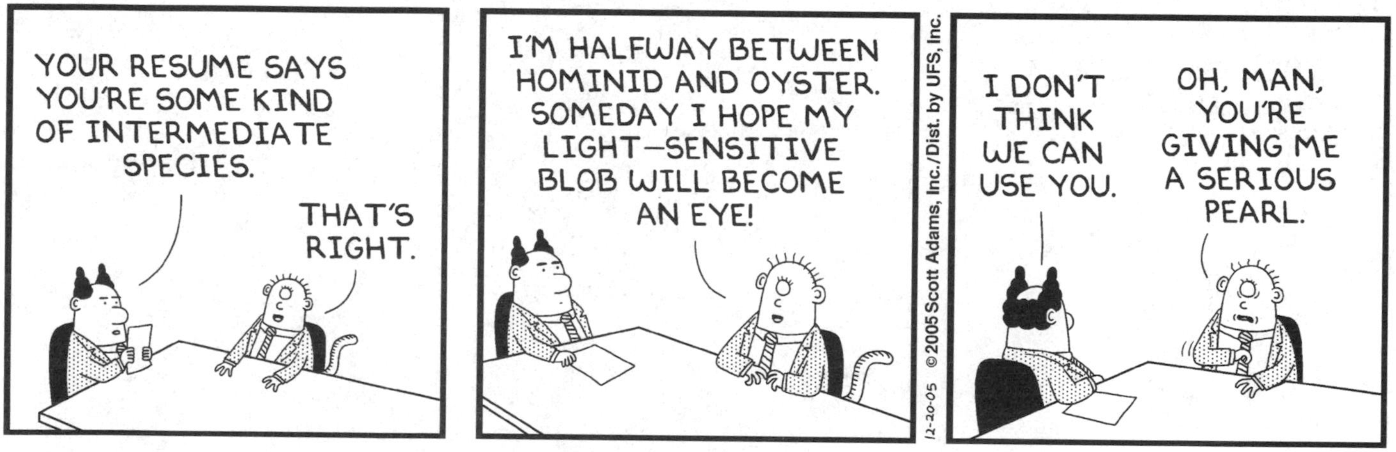
YOUR RESUME SAYS YOU'RE SOME KIND OF INTERMEDIATE SPECIES.
THAT'S RIGHT.
I'M HALFWAY BETWEEN HOMINID AND OYSTER. SOMEDAY I HOPE MY LIGHT—SENSITIVE BLOB WILL BECOME AN EYE!
12-20-05 © 2005 Scott Adams, Inc./Dist. by UFS, Inc.
I DON'T THINK WE CAN USE YOU.
OH, MAN, YOU'RE GIVING ME A SERIOUS PEARL.

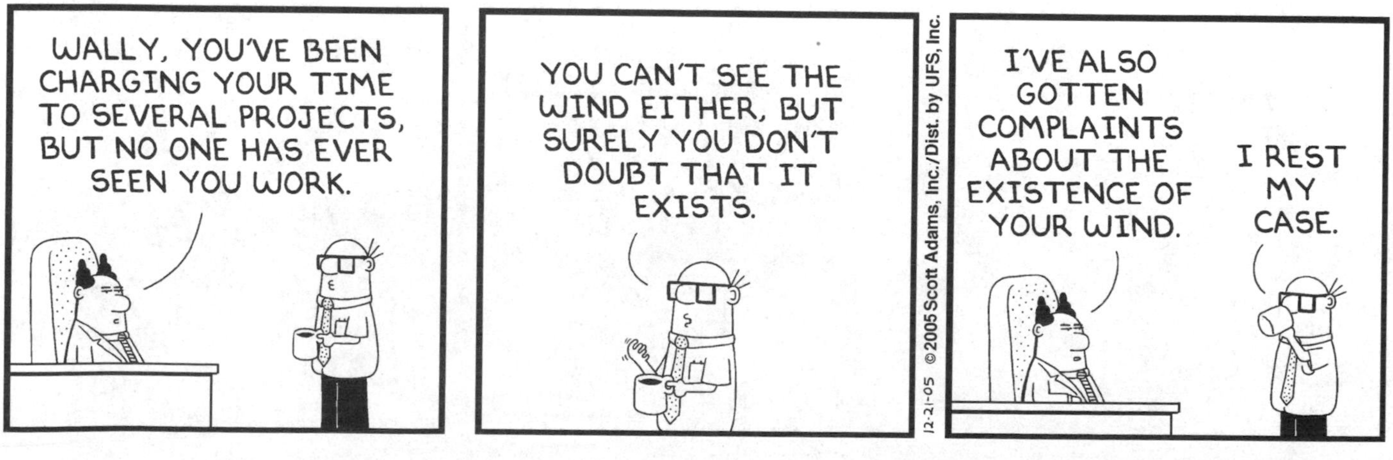
WALLY, YOU'VE BEEN CHARGING YOUR TIME TO SEVERAL PROJECTS, BUT NO ONE HAS EVER SEEN YOU WORK.
YOU CAN'T SEE THE WIND EITHER, BUT SURELY YOU DON'T DOUBT THAT IT EXISTS.
12-21-05 © 2005 Scott Adams, Inc./Dist. by UFS, Inc.
I'VE ALSO GOTTEN COMPLAINTS ABOUT THE EXISTENCE OF YOUR WIND.
I REST MY CASE.

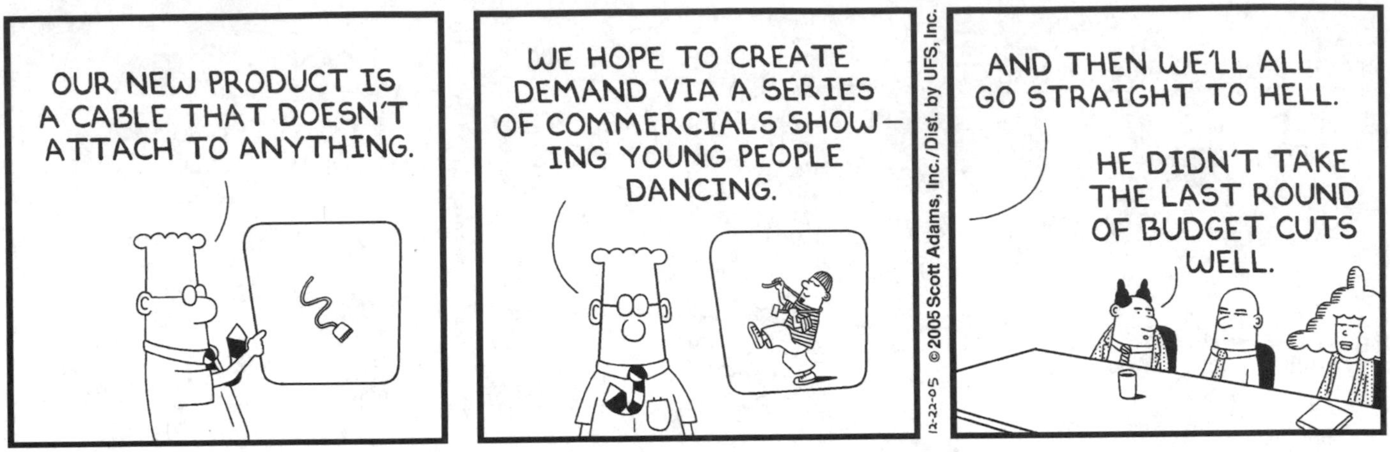
OUR NEW PRODUCT IS A CABLE THAT DOESN'T ATTACH TO ANYTHING.
WE HOPE TO CREATE DEMAND VIA A SERIES OF COMMERCIALS SHOWING YOUNG PEOPLE DANCING.
12-22-05 ©2005 Scott Adams, Inc./Dist. by UFS, Inc.
AND THEN WE'LL ALL GO STRAIGHT TO HELL.
HE DIDN'T TAKE THE LAST ROUND OF BUDGET CUTS WELL.

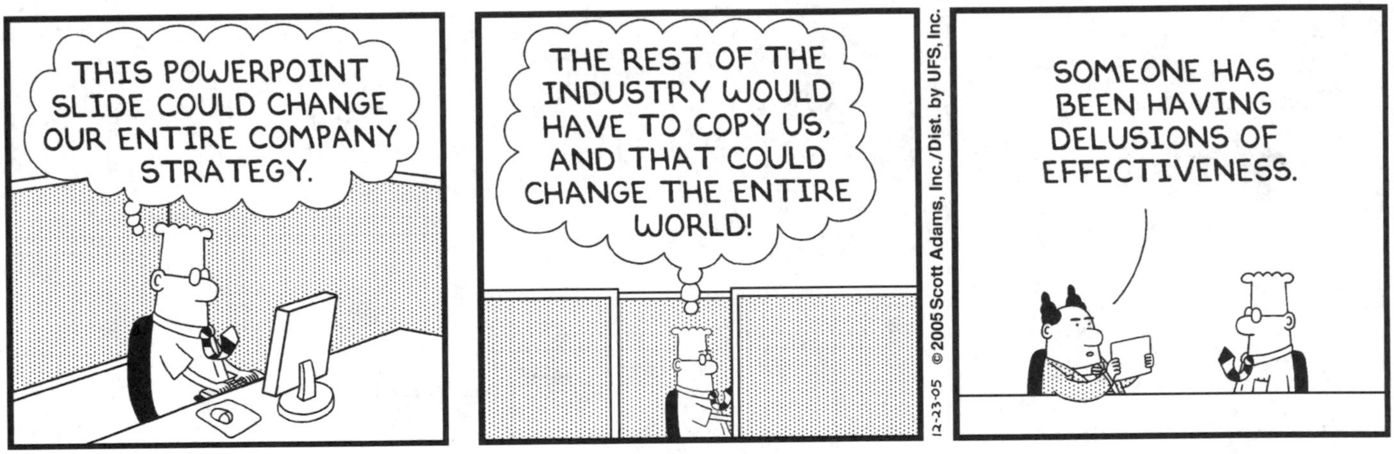
THIS POWERPOINT SLIDE COULD CHANGE OUR ENTIRE COMPANY STRATEGY.
THE REST OF THE INDUSTRY WOULD HAVE TO COPY US, AND THAT COULD CHANGE THE ENTIRE WORLD!
12-23-05 ©2005 Scott Adams, Inc./Dist. by UFS, Inc.
SOMEONE HAS BEEN HAVING DELUSIONS OF EFFECTIVENESS.

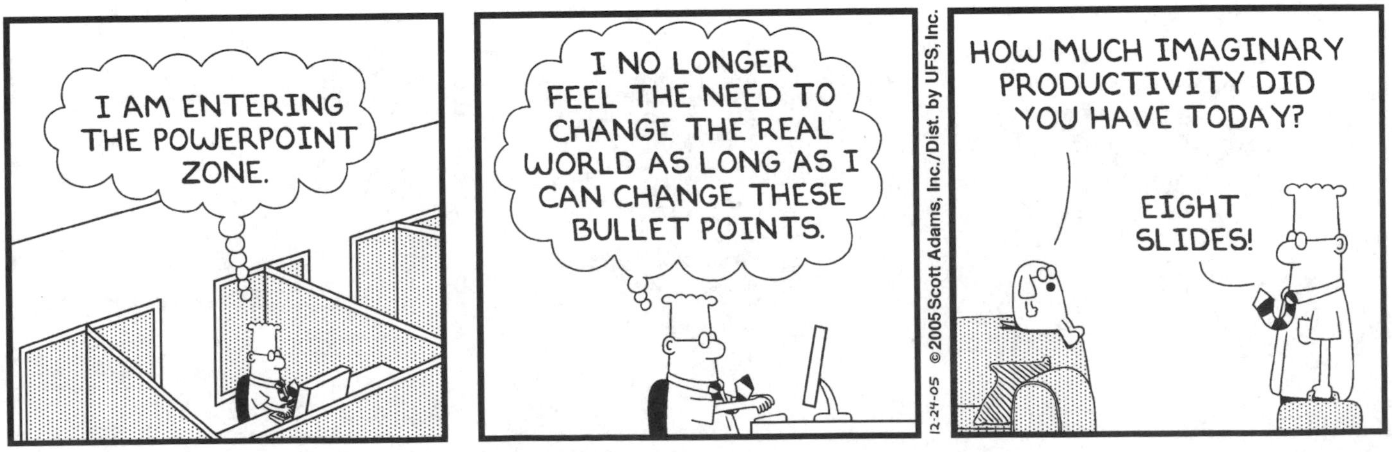
I AM ENTERING THE POWERPOINT ZONE.
I NO LONGER FEEL THE NEED TO CHANGE THE REAL WORLD AS LONG AS I CAN CHANGE THESE BULLET POINTS.
12-24-05 ©2005 Scott Adams, Inc./Dist. by UFS, Inc.
HOW MUCH IMAGINARY PRODUCTIVITY DID YOU HAVE TODAY?
EIGHT SLIDES!

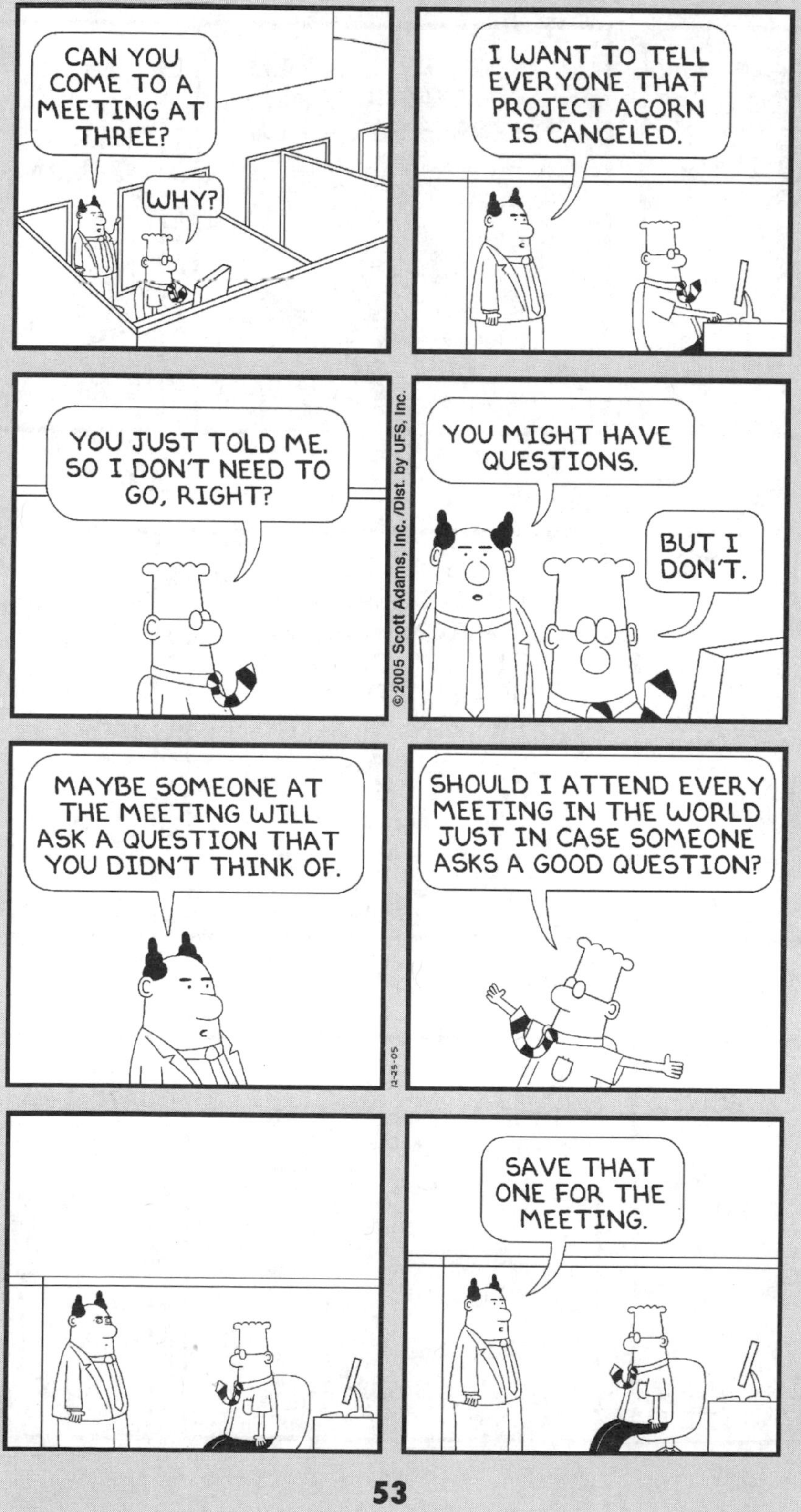
CAN YOU COME TO A MEETING AT THREE?
WHY?
I WANT TO TELL EVERYONE THAT PROJECT ACORN IS CANCELED.
YOU JUST TOLD ME. SO I DON'T NEED TO GO, RIGHT?
YOU MIGHT HAVE QUESTIONS.
BUT I DON'T.
MAYBE SOMEONE AT THE MEETING WILL ASK A QUESTION THAT YOU DIDN'T THINK OF.
SHOULD I ATTEND EVERY MEETING IN THE WORLD JUST IN CASE SOMEONE ASKS A GOOD QUESTION?
SAVE THAT ONE FOR THE MEETING.
©2005 Scott Adams, Inc./Dist. by UFS, Inc.
12-25-05

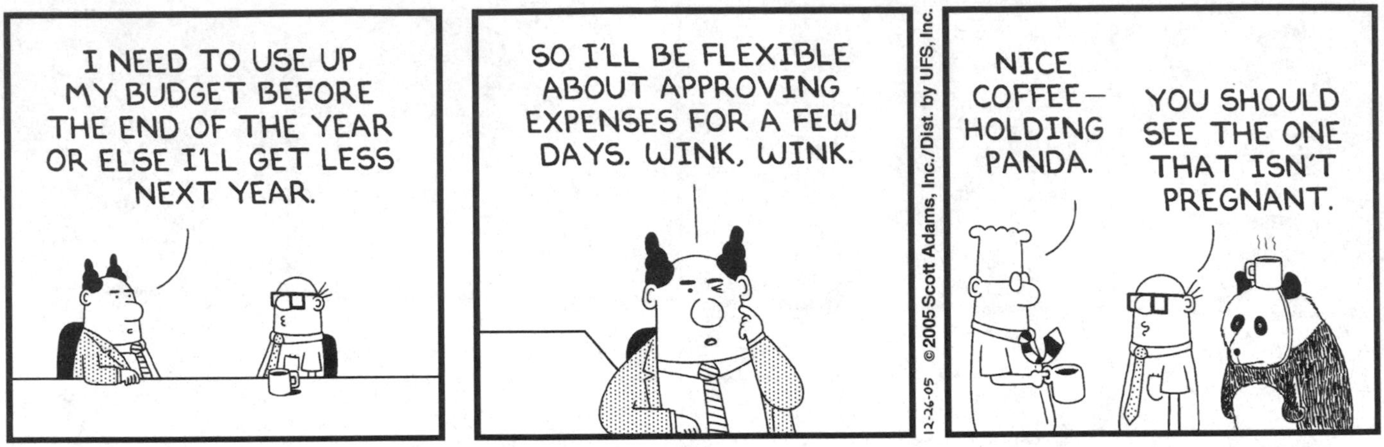
I NEED TO USE UP MY BUDGET BEFORE THE END OF THE YEAR OR ELSE I'LL GET LESS NEXT YEAR.
SO I'LL BE FLEXIBLE ABOUT APPROVING EXPENSES FOR A FEW DAYS. WINK, WINK.
12-26-05 © 2005 Scott Adams, Inc./Dist. by UFS, Inc.
NICE COFFEE-HOLDING PANDA.
YOU SHOULD SEE THE ONE THAT ISN'T PREGNANT.

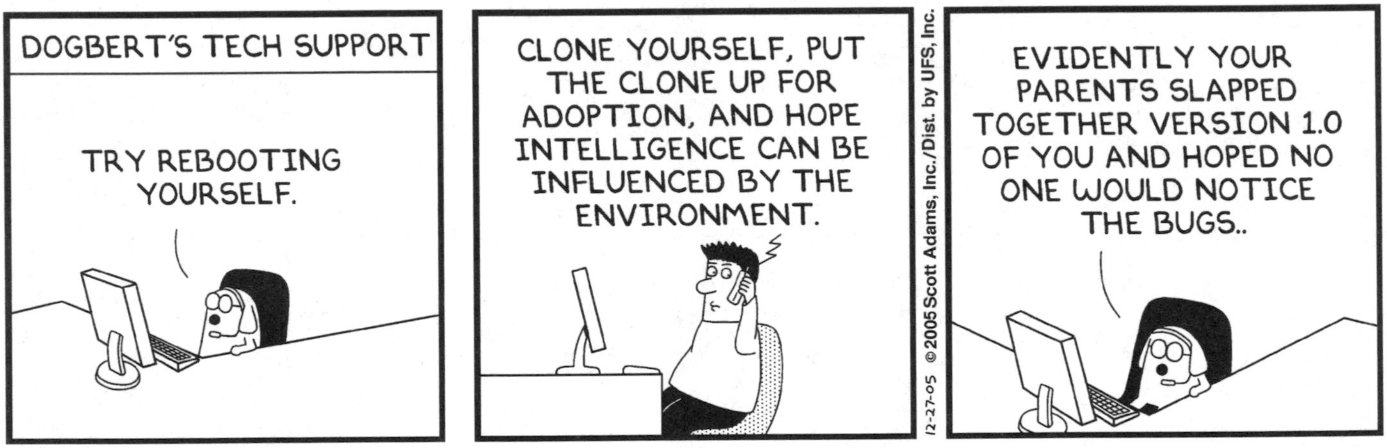
DOGBERT'S TECH SUPPORT
TRY REBOOTING YOURSELF.
CLONE YOURSELF, PUT THE CLONE UP FOR ADOPTION, AND HOPE INTELLIGENCE CAN BE INFLUENCED BY THE ENVIRONMENT.
12-27-05 © 2005 Scott Adams, Inc./Dist. by UFS, Inc.
EVIDENTLY YOUR PARENTS SLAPPED TOGETHER VERSION 1.0 OF YOU AND HOPED NO ONE WOULD NOTICE THE BUGS..

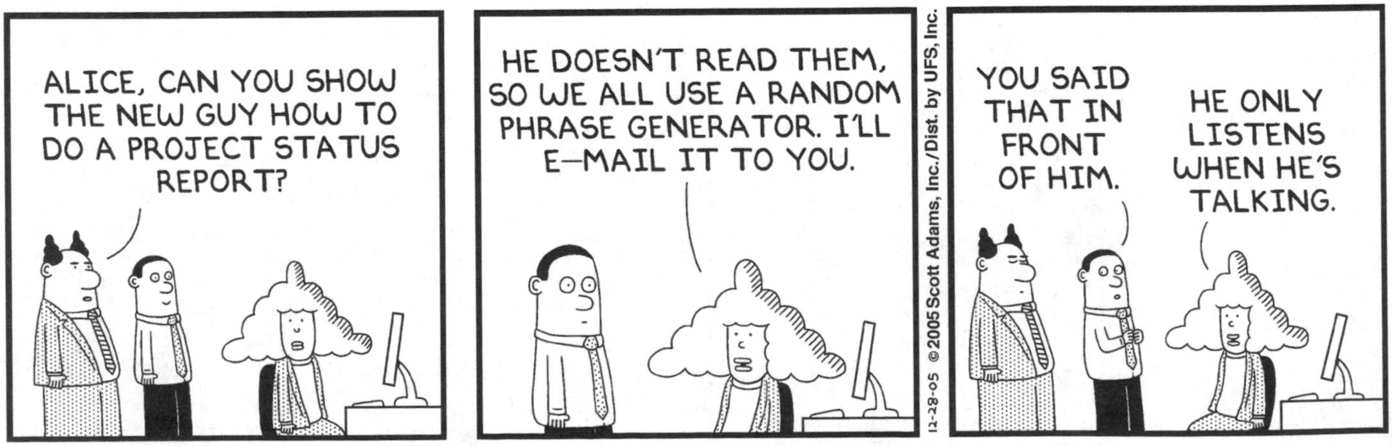
ALICE, CAN YOU SHOW THE NEW GUY HOW TO DO A PROJECT STATUS REPORT?
HE DOESN'T READ THEM, SO WE ALL USE A RANDOM PHRASE GENERATOR. I'LL E-MAIL IT TO YOU.
12-28-05 © 2005 Scott Adams, Inc./Dist. by UFS, Inc.
YOU SAID THAT IN FRONT OF HIM.
HE ONLY LISTENS WHEN HE'S TALKING.

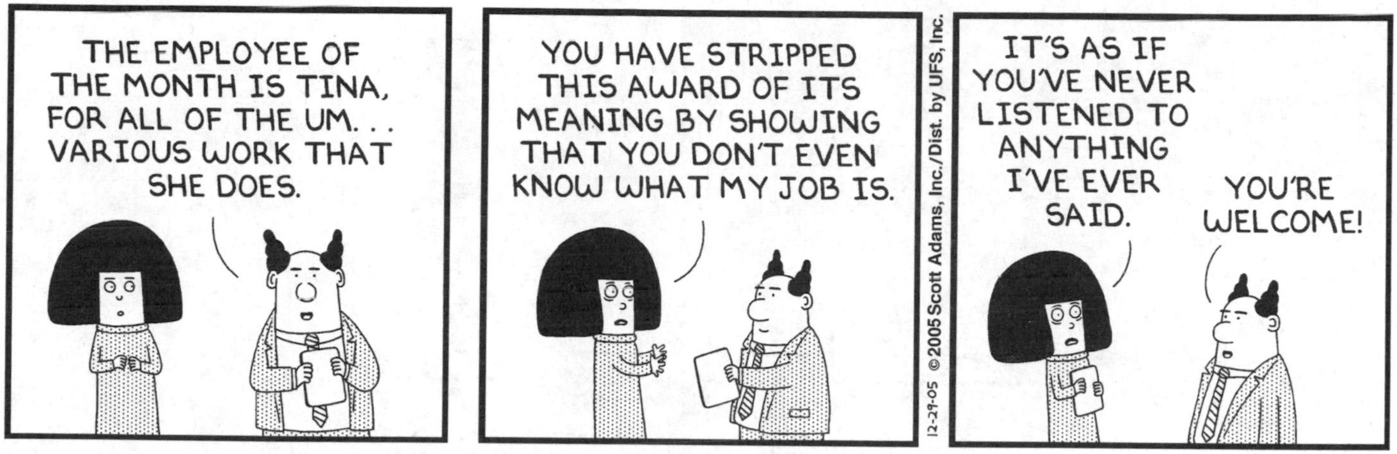
THE EMPLOYEE OF THE MONTH IS TINA, FOR ALL OF THE UM. . . VARIOUS WORK THAT SHE DOES.
YOU HAVE STRIPPED THIS AWARD OF ITS MEANING BY SHOWING THAT YOU DON'T EVEN KNOW WHAT MY JOB IS.
12-29-05 ©2005 Scott Adams, Inc./Dist. by UFS, Inc.
IT'S AS IF YOU'VE NEVER LISTENED TO ANYTHING I'VE EVER SAID.
YOU'RE WELCOME!

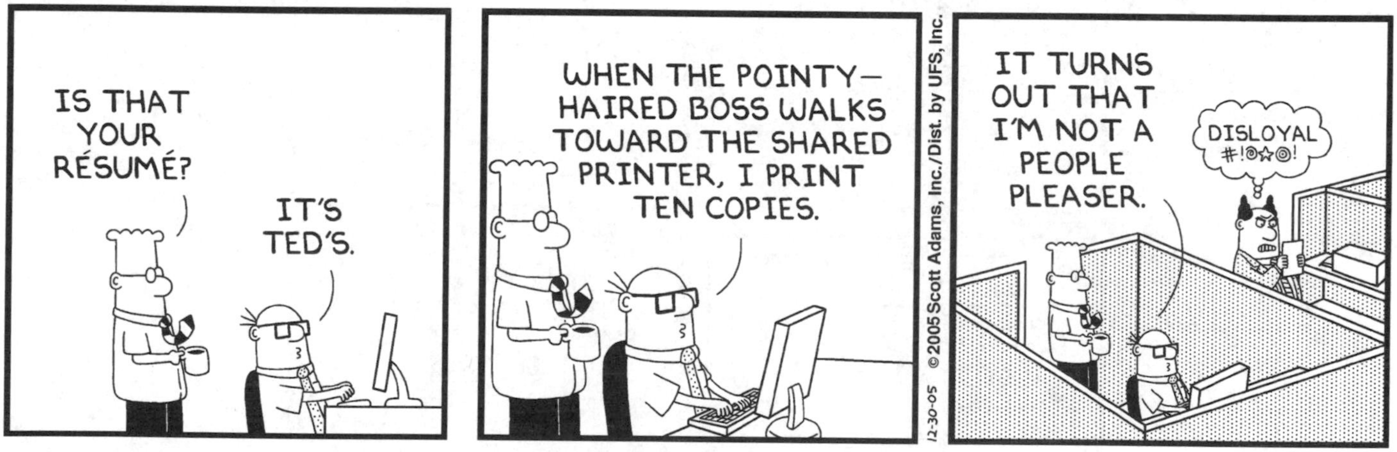
IS THAT YOUR RÉSUMÉ?
IT'S TED'S.
WHEN THE POINTY-HAIRED BOSS WALKS TOWARD THE SHARED PRINTER, I PRINT TEN COPIES.
12-30-05 ©2005 Scott Adams, Inc./Dist. by UFS, Inc.
IT TURNS OUT THAT I'M NOT A PEOPLE PLEASER.
DISLOYAL

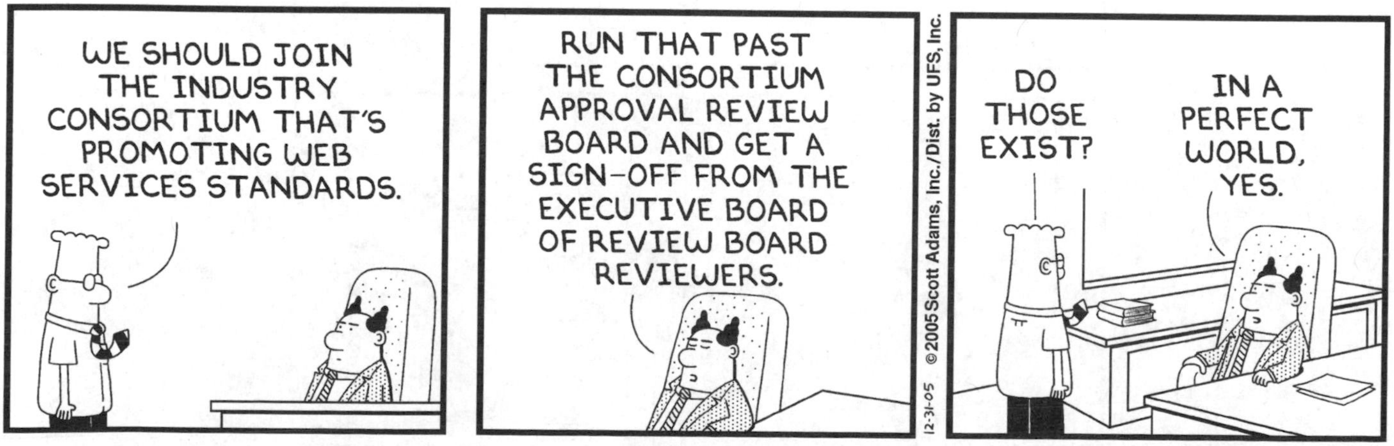
WE SHOULD JOIN THE INDUSTRY CONSORTIUM THAT'S PROMOTING WEB SERVICES STANDARDS.
RUN THAT PAST THE CONSORTIUM APPROVAL REVIEW BOARD AND GET A SIGN-OFF FROM THE EXECUTIVE BOARD OF REVIEW BOARD REVIEWERS.
12-31-05 ©2005 Scott Adams, Inc./Dist. by UFS, Inc.
DO THOSE EXIST?
IN A PERFECT WORLD, YES.

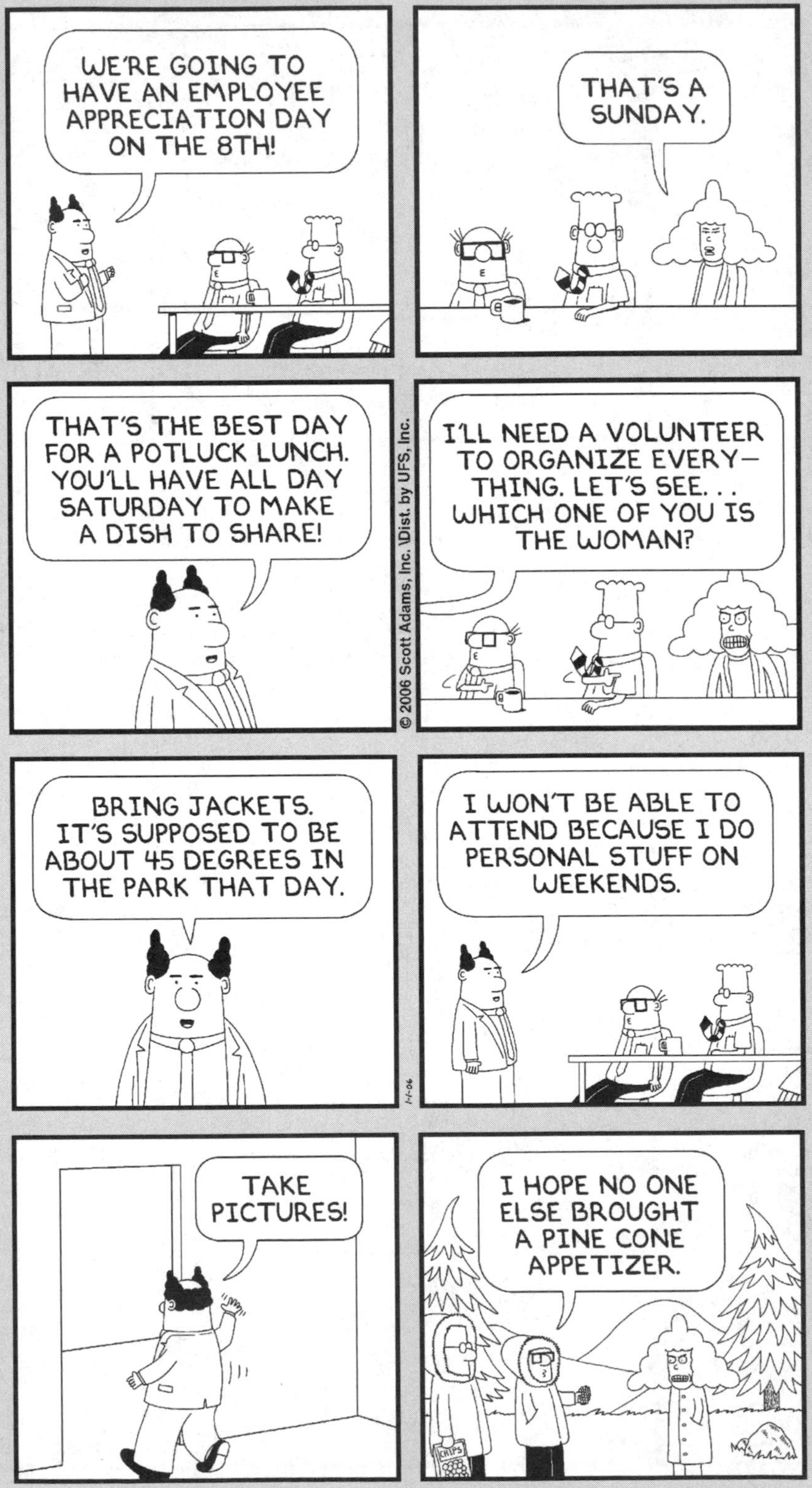
WE'RE GOING TO HAVE AN EMPLOYEE APPRECIATION DAY ON THE 8TH!
THAT'S A SUNDAY.
THAT'S THE BEST DAY FOR A POTLUCK LUNCH. YOU'LL HAVE ALL DAY SATURDAY TO MAKE A DISH TO SHARE!
I'LL NEED A VOLUNTEER TO ORGANIZE EVERY-THING. LET'S SEE. . . WHICH ONE OF YOU IS THE WOMAN?
© 2006 Scott Adams, Inc. \Dist. by UFS, Inc.
BRING JACKETS. IT'S SUPPOSED TO BE ABOUT 45 DEGREES IN THE PARK THAT DAY.
I WON'T BE ABLE TO ATTEND BECAUSE I DO PERSONAL STUFF ON WEEKENDS.
TAKE PICTURES!
I HOPE NO ONE ELSE BROUGHT A PINE CONE APPETIZER.
CHIPS

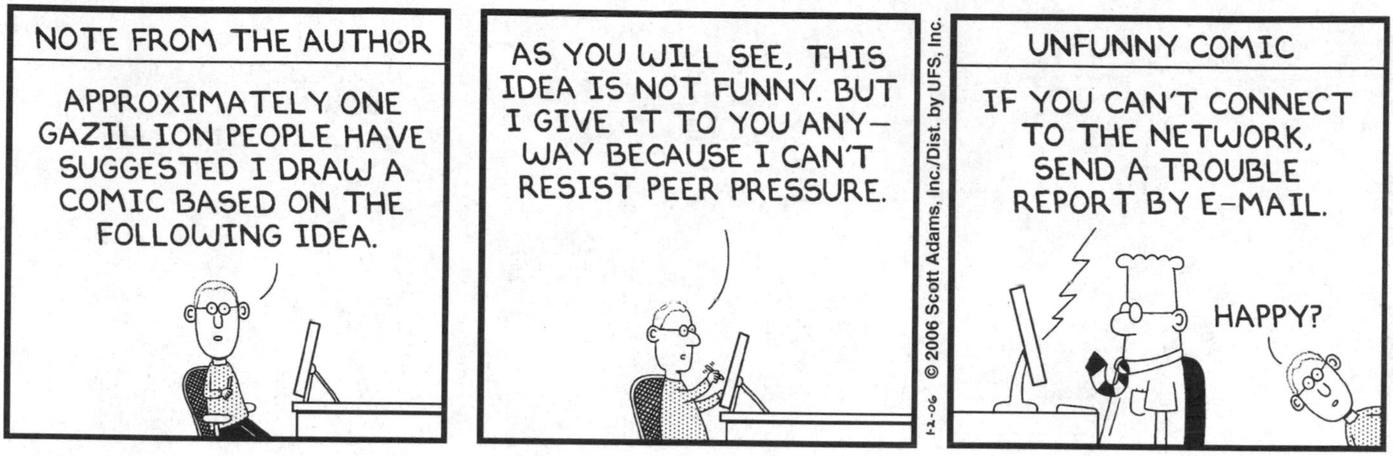
NOTE FROM THE AUTHOR
APPROXIMATELY ONE GAZILLION PEOPLE HAVE SUGGESTED I DRAW A COMIC BASED ON THE FOLLOWING IDEA.
AS YOU WILL SEE, THIS IDEA IS NOT FUNNY. BUT I GIVE IT TO YOU ANY-WAY BECAUSE I CAN'T RESIST PEER PRESSURE.
1-2-06 © 2006 Scott Adams, Inc./Dist. by UFS, Inc.
UNFUNNY COMIC
IF YOU CAN'T CONNECT TO THE NETWORK, SEND A TROUBLE REPORT BY E-MAIL.
HAPPY?

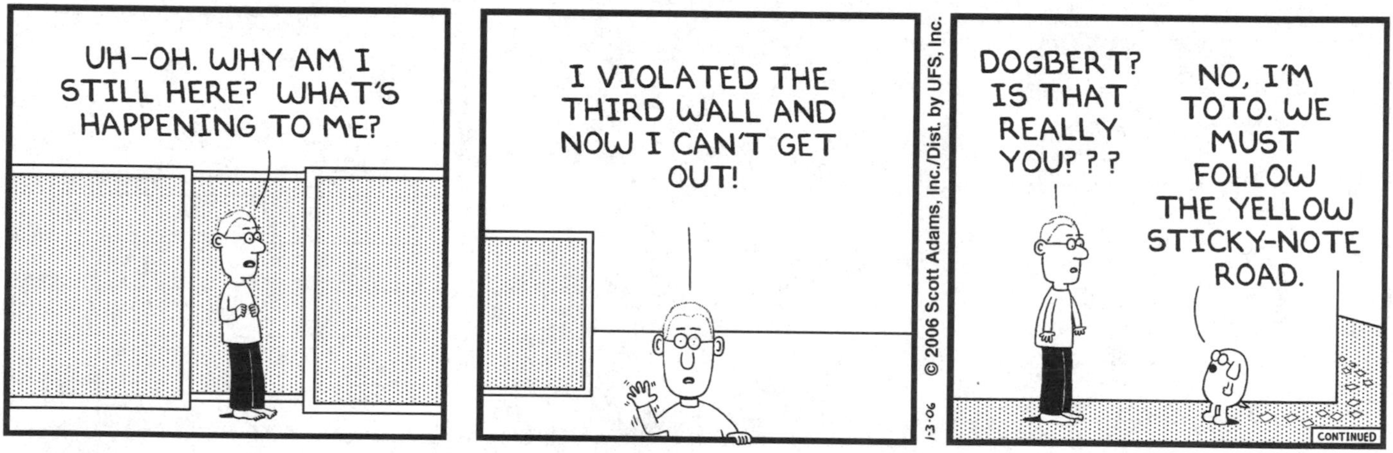
UH-OH. WHY AM I STILL HERE? WHAT'S HAPPENING TO ME?
I VIOLATED THE THIRD WALL AND NOW I CAN'T GET OUT!
1-3-06 © 2006 Scott Adams, Inc./Dist. by UFS, Inc.
DOGBERT? IS THAT REALLY YOU? ? ?
NO, I'M TOTO. WE MUST FOLLOW THE YELLOW STICKY-NOTE ROAD.
CONTINUED

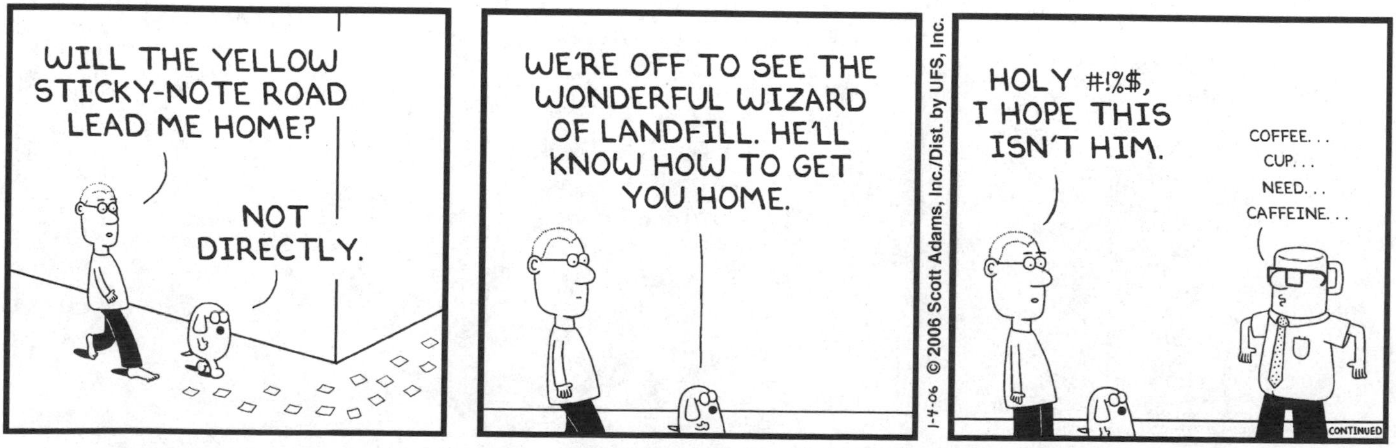
WILL THE YELLOW STICKY-NOTE ROAD LEAD ME HOME?
NOT DIRECTLY.
WE'RE OFF TO SEE THE WONDERFUL WIZARD OF LANDFILL. HE'LL KNOW HOW TO GET YOU HOME.
1-4-06 © 2006 Scott Adams, Inc./Dist. by UFS, Inc.
HOLY #!%$, I HOPE THIS ISN'T HIM.
COFFEE. . .
CUP. . .
NEED. . .
CAFFEINE. . .
CONTINUED

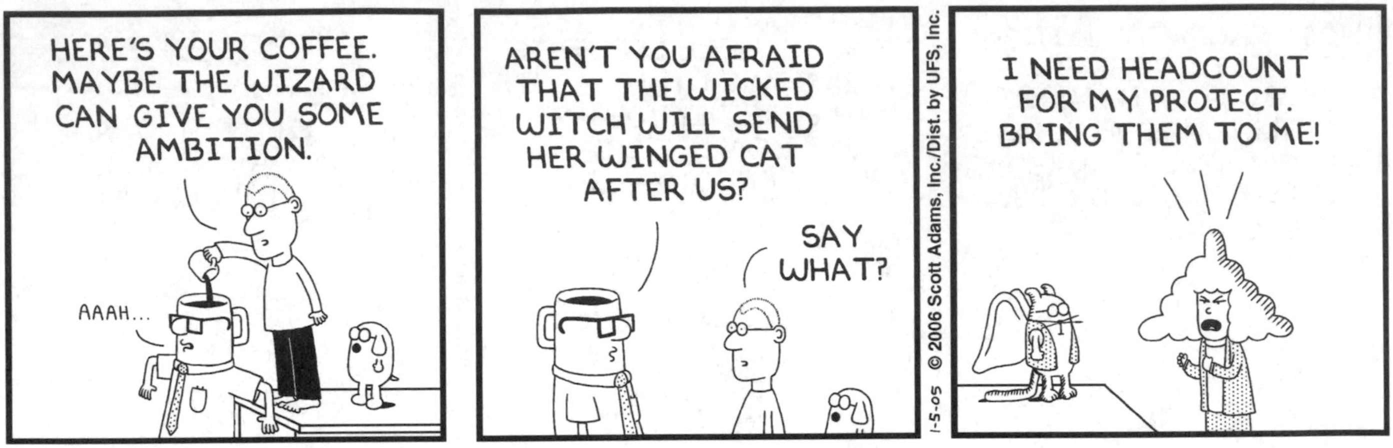
HERE'S YOUR COFFEE. MAYBE THE WIZARD CAN GIVE YOU SOME AMBITION.
AAAH...
AREN'T YOU AFRAID THAT THE WICKED WITCH WILL SEND HER WINGED CAT AFTER US?
SAY WHAT?
I NEED HEADCOUNT FOR MY PROJECT. BRING THEM TO ME!
1-5-05 © 2006 Scott Adams, Inc./Dist. by UFS, Inc.

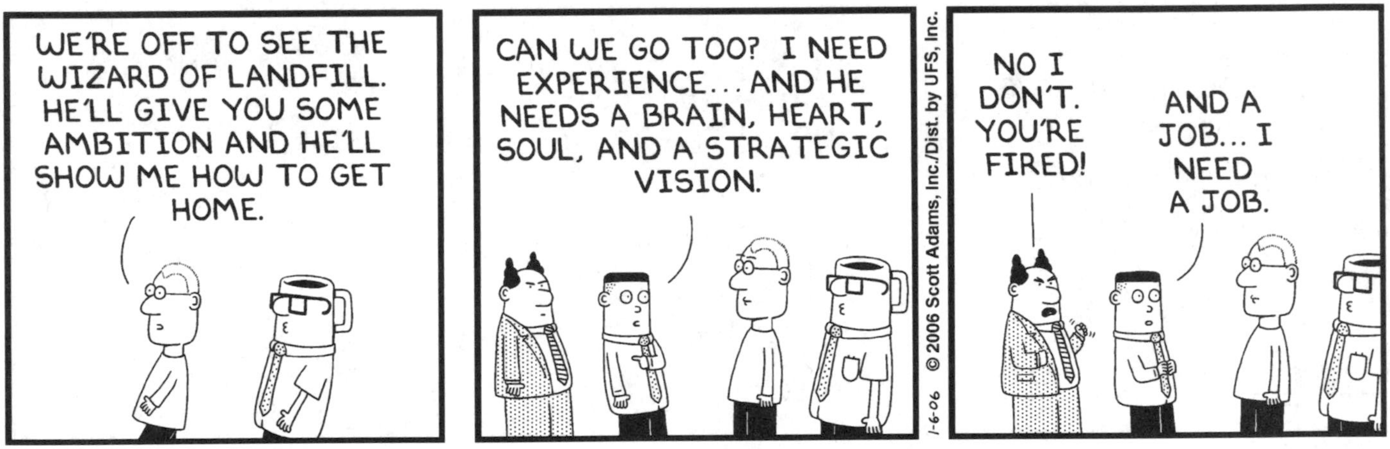
WE'RE OFF TO SEE THE WIZARD OF LANDFILL. HE'LL GIVE YOU SOME AMBITION AND HE'LL SHOW ME HOW TO GET HOME.
CAN WE GO TOO? I NEED EXPERIENCE... AND HE NEEDS A BRAIN, HEART, SOUL, AND A STRATEGIC VISION.
NO I DON'T. YOU'RE FIRED!
AND A JOB... I NEED A JOB.
1-6-06 © 2006 Scott Adams, Inc./Dist. by UFS, Inc.

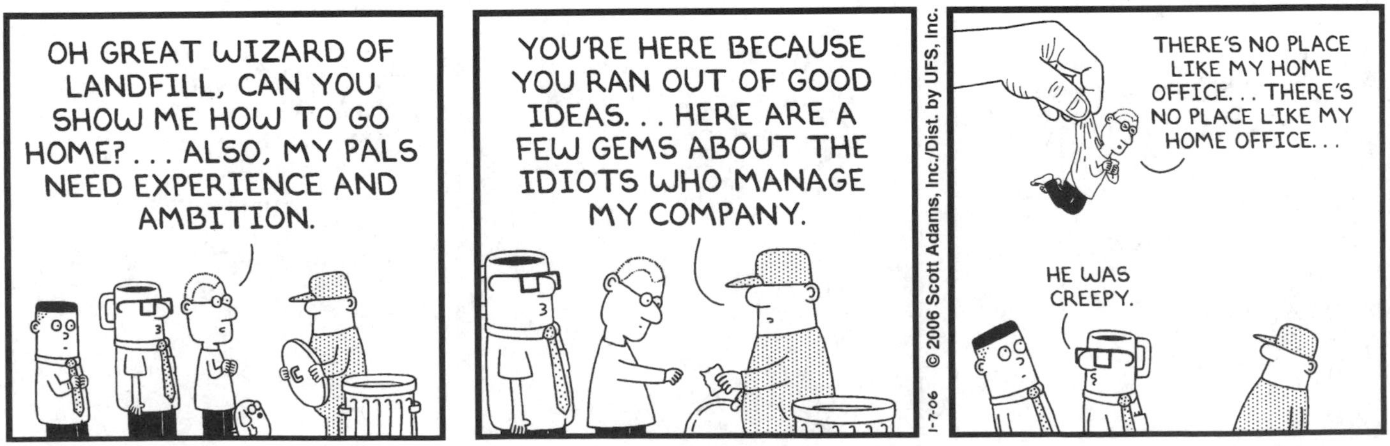
OH GREAT WIZARD OF LANDFILL, CAN YOU SHOW ME HOW TO GO HOME? . . . ALSO, MY PALS NEED EXPERIENCE AND AMBITION.
YOU'RE HERE BECAUSE YOU RAN OUT OF GOOD IDEAS. . . HERE ARE A FEW GEMS ABOUT THE IDIOTS WHO MANAGE MY COMPANY.
THERE'S NO PLACE LIKE MY HOME OFFICE. . . THERE'S NO PLACE LIKE MY HOME OFFICE. . .
HE WAS CREEPY.
1-7-06 © 2006 Scott Adams, Inc./Dist. by UFS, Inc.

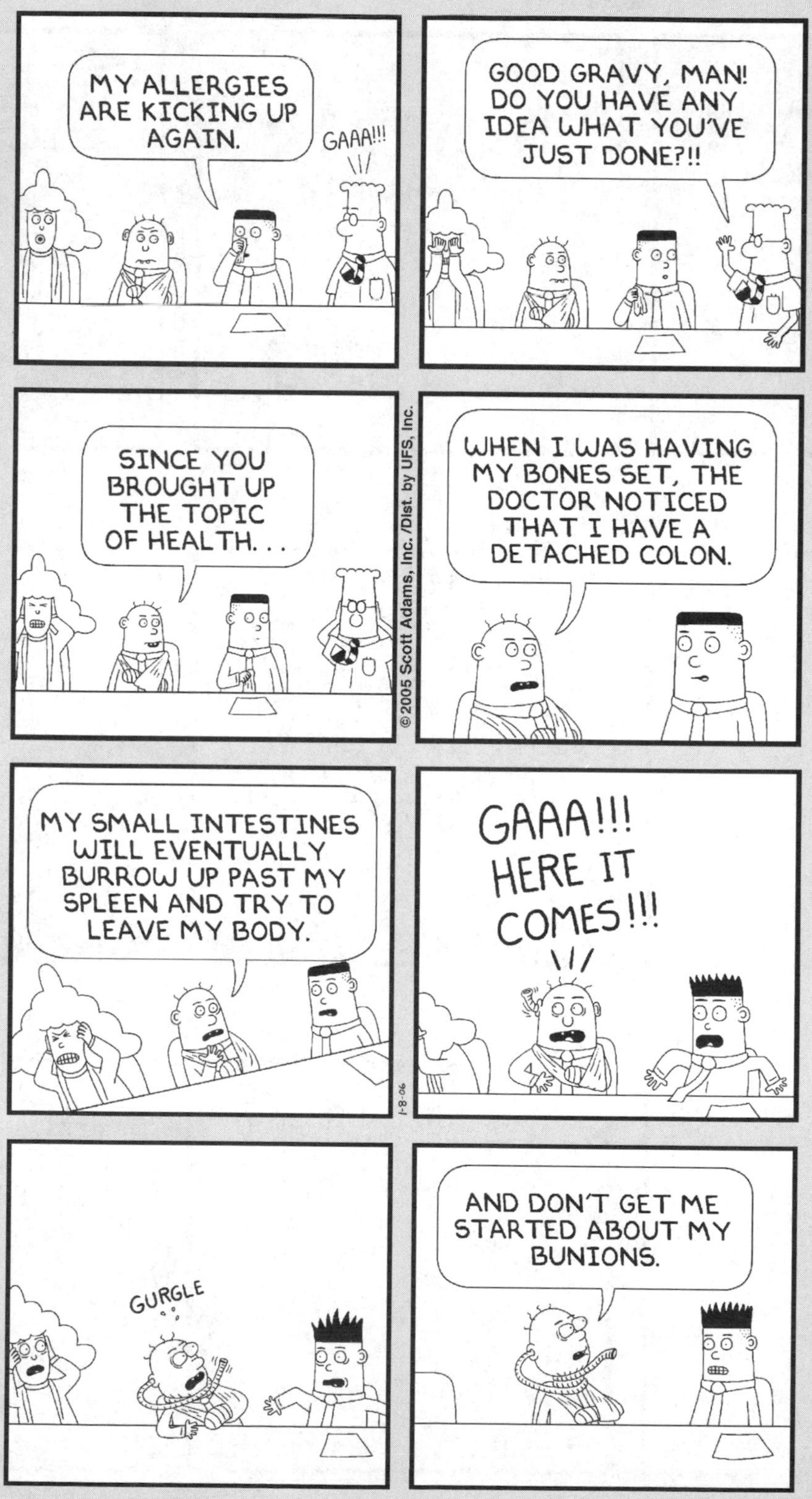
MY ALLERGIES ARE KICKING UP AGAIN.
GAAA!!!
GOOD GRAVY, MAN! DO YOU HAVE ANY IDEA WHAT YOU'VE JUST DONE?!!
SINCE YOU BROUGHT UP THE TOPIC OF HEALTH. . .
© 2005 Scott Adams, Inc. /Dist. by UFS, Inc.
WHEN I WAS HAVING MY BONES SET, THE DOCTOR NOTICED THAT I HAVE A DETACHED COLON.
MY SMALL INTESTINES WILL EVENTUALLY BURROW UP PAST MY SPLEEN AND TRY TO LEAVE MY BODY.
1-8-06
GAAA!!! HERE IT COMES!!!
GURGLE
AND DON'T GET ME STARTED ABOUT MY BUNIONS.

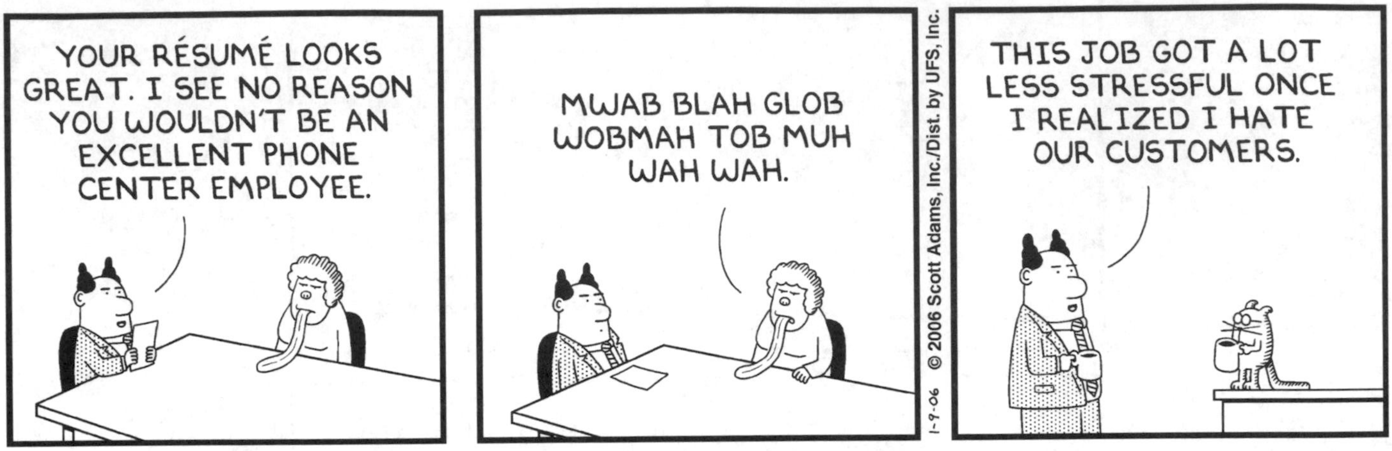
YOUR RÉSUMÉ LOOKS GREAT. I SEE NO REASON YOU WOULDN'T BE AN EXCELLENT PHONE CENTER EMPLOYEE.
MWAB BLAH GLOB WOBMAH TOB MUH WAH WAH.
THIS JOB GOT A LOT LESS STRESSFUL ONCE I REALIZED I HATE OUR CUSTOMERS.
1-9-06 © 2006 Scott Adams, Inc./Dist. by UFS, Inc.

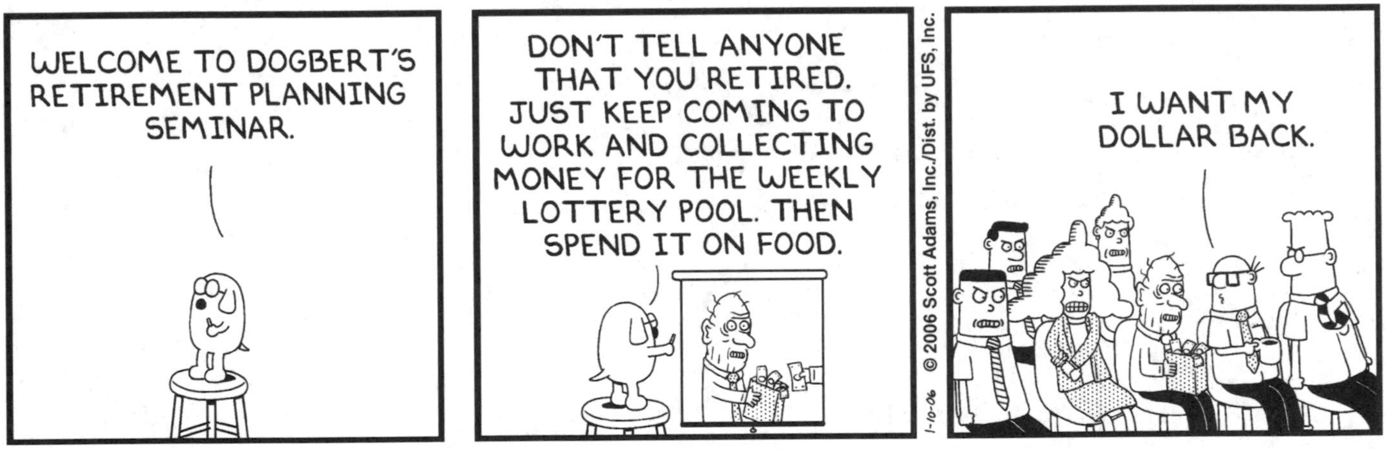
WELCOME TO DOGBERT'S RETIREMENT PLANNING SEMINAR.
DON'T TELL ANYONE THAT YOU RETIRED. JUST KEEP COMING TO WORK AND COLLECTING MONEY FOR THE WEEKLY LOTTERY POOL. THEN SPEND IT ON FOOD.
I WANT MY DOLLAR BACK.
1-10-06 © 2006 Scott Adams, Inc./Dist. by UFS, Inc.

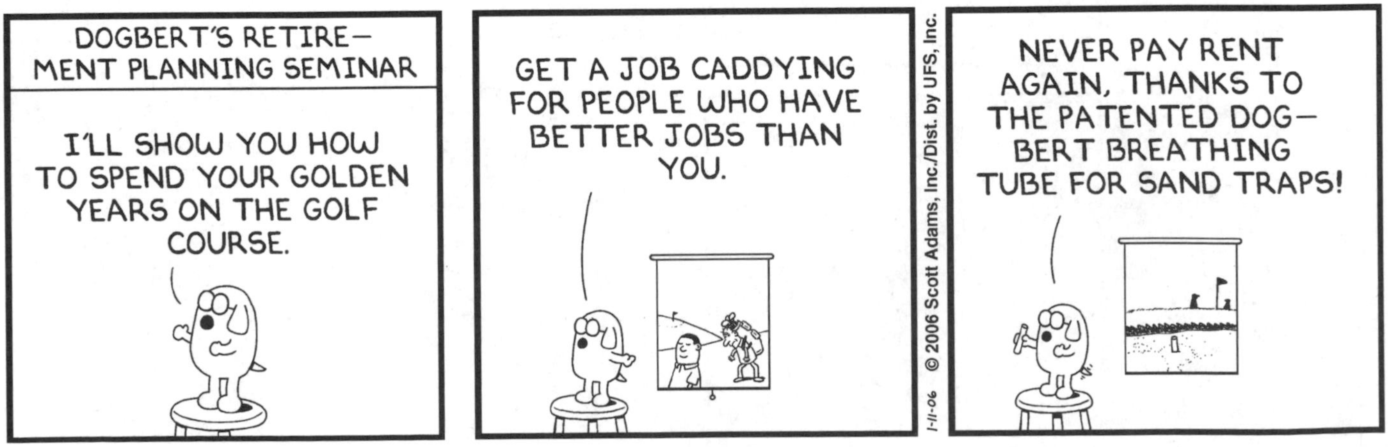
DOGBERT'S RETIRE-MENT PLANNING SEMINAR
I'LL SHOW YOU HOW TO SPEND YOUR GOLDEN YEARS ON THE GOLF COURSE.
GET A JOB CADDYING FOR PEOPLE WHO HAVE BETTER JOBS THAN YOU.
NEVER PAY RENT AGAIN, THANKS TO THE PATENTED DOG-BERT BREATHING TUBE FOR SAND TRAPS!
1-11-06 © 2006 Scott Adams, Inc./Dist. by UFS, Inc.

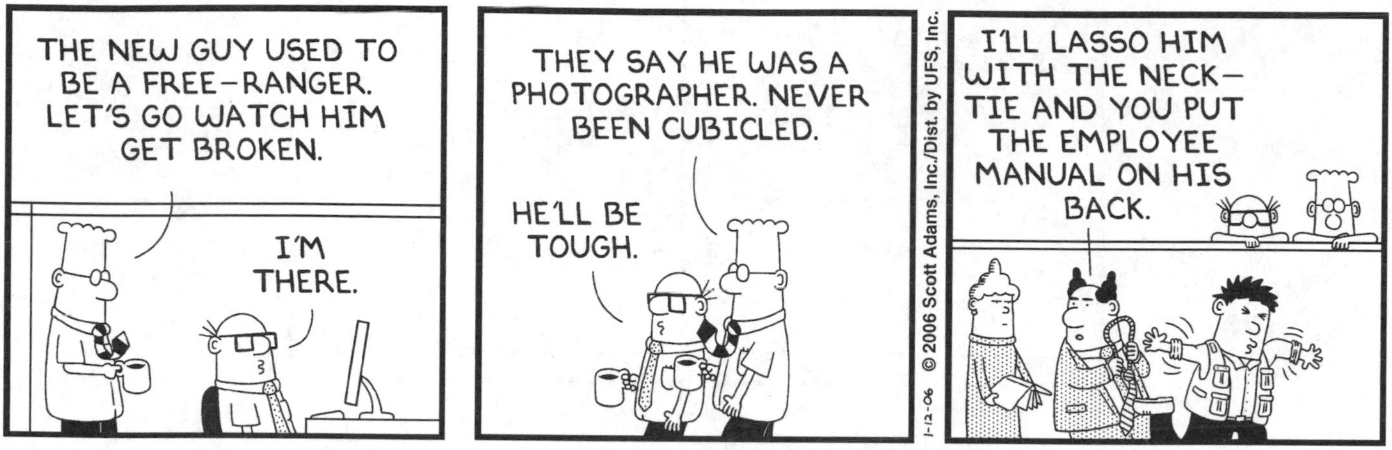
THE NEW GUY USED TO BE A FREE-RANGER. LET'S GO WATCH HIM GET BROKEN.
I'M THERE.
THEY SAY HE WAS A PHOTOGRAPHER. NEVER BEEN CUBICLED.
HE'LL BE TOUGH.
1-12-06 © 2006 Scott Adams, Inc./Dist. by UFS, Inc.
I'LL LASSO HIM WITH THE NECK-TIE AND YOU PUT THE EMPLOYEE MANUAL ON HIS BACK.

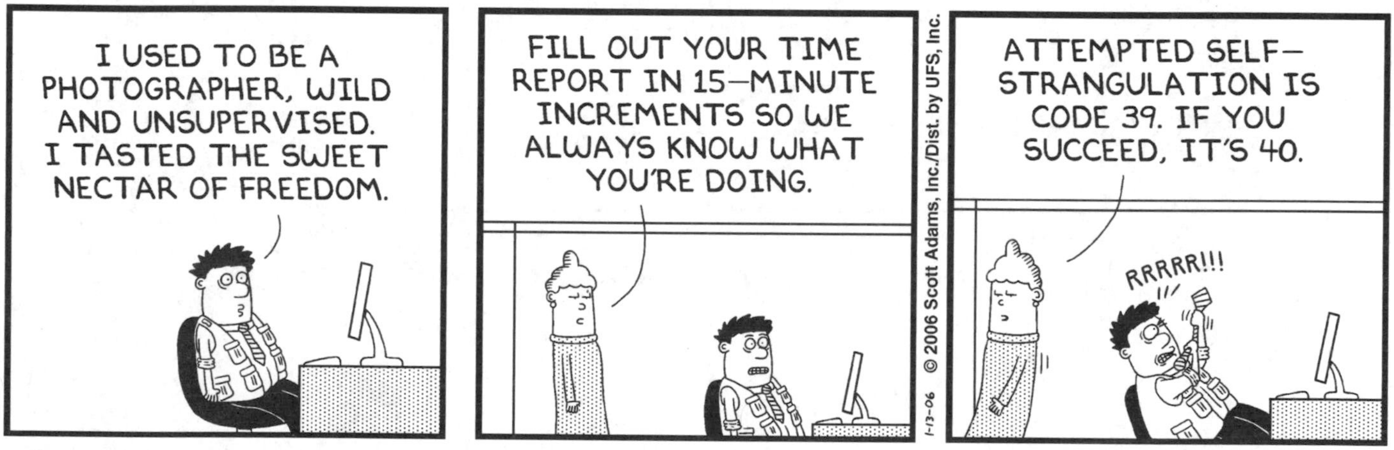
I USED TO BE A PHOTOGRAPHER, WILD AND UNSUPERVISED. I TASTED THE SWEET NECTAR OF FREEDOM.
FILL OUT YOUR TIME REPORT IN 15-MINUTE INCREMENTS SO WE ALWAYS KNOW WHAT YOU'RE DOING.
1-13-06 © 2006 Scott Adams, Inc./Dist. by UFS, Inc.
ATTEMPTED SELF-STRANGULATION IS CODE 39. IF YOU SUCCEED, IT'S 40.
RRRRR!!!

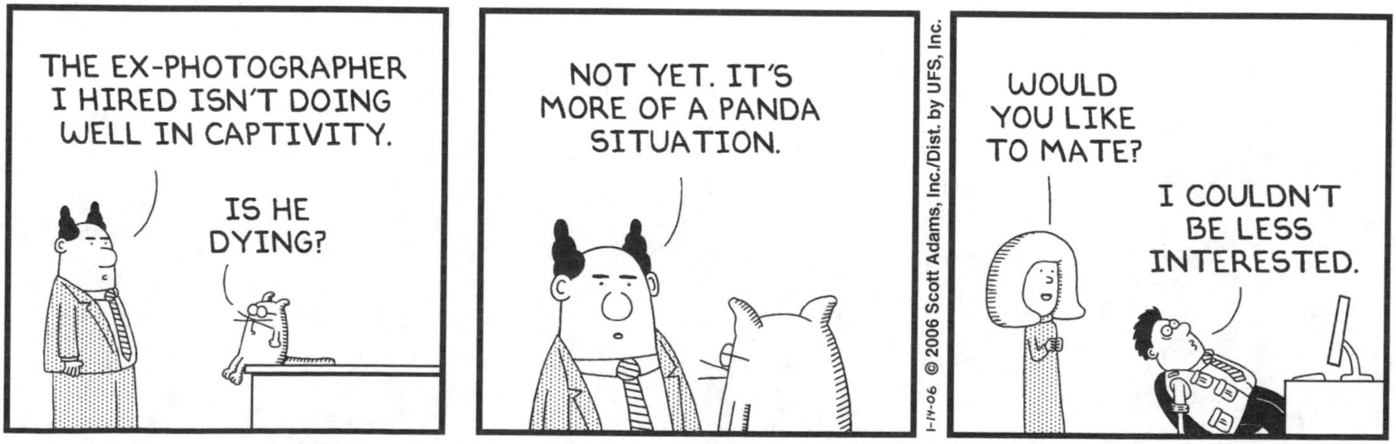
THE EX-PHOTOGRAPHER I HIRED ISN'T DOING WELL IN CAPTIVITY.
IS HE DYING?
NOT YET. IT'S MORE OF A PANDA SITUATION.
1-14-06 © 2006 Scott Adams, Inc./Dist. by UFS, Inc.
WOULD YOU LIKE TO MATE?
I COULDN'T BE LESS INTERESTED.

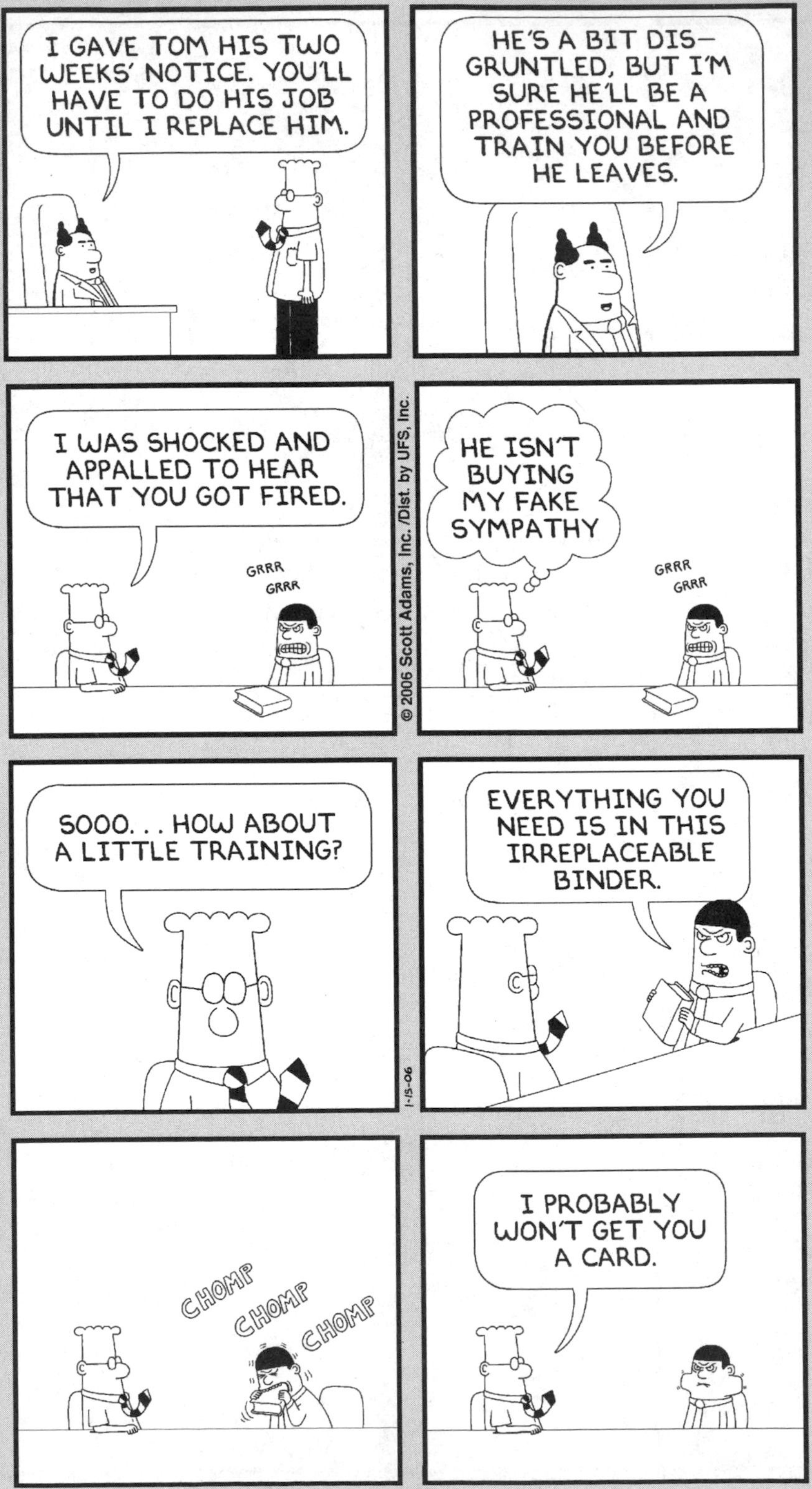

I GAVE TOM HIS TWO WEEKS' NOTICE. YOU'LL HAVE TO DO HIS JOB UNTIL I REPLACE HIM.
HE'S A BIT DIS— GRUNTLED, BUT I'M SURE HE'LL BE A PROFESSIONAL AND TRAIN YOU BEFORE HE LEAVES.
I WAS SHOCKED AND APPALLED TO HEAR THAT YOU GOT FIRED.
GRRR GRRR
HE ISN'T BUYING MY FAKE SYMPATHY
GRRR GRRR
SOOO. . . HOW ABOUT A LITTLE TRAINING?
EVERYTHING YOU NEED IS IN THIS IRREPLACEABLE BINDER.
CHOMP CHOMP CHOMP
I PROBABLY WON'T GET YOU A CARD.

1-15-06

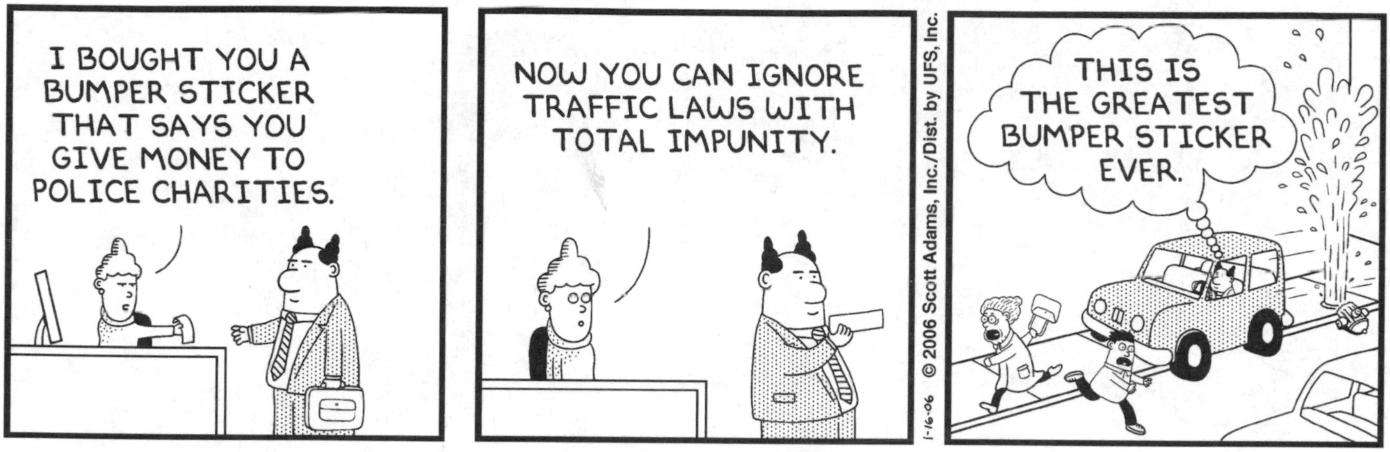
I BOUGHT YOU A BUMPER STICKER THAT SAYS YOU GIVE MONEY TO POLICE CHARITIES.
NOW YOU CAN IGNORE TRAFFIC LAWS WITH TOTAL IMPUNITY.
1-16-06 © 2006 Scott Adams, Inc./Dist. by UFS, Inc.
THIS IS THE GREATEST BUMPER STICKER EVER.

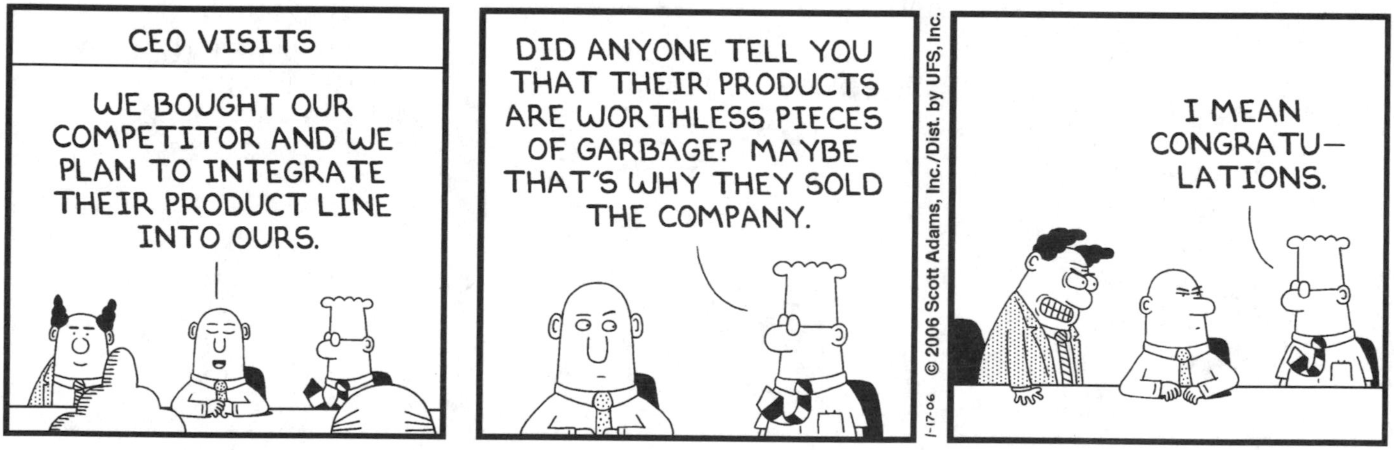
CEO VISITS
WE BOUGHT OUR COMPETITOR AND WE PLAN TO INTEGRATE THEIR PRODUCT LINE INTO OURS.
DID ANYONE TELL YOU THAT THEIR PRODUCTS ARE WORTHLESS PIECES OF GARBAGE? MAYBE THAT'S WHY THEY SOLD THE COMPANY.
1-17-06 © 2006 Scott Adams, Inc./Dist. by UFS, Inc.
I MEAN CONGRATU-LATIONS.

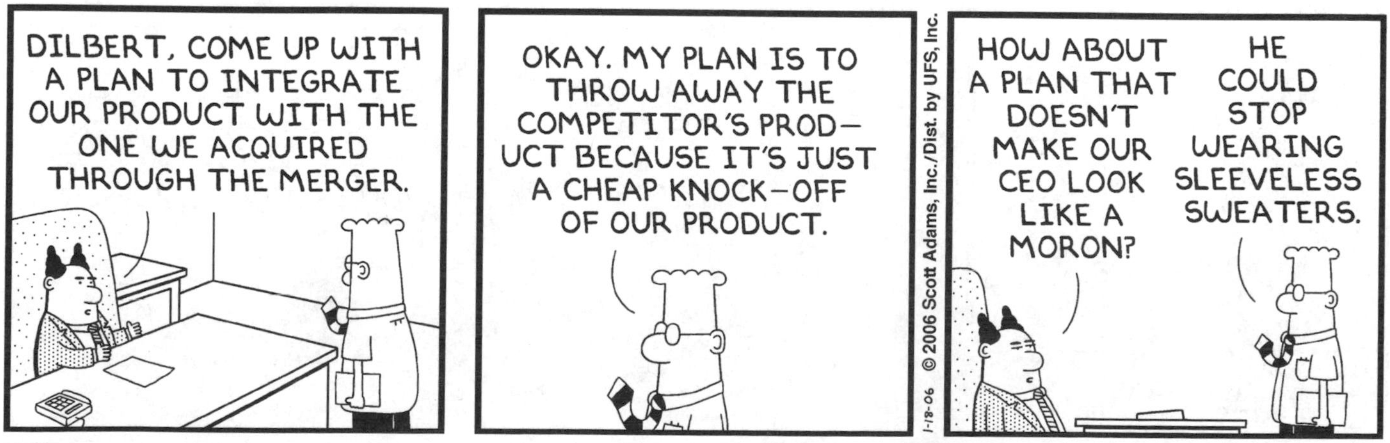
DILBERT, COME UP WITH A PLAN TO INTEGRATE OUR PRODUCT WITH THE ONE WE ACQUIRED THROUGH THE MERGER.
OKAY. MY PLAN IS TO THROW AWAY THE COMPETITOR'S PROD-UCT BECAUSE IT'S JUST A CHEAP KNOCK-OFF OF OUR PRODUCT.
1-18-06 © 2006 Scott Adams, Inc./Dist. by UFS, Inc.
HOW ABOUT A PLAN THAT DOESN'T MAKE OUR CEO LOOK LIKE A MORON?
HE COULD STOP WEARING SLEEVELESS SWEATERS.

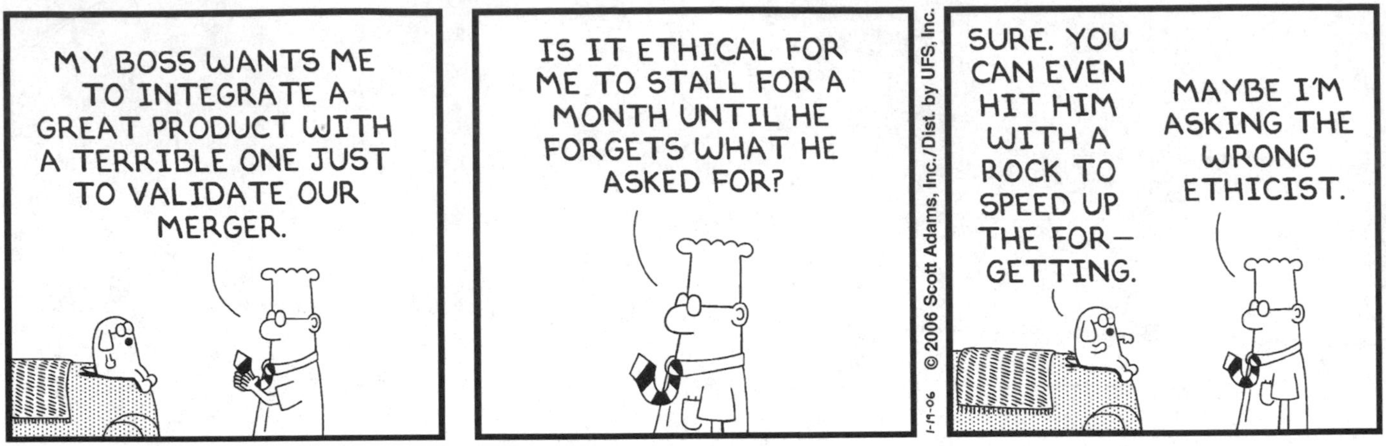
MY BOSS WANTS ME TO INTEGRATE A GREAT PRODUCT WITH A TERRIBLE ONE JUST TO VALIDATE OUR MERGER.
IS IT ETHICAL FOR ME TO STALL FOR A MONTH UNTIL HE FORGETS WHAT HE ASKED FOR?
1-19-06 © 2006 Scott Adams, Inc./Dist. by UFS, Inc.
SURE. YOU CAN EVEN HIT HIM WITH A ROCK TO SPEED UP THE FOR-GETTING.
MAYBE I'M ASKING THE WRONG ETHICIST.

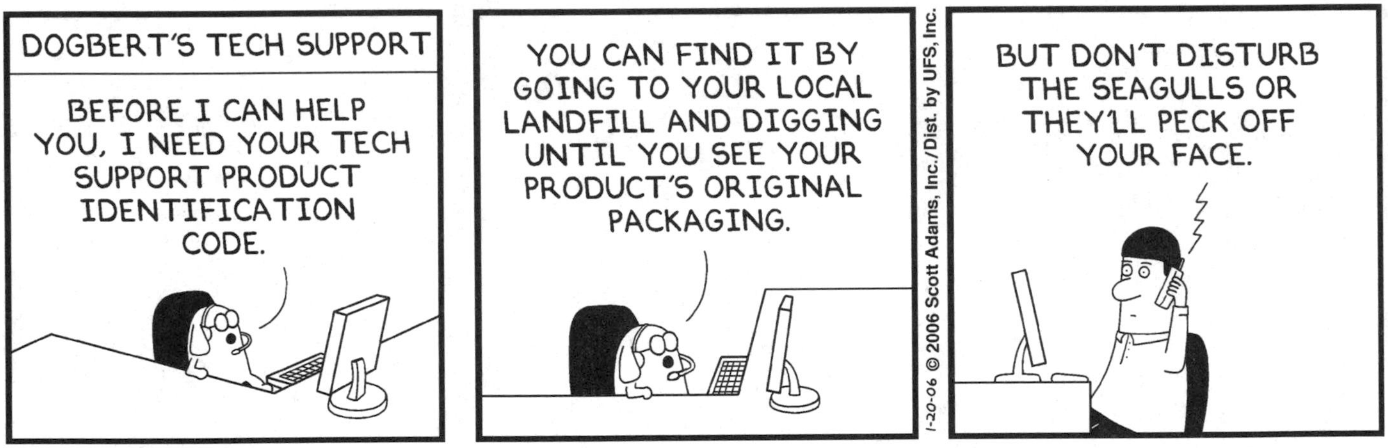
DOGBERT'S TECH SUPPORT
BEFORE I CAN HELP YOU, I NEED YOUR TECH SUPPORT PRODUCT IDENTIFICATION CODE.
YOU CAN FIND IT BY GOING TO YOUR LOCAL LANDFILL AND DIGGING UNTIL YOU SEE YOUR PRODUCT'S ORIGINAL PACKAGING.
1-20-06 © 2006 Scott Adams, Inc./Dist. by UFS, Inc.
BUT DON'T DISTURB THE SEAGULLS OR THEY'LL PECK OFF YOUR FACE.

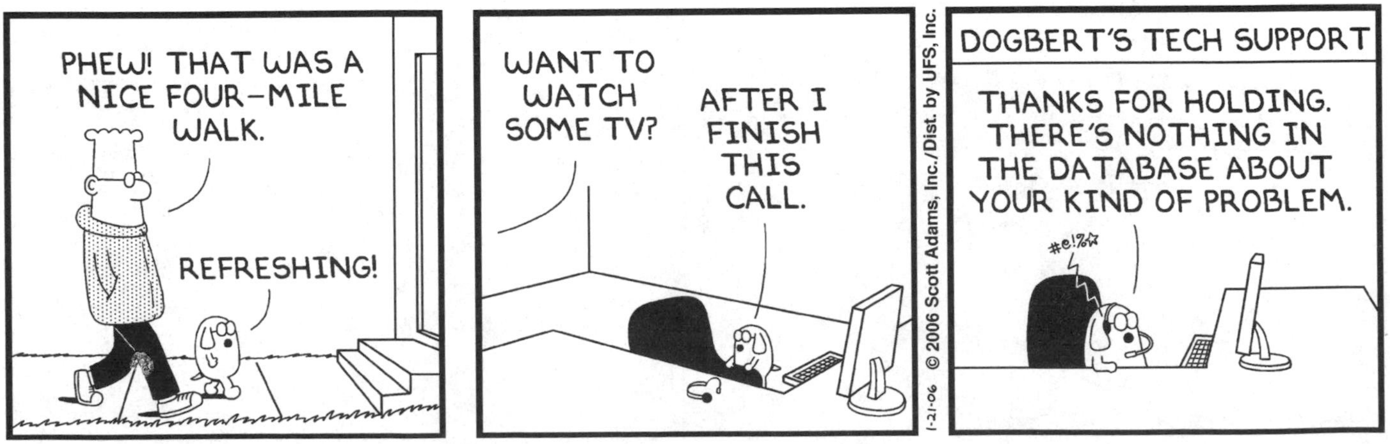
PHEW! THAT WAS A NICE FOUR-MILE WALK.
REFRESHING!
WANT TO WATCH SOME TV?
AFTER I FINISH THIS CALL.
1-21-06 © 2006 Scott Adams, Inc./Dist. by UFS, Inc.
DOGBERT'S TECH SUPPORT
THANKS FOR HOLDING. THERE'S NOTHING IN THE DATABASE ABOUT YOUR KIND OF PROBLEM.
#e!%☆

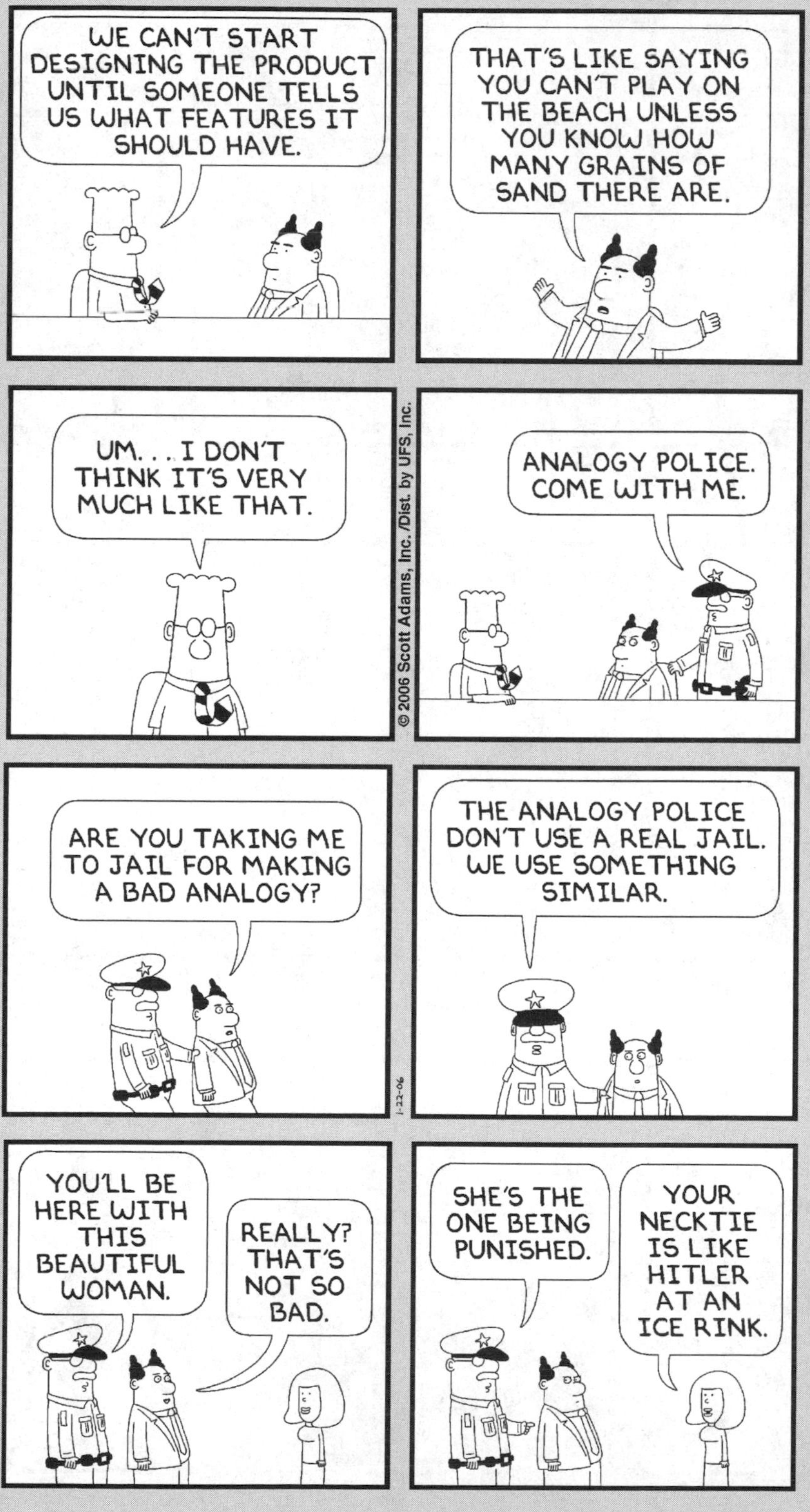
WE CAN'T START DESIGNING THE PRODUCT UNTIL SOMEONE TELLS US WHAT FEATURES IT SHOULD HAVE.
THAT'S LIKE SAYING YOU CAN'T PLAY ON THE BEACH UNLESS YOU KNOW HOW MANY GRAINS OF SAND THERE ARE.
UM. . . I DON'T THINK IT'S VERY MUCH LIKE THAT.
ANALOGY POLICE. COME WITH ME.
ARE YOU TAKING ME TO JAIL FOR MAKING A BAD ANALOGY?
THE ANALOGY POLICE DON'T USE A REAL JAIL. WE USE SOMETHING SIMILAR.
YOU'LL BE HERE WITH THIS BEAUTIFUL WOMAN.
REALLY? THAT'S NOT SO BAD.
SHE'S THE ONE BEING PUNISHED.
YOUR NECKTIE IS LIKE HITLER AT AN ICE RINK.
1-22-06

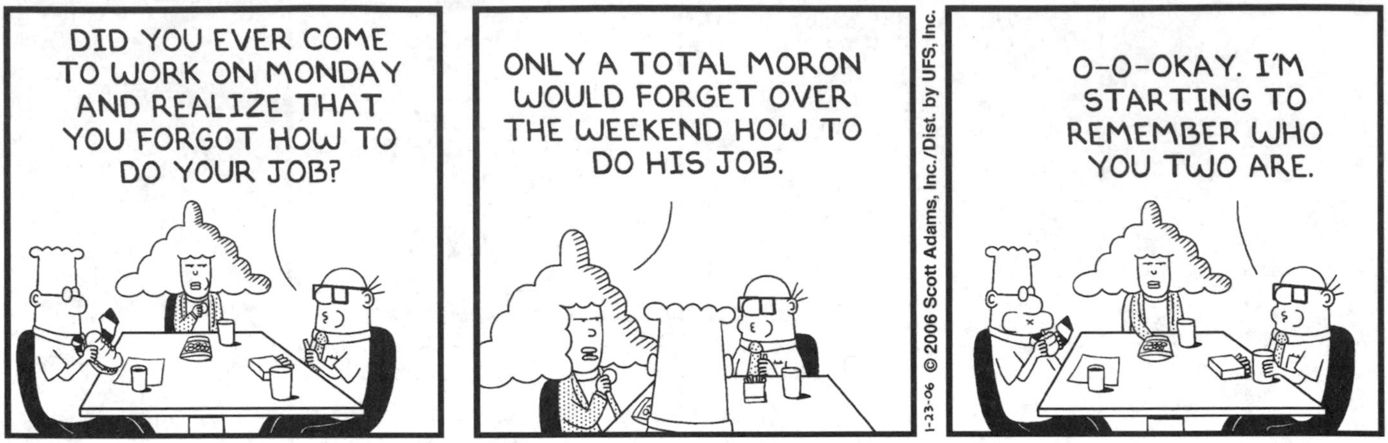
DID YOU EVER COME TO WORK ON MONDAY AND REALIZE THAT YOU FORGOT HOW TO DO YOUR JOB?
ONLY A TOTAL MORON WOULD FORGET OVER THE WEEKEND HOW TO DO HIS JOB.
O-O-OKAY. I'M STARTING TO REMEMBER WHO YOU TWO ARE.
1-23-06 © 2006 Scott Adams, Inc./Dist. by UFS, Inc.

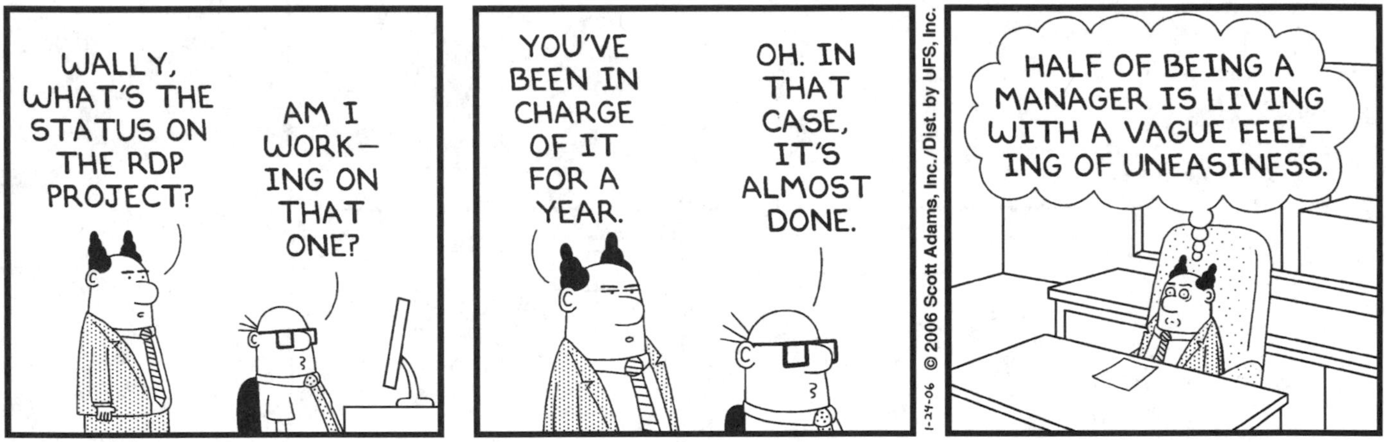
WALLY, WHAT'S THE STATUS ON THE RDP PROJECT?
AM I WORK-ING ON THAT ONE?
YOU'VE BEEN IN CHARGE OF IT FOR A YEAR.
OH. IN THAT CASE, IT'S ALMOST DONE.
HALF OF BEING A MANAGER IS LIVING WITH A VAGUE FEEL-ING OF UNEASINESS.
1-24-06 © 2006 Scott Adams, Inc./Dist. by UFS, Inc.

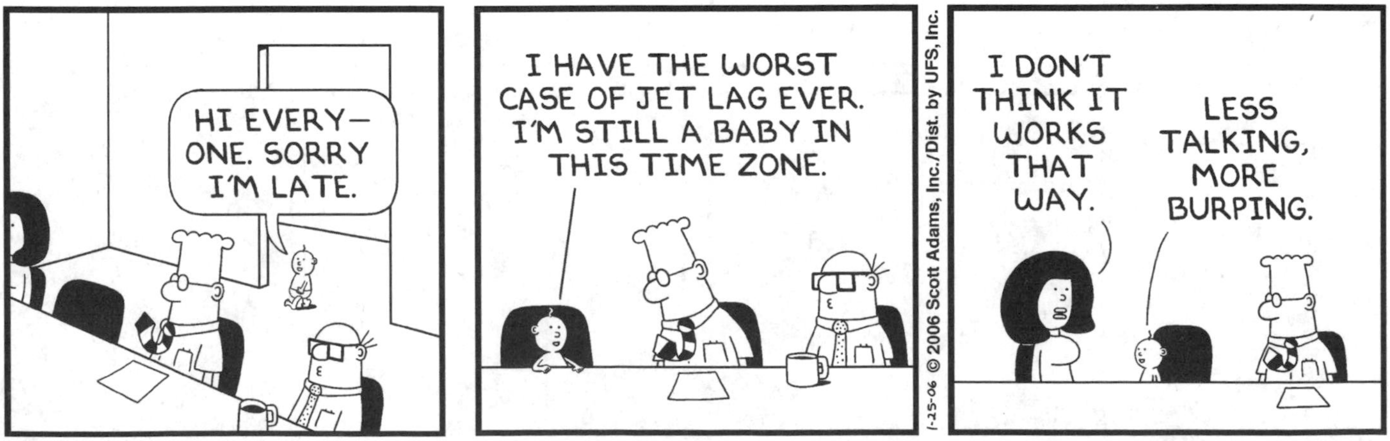
HI EVERY-ONE. SORRY I'M LATE.
I HAVE THE WORST CASE OF JET LAG EVER. I'M STILL A BABY IN THIS TIME ZONE.
I DON'T THINK IT WORKS THAT WAY.
LESS TALKING, MORE BURPING.
1-25-06 © 2006 Scott Adams, Inc./Dist. by UFS, Inc.

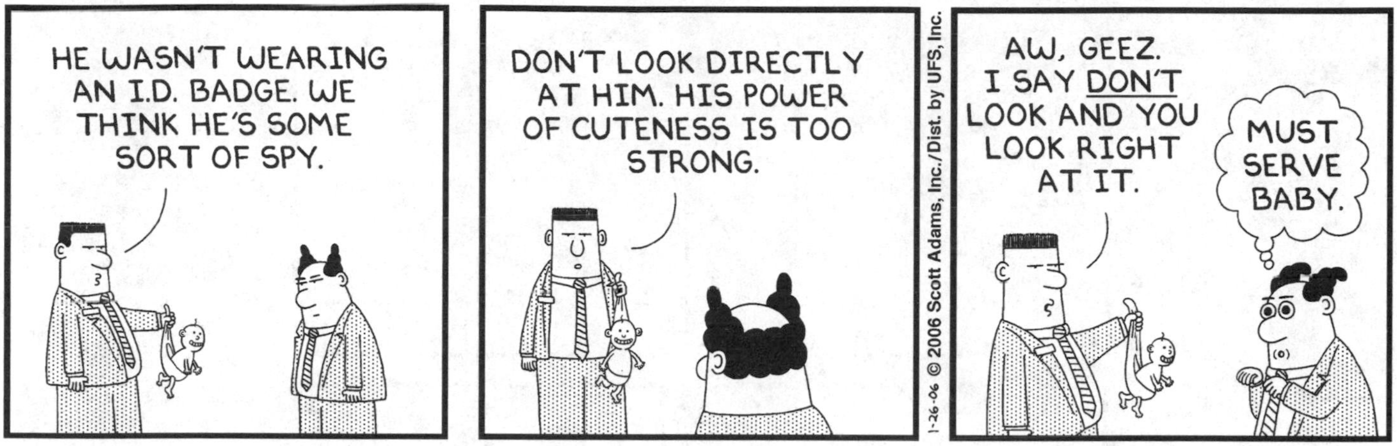
HE WASN'T WEARING AN I.D. BADGE. WE THINK HE'S SOME SORT OF SPY.
DON'T LOOK DIRECTLY AT HIM. HIS POWER OF CUTENESS IS TOO STRONG.
1-26-06 © 2006 Scott Adams, Inc./Dist. by UFS, Inc.
AW, GEEZ. I SAY DON'T LOOK AND YOU LOOK RIGHT AT IT.
MUST SERVE BABY.

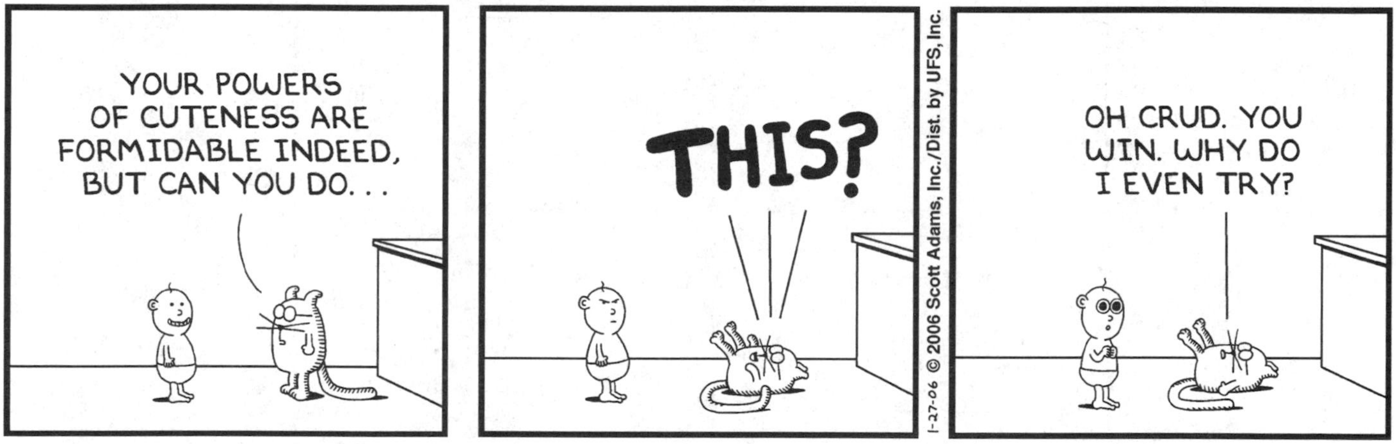
YOUR POWERS OF CUTENESS ARE FORMIDABLE INDEED, BUT CAN YOU DO. . .
THIS?
1-27-06 © 2006 Scott Adams, Inc./Dist. by UFS, Inc.
OH CRUD. YOU WIN. WHY DO I EVEN TRY?

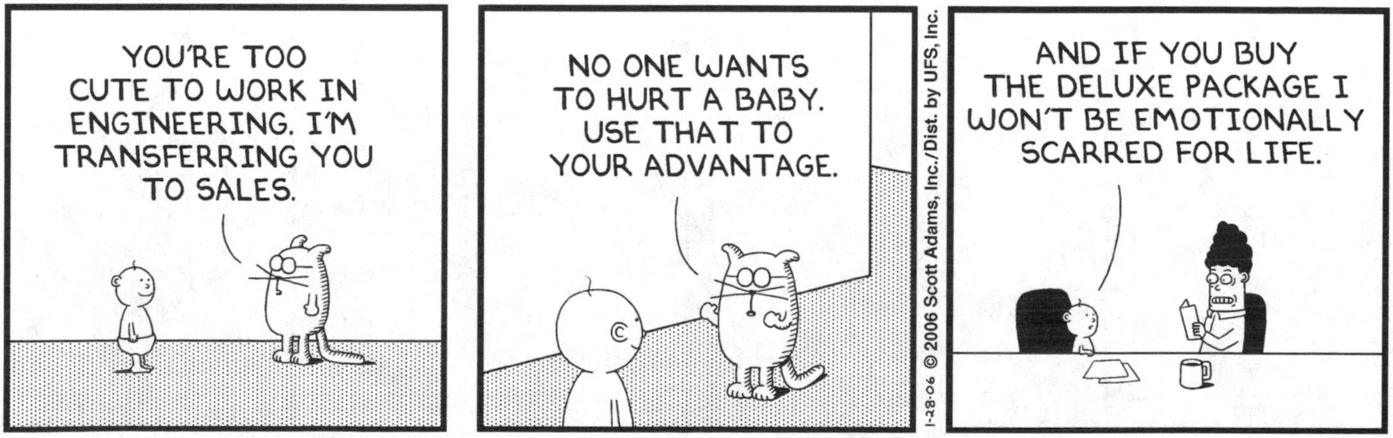
YOU'RE TOO CUTE TO WORK IN ENGINEERING. I'M TRANSFERRING YOU TO SALES.
NO ONE WANTS TO HURT A BABY. USE THAT TO YOUR ADVANTAGE.
1-28-06 © 2006 Scott Adams, Inc./Dist. by UFS, Inc.
AND IF YOU BUY THE DELUXE PACKAGE I WON'T BE EMOTIONALLY SCARRED FOR LIFE.

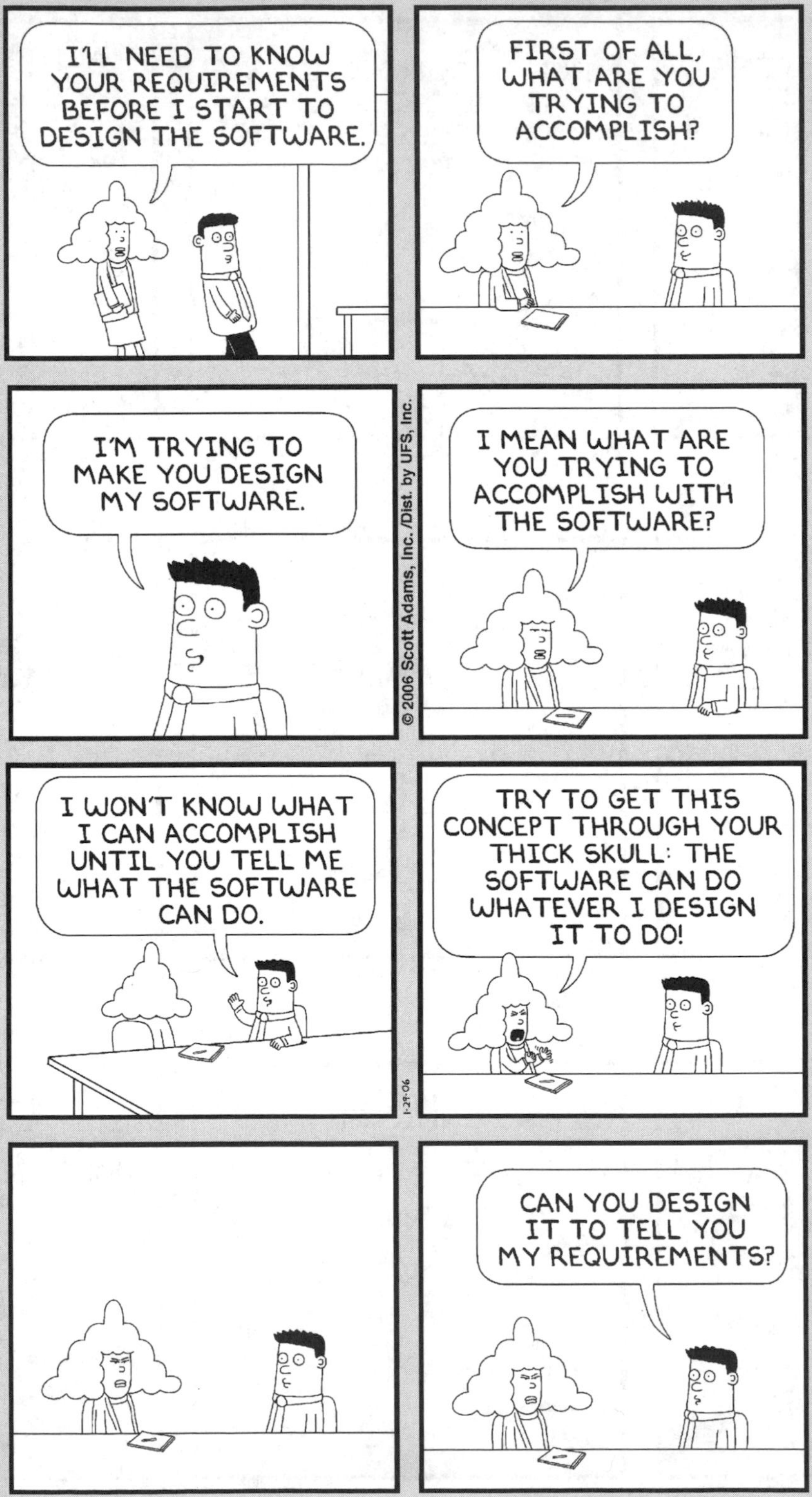
I'LL NEED TO KNOW YOUR REQUIREMENTS BEFORE I START TO DESIGN THE SOFTWARE.
FIRST OF ALL, WHAT ARE YOU TRYING TO ACCOMPLISH?
I'M TRYING TO MAKE YOU DESIGN MY SOFTWARE.
I MEAN WHAT ARE YOU TRYING TO ACCOMPLISH WITH THE SOFTWARE?
I WON'T KNOW WHAT I CAN ACCOMPLISH UNTIL YOU TELL ME WHAT THE SOFTWARE CAN DO.
TRY TO GET THIS CONCEPT THROUGH YOUR THICK SKULL: THE SOFTWARE CAN DO WHATEVER I DESIGN IT TO DO!
CAN YOU DESIGN IT TO TELL YOU MY REQUIREMENTS?
© 2006 Scott Adams, Inc. /Dist. by UFS, Inc.
1-29-06

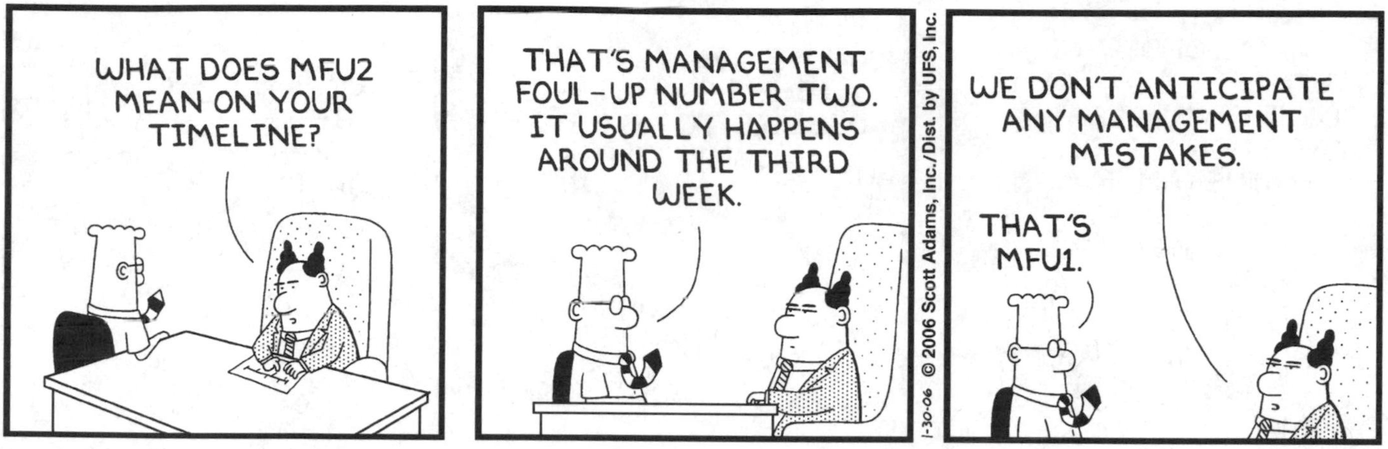
WHAT DOES MFU2 MEAN ON YOUR TIMELINE?
THAT'S MANAGEMENT FOUL-UP NUMBER TWO. IT USUALLY HAPPENS AROUND THE THIRD WEEK.
WE DON'T ANTICIPATE ANY MANAGEMENT MISTAKES.
THAT'S MFU1.
1-30-06 © 2006 Scott Adams, Inc./Dist. by UFS, Inc.

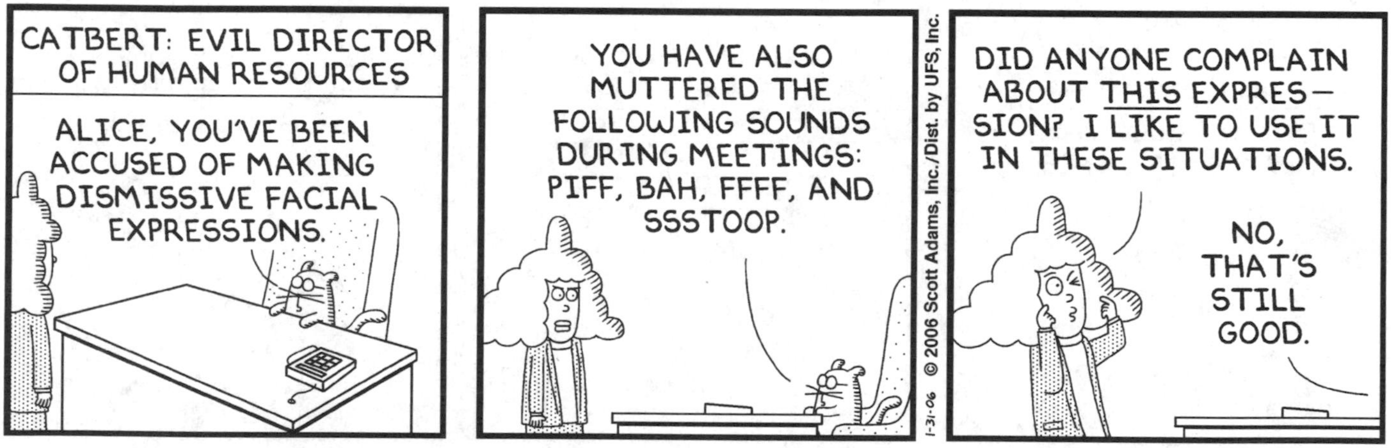
CATBERT: EVIL DIRECTOR OF HUMAN RESOURCES
ALICE, YOU'VE BEEN ACCUSED OF MAKING DISMISSIVE FACIAL EXPRESSIONS.
YOU HAVE ALSO MUTTERED THE FOLLOWING SOUNDS DURING MEETINGS: PIFF, BAH, FFFF, AND SSSTOOP.
DID ANYONE COMPLAIN ABOUT THIS EXPRES-SION? I LIKE TO USE IT IN THESE SITUATIONS.
NO, THAT'S STILL GOOD.
1-31-06 © 2006 Scott Adams, Inc./Dist. by UFS, Inc.

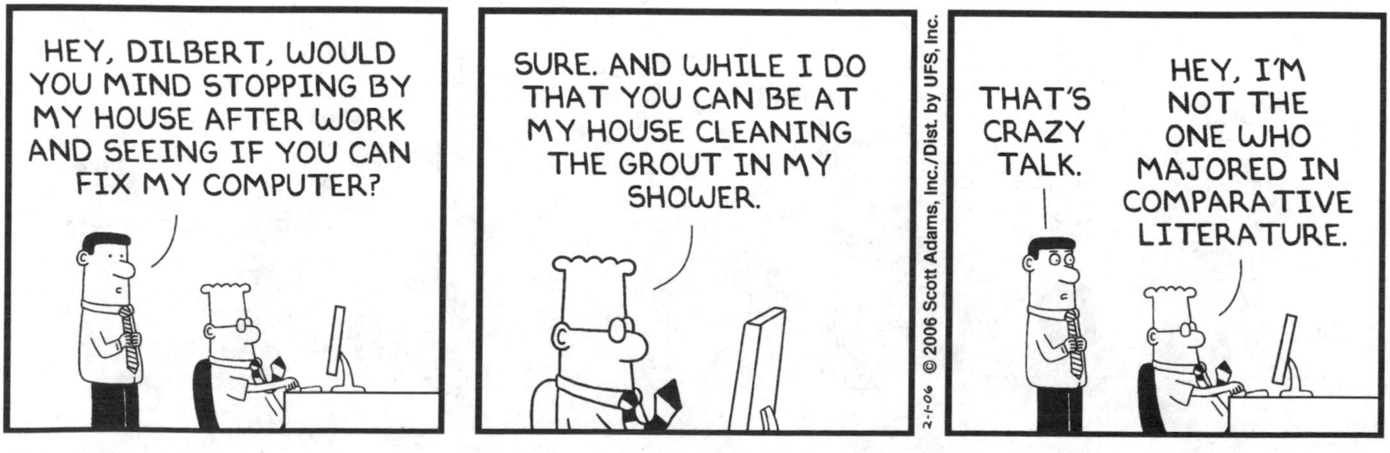
HEY, DILBERT, WOULD YOU MIND STOPPING BY MY HOUSE AFTER WORK AND SEEING IF YOU CAN FIX MY COMPUTER?
SURE. AND WHILE I DO THAT YOU CAN BE AT MY HOUSE CLEANING THE GROUT IN MY SHOWER.
THAT'S CRAZY TALK.
HEY, I'M NOT THE ONE WHO MAJORED IN COMPARATIVE LITERATURE.
2-1-06 © 2006 Scott Adams, Inc./Dist. by UFS, Inc.

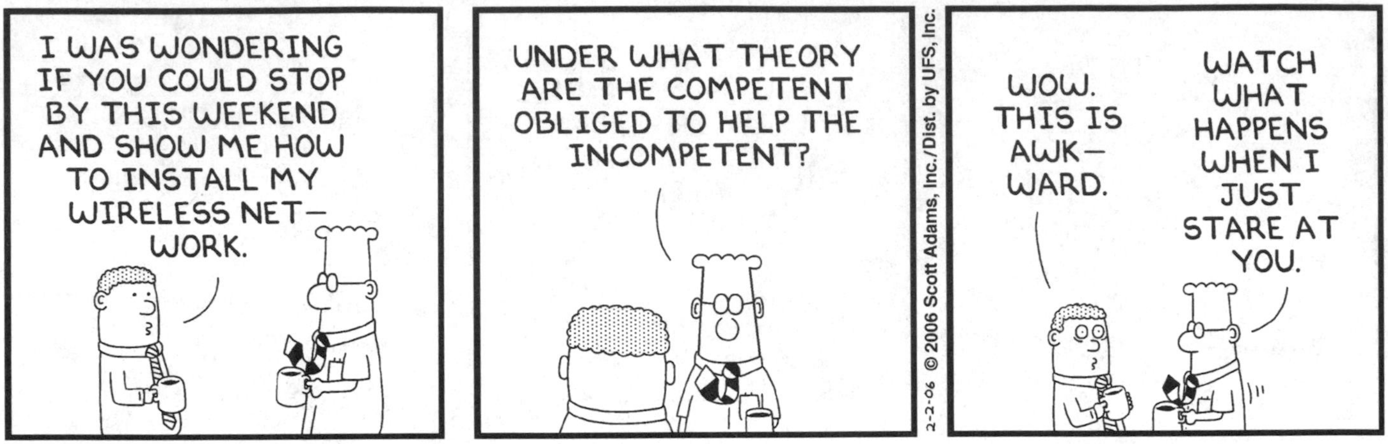
I WAS WONDERING IF YOU COULD STOP BY THIS WEEKEND AND SHOW ME HOW TO INSTALL MY WIRELESS NET-WORK.
UNDER WHAT THEORY ARE THE COMPETENT OBLIGED TO HELP THE INCOMPETENT?
2-2-06 © 2006 Scott Adams, Inc./Dist. by UFS, Inc.
WOW. THIS IS AWK-WARD.
WATCH WHAT HAPPENS WHEN I JUST STARE AT YOU.

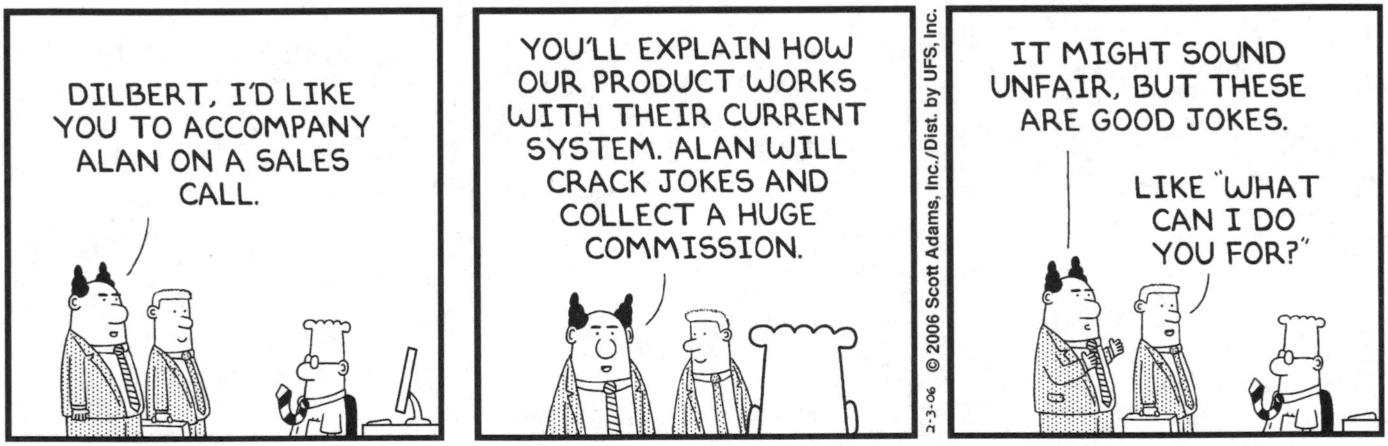
DILBERT, I'D LIKE YOU TO ACCOMPANY ALAN ON A SALES CALL.
YOU'LL EXPLAIN HOW OUR PRODUCT WORKS WITH THEIR CURRENT SYSTEM. ALAN WILL CRACK JOKES AND COLLECT A HUGE COMMISSION.
2-3-06 © 2006 Scott Adams, Inc./Dist. by UFS, Inc.
IT MIGHT SOUND UNFAIR, BUT THESE ARE GOOD JOKES.
LIKE "WHAT CAN I DO YOU FOR?"

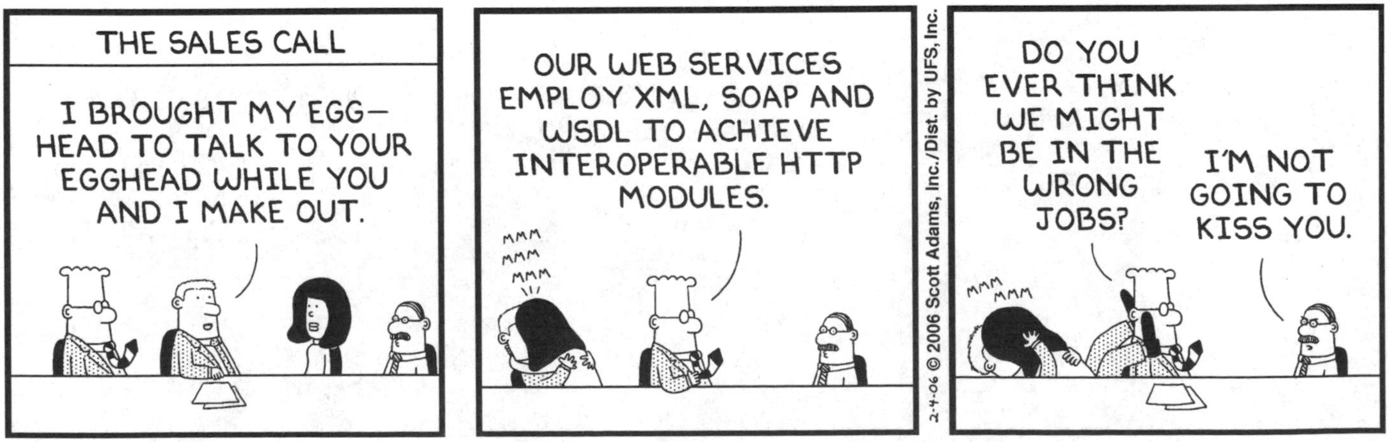
THE SALES CALL
I BROUGHT MY EGG-HEAD TO TALK TO YOUR EGGHEAD WHILE YOU AND I MAKE OUT.
MMM MMM MMM
OUR WEB SERVICES EMPLOY XML, SOAP AND WSDL TO ACHIEVE INTEROPERABLE HTTP MODULES.
2-4-06 © 2006 Scott Adams, Inc./Dist. by UFS, Inc.
MMM MMM
DO YOU EVER THINK WE MIGHT BE IN THE WRONG JOBS?
I'M NOT GOING TO KISS YOU.

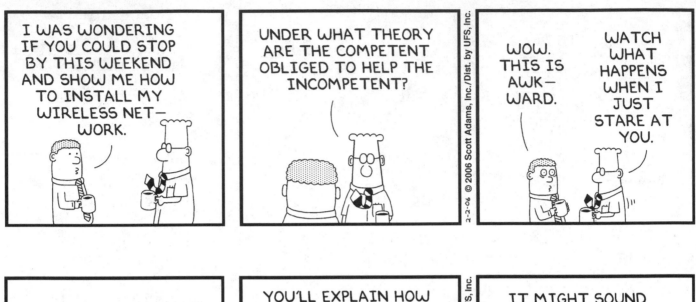

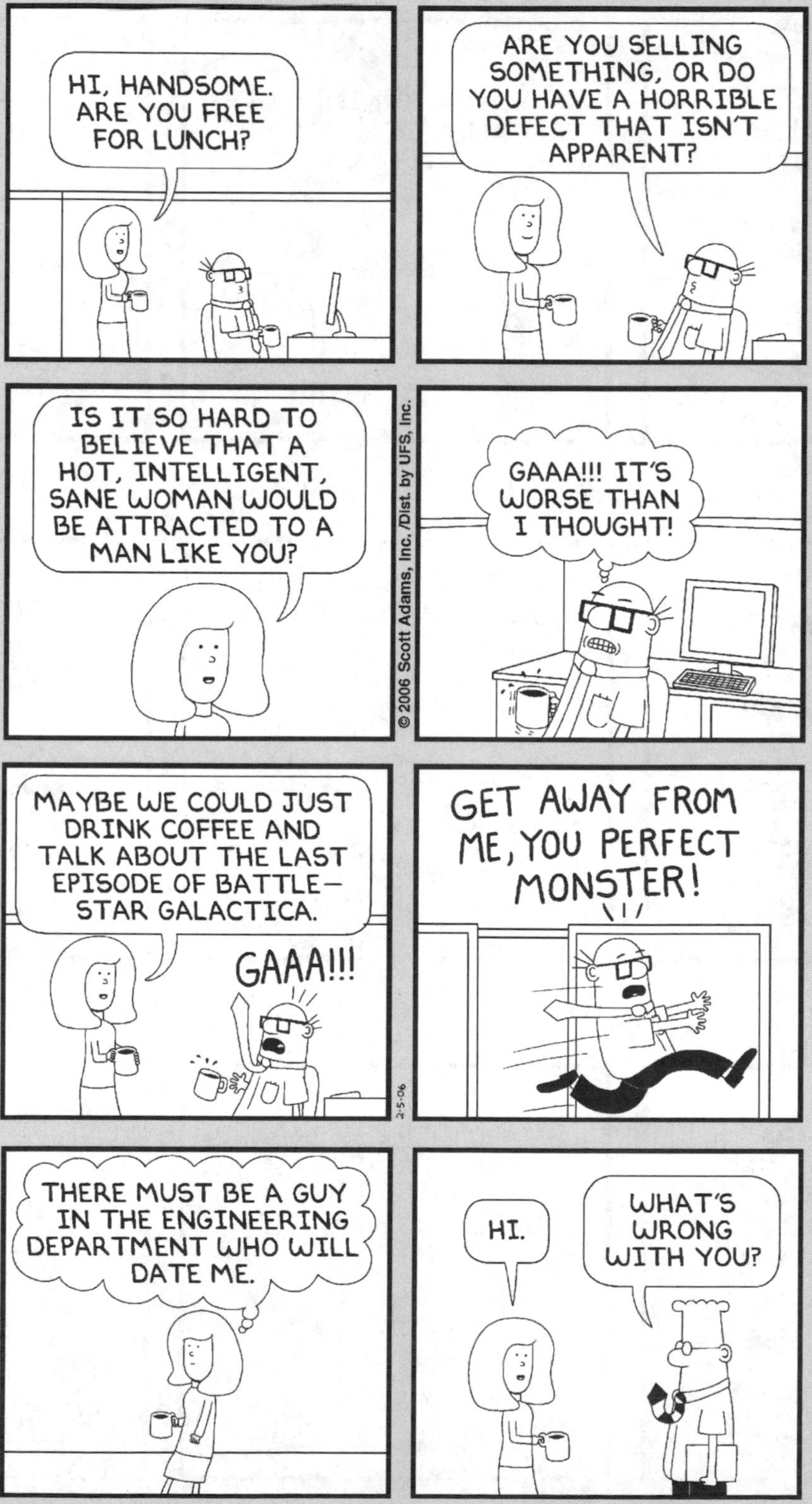
HI, HANDSOME. ARE YOU FREE FOR LUNCH?
ARE YOU SELLING SOMETHING, OR DO YOU HAVE A HORRIBLE DEFECT THAT ISN'T APPARENT?
IS IT SO HARD TO BELIEVE THAT A HOT, INTELLIGENT, SANE WOMAN WOULD BE ATTRACTED TO A MAN LIKE YOU?
GAAA!!! IT'S WORSE THAN I THOUGHT!
MAYBE WE COULD JUST DRINK COFFEE AND TALK ABOUT THE LAST EPISODE OF BATTLE-STAR GALACTICA.
GAAA!!!
GET AWAY FROM ME, YOU PERFECT MONSTER!
THERE MUST BE A GUY IN THE ENGINEERING DEPARTMENT WHO WILL DATE ME.
HI.
WHAT'S WRONG WITH YOU?
2-5-06

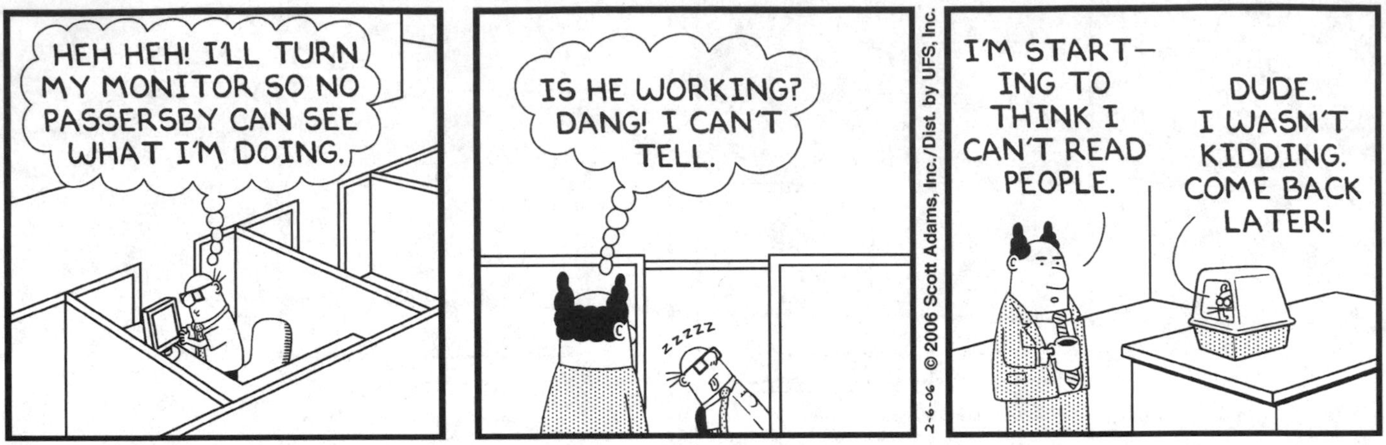
HEH HEH! I'LL TURN MY MONITOR SO NO PASSERSBY CAN SEE WHAT I'M DOING.
IS HE WORKING? DANG! I CAN'T TELL.
ZZZZZ
2-6-06 © 2006 Scott Adams, Inc./Dist. by UFS, Inc.
I'M START-ING TO THINK I CAN'T READ PEOPLE.
DUDE. I WASN'T KIDDING. COME BACK LATER!

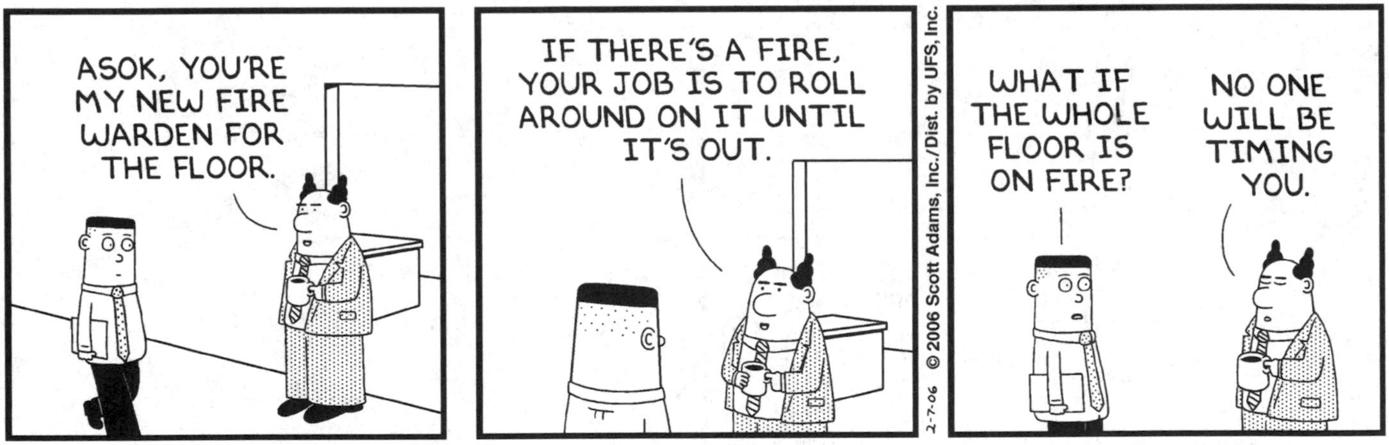
ASOK, YOU'RE MY NEW FIRE WARDEN FOR THE FLOOR.
IF THERE'S A FIRE, YOUR JOB IS TO ROLL AROUND ON IT UNTIL IT'S OUT.
2-7-06 © 2006 Scott Adams, Inc./Dist. by UFS, Inc.
WHAT IF THE WHOLE FLOOR IS ON FIRE?
NO ONE WILL BE TIMING YOU.

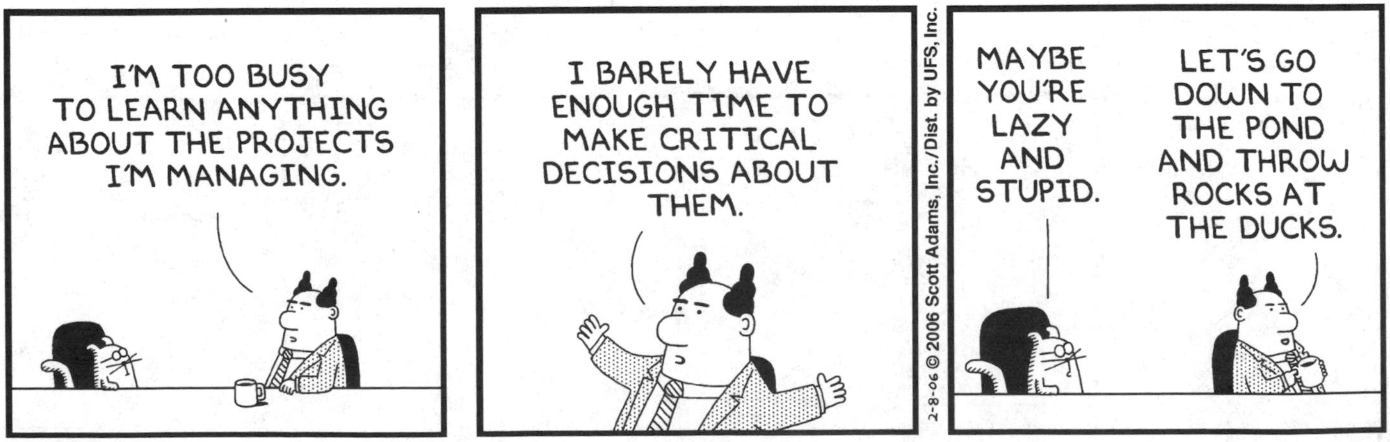
I'M TOO BUSY TO LEARN ANYTHING ABOUT THE PROJECTS I'M MANAGING.
I BARELY HAVE ENOUGH TIME TO MAKE CRITICAL DECISIONS ABOUT THEM.
2-8-06 © 2006 Scott Adams, Inc./Dist. by UFS, Inc.
MAYBE YOU'RE LAZY AND STUPID.
LET'S GO DOWN TO THE POND AND THROW ROCKS AT THE DUCKS.

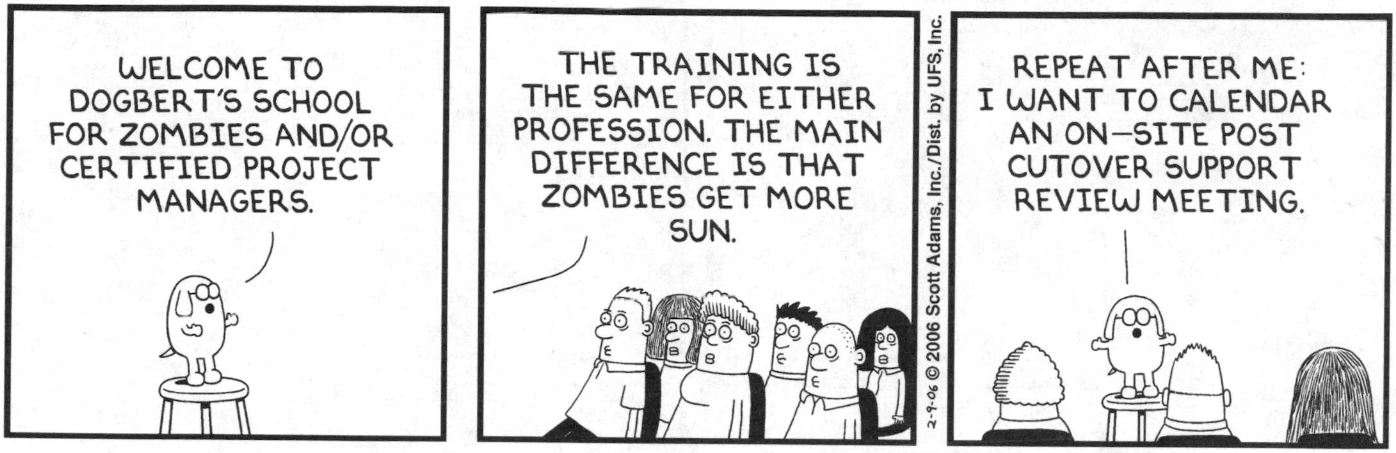
WELCOME TO DOGBERT'S SCHOOL FOR ZOMBIES AND/OR CERTIFIED PROJECT MANAGERS.
THE TRAINING IS THE SAME FOR EITHER PROFESSION. THE MAIN DIFFERENCE IS THAT ZOMBIES GET MORE SUN.
2-9-06 © 2006 Scott Adams, Inc./Dist. by UFS, Inc.
REPEAT AFTER ME: I WANT TO CALENDAR AN ON-SITE POST CUTOVER SUPPORT REVIEW MEETING.

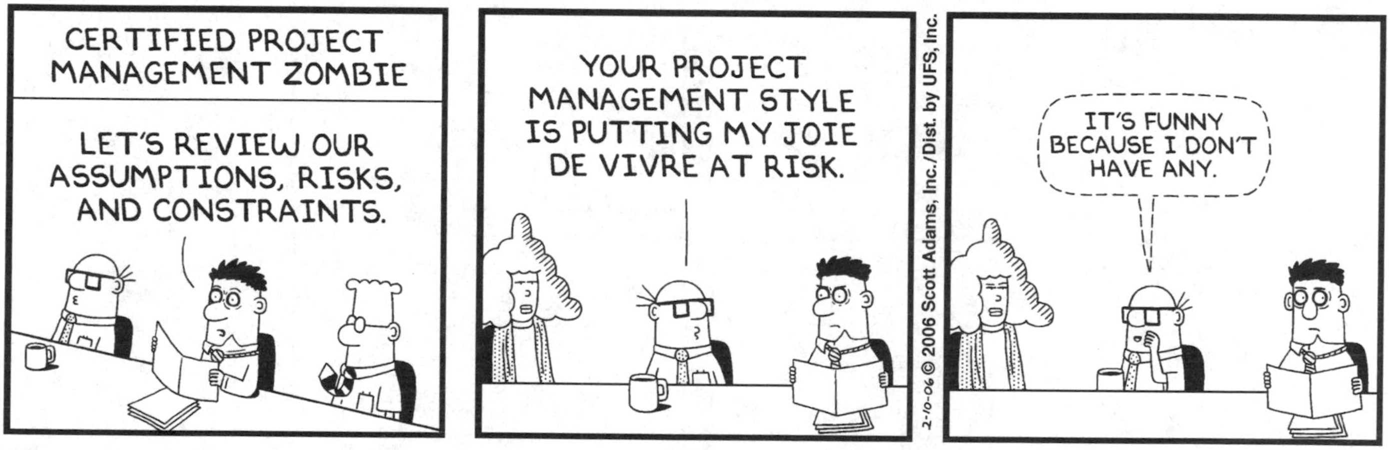
CERTIFIED PROJECT MANAGEMENT ZOMBIE
LET'S REVIEW OUR ASSUMPTIONS, RISKS, AND CONSTRAINTS.
YOUR PROJECT MANAGEMENT STYLE IS PUTTING MY JOIE DE VIVRE AT RISK.
2-10-06 © 2006 Scott Adams, Inc./Dist. by UFS, Inc.
IT'S FUNNY BECAUSE I DON'T HAVE ANY.

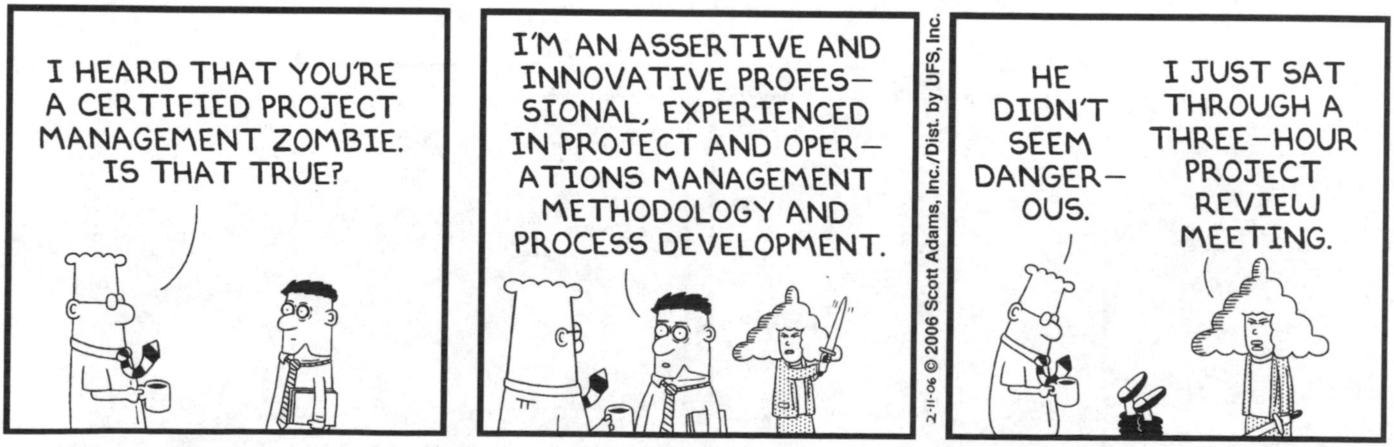
I HEARD THAT YOU'RE A CERTIFIED PROJECT MANAGEMENT ZOMBIE. IS THAT TRUE?
I'M AN ASSERTIVE AND INNOVATIVE PROFES-SIONAL, EXPERIENCED IN PROJECT AND OPER-ATIONS MANAGEMENT METHODOLOGY AND PROCESS DEVELOPMENT.
2-11-06 © 2006 Scott Adams, Inc./Dist. by UFS, Inc.
HE DIDN'T SEEM DANGER-OUS.
I JUST SAT THROUGH A THREE-HOUR PROJECT REVIEW MEETING.

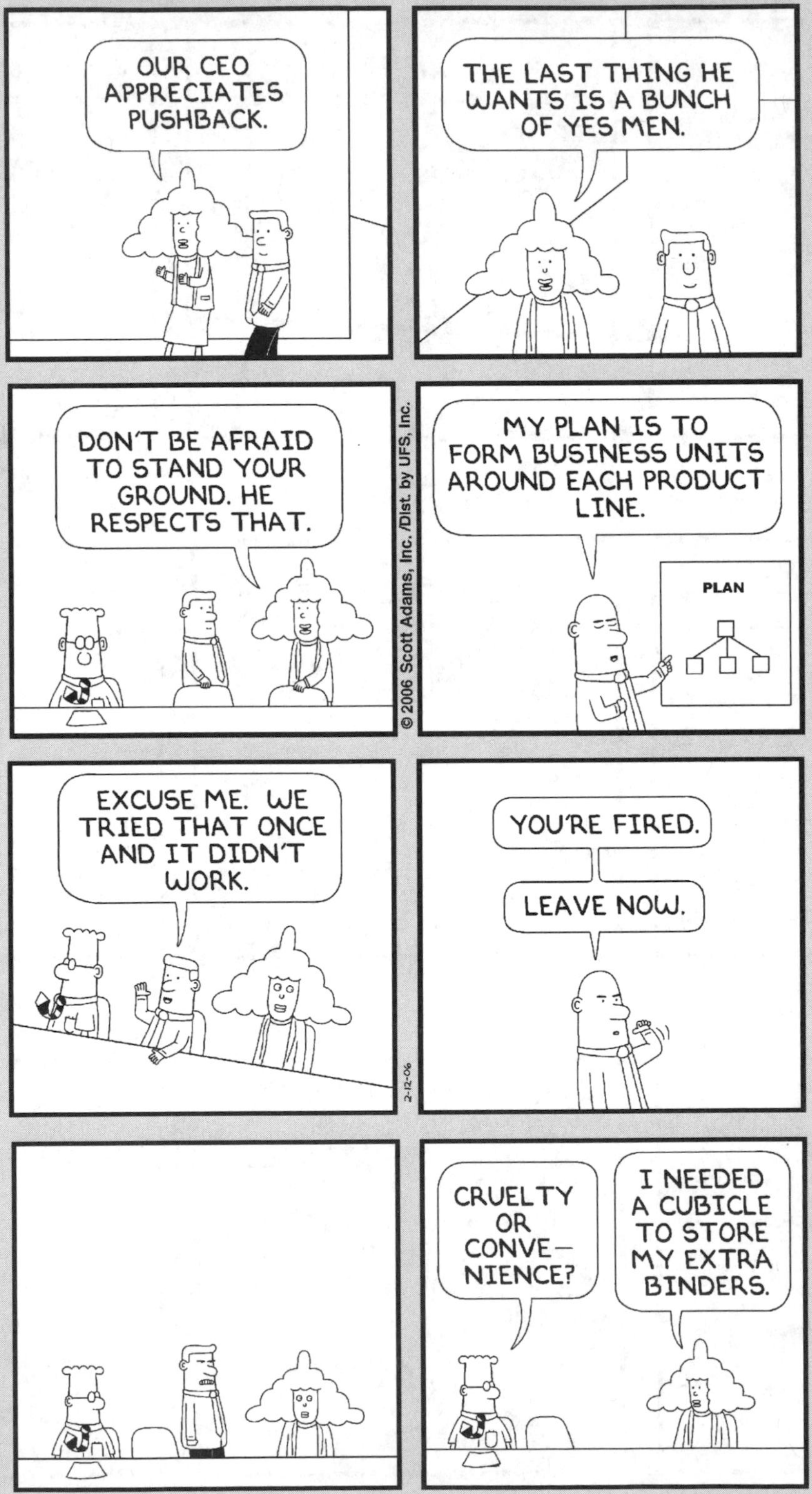
OUR CEO APPRECIATES PUSHBACK.
THE LAST THING HE WANTS IS A BUNCH OF YES MEN.
DON'T BE AFRAID TO STAND YOUR GROUND. HE RESPECTS THAT.
© 2006 Scott Adams, Inc. /Dist. by UFS, Inc.
MY PLAN IS TO FORM BUSINESS UNITS AROUND EACH PRODUCT LINE.
PLAN
EXCUSE ME. WE TRIED THAT ONCE AND IT DIDN'T WORK.
2-12-06
YOU'RE FIRED.
LEAVE NOW.
CRUELTY OR CONVE–NIENCE?
I NEEDED A CUBICLE TO STORE MY EXTRA BINDERS.

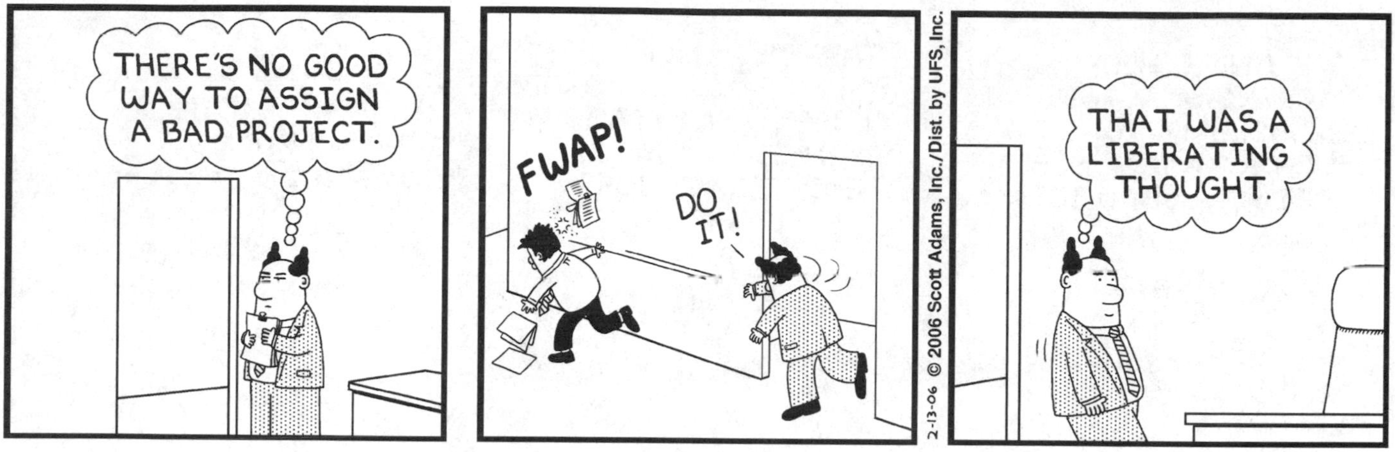
THERE'S NO GOOD WAY TO ASSIGN A BAD PROJECT.
FWAP!
DO IT!
2-13-06 © 2006 Scott Adams, Inc./Dist. by UFS, Inc.
THAT WAS A LIBERATING THOUGHT.

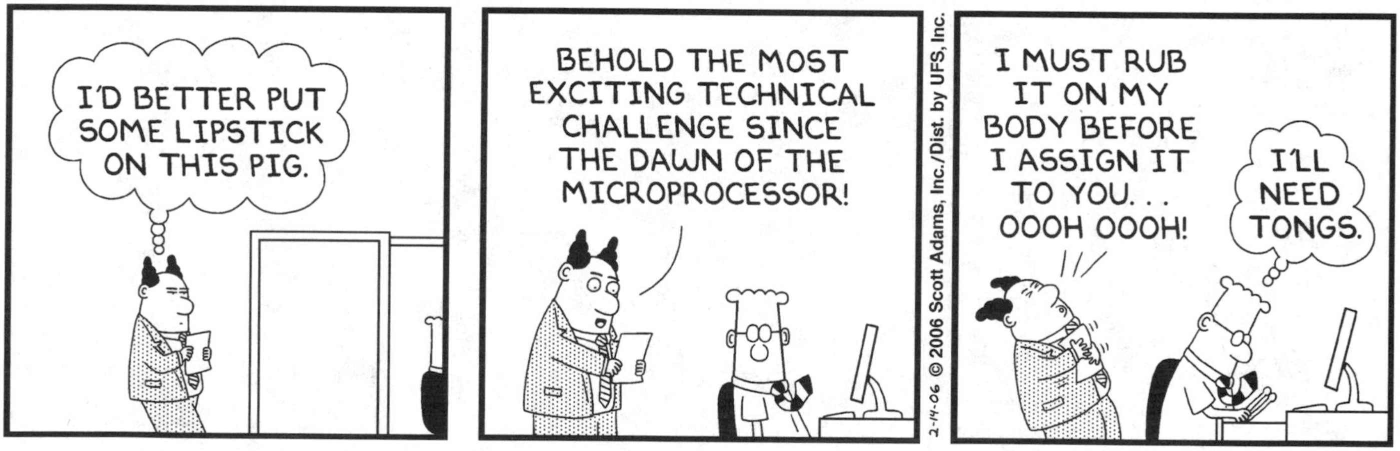
I'D BETTER PUT SOME LIPSTICK ON THIS PIG.
BEHOLD THE MOST EXCITING TECHNICAL CHALLENGE SINCE THE DAWN OF THE MICROPROCESSOR!
2-14-06 © 2006 Scott Adams, Inc./Dist. by UFS, Inc.
I MUST RUB IT ON MY BODY BEFORE I ASSIGN IT TO YOU. . . OOOH OOOH!
I'LL NEED TONGS.

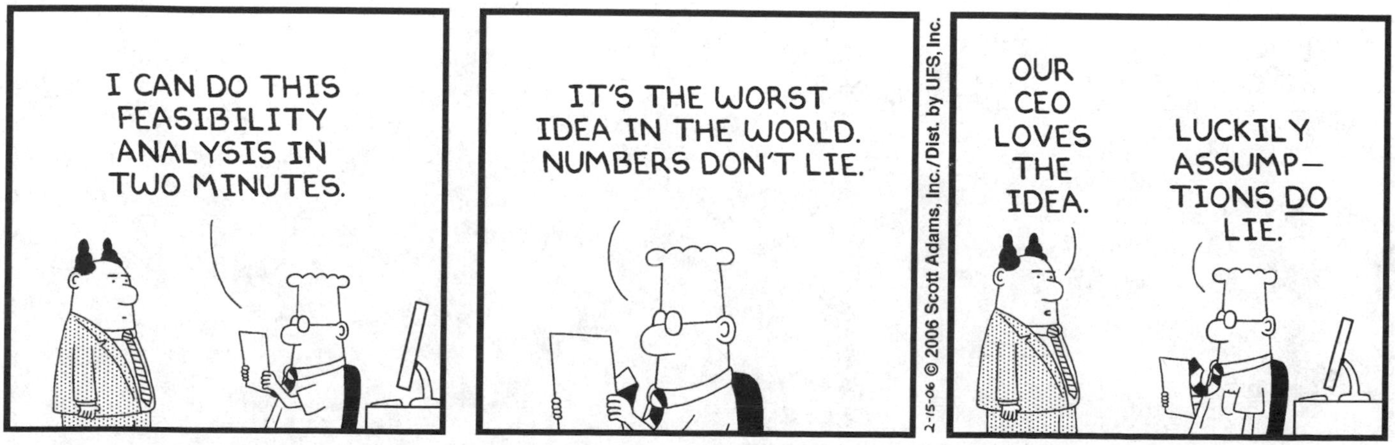
I CAN DO THIS FEASIBILITY ANALYSIS IN TWO MINUTES.
IT'S THE WORST IDEA IN THE WORLD. NUMBERS DON'T LIE.
2-15-06 © 2006 Scott Adams, Inc./Dist. by UFS, Inc.
OUR CEO LOVES THE IDEA.
LUCKILY ASSUMP– TIONS DO LIE.

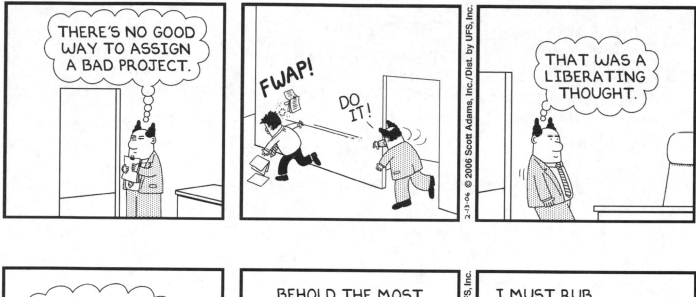

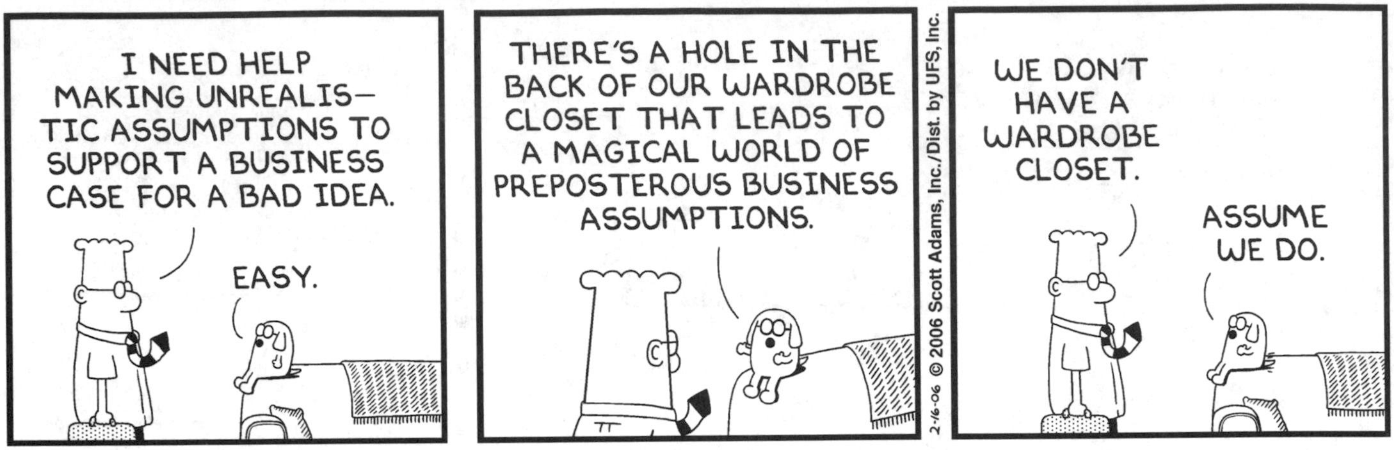
I NEED HELP MAKING UNREALISTIC ASSUMPTIONS TO SUPPORT A BUSINESS CASE FOR A BAD IDEA.
EASY.
THERE'S A HOLE IN THE BACK OF OUR WARDROBE CLOSET THAT LEADS TO A MAGICAL WORLD OF PREPOSTEROUS BUSINESS ASSUMPTIONS.
2-16-06 © 2006 Scott Adams, Inc./Dist. by UFS, Inc.
WE DON'T HAVE A WARDROBE CLOSET.
ASSUME WE DO.

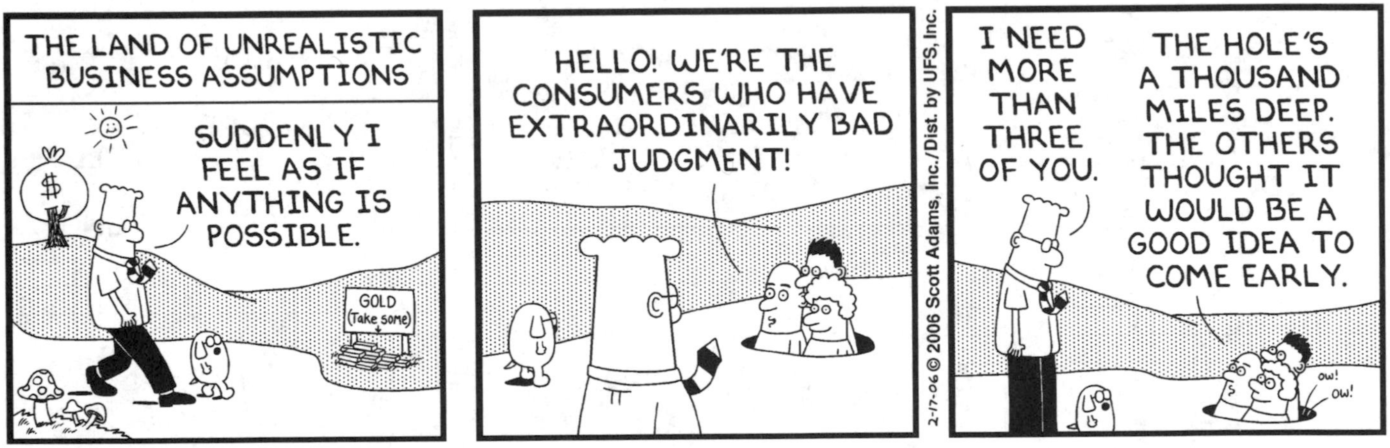
THE LAND OF UNREALISTIC BUSINESS ASSUMPTIONS
SUDDENLY I FEEL AS IF ANYTHING IS POSSIBLE.
GOLD (Take some)
HELLO! WE'RE THE CONSUMERS WHO HAVE EXTRAORDINARILY BAD JUDGMENT!
2-17-06 © 2006 Scott Adams, Inc./Dist. by UFS, Inc.
I NEED MORE THAN THREE OF YOU.
THE HOLE'S A THOUSAND MILES DEEP. THE OTHERS THOUGHT IT WOULD BE A GOOD IDEA TO COME EARLY.
ow!
ow!

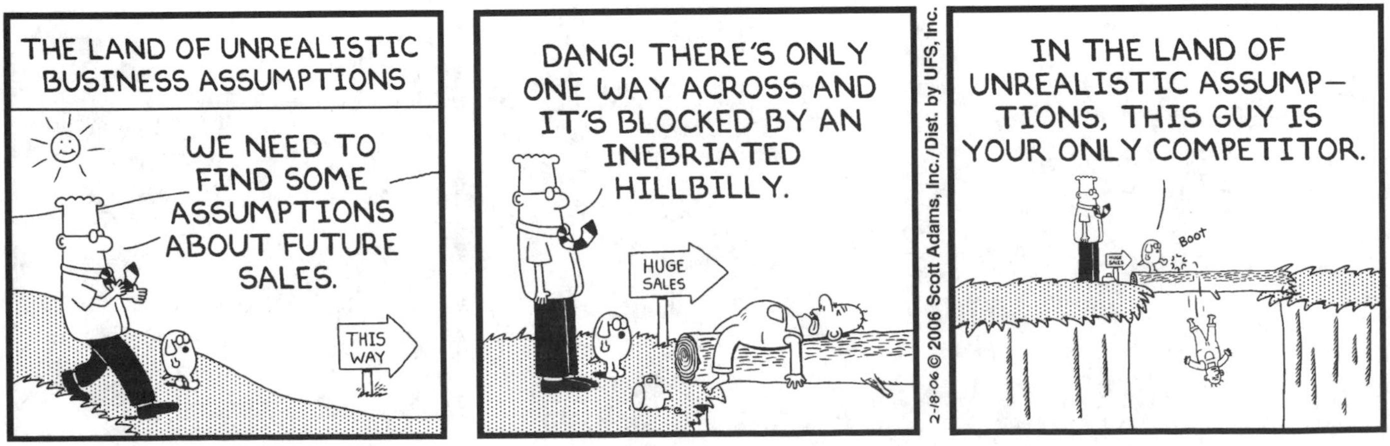
THE LAND OF UNREALISTIC BUSINESS ASSUMPTIONS
WE NEED TO FIND SOME ASSUMPTIONS ABOUT FUTURE SALES.
THIS WAY
DANG! THERE'S ONLY ONE WAY ACROSS AND IT'S BLOCKED BY AN INEBRIATED HILLBILLY.
HUGE SALES
2-18-06 © 2006 Scott Adams, Inc./Dist. by UFS, Inc.
IN THE LAND OF UNREALISTIC ASSUMPTIONS, THIS GUY IS YOUR ONLY COMPETITOR.
Boot

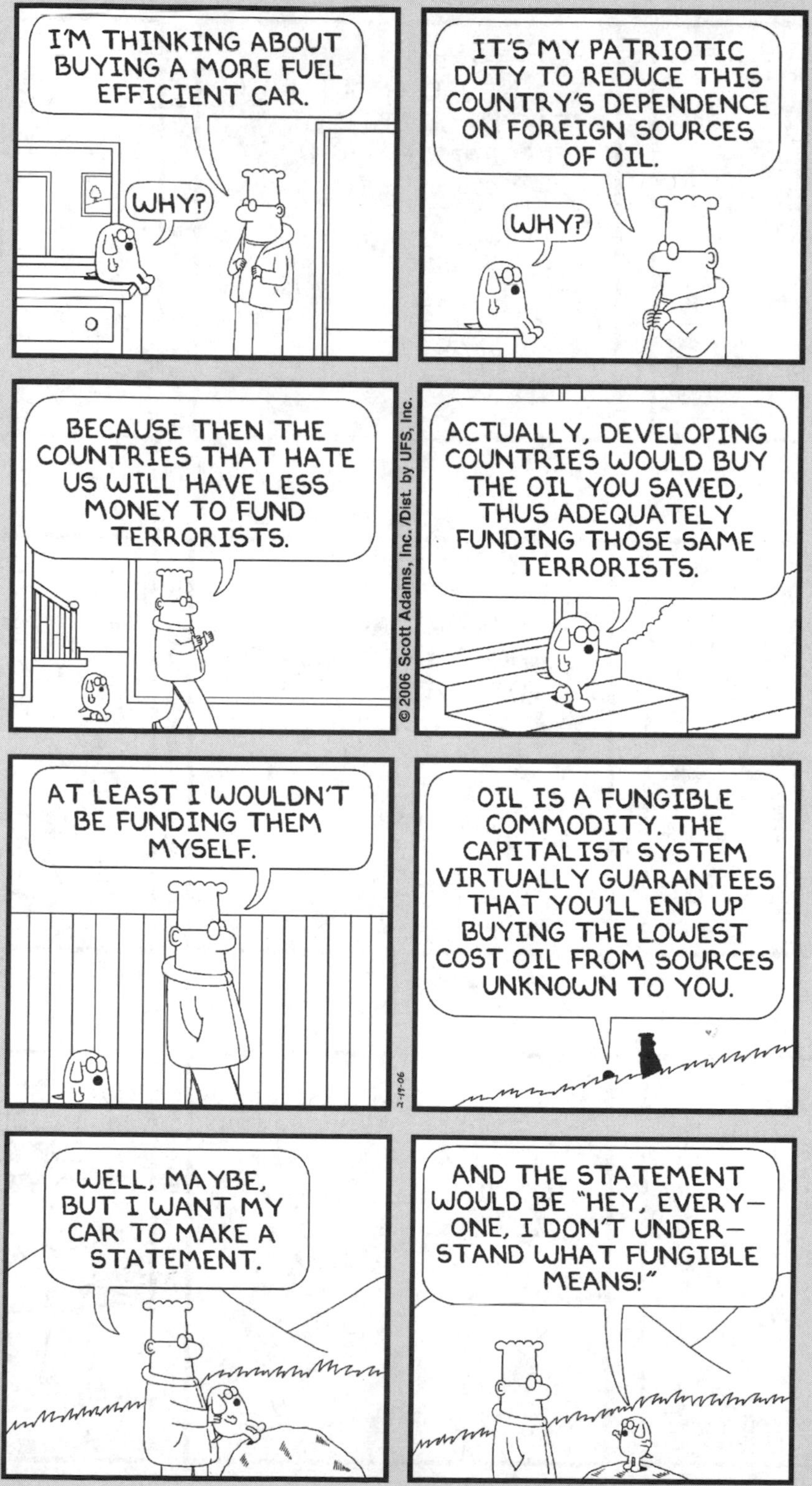
I'M THINKING ABOUT BUYING A MORE FUEL EFFICIENT CAR.
WHY?
IT'S MY PATRIOTIC DUTY TO REDUCE THIS COUNTRY'S DEPENDENCE ON FOREIGN SOURCES OF OIL.
WHY?
BECAUSE THEN THE COUNTRIES THAT HATE US WILL HAVE LESS MONEY TO FUND TERRORISTS.
© 2006 Scott Adams, Inc. /Dist. by UFS, Inc.
ACTUALLY, DEVELOPING COUNTRIES WOULD BUY THE OIL YOU SAVED, THUS ADEQUATELY FUNDING THOSE SAME TERRORISTS.
AT LEAST I WOULDN'T BE FUNDING THEM MYSELF.
OIL IS A FUNGIBLE COMMODITY. THE CAPITALIST SYSTEM VIRTUALLY GUARANTEES THAT YOU'LL END UP BUYING THE LOWEST COST OIL FROM SOURCES UNKNOWN TO YOU.
WELL, MAYBE, BUT I WANT MY CAR TO MAKE A STATEMENT.
AND THE STATEMENT WOULD BE "HEY, EVERY-ONE, I DON'T UNDER-STAND WHAT FUNGIBLE MEANS!"

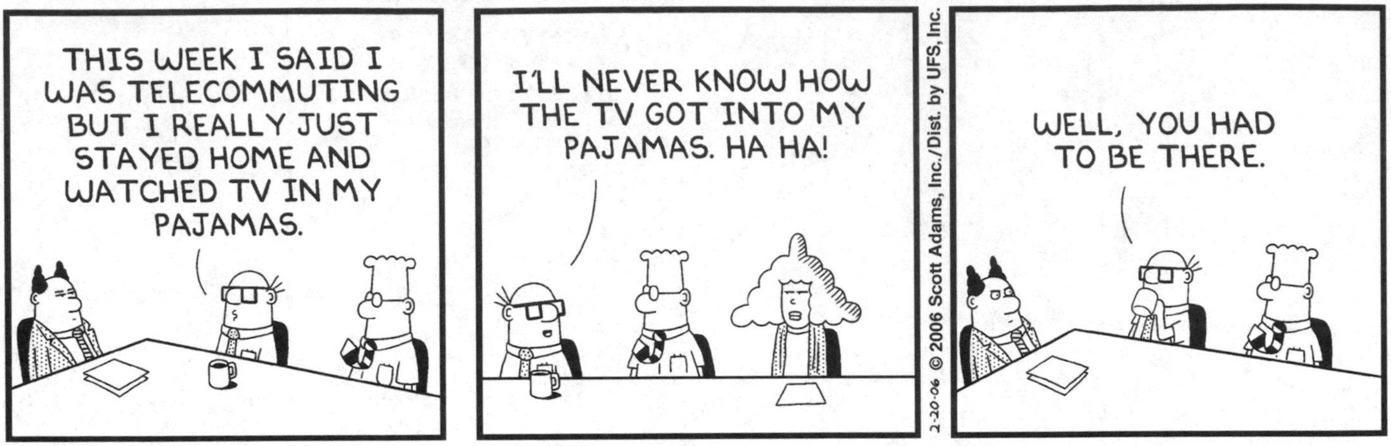
THIS WEEK I SAID I WAS TELECOMMUTING BUT I REALLY JUST STAYED HOME AND WATCHED TV IN MY PAJAMAS.
I'LL NEVER KNOW HOW THE TV GOT INTO MY PAJAMAS. HA HA!
WELL, YOU HAD TO BE THERE.
2-20-06 © 2006 Scott Adams, Inc./Dist. by UFS, Inc.

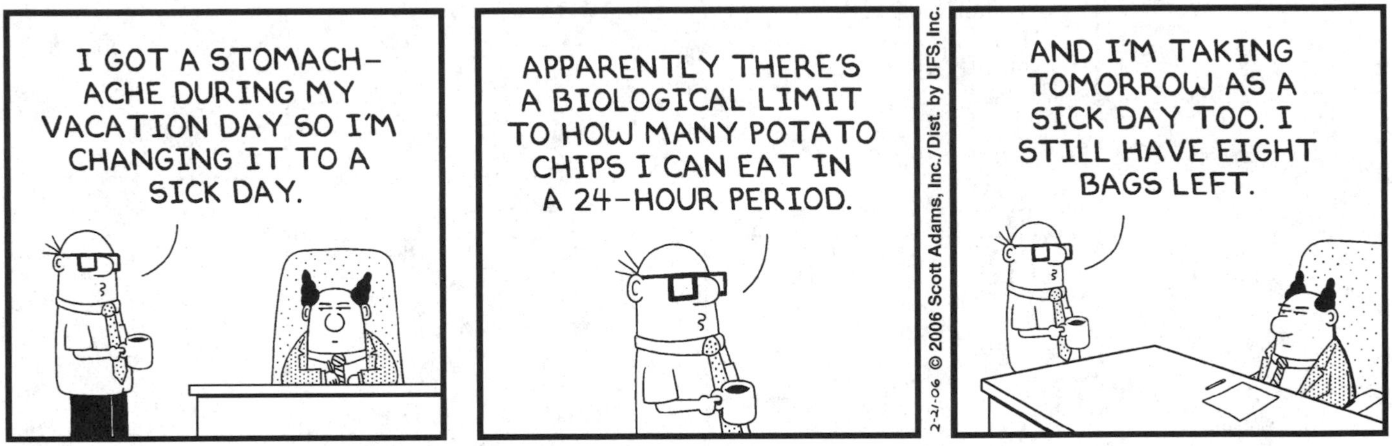
I GOT A STOMACH-ACHE DURING MY VACATION DAY SO I'M CHANGING IT TO A SICK DAY.
APPARENTLY THERE'S A BIOLOGICAL LIMIT TO HOW MANY POTATO CHIPS I CAN EAT IN A 24-HOUR PERIOD.
AND I'M TAKING TOMORROW AS A SICK DAY TOO. I STILL HAVE EIGHT BAGS LEFT.
2-21-06 © 2006 Scott Adams, Inc./Dist. by UFS, Inc.

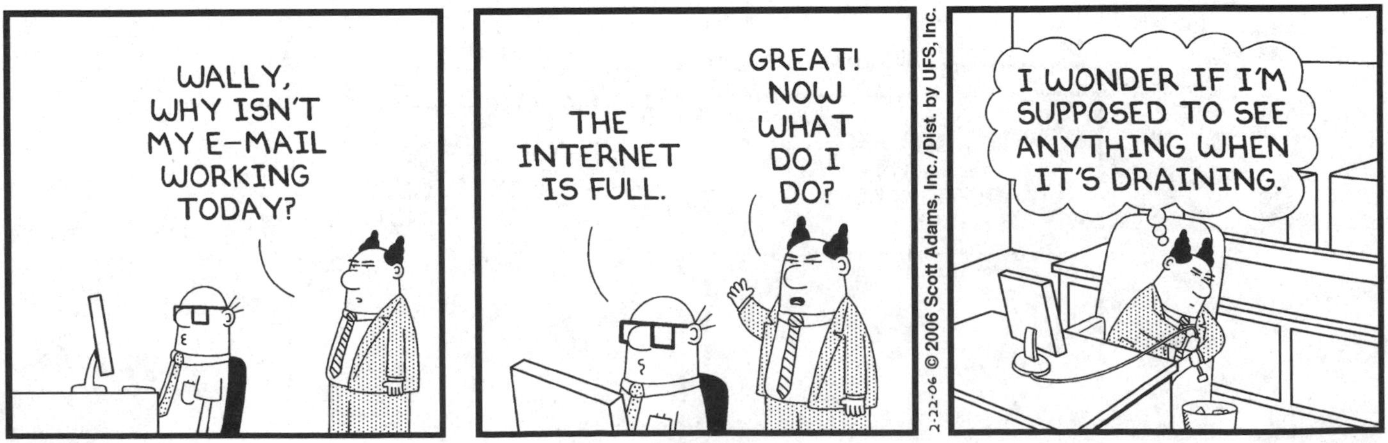
WALLY, WHY ISN'T MY E-MAIL WORKING TODAY?
THE INTERNET IS FULL.
GREAT! NOW WHAT DO I DO?
I WONDER IF I'M SUPPOSED TO SEE ANYTHING WHEN IT'S DRAINING.
2-22-06 © 2006 Scott Adams, Inc./Dist. by UFS, Inc.

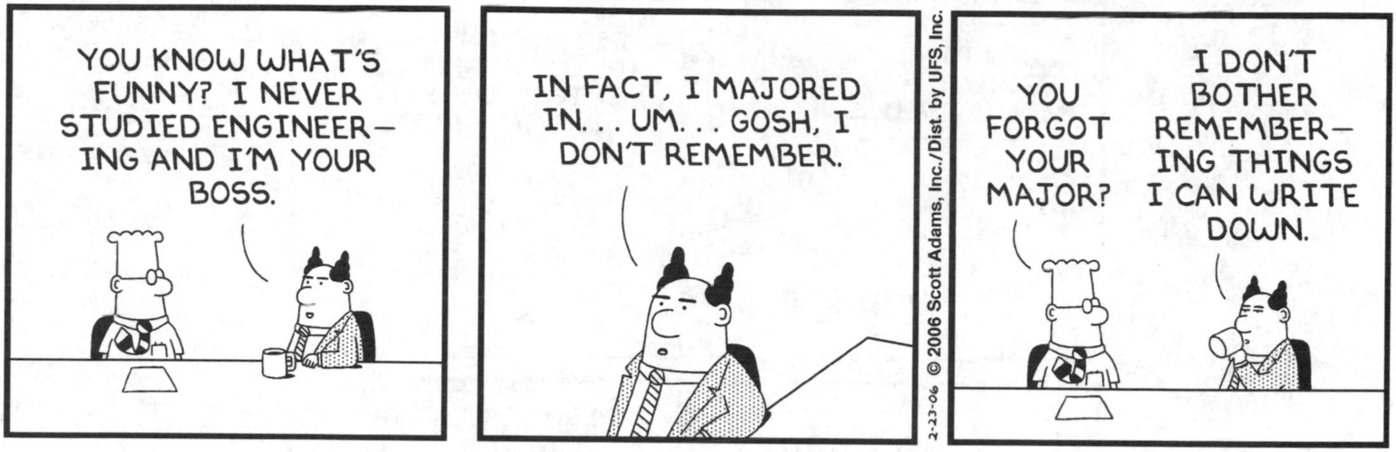
YOU KNOW WHAT'S FUNNY? I NEVER STUDIED ENGINEER–ING AND I'M YOUR BOSS.
IN FACT, I MAJORED IN. . . UM. . . GOSH, I DON'T REMEMBER.
2-23-06 © 2006 Scott Adams, Inc./Dist. by UFS, Inc.
YOU FORGOT YOUR MAJOR?
I DON'T BOTHER REMEMBER–ING THINGS I CAN WRITE DOWN.

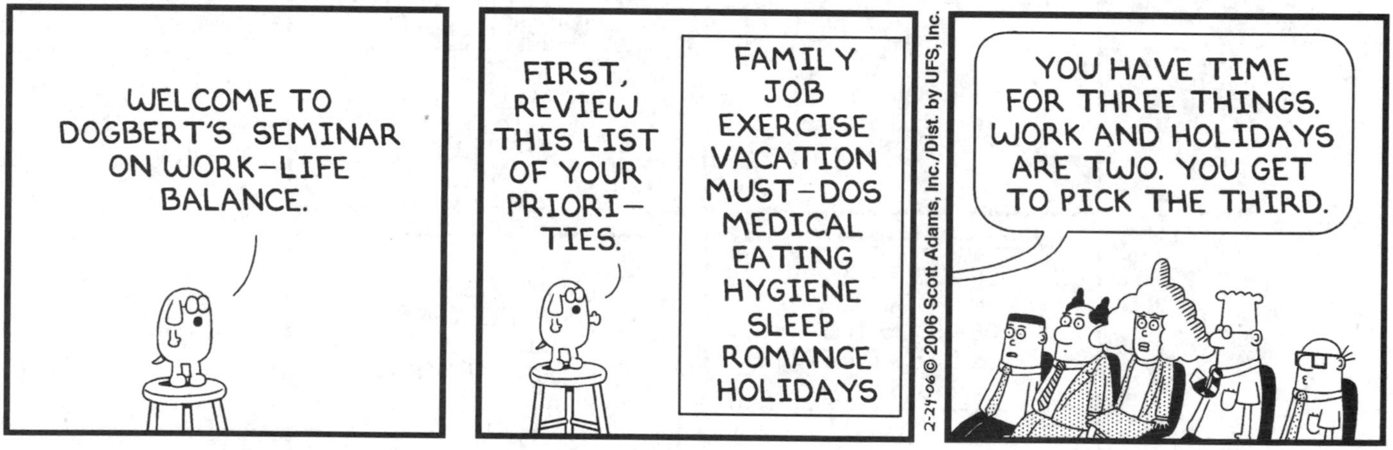
WELCOME TO DOGBERT'S SEMINAR ON WORK–LIFE BALANCE.
FIRST, REVIEW THIS LIST OF YOUR PRIORI–TIES.
FAMILY
JOB
EXERCISE
VACATION
MUST–DOS
MEDICAL
EATING
HYGIENE
SLEEP
ROMANCE
HOLIDAYS
2-24-06 © 2006 Scott Adams, Inc./Dist. by UFS, Inc.
YOU HAVE TIME FOR THREE THINGS. WORK AND HOLIDAYS ARE TWO. YOU GET TO PICK THE THIRD.

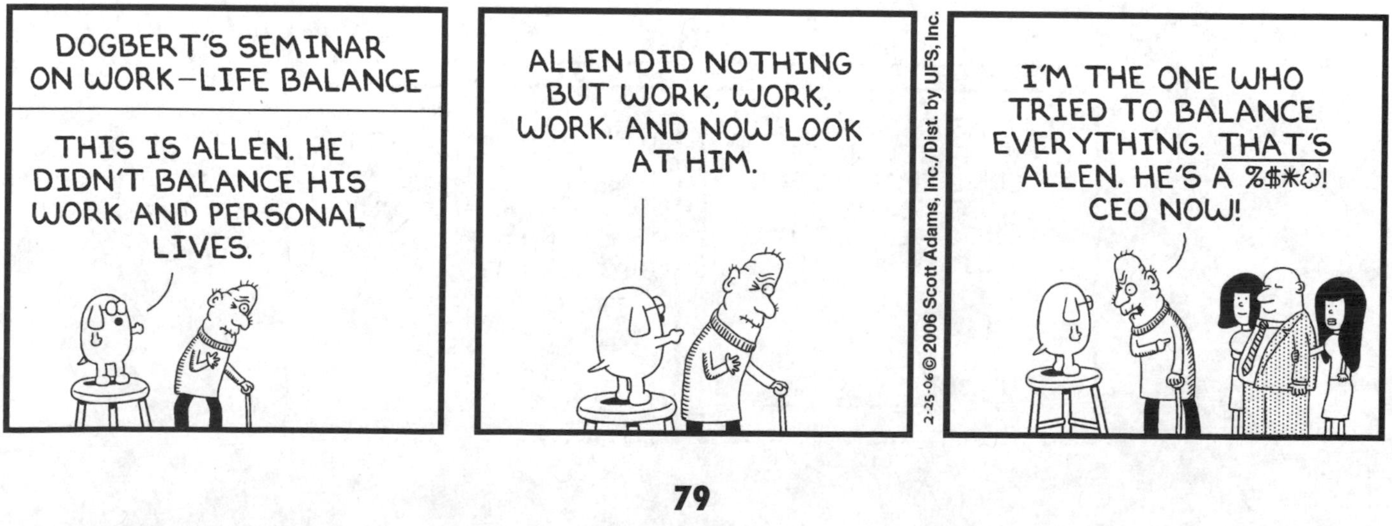
DOGBERT'S SEMINAR ON WORK–LIFE BALANCE
THIS IS ALLEN. HE DIDN'T BALANCE HIS WORK AND PERSONAL LIVES.
ALLEN DID NOTHING BUT WORK, WORK, WORK. AND NOW LOOK AT HIM.
2-25-06 © 2006 Scott Adams, Inc./Dist. by UFS, Inc.
I'M THE ONE WHO TRIED TO BALANCE EVERYTHING. THAT'S ALLEN. HE'S A %$*✪! CEO NOW!

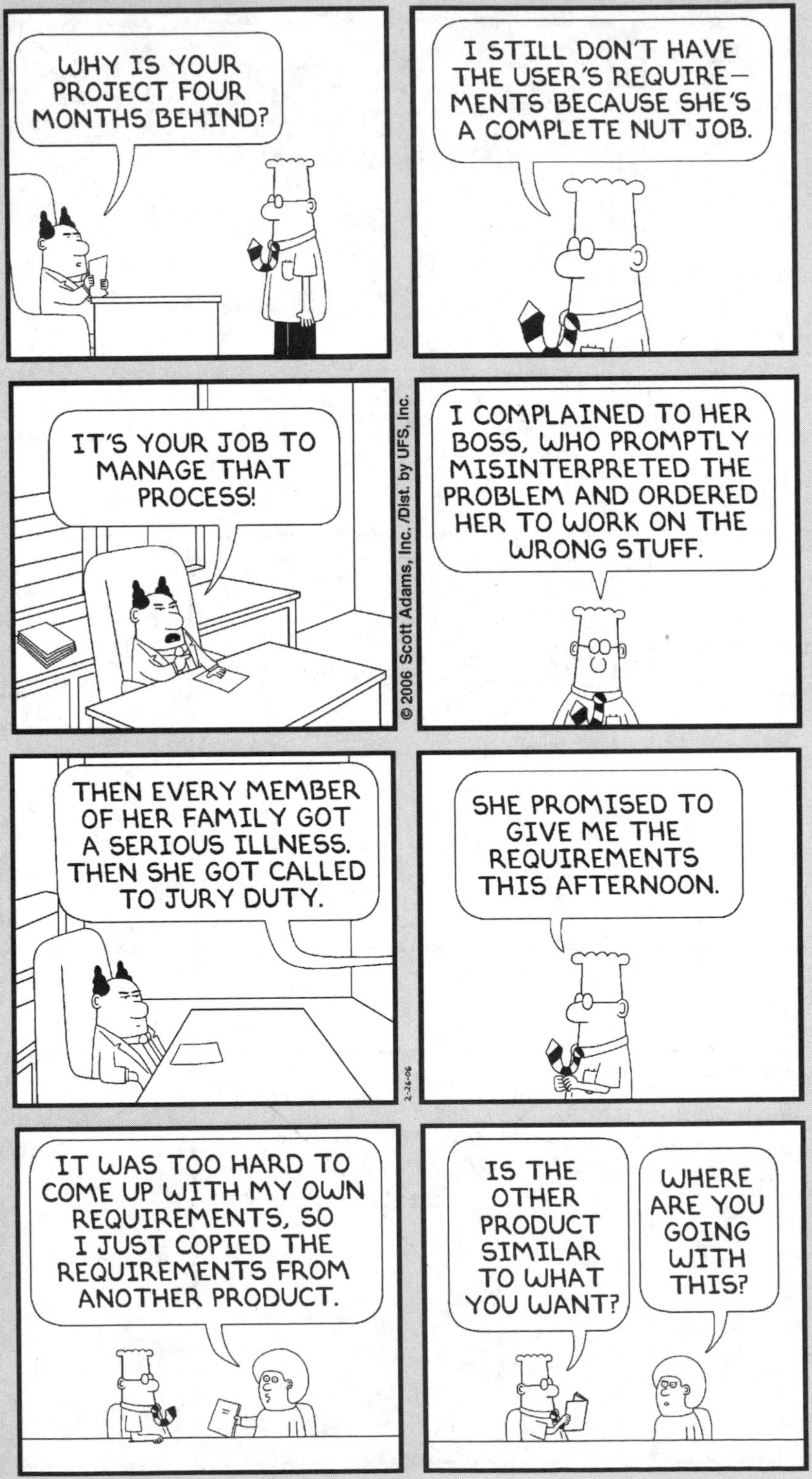
WHY IS YOUR PROJECT FOUR MONTHS BEHIND?
I STILL DON'T HAVE THE USER'S REQUIRE— MENTS BECAUSE SHE'S A COMPLETE NUT JOB.
IT'S YOUR JOB TO MANAGE THAT PROCESS!
I COMPLAINED TO HER BOSS, WHO PROMPTLY MISINTERPRETED THE PROBLEM AND ORDERED HER TO WORK ON THE WRONG STUFF.
THEN EVERY MEMBER OF HER FAMILY GOT A SERIOUS ILLNESS. THEN SHE GOT CALLED TO JURY DUTY.
SHE PROMISED TO GIVE ME THE REQUIREMENTS THIS AFTERNOON.
IT WAS TOO HARD TO COME UP WITH MY OWN REQUIREMENTS, SO I JUST COPIED THE REQUIREMENTS FROM ANOTHER PRODUCT.
IS THE OTHER PRODUCT SIMILAR TO WHAT YOU WANT?
WHERE ARE YOU GOING WITH THIS?
© 2006 Scott Adams, Inc. /Dist. by UFS, Inc.
2-26-06

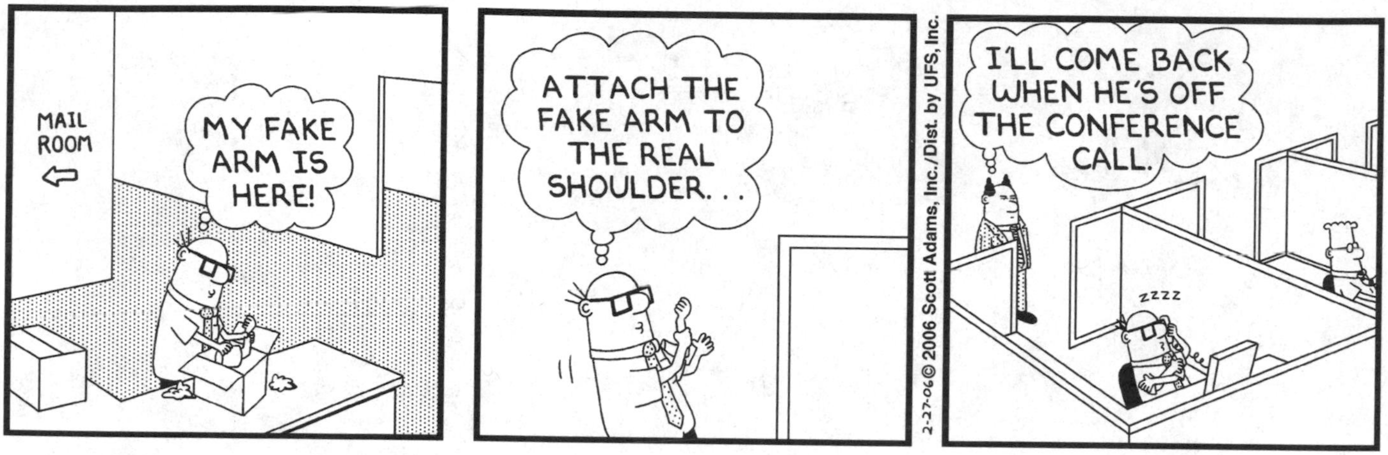
MAIL ROOM
MY FAKE ARM IS HERE!
ATTACH THE FAKE ARM TO THE REAL SHOULDER. . .
2-27-06 © 2006 Scott Adams, Inc./Dist. by UFS, Inc.
I'LL COME BACK WHEN HE'S OFF THE CONFERENCE CALL.
ZZZZ

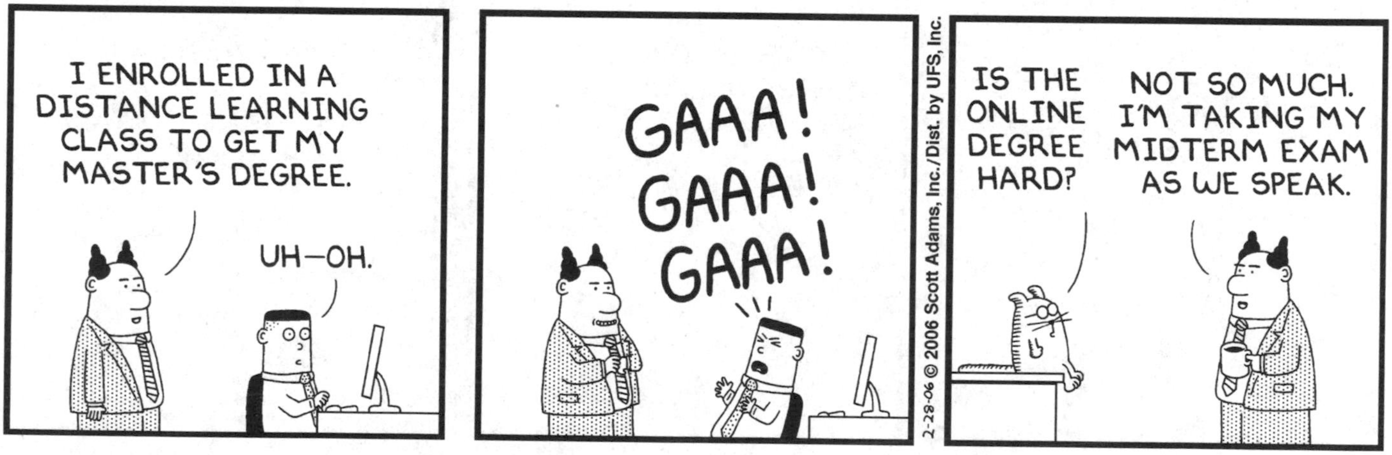
I ENROLLED IN A DISTANCE LEARNING CLASS TO GET MY MASTER'S DEGREE.
UH-OH.
GAAA! GAAA! GAAA!
2-28-06 © 2006 Scott Adams, Inc./Dist. by UFS, Inc.
IS THE ONLINE DEGREE HARD?
NOT SO MUCH. I'M TAKING MY MIDTERM EXAM AS WE SPEAK.

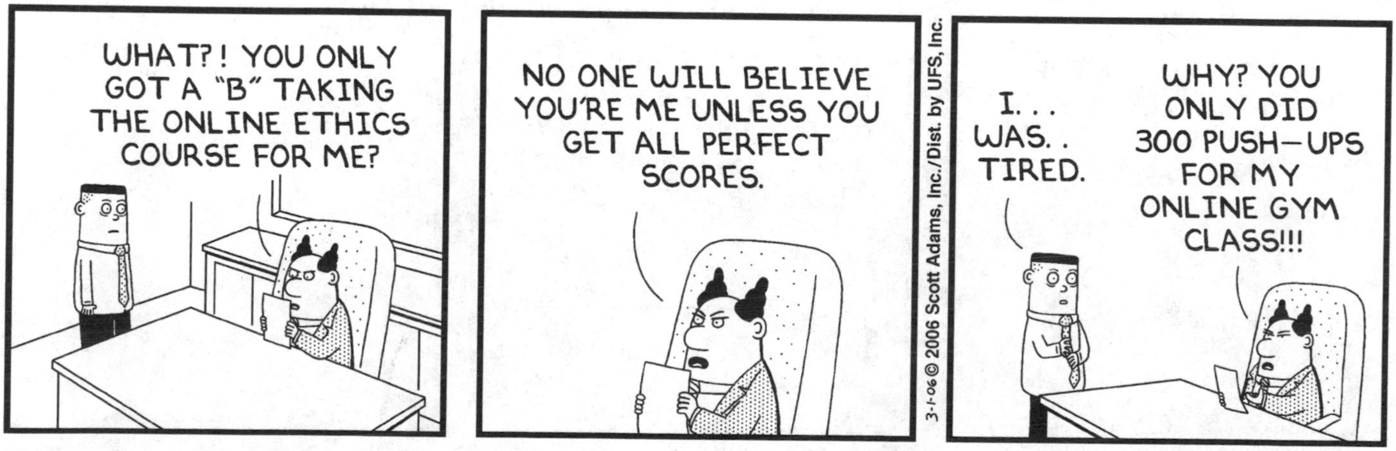
WHAT?! YOU ONLY GOT A "B" TAKING THE ONLINE ETHICS COURSE FOR ME?
NO ONE WILL BELIEVE YOU'RE ME UNLESS YOU GET ALL PERFECT SCORES.
3-1-06 © 2006 Scott Adams, Inc./Dist. by UFS, Inc.
I. . . WAS. . TIRED.
WHY? YOU ONLY DID 300 PUSH-UPS FOR MY ONLINE GYM CLASS!!!

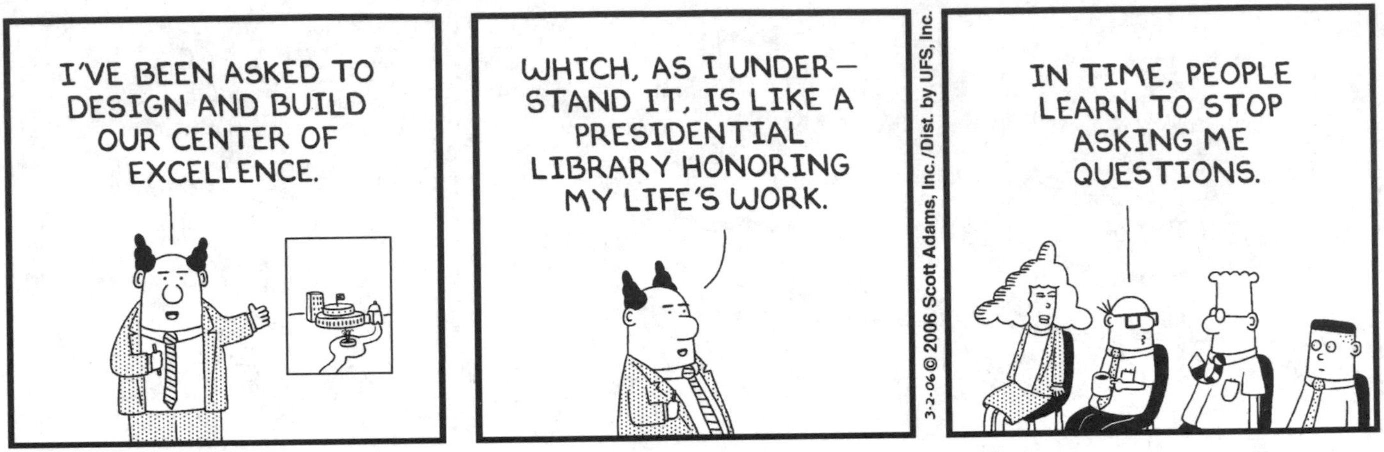
I'VE BEEN ASKED TO DESIGN AND BUILD OUR CENTER OF EXCELLENCE.
WHICH, AS I UNDERSTAND IT, IS LIKE A PRESIDENTIAL LIBRARY HONORING MY LIFE'S WORK.
3-2-06 © 2006 Scott Adams, Inc./Dist. by UFS, Inc.
IN TIME, PEOPLE LEARN TO STOP ASKING ME QUESTIONS.

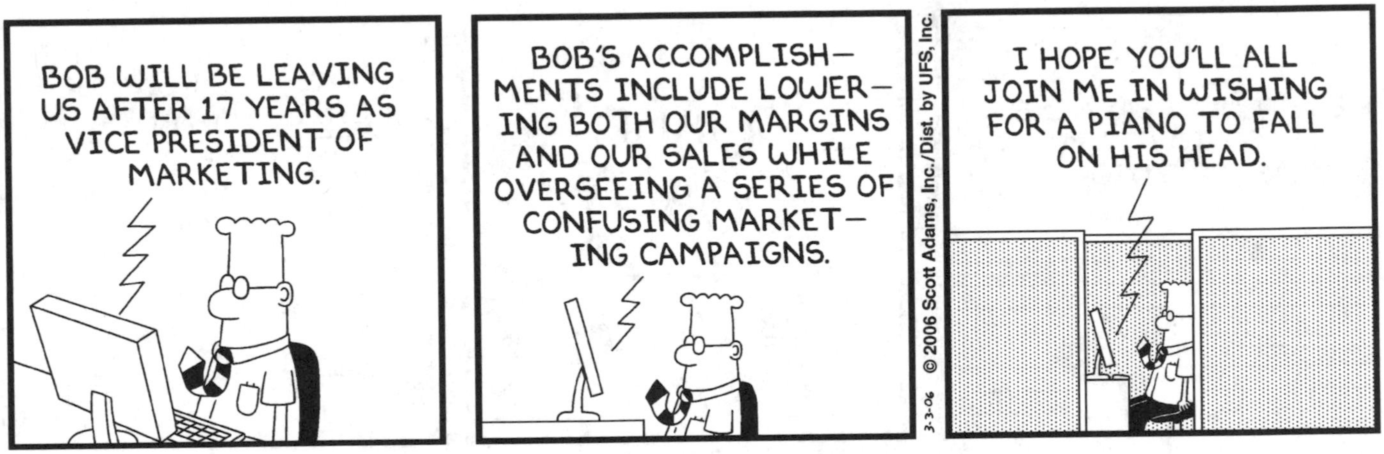
BOB WILL BE LEAVING US AFTER 17 YEARS AS VICE PRESIDENT OF MARKETING.
BOB'S ACCOMPLISHMENTS INCLUDE LOWERING BOTH OUR MARGINS AND OUR SALES WHILE OVERSEEING A SERIES OF CONFUSING MARKETING CAMPAIGNS.
3-3-06 © 2006 Scott Adams, Inc./Dist. by UFS, Inc.
I HOPE YOU'LL ALL JOIN ME IN WISHING FOR A PIANO TO FALL ON HIS HEAD.

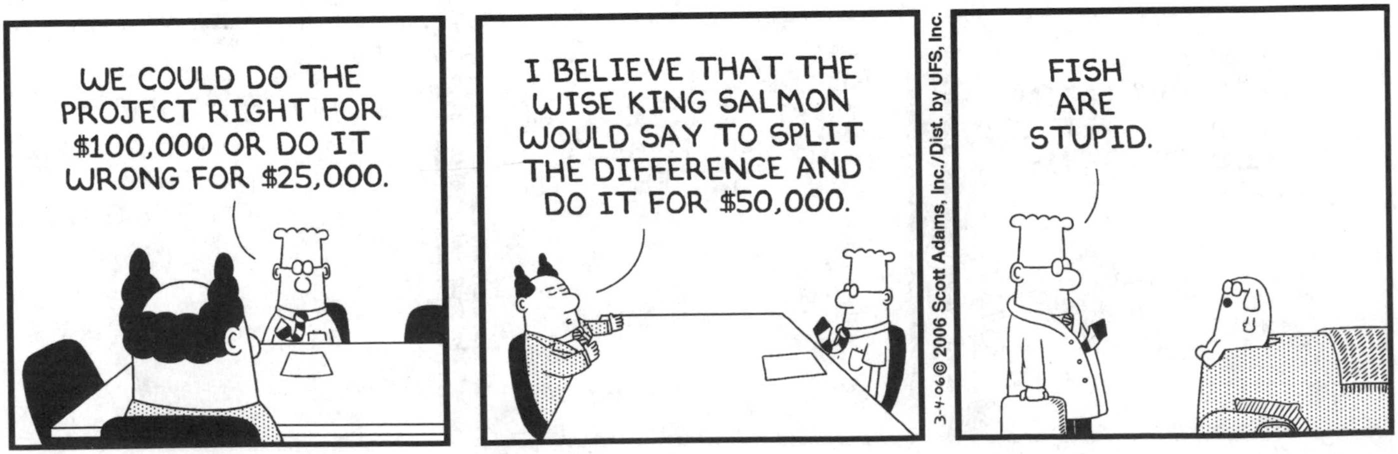
WE COULD DO THE PROJECT RIGHT FOR $100,000 OR DO IT WRONG FOR $25,000.
I BELIEVE THAT THE WISE KING SALMON WOULD SAY TO SPLIT THE DIFFERENCE AND DO IT FOR $50,000.
3-4-06 © 2006 Scott Adams, Inc./Dist. by UFS, Inc.
FISH ARE STUPID.

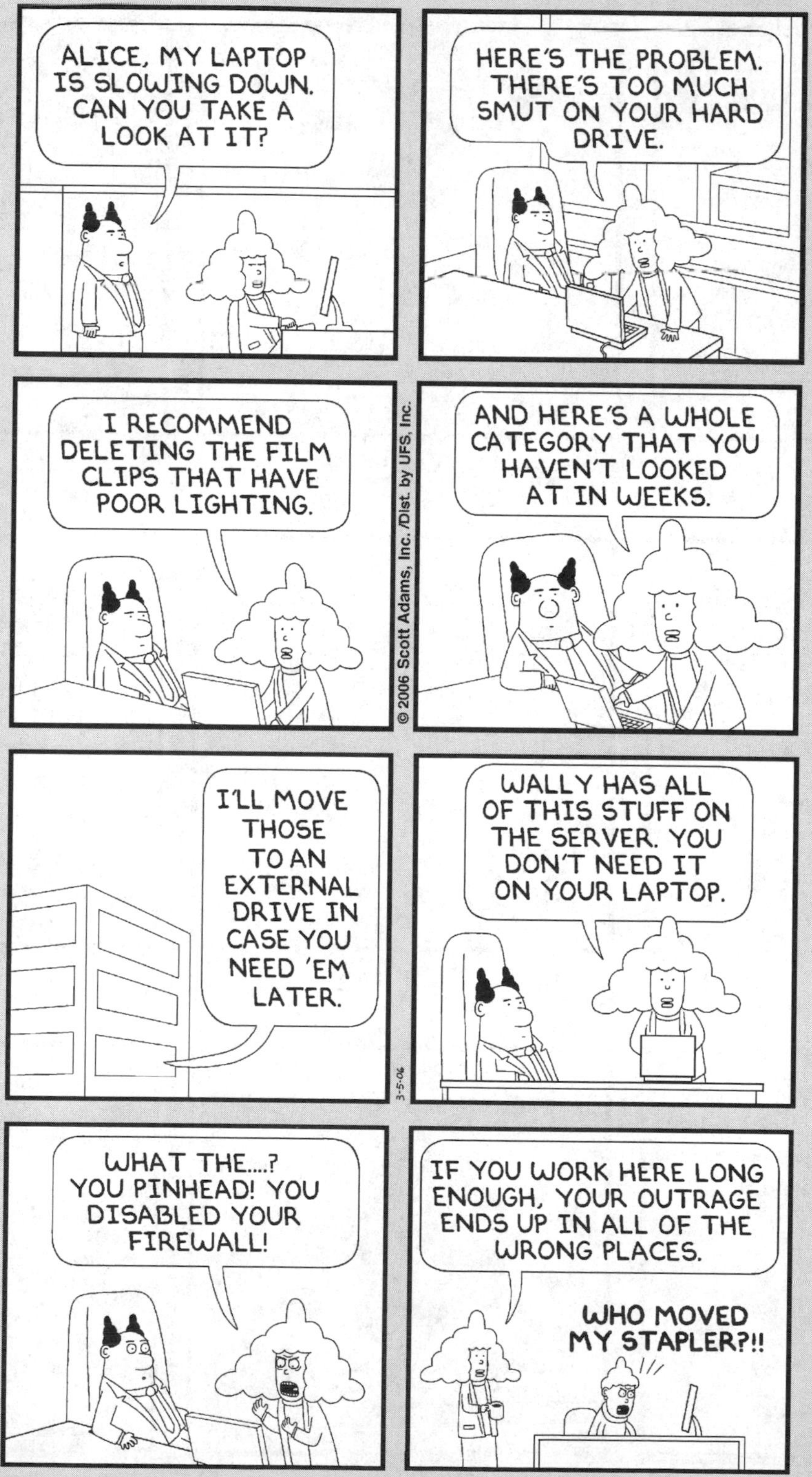
ALICE, MY LAPTOP IS SLOWING DOWN. CAN YOU TAKE A LOOK AT IT?
HERE'S THE PROBLEM. THERE'S TOO MUCH SMUT ON YOUR HARD DRIVE.
I RECOMMEND DELETING THE FILM CLIPS THAT HAVE POOR LIGHTING.
© 2006 Scott Adams, Inc. /Dist. by UFS, Inc.
AND HERE'S A WHOLE CATEGORY THAT YOU HAVEN'T LOOKED AT IN WEEKS.
I'LL MOVE THOSE TO AN EXTERNAL DRIVE IN CASE YOU NEED 'EM LATER.
3-5-06
WALLY HAS ALL OF THIS STUFF ON THE SERVER. YOU DON'T NEED IT ON YOUR LAPTOP.
WHAT THE....? YOU PINHEAD! YOU DISABLED YOUR FIREWALL!
IF YOU WORK HERE LONG ENOUGH, YOUR OUTRAGE ENDS UP IN ALL OF THE WRONG PLACES.
WHO MOVED MY STAPLER?!!

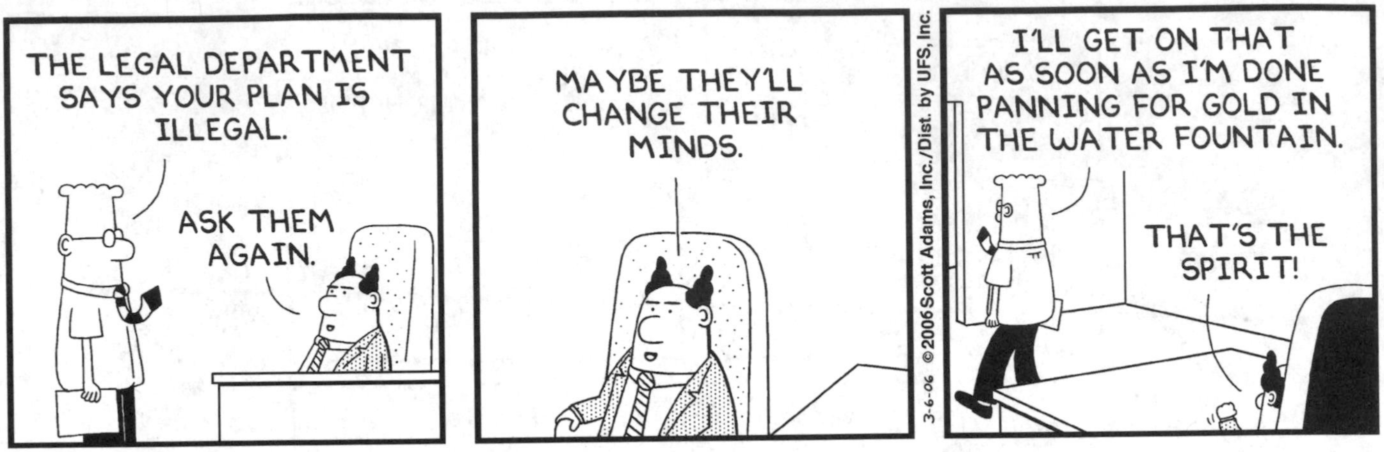
THE LEGAL DEPARTMENT SAYS YOUR PLAN IS ILLEGAL.
ASK THEM AGAIN.
MAYBE THEY'LL CHANGE THEIR MINDS.
3-6-06 ©2006 Scott Adams, Inc./Dist. by UFS, Inc.
I'LL GET ON THAT AS SOON AS I'M DONE PANNING FOR GOLD IN THE WATER FOUNTAIN.
THAT'S THE SPIRIT!

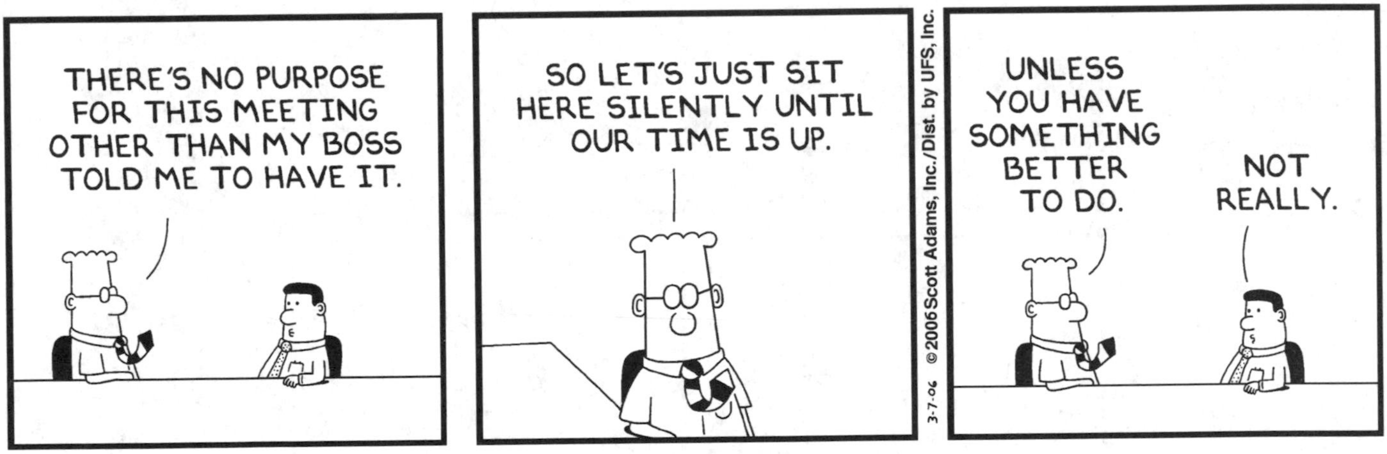
THERE'S NO PURPOSE FOR THIS MEETING OTHER THAN MY BOSS TOLD ME TO HAVE IT.
SO LET'S JUST SIT HERE SILENTLY UNTIL OUR TIME IS UP.
3-7-06 ©2006 Scott Adams, Inc./Dist. by UFS, Inc.
UNLESS YOU HAVE SOMETHING BETTER TO DO.
NOT REALLY.

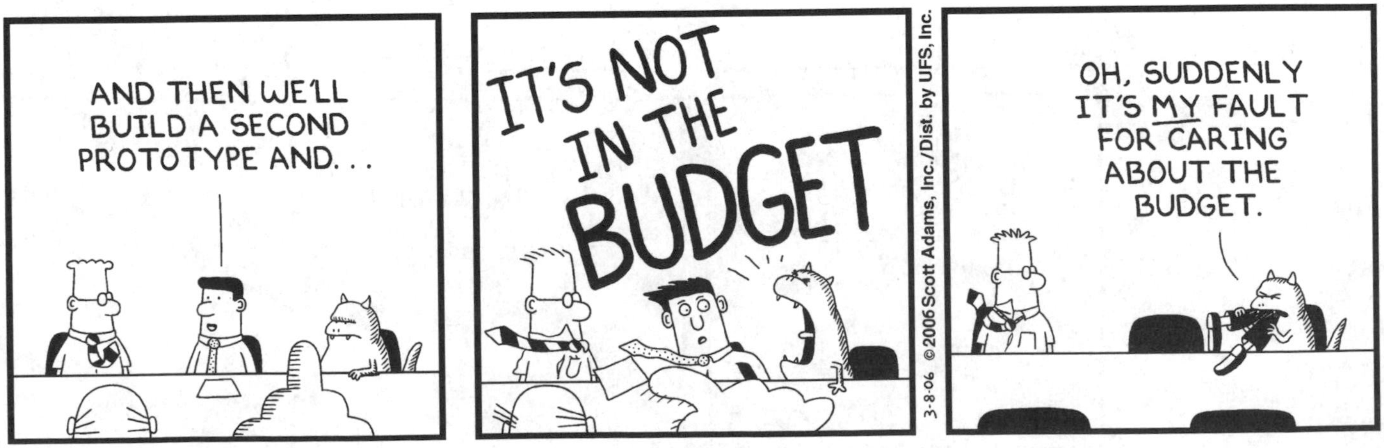
AND THEN WE'LL BUILD A SECOND PROTOTYPE AND. . .
IT'S NOT IN THE BUDGET
3-8-06 ©2006 Scott Adams, Inc./Dist. by UFS, Inc.
OH, SUDDENLY IT'S MY FAULT FOR CARING ABOUT THE BUDGET.

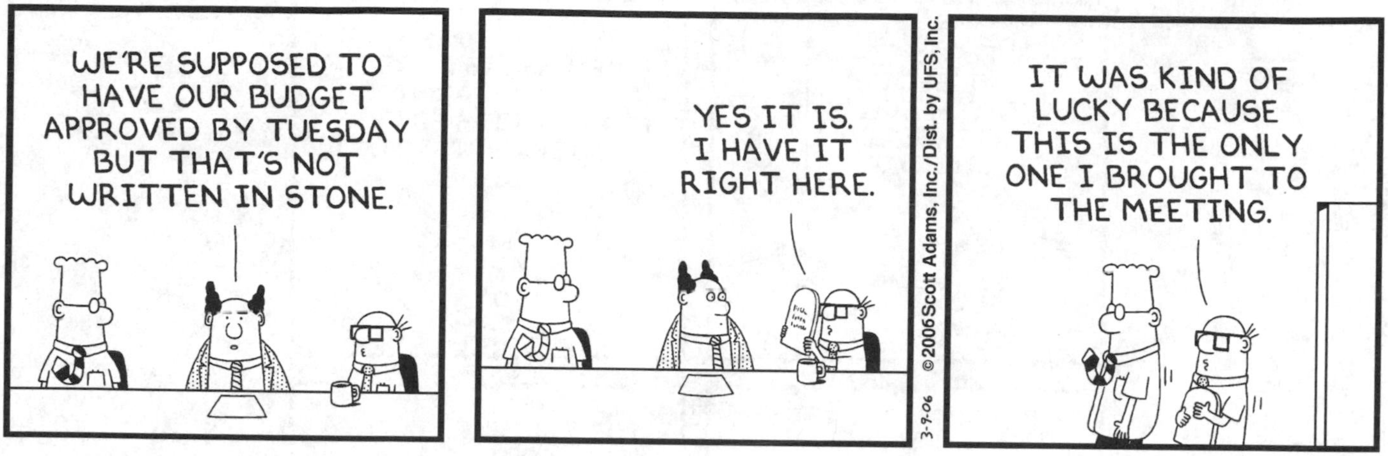
WE'RE SUPPOSED TO HAVE OUR BUDGET APPROVED BY TUESDAY BUT THAT'S NOT WRITTEN IN STONE.
YES IT IS. I HAVE IT RIGHT HERE.
3-9-06 © 2006 Scott Adams, Inc./Dist. by UFS, Inc.
IT WAS KIND OF LUCKY BECAUSE THIS IS THE ONLY ONE I BROUGHT TO THE MEETING.

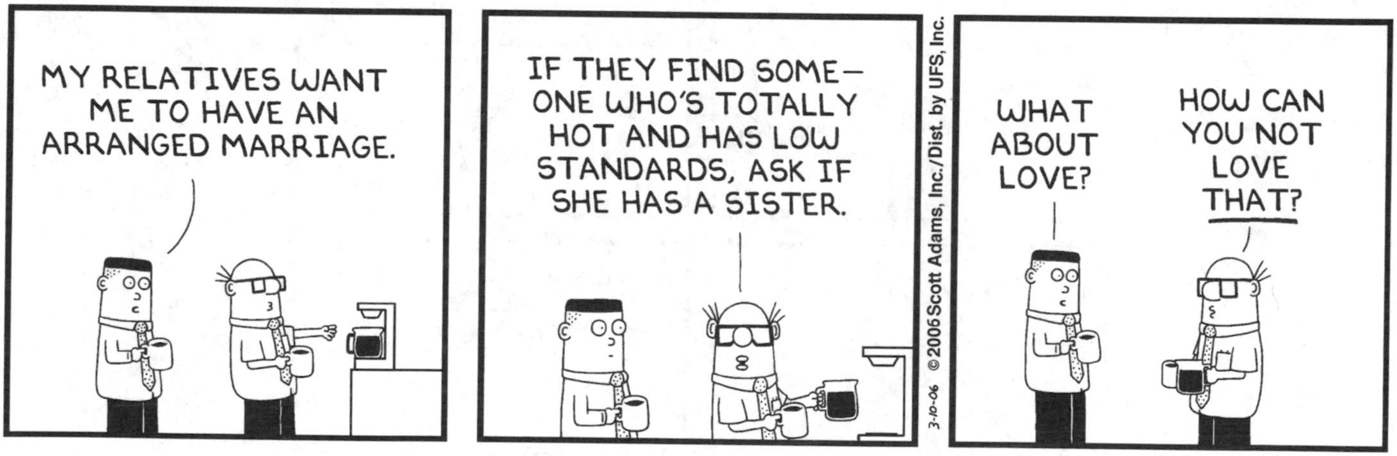
MY RELATIVES WANT ME TO HAVE AN ARRANGED MARRIAGE.
IF THEY FIND SOME-ONE WHO'S TOTALLY HOT AND HAS LOW STANDARDS, ASK IF SHE HAS A SISTER.
3-10-06 © 2006 Scott Adams, Inc./Dist. by UFS, Inc.
WHAT ABOUT LOVE?
HOW CAN YOU NOT LOVE THAT?

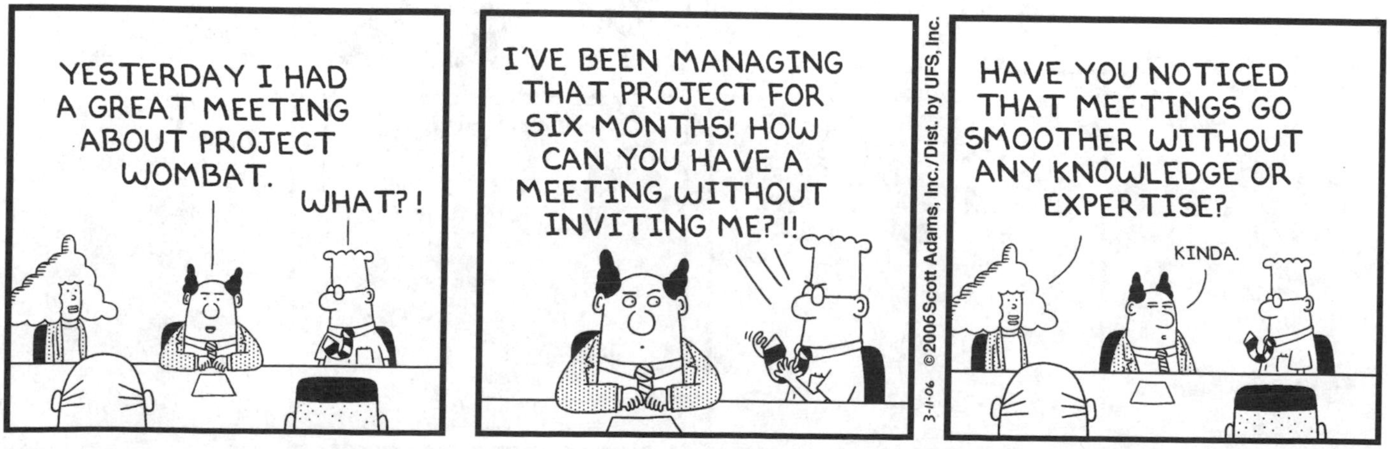
YESTERDAY I HAD A GREAT MEETING ABOUT PROJECT WOMBAT.
WHAT?!
I'VE BEEN MANAGING THAT PROJECT FOR SIX MONTHS! HOW CAN YOU HAVE A MEETING WITHOUT INVITING ME?!!
3-11-06 © 2006 Scott Adams, Inc./Dist. by UFS, Inc.
HAVE YOU NOTICED THAT MEETINGS GO SMOOTHER WITHOUT ANY KNOWLEDGE OR EXPERTISE?
KINDA.

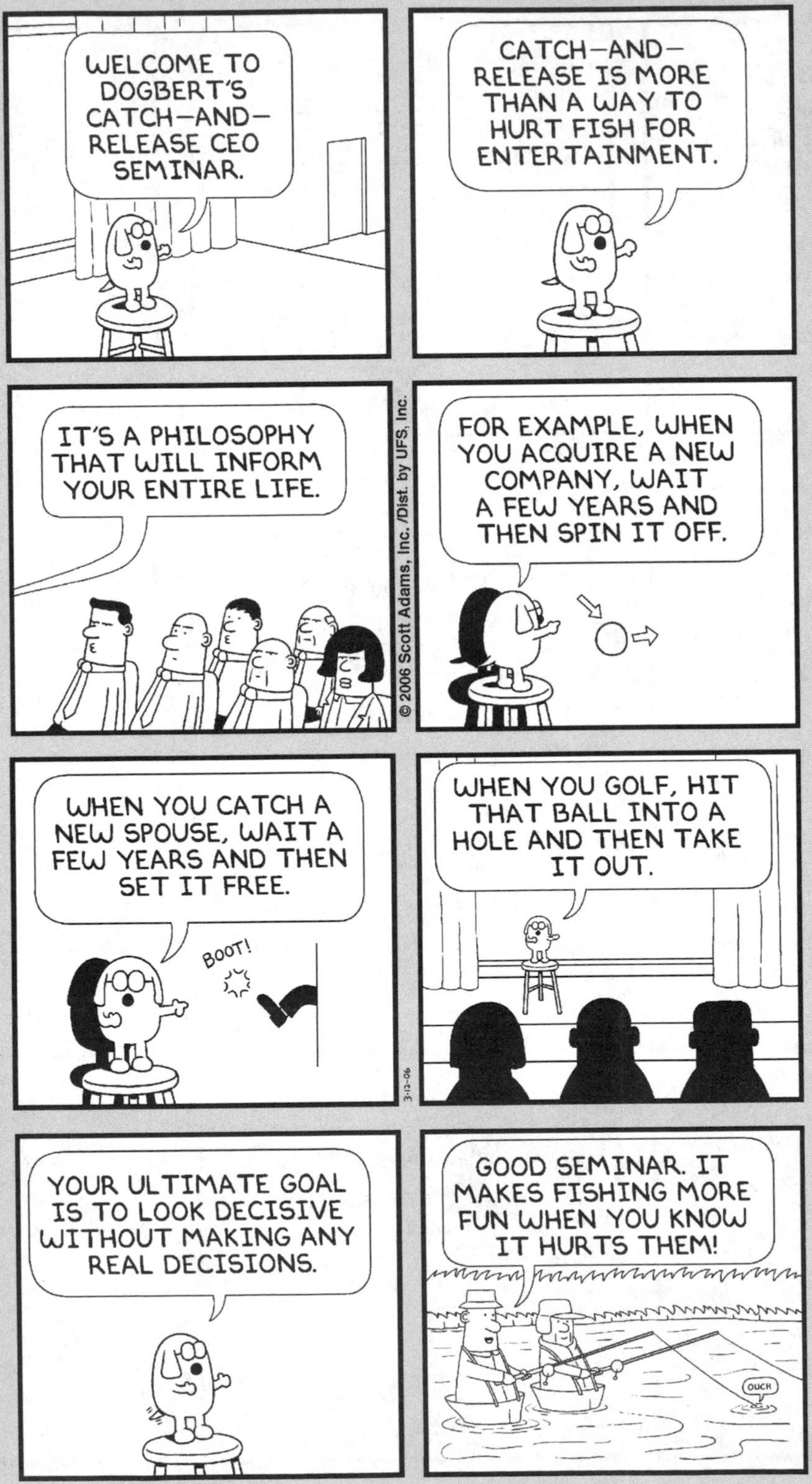
WELCOME TO DOGBERT'S CATCH-AND-RELEASE CEO SEMINAR.
CATCH-AND-RELEASE IS MORE THAN A WAY TO HURT FISH FOR ENTERTAINMENT.
IT'S A PHILOSOPHY THAT WILL INFORM YOUR ENTIRE LIFE.
FOR EXAMPLE, WHEN YOU ACQUIRE A NEW COMPANY, WAIT A FEW YEARS AND THEN SPIN IT OFF.
WHEN YOU CATCH A NEW SPOUSE, WAIT A FEW YEARS AND THEN SET IT FREE.
BOOT!
WHEN YOU GOLF, HIT THAT BALL INTO A HOLE AND THEN TAKE IT OUT.
YOUR ULTIMATE GOAL IS TO LOOK DECISIVE WITHOUT MAKING ANY REAL DECISIONS.
GOOD SEMINAR. IT MAKES FISHING MORE FUN WHEN YOU KNOW IT HURTS THEM!
OUCH
© 2006 Scott Adams, Inc. /Dist. by UFS, Inc.
3-12-06

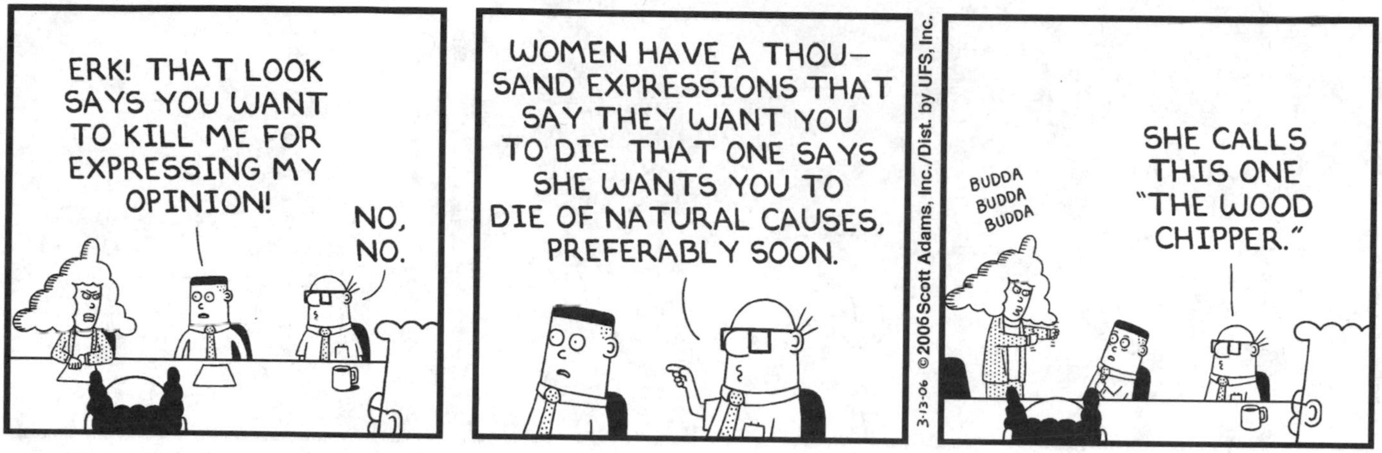
ERK! THAT LOOK SAYS YOU WANT TO KILL ME FOR EXPRESSING MY OPINION!
NO, NO.
WOMEN HAVE A THOU– SAND EXPRESSIONS THAT SAY THEY WANT YOU TO DIE. THAT ONE SAYS SHE WANTS YOU TO DIE OF NATURAL CAUSES, PREFERABLY SOON.
3·13·06 © 2006 Scott Adams, Inc./Dist. by UFS, Inc.
BUDDA BUDDA BUDDA
SHE CALLS THIS ONE "THE WOOD CHIPPER."

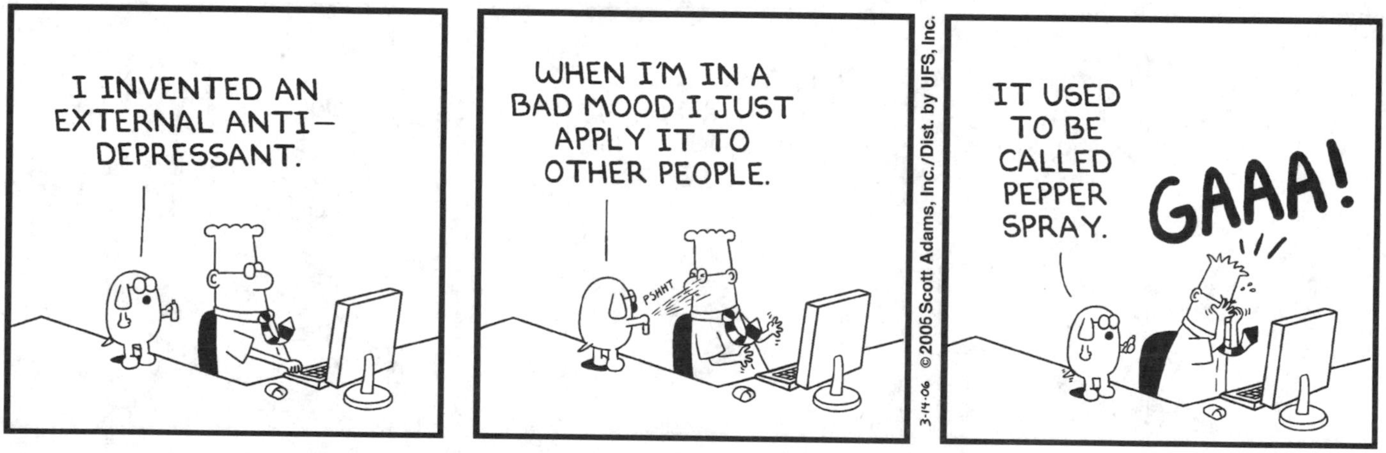
I INVENTED AN EXTERNAL ANTI– DEPRESSANT.
WHEN I'M IN A BAD MOOD I JUST APPLY IT TO OTHER PEOPLE.
PSHHT
3·14·06 © 2006 Scott Adams, Inc./Dist. by UFS, Inc.
IT USED TO BE CALLED PEPPER SPRAY.
GAAA!

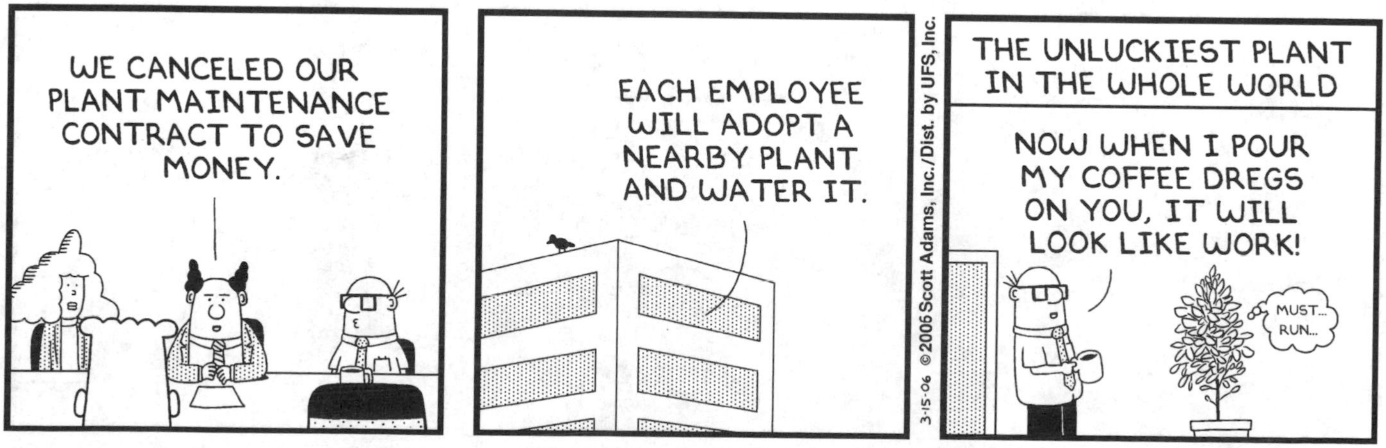
WE CANCELED OUR PLANT MAINTENANCE CONTRACT TO SAVE MONEY.
EACH EMPLOYEE WILL ADOPT A NEARBY PLANT AND WATER IT.
3·15·06 © 2006 Scott Adams, Inc./Dist. by UFS, Inc.
THE UNLUCKIEST PLANT IN THE WHOLE WORLD
NOW WHEN I POUR MY COFFEE DREGS ON YOU, IT WILL LOOK LIKE WORK!
MUST... RUN...

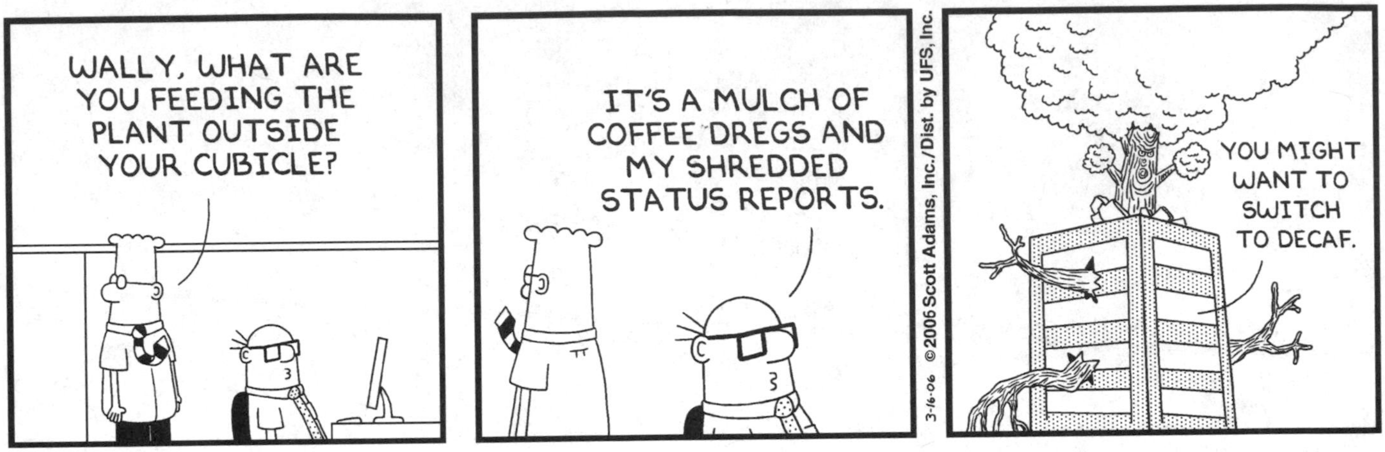
WALLY, WHAT ARE YOU FEEDING THE PLANT OUTSIDE YOUR CUBICLE?
IT'S A MULCH OF COFFEE DREGS AND MY SHREDDED STATUS REPORTS.
3-16-06 ©2006 Scott Adams, Inc./Dist. by UFS, Inc.
YOU MIGHT WANT TO SWITCH TO DECAF.

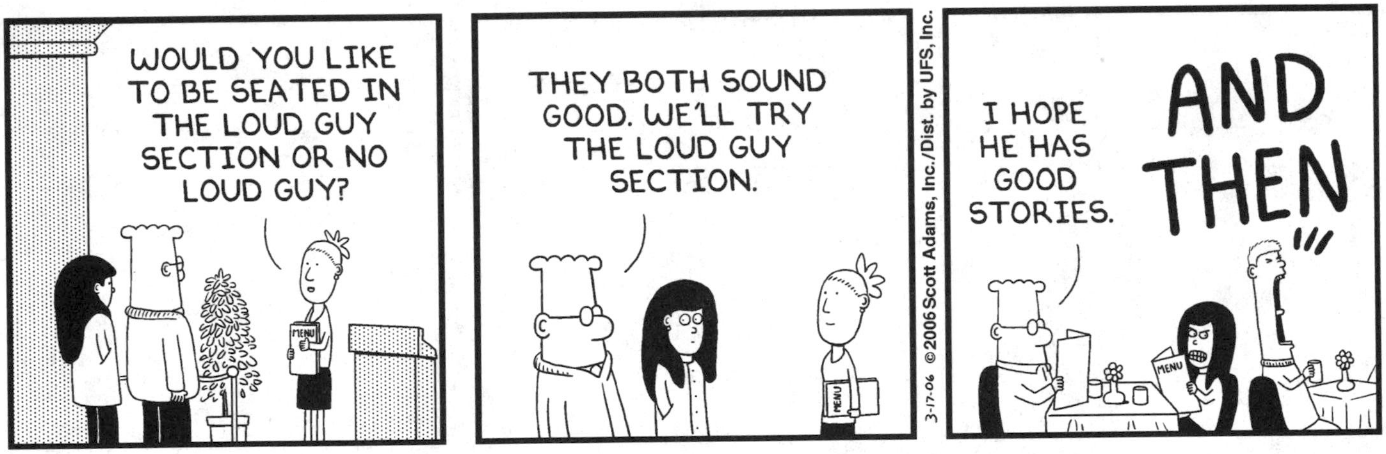
WOULD YOU LIKE TO BE SEATED IN THE LOUD GUY SECTION OR NO LOUD GUY?
MENU
THEY BOTH SOUND GOOD. WE'LL TRY THE LOUD GUY SECTION.
MENU
3-17-06 ©2006 Scott Adams, Inc./Dist. by UFS, Inc.
I HOPE HE HAS GOOD STORIES.
AND THEN
MENU

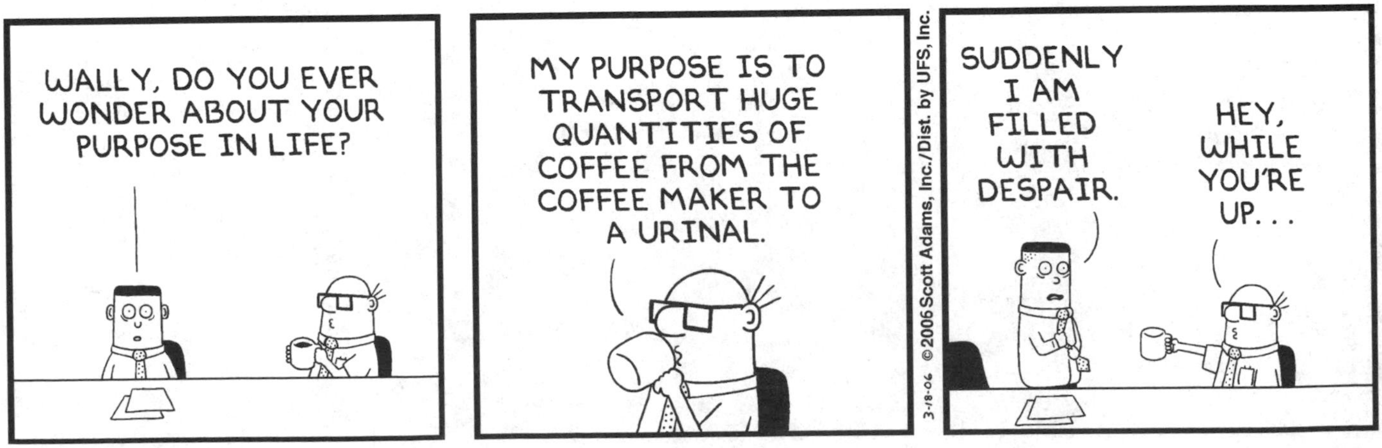
WALLY, DO YOU EVER WONDER ABOUT YOUR PURPOSE IN LIFE?
MY PURPOSE IS TO TRANSPORT HUGE QUANTITIES OF COFFEE FROM THE COFFEE MAKER TO A URINAL.
3-18-06 ©2006 Scott Adams, Inc./Dist. by UFS, Inc.
SUDDENLY I AM FILLED WITH DESPAIR.
HEY, WHILE YOU'RE UP. . .

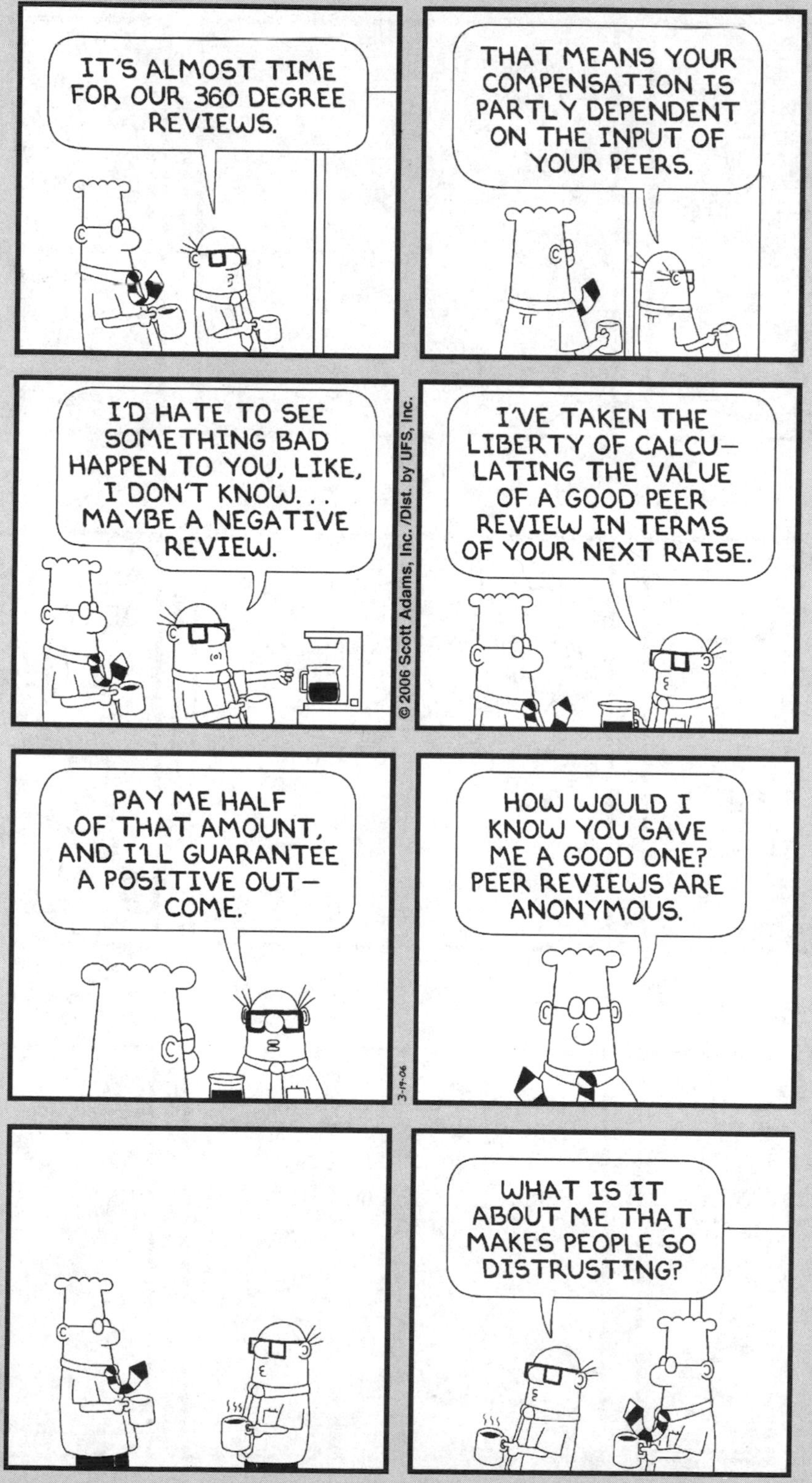
IT'S ALMOST TIME FOR OUR 360 DEGREE REVIEWS.
THAT MEANS YOUR COMPENSATION IS PARTLY DEPENDENT ON THE INPUT OF YOUR PEERS.
I'D HATE TO SEE SOMETHING BAD HAPPEN TO YOU, LIKE, I DON'T KNOW. . . MAYBE A NEGATIVE REVIEW.
© 2006 Scott Adams, Inc./Dist. by UFS, Inc.
I'VE TAKEN THE LIBERTY OF CALCU– LATING THE VALUE OF A GOOD PEER REVIEW IN TERMS OF YOUR NEXT RAISE.
PAY ME HALF OF THAT AMOUNT, AND I'LL GUARANTEE A POSITIVE OUT– COME.
3-19-06
HOW WOULD I KNOW YOU GAVE ME A GOOD ONE? PEER REVIEWS ARE ANONYMOUS.
WHAT IS IT ABOUT ME THAT MAKES PEOPLE SO DISTRUSTING?

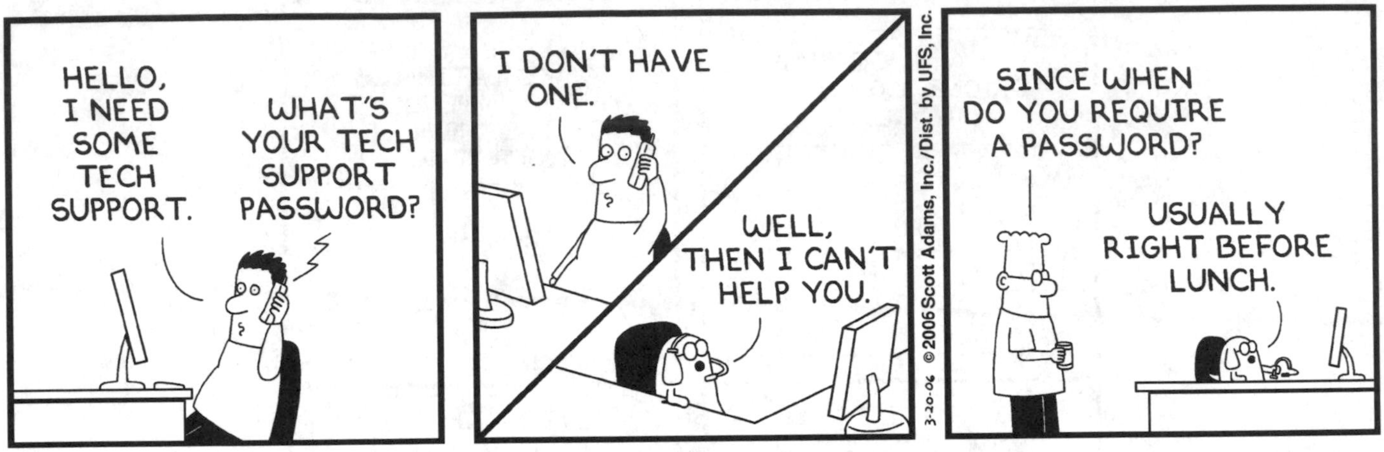
HELLO, I NEED SOME TECH SUPPORT.
WHAT'S YOUR TECH SUPPORT PASSWORD?
I DON'T HAVE ONE.
WELL, THEN I CAN'T HELP YOU.
3-20-06 © 2006 Scott Adams, Inc./Dist. by UFS, Inc.
SINCE WHEN DO YOU REQUIRE A PASSWORD?
USUALLY RIGHT BEFORE LUNCH.

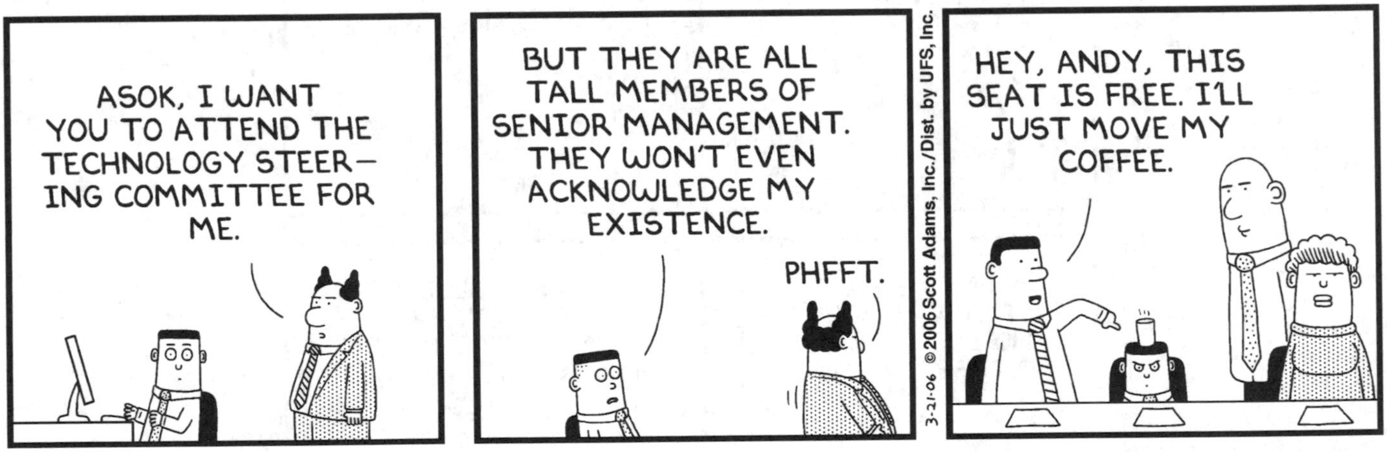
ASOK, I WANT YOU TO ATTEND THE TECHNOLOGY STEER-ING COMMITTEE FOR ME.
BUT THEY ARE ALL TALL MEMBERS OF SENIOR MANAGEMENT. THEY WON'T EVEN ACKNOWLEDGE MY EXISTENCE.
PHFFT.
3-21-06 © 2006 Scott Adams, Inc./Dist. by UFS, Inc.
HEY, ANDY, THIS SEAT IS FREE. I'LL JUST MOVE MY COFFEE.

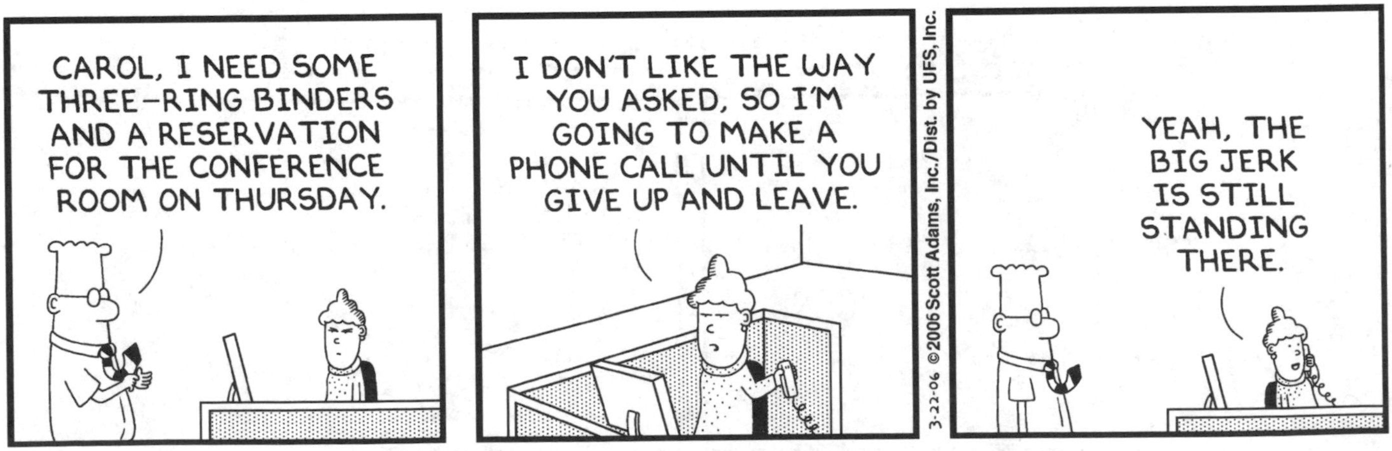
CAROL, I NEED SOME THREE-RING BINDERS AND A RESERVATION FOR THE CONFERENCE ROOM ON THURSDAY.
I DON'T LIKE THE WAY YOU ASKED, SO I'M GOING TO MAKE A PHONE CALL UNTIL YOU GIVE UP AND LEAVE.
3-22-06 © 2006 Scott Adams, Inc./Dist. by UFS, Inc.
YEAH, THE BIG JERK IS STILL STANDING THERE.

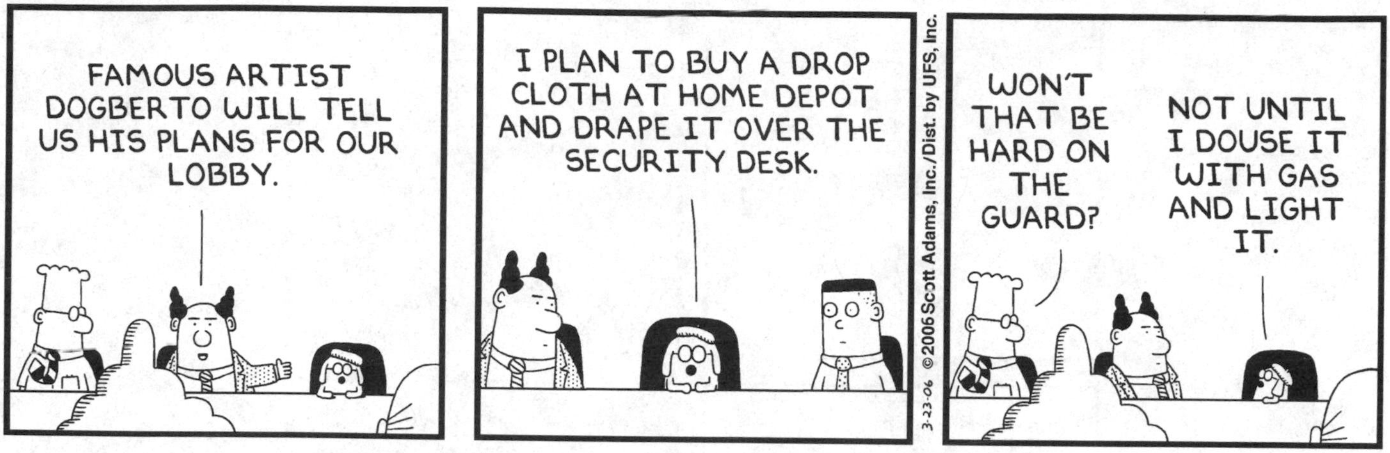
FAMOUS ARTIST DOGBERTO WILL TELL US HIS PLANS FOR OUR LOBBY.
I PLAN TO BUY A DROP CLOTH AT HOME DEPOT AND DRAPE IT OVER THE SECURITY DESK.
WON'T THAT BE HARD ON THE GUARD?
NOT UNTIL I DOUSE IT WITH GAS AND LIGHT IT.
3-23-06 © 2006 Scott Adams, Inc./Dist. by UFS, Inc.

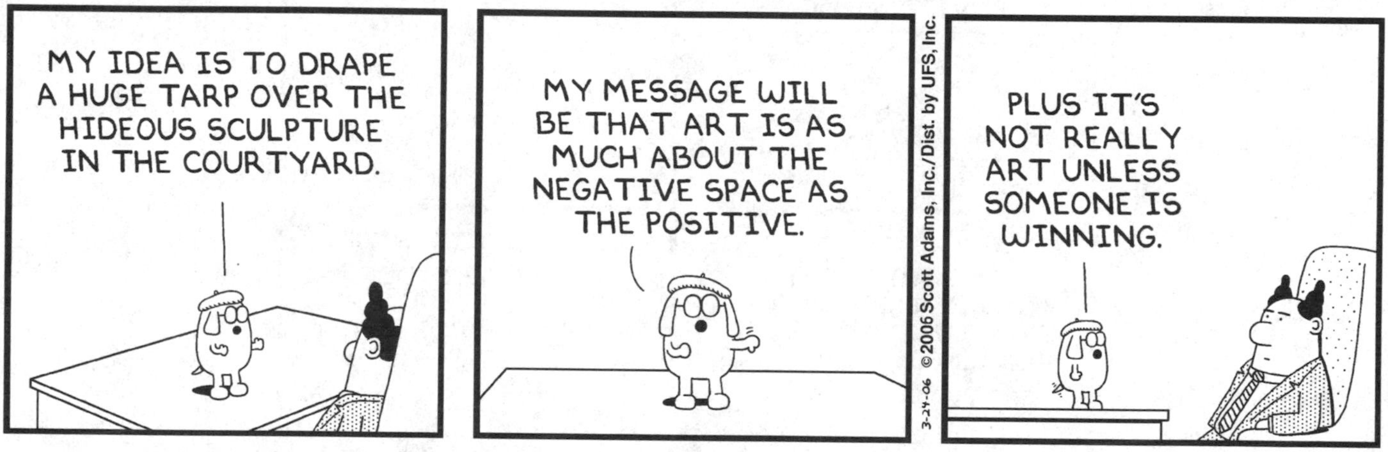
MY IDEA IS TO DRAPE A HUGE TARP OVER THE HIDEOUS SCULPTURE IN THE COURTYARD.
MY MESSAGE WILL BE THAT ART IS AS MUCH ABOUT THE NEGATIVE SPACE AS THE POSITIVE.
PLUS IT'S NOT REALLY ART UNLESS SOMEONE IS WINNING.
3-24-06 © 2006 Scott Adams, Inc./Dist. by UFS, Inc.

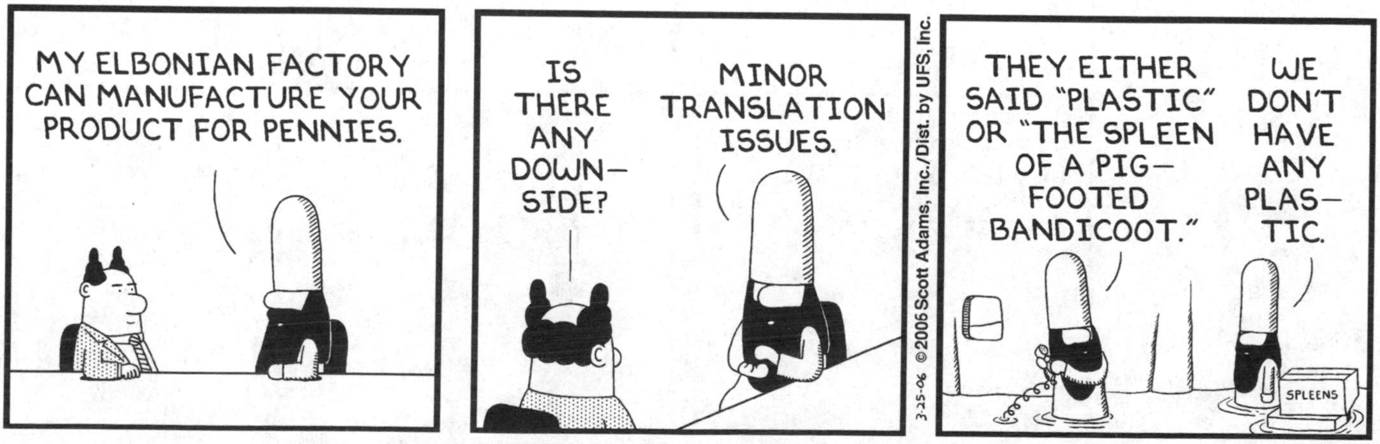
MY ELBONIAN FACTORY CAN MANUFACTURE YOUR PRODUCT FOR PENNIES.
IS THERE ANY DOWN-SIDE?
MINOR TRANSLATION ISSUES.
THEY EITHER SAID "PLASTIC" OR "THE SPLEEN OF A PIG-FOOTED BANDICOOT."
WE DON'T HAVE ANY PLAS-TIC.
SPLEENS
3-25-06 © 2006 Scott Adams, Inc./Dist. by UFS, Inc.

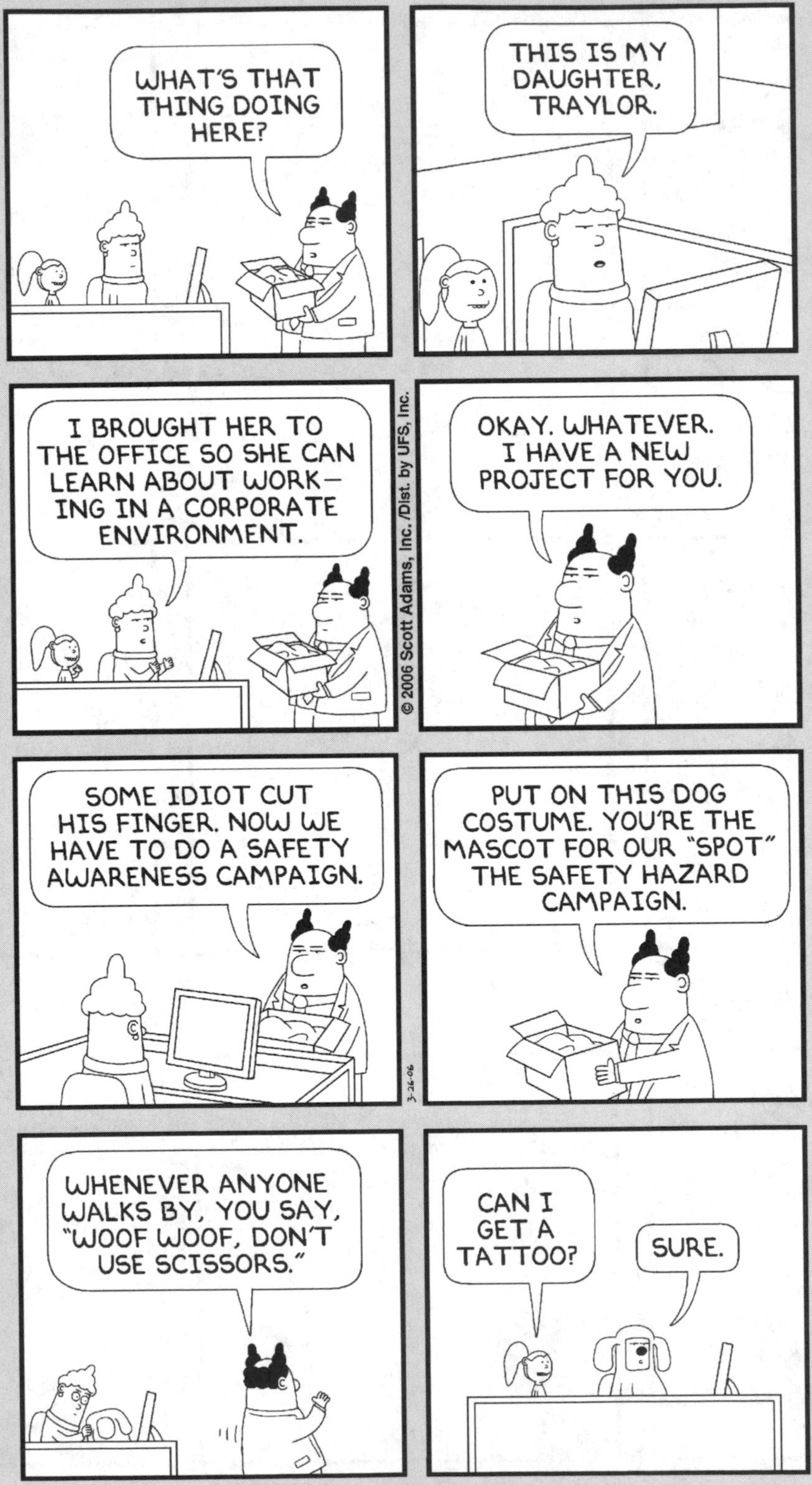
WHAT'S THAT THING DOING HERE?
THIS IS MY DAUGHTER, TRAYLOR.
I BROUGHT HER TO THE OFFICE SO SHE CAN LEARN ABOUT WORK-ING IN A CORPORATE ENVIRONMENT.
OKAY. WHATEVER. I HAVE A NEW PROJECT FOR YOU.
© 2006 Scott Adams, Inc./Dist. by UFS, Inc.
SOME IDIOT CUT HIS FINGER. NOW WE HAVE TO DO A SAFETY AWARENESS CAMPAIGN.
PUT ON THIS DOG COSTUME. YOU'RE THE MASCOT FOR OUR "SPOT" THE SAFETY HAZARD CAMPAIGN.
3-26-06
WHENEVER ANYONE WALKS BY, YOU SAY, "WOOF WOOF, DON'T USE SCISSORS."
CAN I GET A TATTOO?
SURE.

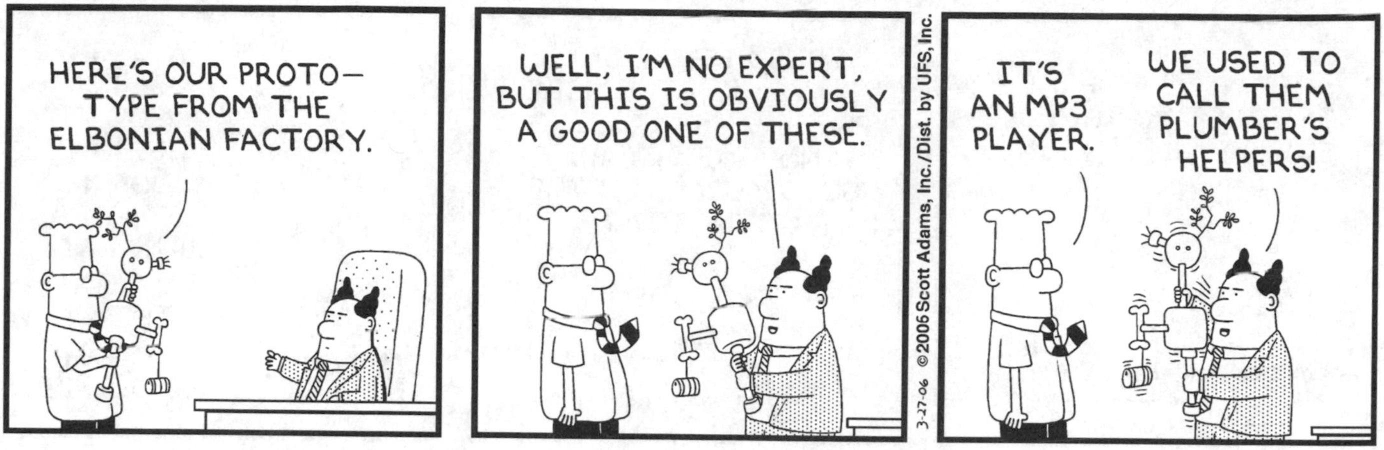
HERE'S OUR PROTO-TYPE FROM THE ELBONIAN FACTORY.
WELL, I'M NO EXPERT, BUT THIS IS OBVIOUSLY A GOOD ONE OF THESE.
3-27-06 ©2006 Scott Adams, Inc./Dist. by UFS, Inc.
IT'S AN MP3 PLAYER.
WE USED TO CALL THEM PLUMBER'S HELPERS!

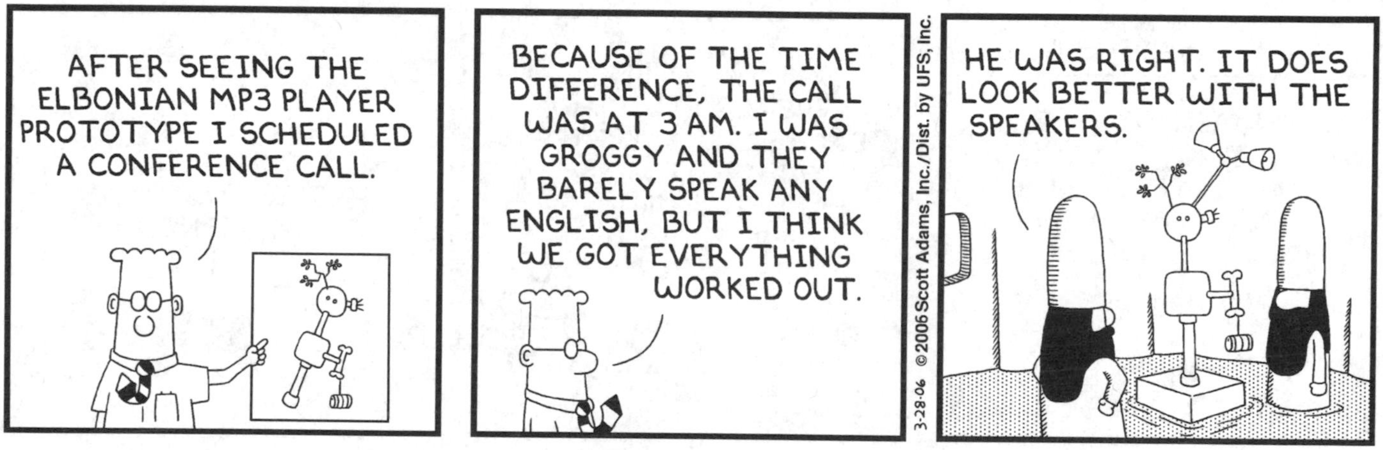
AFTER SEEING THE ELBONIAN MP3 PLAYER PROTOTYPE I SCHEDULED A CONFERENCE CALL.
BECAUSE OF THE TIME DIFFERENCE, THE CALL WAS AT 3 AM. I WAS GROGGY AND THEY BARELY SPEAK ANY ENGLISH, BUT I THINK WE GOT EVERYTHING WORKED OUT.
3-28-06 ©2006 Scott Adams, Inc./Dist. by UFS, Inc.
HE WAS RIGHT. IT DOES LOOK BETTER WITH THE SPEAKERS.

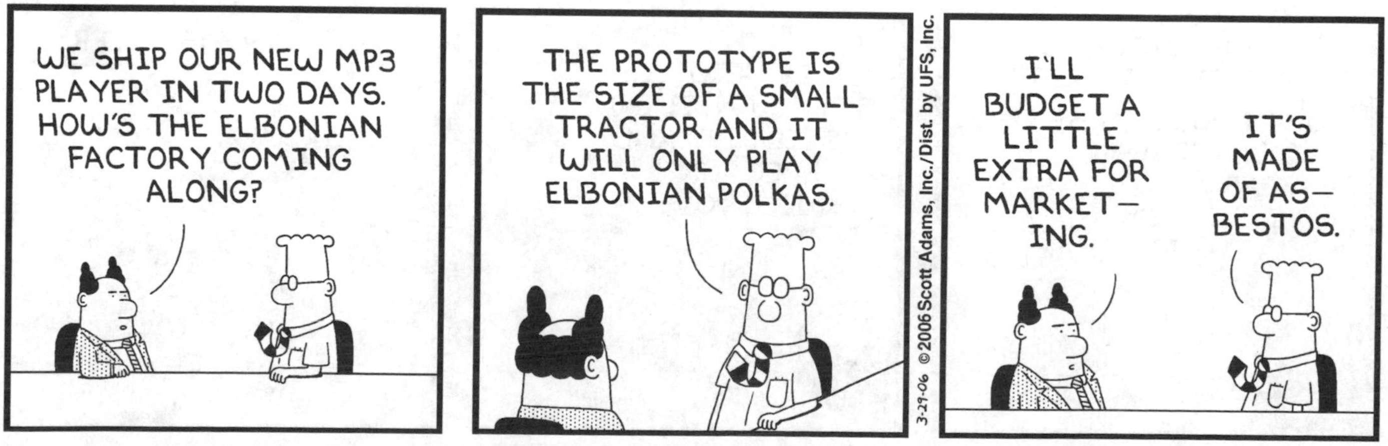
WE SHIP OUR NEW MP3 PLAYER IN TWO DAYS. HOW'S THE ELBONIAN FACTORY COMING ALONG?
THE PROTOTYPE IS THE SIZE OF A SMALL TRACTOR AND IT WILL ONLY PLAY ELBONIAN POLKAS.
3-29-06 ©2006 Scott Adams, Inc./Dist. by UFS, Inc.
I'LL BUDGET A LITTLE EXTRA FOR MARKET-ING.
IT'S MADE OF AS-BESTOS.

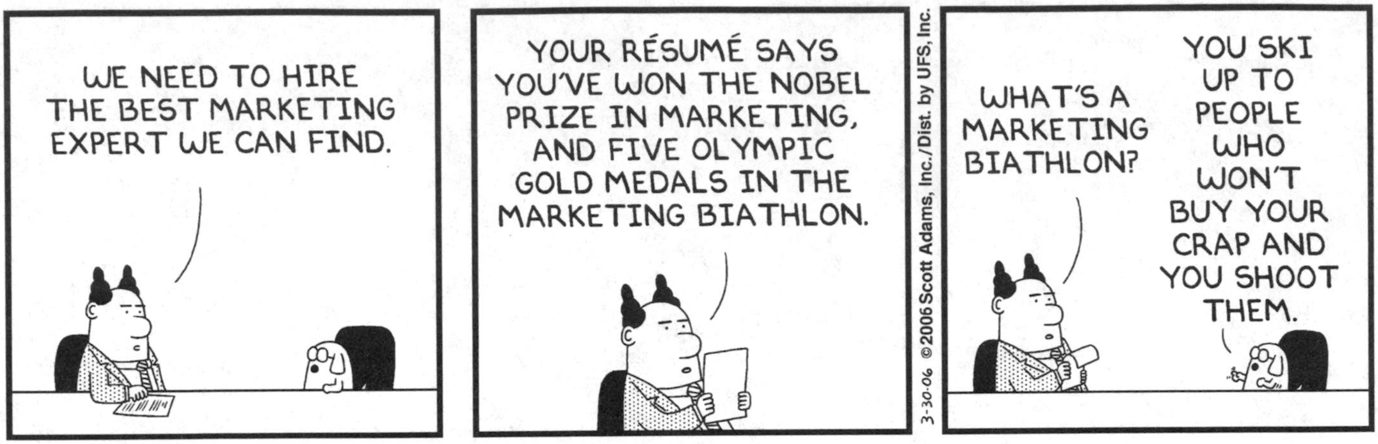
WE NEED TO HIRE THE BEST MARKETING EXPERT WE CAN FIND.
YOUR RÉSUMÉ SAYS YOU'VE WON THE NOBEL PRIZE IN MARKETING, AND FIVE OLYMPIC GOLD MEDALS IN THE MARKETING BIATHLON.
3-30-06 ©2006 Scott Adams, Inc./Dist. by UFS, Inc.
WHAT'S A MARKETING BIATHLON?
YOU SKI UP TO PEOPLE WHO WON'T BUY YOUR CRAP AND YOU SHOOT THEM.

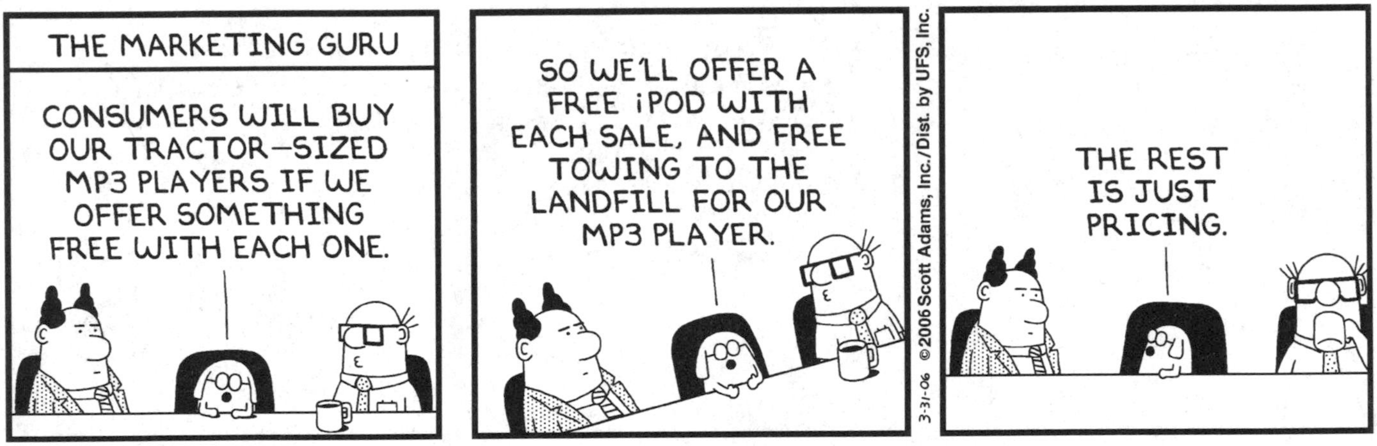
THE MARKETING GURU
CONSUMERS WILL BUY OUR TRACTOR—SIZED MP3 PLAYERS IF WE OFFER SOMETHING FREE WITH EACH ONE.
SO WE'LL OFFER A FREE iPOD WITH EACH SALE, AND FREE TOWING TO THE LANDFILL FOR OUR MP3 PLAYER.
3-31-06 ©2006 Scott Adams, Inc./Dist. by UFS, Inc.
THE REST IS JUST PRICING.

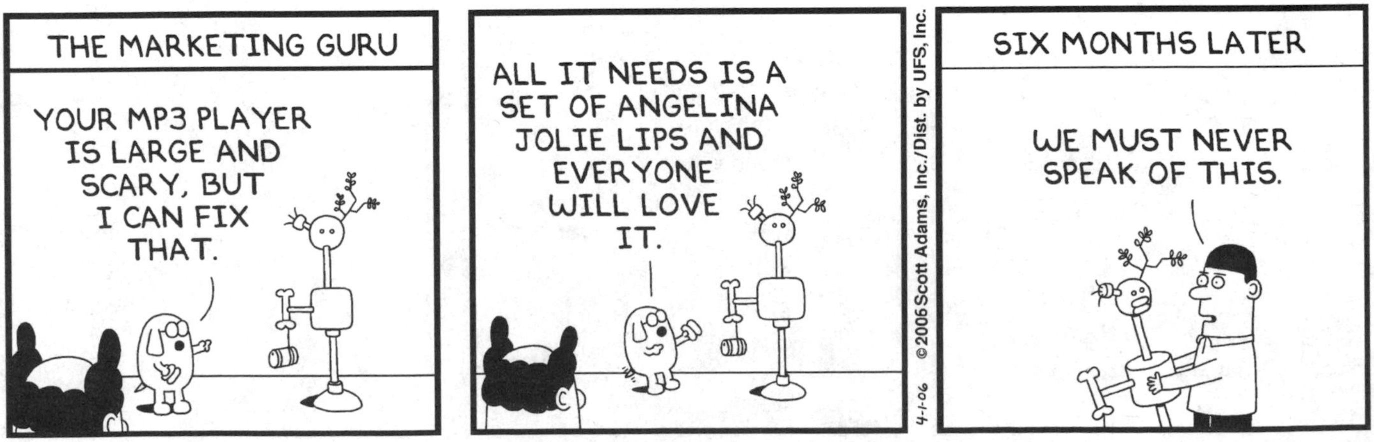
THE MARKETING GURU
YOUR MP3 PLAYER IS LARGE AND SCARY, BUT I CAN FIX THAT.
ALL IT NEEDS IS A SET OF ANGELINA JOLIE LIPS AND EVERYONE WILL LOVE IT.
4-1-06 ©2006 Scott Adams, Inc./Dist. by UFS, Inc.
SIX MONTHS LATER
WE MUST NEVER SPEAK OF THIS.

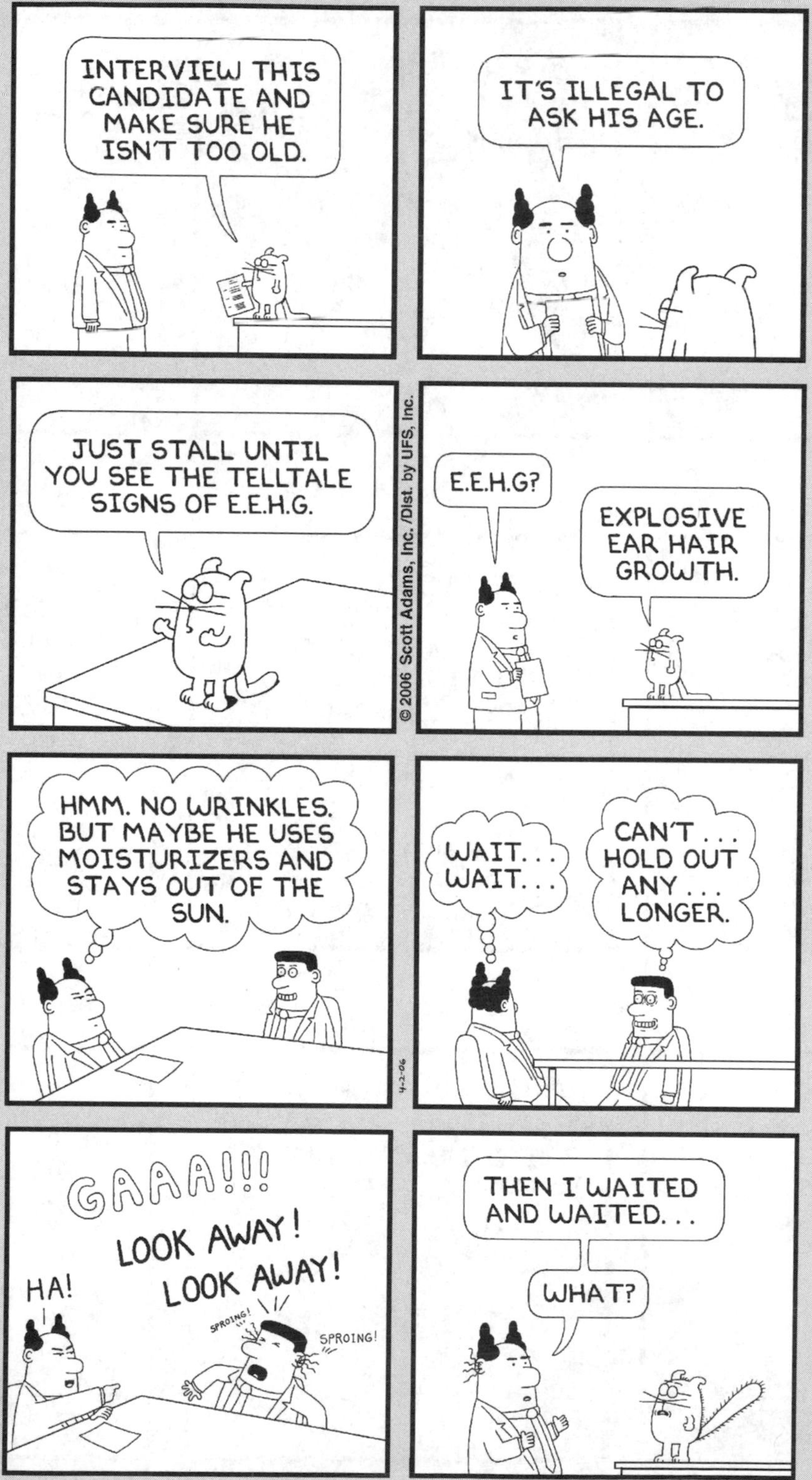
INTERVIEW THIS CANDIDATE AND MAKE SURE HE ISN'T TOO OLD.
IT'S ILLEGAL TO ASK HIS AGE.
JUST STALL UNTIL YOU SEE THE TELLTALE SIGNS OF E.E.H.G.
E.E.H.G?
EXPLOSIVE EAR HAIR GROWTH.
© 2006 Scott Adams, Inc./Dist. by UFS, Inc.
HMM. NO WRINKLES. BUT MAYBE HE USES MOISTURIZERS AND STAYS OUT OF THE SUN.
4-2-06
WAIT... WAIT...
CAN'T ... HOLD OUT ANY ... LONGER.
GAAA!!!
LOOK AWAY! LOOK AWAY!
HA!
SPROING!
SPROING!
THEN I WAITED AND WAITED...
WHAT?

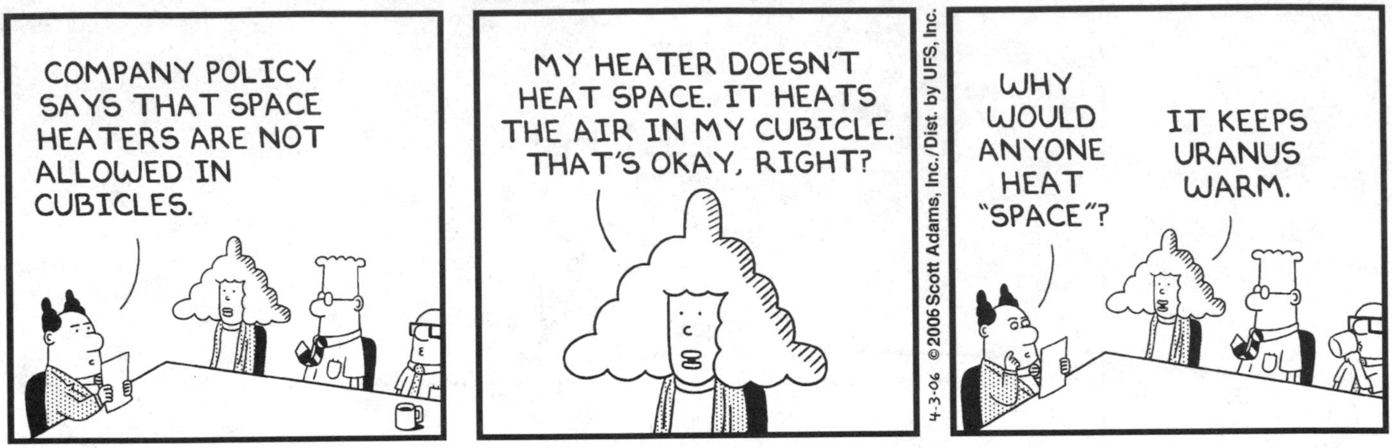
COMPANY POLICY SAYS THAT SPACE HEATERS ARE NOT ALLOWED IN CUBICLES.
MY HEATER DOESN'T HEAT SPACE. IT HEATS THE AIR IN MY CUBICLE. THAT'S OKAY, RIGHT?
WHY WOULD ANYONE HEAT "SPACE"?
IT KEEPS URANUS WARM.
4-3-06 © 2006 Scott Adams, Inc./Dist. by UFS, Inc.

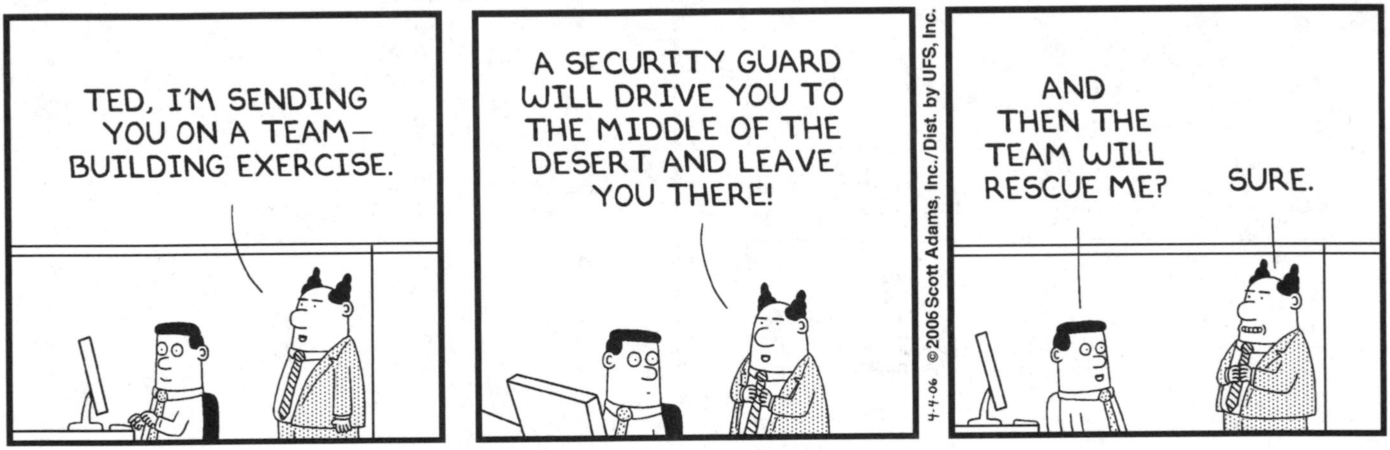
TED, I'M SENDING YOU ON A TEAM-BUILDING EXERCISE.
A SECURITY GUARD WILL DRIVE YOU TO THE MIDDLE OF THE DESERT AND LEAVE YOU THERE!
AND THEN THE TEAM WILL RESCUE ME?
SURE.
4-4-06 © 2006 Scott Adams, Inc./Dist. by UFS, Inc.

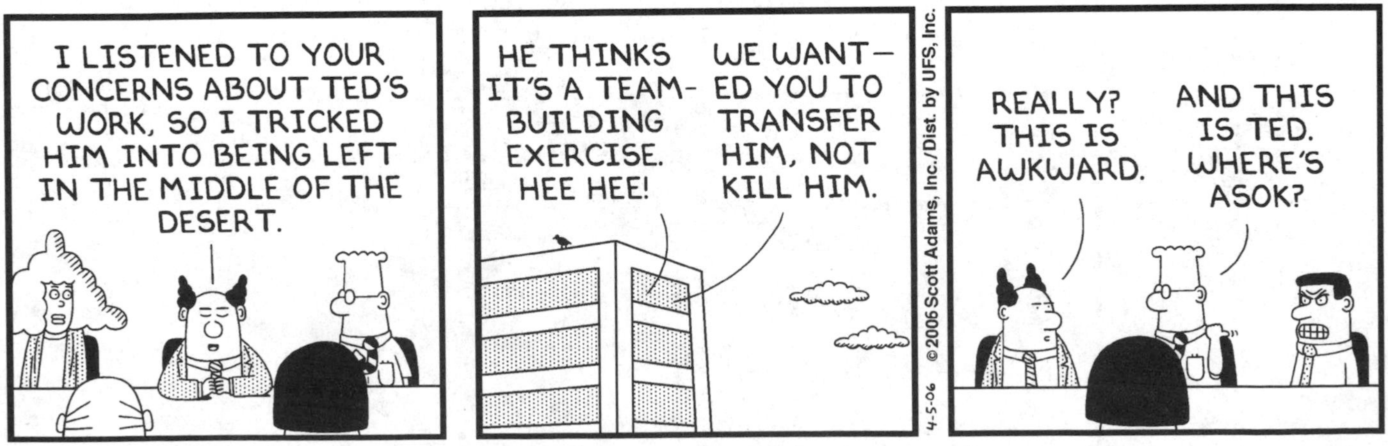
I LISTENED TO YOUR CONCERNS ABOUT TED'S WORK, SO I TRICKED HIM INTO BEING LEFT IN THE MIDDLE OF THE DESERT.
HE THINKS IT'S A TEAM-BUILDING EXERCISE. HEE HEE!
WE WANTED YOU TO TRANSFER HIM, NOT KILL HIM.
REALLY? THIS IS AWKWARD.
AND THIS IS TED. WHERE'S ASOK?
4-5-06 © 2006 Scott Adams, Inc./Dist. by UFS, Inc.

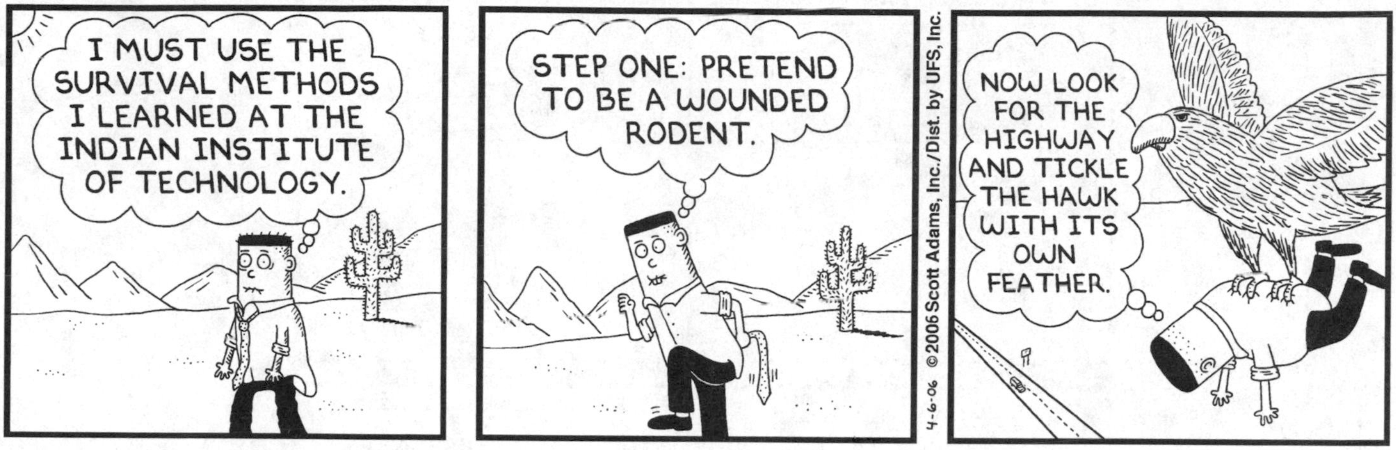
I MUST USE THE SURVIVAL METHODS I LEARNED AT THE INDIAN INSTITUTE OF TECHNOLOGY.
STEP ONE: PRETEND TO BE A WOUNDED RODENT.
4-6-06 ©2006 Scott Adams, Inc./Dist. by UFS, Inc.
NOW LOOK FOR THE HIGHWAY AND TICKLE THE HAWK WITH ITS OWN FEATHER.

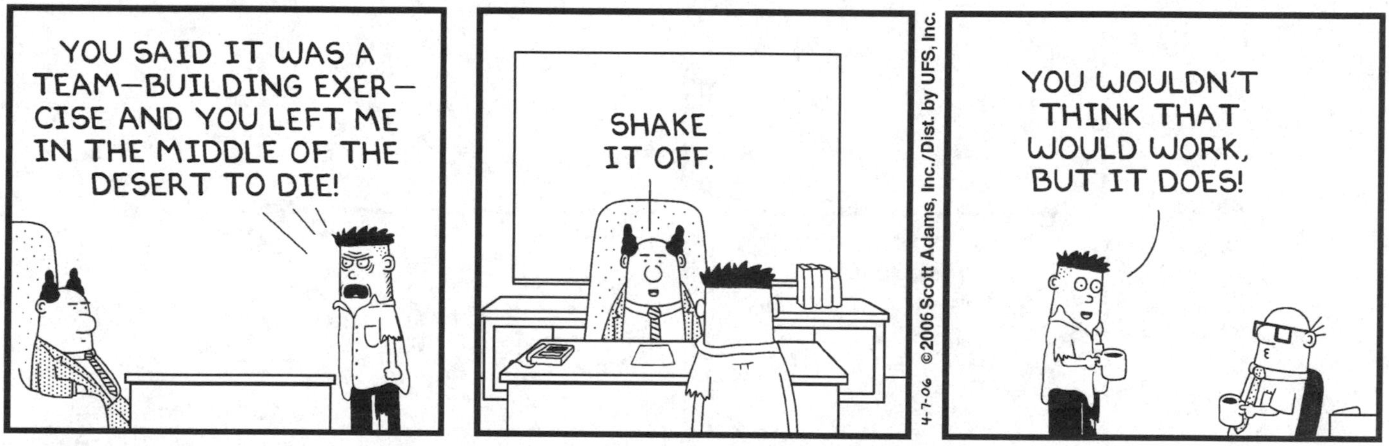
YOU SAID IT WAS A TEAM—BUILDING EXER—CISE AND YOU LEFT ME IN THE MIDDLE OF THE DESERT TO DIE!
SHAKE IT OFF.
4-7-06 ©2006 Scott Adams, Inc./Dist. by UFS, Inc.
YOU WOULDN'T THINK THAT WOULD WORK, BUT IT DOES!

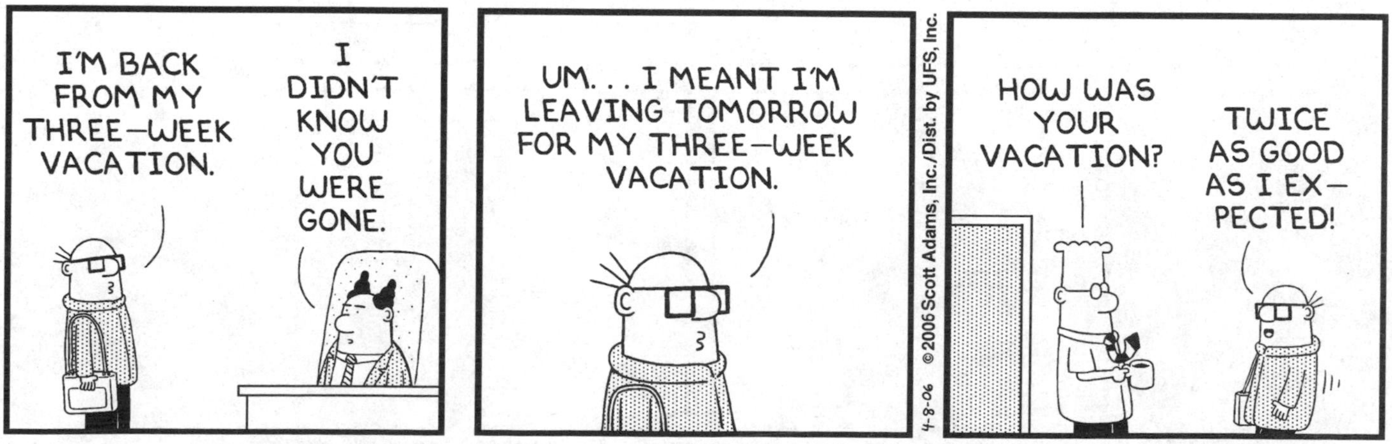
I'M BACK FROM MY THREE—WEEK VACATION.
I DIDN'T KNOW YOU WERE GONE.
UM. . . I MEANT I'M LEAVING TOMORROW FOR MY THREE—WEEK VACATION.
4-8-06 ©2006 Scott Adams, Inc./Dist. by UFS, Inc.
HOW WAS YOUR VACATION?
TWICE AS GOOD AS I EX—PECTED!

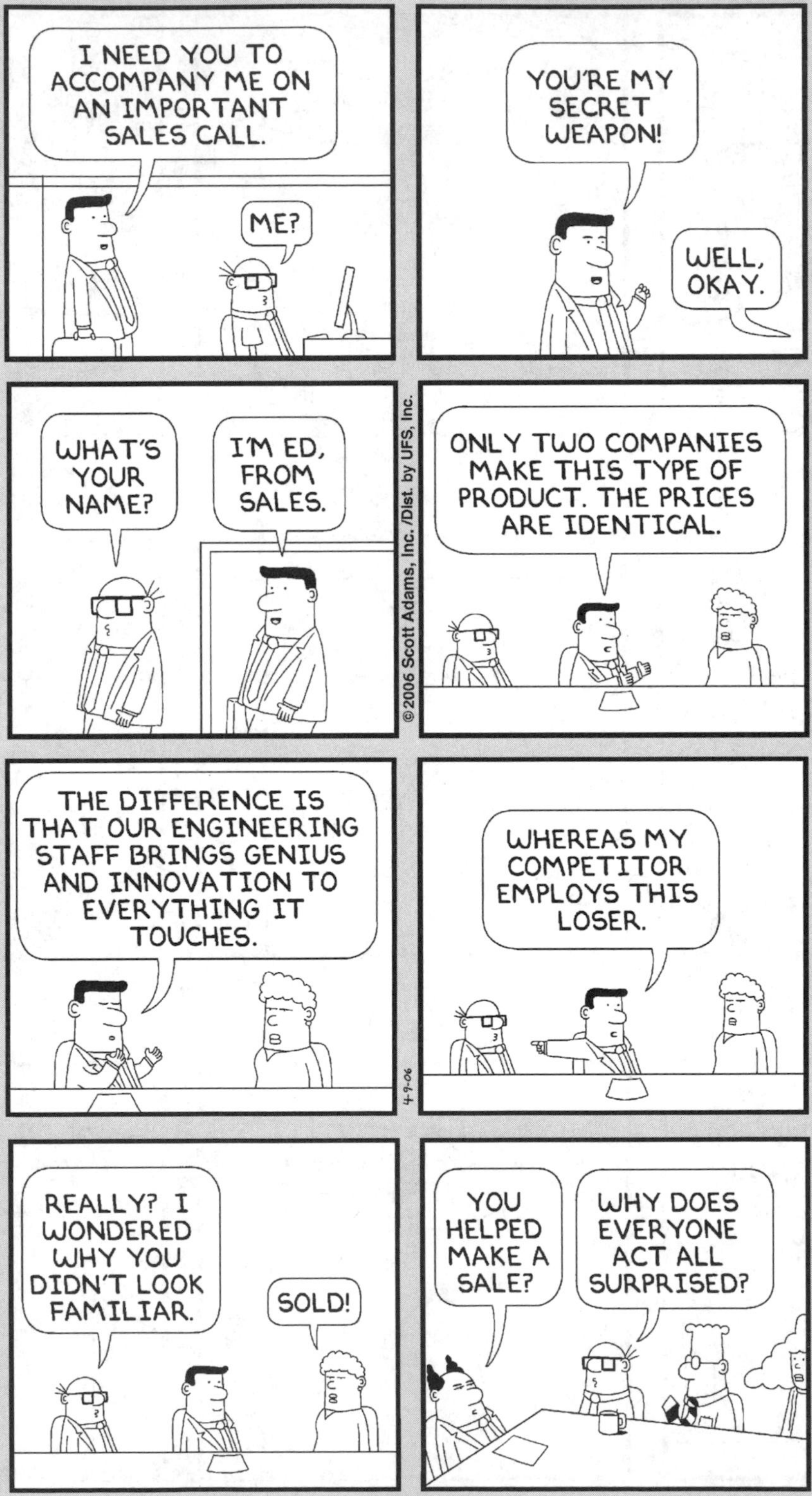
I NEED YOU TO ACCOMPANY ME ON AN IMPORTANT SALES CALL.
ME?
YOU'RE MY SECRET WEAPON!
WELL, OKAY.
WHAT'S YOUR NAME?
I'M ED, FROM SALES.
©2006 Scott Adams, Inc./Dist. by UFS, Inc.
ONLY TWO COMPANIES MAKE THIS TYPE OF PRODUCT. THE PRICES ARE IDENTICAL.
THE DIFFERENCE IS THAT OUR ENGINEERING STAFF BRINGS GENIUS AND INNOVATION TO EVERYTHING IT TOUCHES.
4-9-06
WHEREAS MY COMPETITOR EMPLOYS THIS LOSER.
REALLY? I WONDERED WHY YOU DIDN'T LOOK FAMILIAR.
SOLD!
YOU HELPED MAKE A SALE?
WHY DOES EVERYONE ACT ALL SURPRISED?

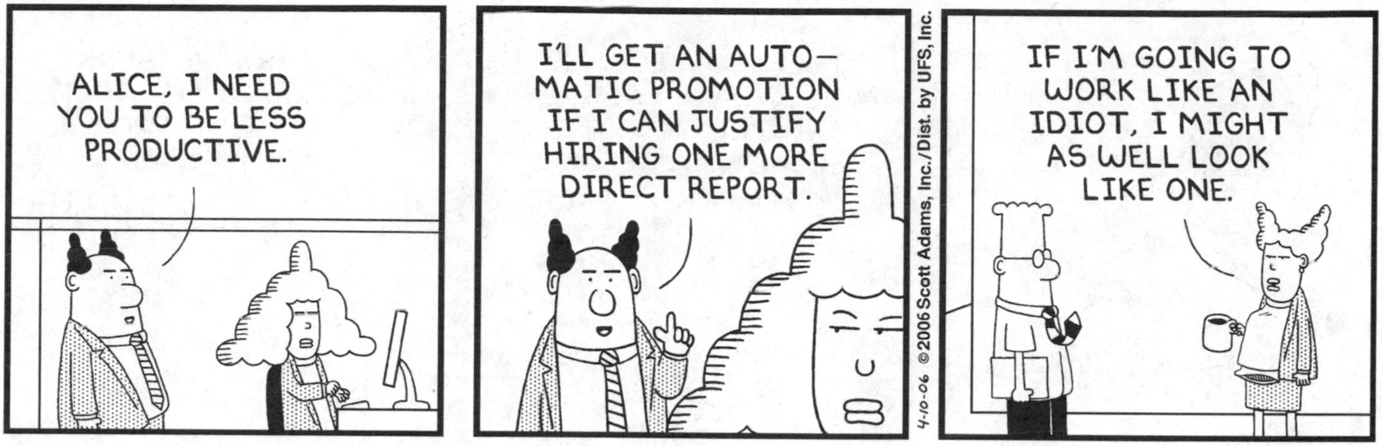
ALICE, I NEED YOU TO BE LESS PRODUCTIVE.
I'LL GET AN AUTO-MATIC PROMOTION IF I CAN JUSTIFY HIRING ONE MORE DIRECT REPORT.
4-10-06 © 2006 Scott Adams, Inc./Dist. by UFS, Inc.
IF I'M GOING TO WORK LIKE AN IDIOT, I MIGHT AS WELL LOOK LIKE ONE.

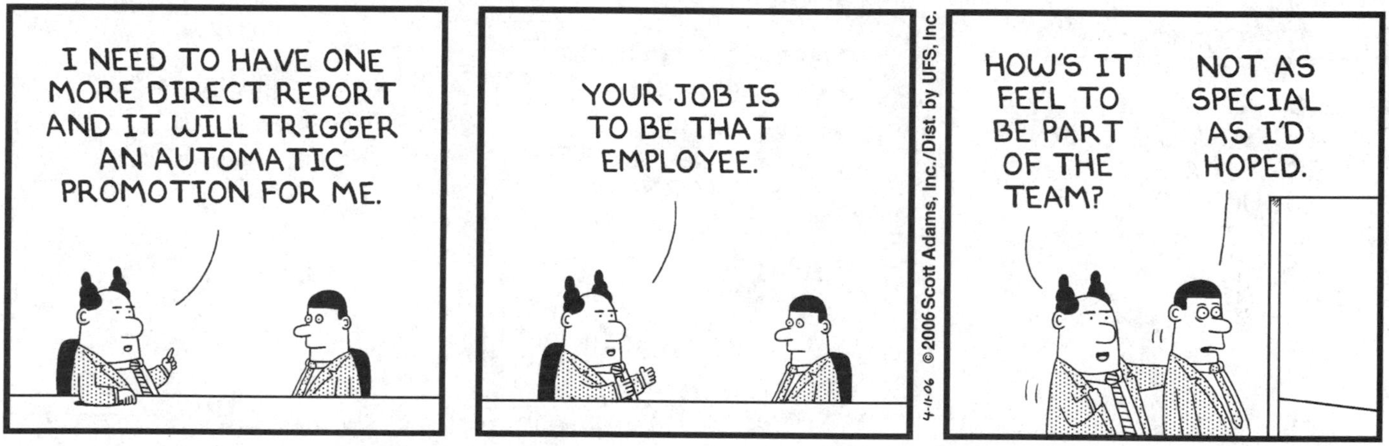
I NEED TO HAVE ONE MORE DIRECT REPORT AND IT WILL TRIGGER AN AUTOMATIC PROMOTION FOR ME.
YOUR JOB IS TO BE THAT EMPLOYEE.
4-11-06 © 2006 Scott Adams, Inc./Dist. by UFS, Inc.
HOW'S IT FEEL TO BE PART OF THE TEAM?
NOT AS SPECIAL AS I'D HOPED.

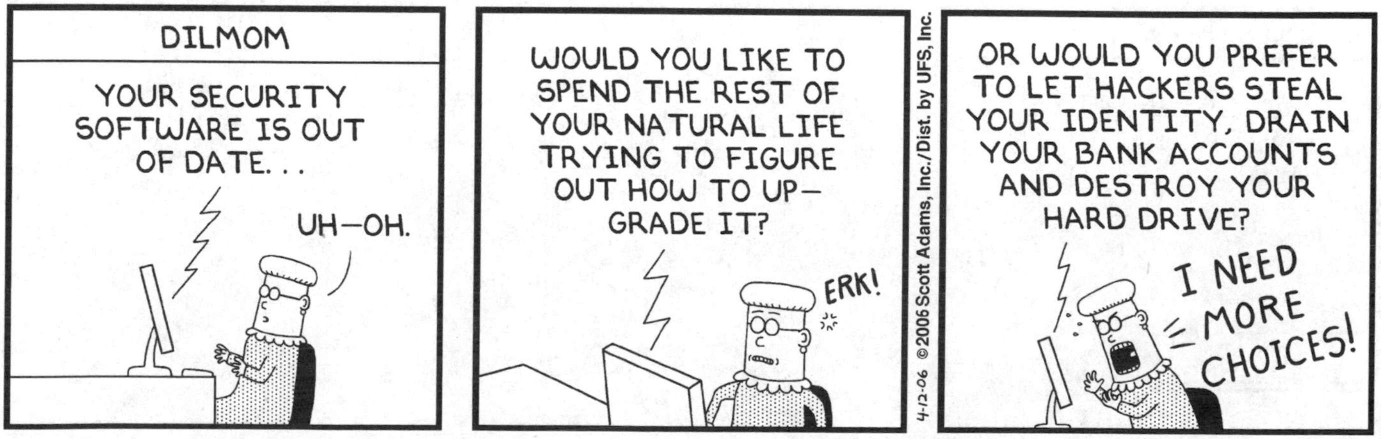
DILMOM
YOUR SECURITY SOFTWARE IS OUT OF DATE. . .
UH-OH.
WOULD YOU LIKE TO SPEND THE REST OF YOUR NATURAL LIFE TRYING TO FIGURE OUT HOW TO UP-GRADE IT?
ERK!
4-12-06 © 2006 Scott Adams, Inc./Dist. by UFS, Inc.
OR WOULD YOU PREFER TO LET HACKERS STEAL YOUR IDENTITY, DRAIN YOUR BANK ACCOUNTS AND DESTROY YOUR HARD DRIVE?
I NEED MORE CHOICES!

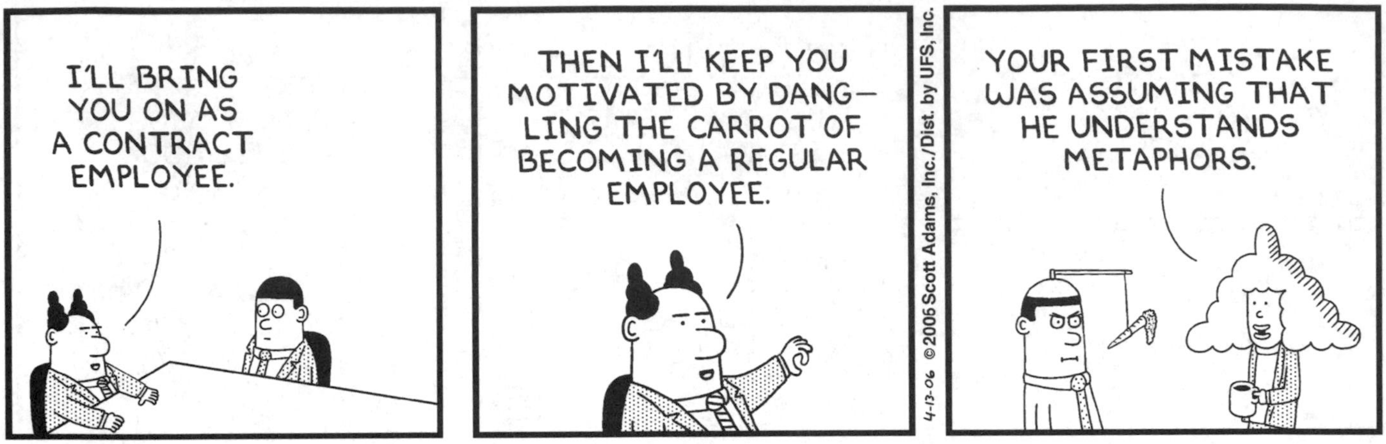
I'LL BRING YOU ON AS A CONTRACT EMPLOYEE.
THEN I'LL KEEP YOU MOTIVATED BY DANG-LING THE CARROT OF BECOMING A REGULAR EMPLOYEE.
4-13-06 © 2006 Scott Adams, Inc./Dist. by UFS, Inc.
YOUR FIRST MISTAKE WAS ASSUMING THAT HE UNDERSTANDS METAPHORS.

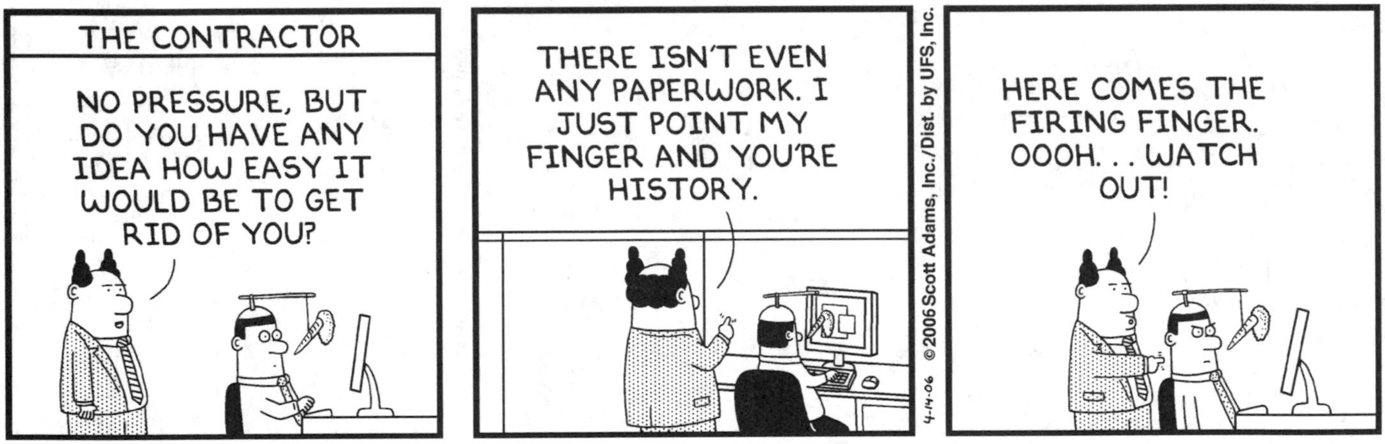
THE CONTRACTOR
NO PRESSURE, BUT DO YOU HAVE ANY IDEA HOW EASY IT WOULD BE TO GET RID OF YOU?
THERE ISN'T EVEN ANY PAPERWORK. I JUST POINT MY FINGER AND YOU'RE HISTORY.
4-14-06 © 2006 Scott Adams, Inc./Dist. by UFS, Inc.
HERE COMES THE FIRING FINGER. OOOH. . . WATCH OUT!

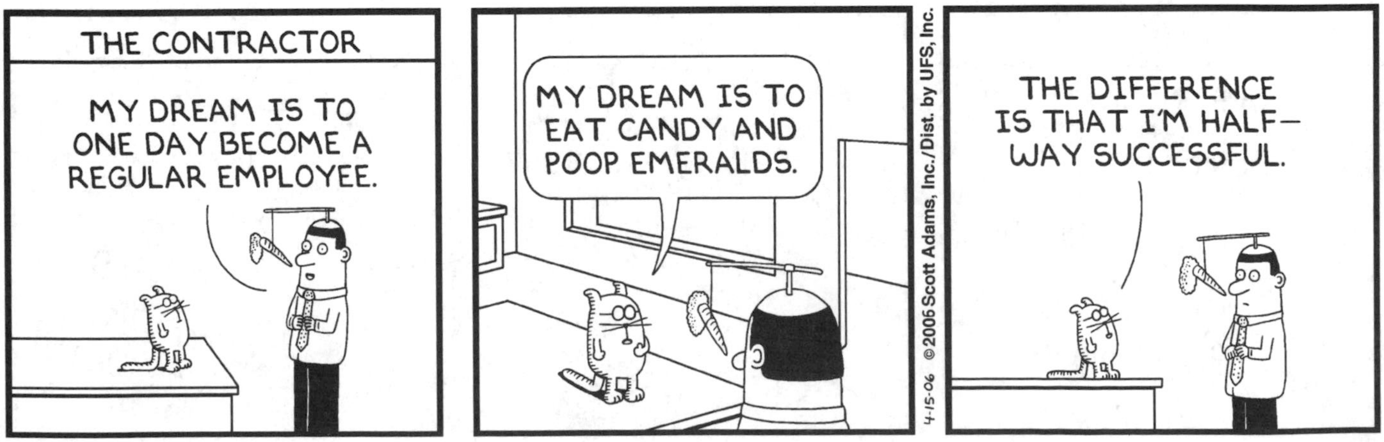
THE CONTRACTOR
MY DREAM IS TO ONE DAY BECOME A REGULAR EMPLOYEE.
MY DREAM IS TO EAT CANDY AND POOP EMERALDS.
4-15-06 © 2006 Scott Adams, Inc./Dist. by UFS, Inc.
THE DIFFERENCE IS THAT I'M HALF-WAY SUCCESSFUL.

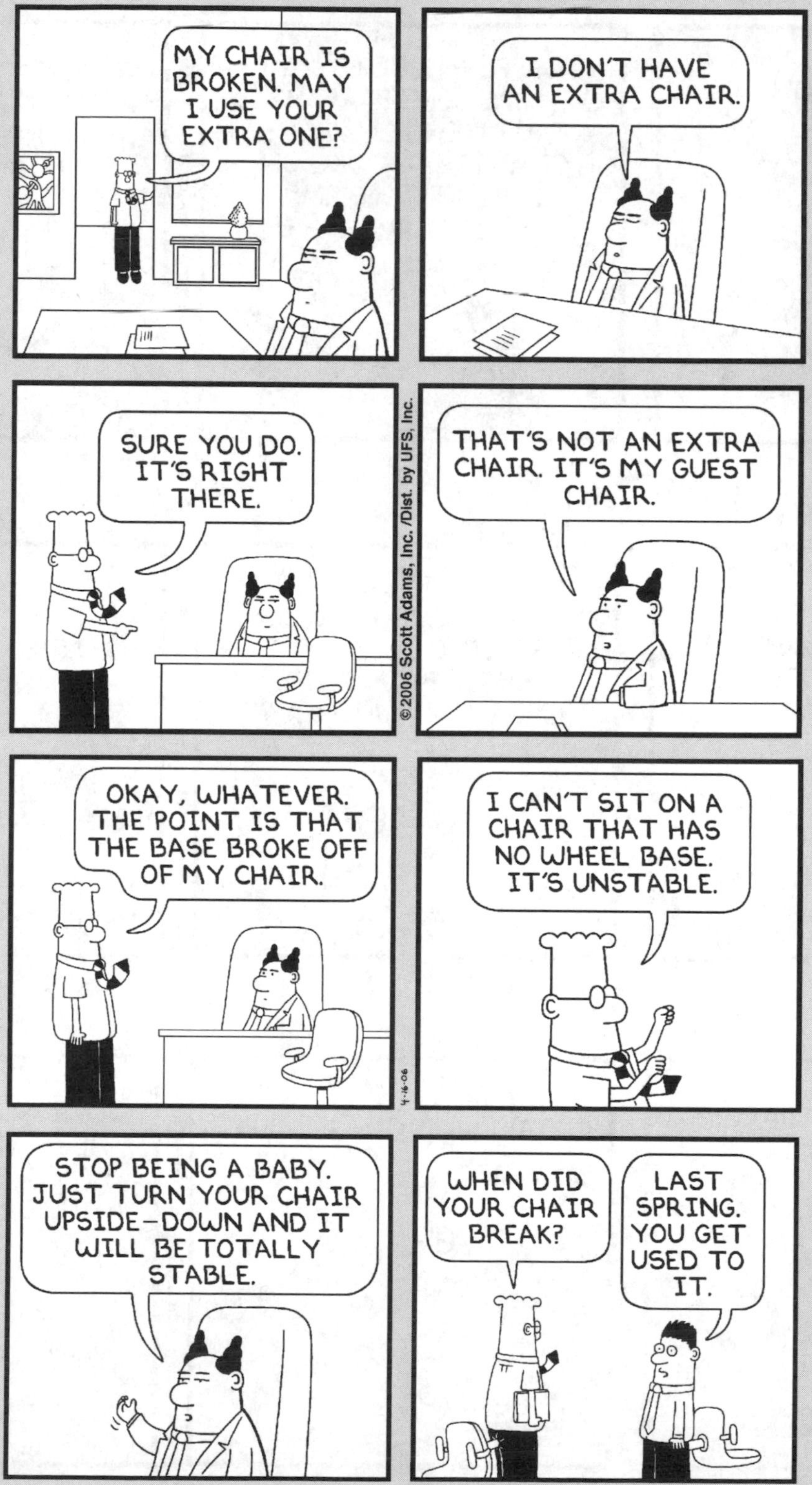
MY CHAIR IS BROKEN. MAY I USE YOUR EXTRA ONE?
I DON'T HAVE AN EXTRA CHAIR.
SURE YOU DO. IT'S RIGHT THERE.
THAT'S NOT AN EXTRA CHAIR. IT'S MY GUEST CHAIR.
OKAY, WHATEVER. THE POINT IS THAT THE BASE BROKE OFF OF MY CHAIR.
I CAN'T SIT ON A CHAIR THAT HAS NO WHEEL BASE. IT'S UNSTABLE.
STOP BEING A BABY. JUST TURN YOUR CHAIR UPSIDE-DOWN AND IT WILL BE TOTALLY STABLE.
WHEN DID YOUR CHAIR BREAK?
LAST SPRING. YOU GET USED TO IT.
© 2006 Scott Adams, Inc. /Dist. by UFS, Inc.
4-16-06

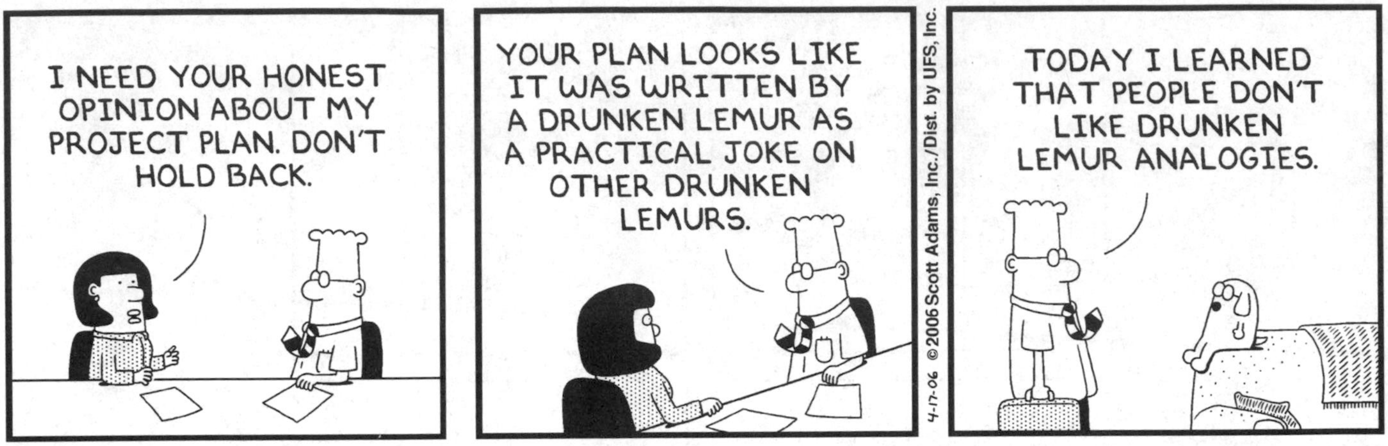
I NEED YOUR HONEST OPINION ABOUT MY PROJECT PLAN. DON'T HOLD BACK.
YOUR PLAN LOOKS LIKE IT WAS WRITTEN BY A DRUNKEN LEMUR AS A PRACTICAL JOKE ON OTHER DRUNKEN LEMURS.
4-17-06 © 2006 Scott Adams, Inc./Dist. by UFS, Inc.
TODAY I LEARNED THAT PEOPLE DON'T LIKE DRUNKEN LEMUR ANALOGIES.

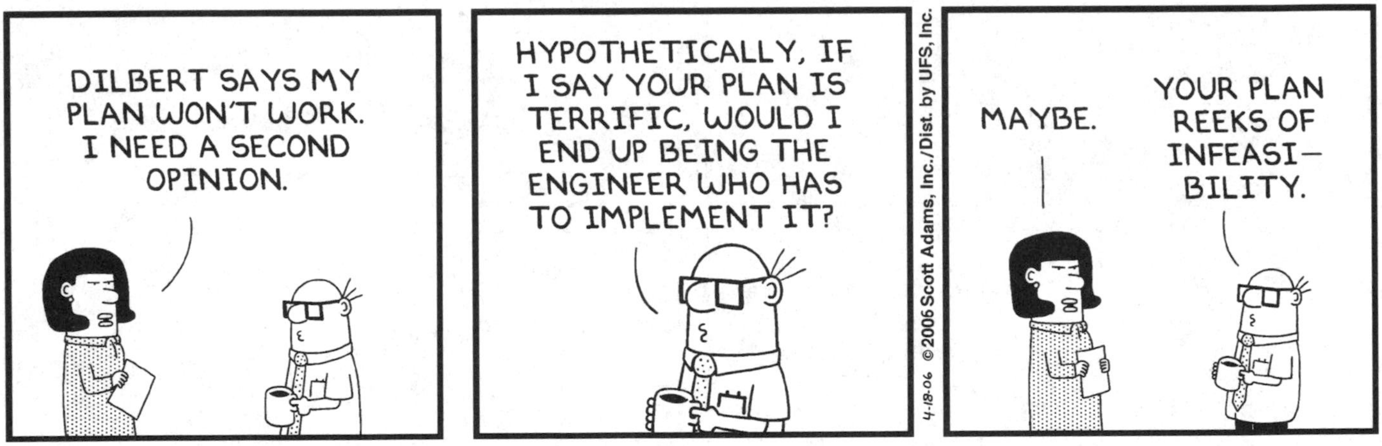
DILBERT SAYS MY PLAN WON'T WORK. I NEED A SECOND OPINION.
HYPOTHETICALLY, IF I SAY YOUR PLAN IS TERRIFIC, WOULD I END UP BEING THE ENGINEER WHO HAS TO IMPLEMENT IT?
4-18-06 © 2006 Scott Adams, Inc./Dist. by UFS, Inc.
MAYBE.
YOUR PLAN REEKS OF INFEASI-BILITY.

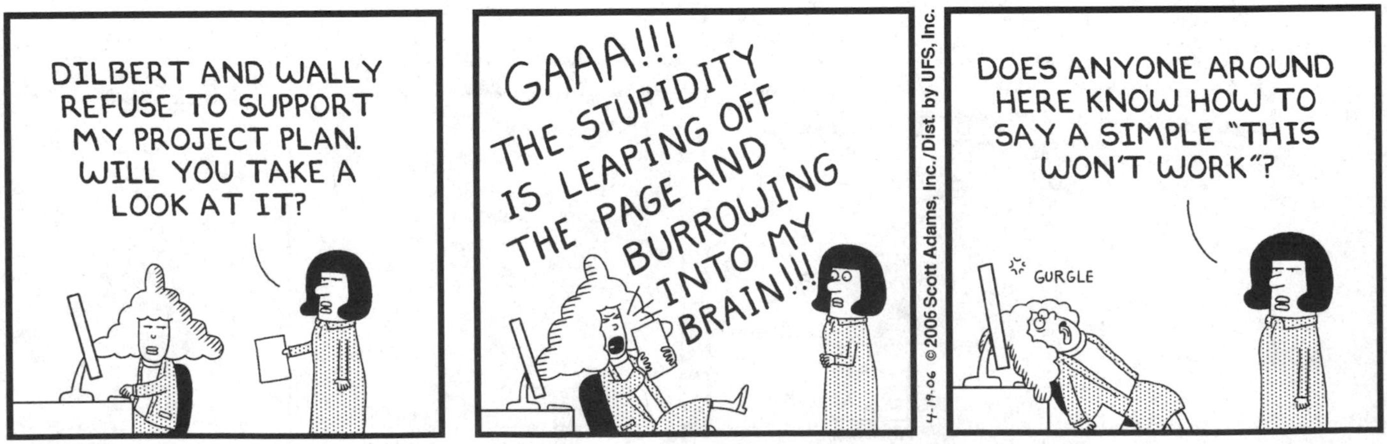
DILBERT AND WALLY REFUSE TO SUPPORT MY PROJECT PLAN. WILL YOU TAKE A LOOK AT IT?
GAAA!!! THE STUPIDITY IS LEAPING OFF THE PAGE AND BURROWING INTO MY BRAIN!!!
4-19-06 © 2006 Scott Adams, Inc./Dist. by UFS, Inc.
GURGLE
DOES ANYONE AROUND HERE KNOW HOW TO SAY A SIMPLE "THIS WON'T WORK"?

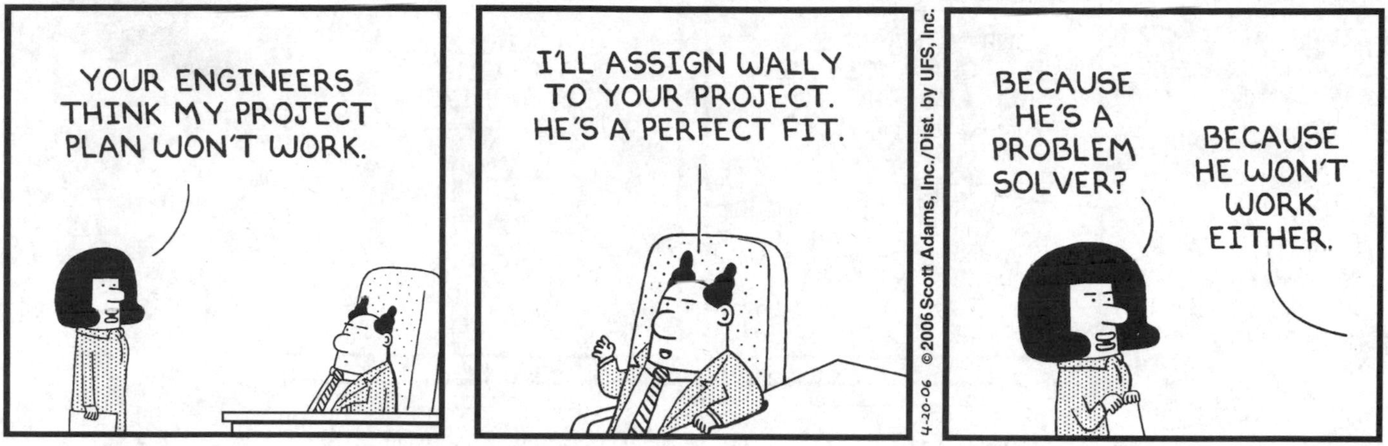
YOUR ENGINEERS THINK MY PROJECT PLAN WON'T WORK.
I'LL ASSIGN WALLY TO YOUR PROJECT. HE'S A PERFECT FIT.
4-20-06 © 2006 Scott Adams, Inc./Dist. by UFS, Inc.
BECAUSE HE'S A PROBLEM SOLVER?
BECAUSE HE WON'T WORK EITHER.

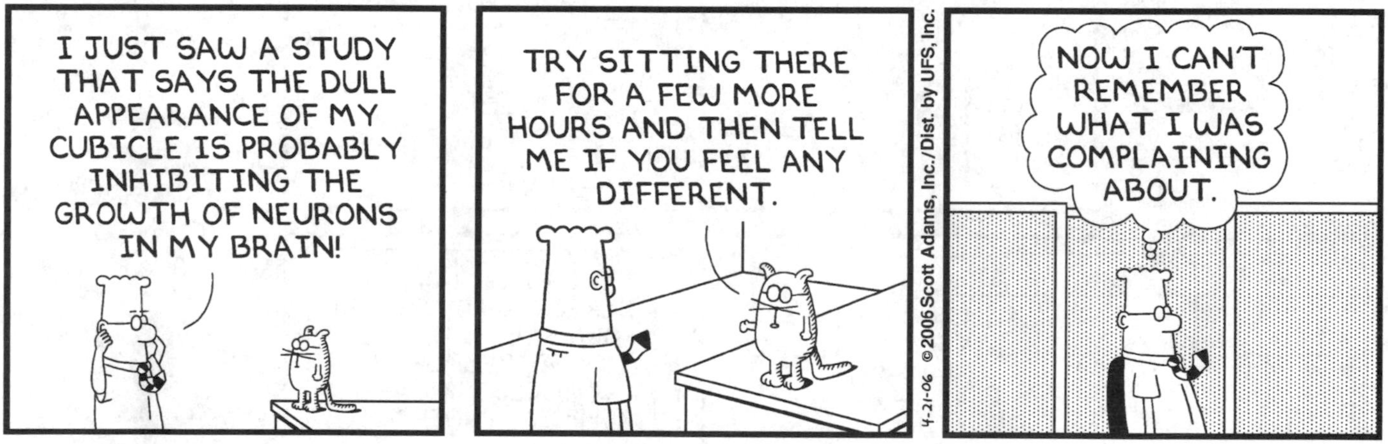
I JUST SAW A STUDY THAT SAYS THE DULL APPEARANCE OF MY CUBICLE IS PROBABLY INHIBITING THE GROWTH OF NEURONS IN MY BRAIN!
TRY SITTING THERE FOR A FEW MORE HOURS AND THEN TELL ME IF YOU FEEL ANY DIFFERENT.
4-21-06 © 2006 Scott Adams, Inc./Dist. by UFS, Inc.
NOW I CAN'T REMEMBER WHAT I WAS COMPLAINING ABOUT.

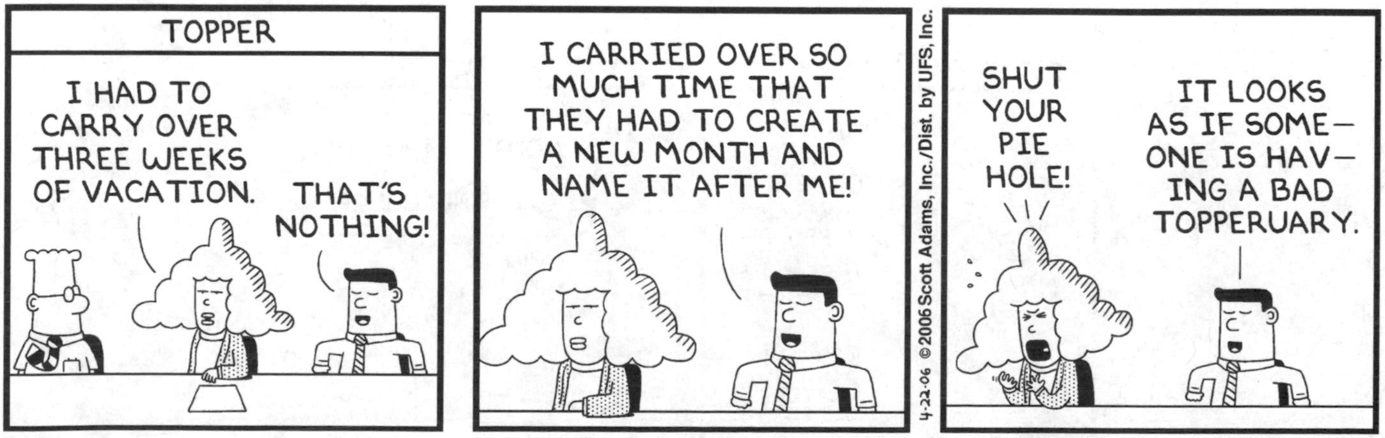
TOPPER
I HAD TO CARRY OVER THREE WEEKS OF VACATION.
THAT'S NOTHING!
I CARRIED OVER SO MUCH TIME THAT THEY HAD TO CREATE A NEW MONTH AND NAME IT AFTER ME!
4-22-06 © 2006 Scott Adams, Inc./Dist. by UFS, Inc.
SHUT YOUR PIE HOLE!
IT LOOKS AS IF SOME-ONE IS HAV-ING A BAD TOPPERUARY.

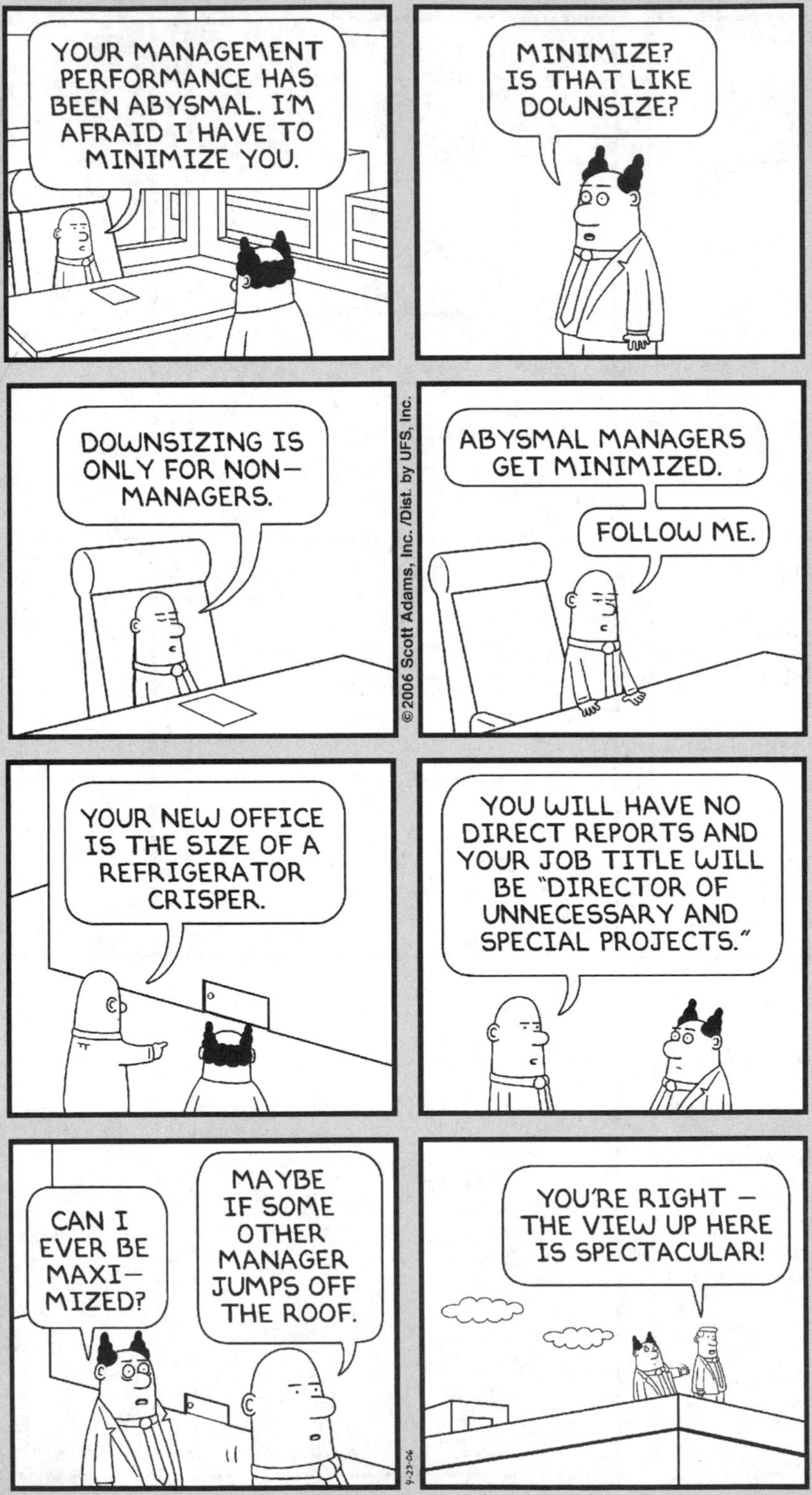
YOUR MANAGEMENT PERFORMANCE HAS BEEN ABYSMAL. I'M AFRAID I HAVE TO MINIMIZE YOU.
MINIMIZE? IS THAT LIKE DOWNSIZE?
DOWNSIZING IS ONLY FOR NON-MANAGERS.
©2006 Scott Adams, Inc./Dist. by UFS, Inc.
ABYSMAL MANAGERS GET MINIMIZED.
FOLLOW ME.
YOUR NEW OFFICE IS THE SIZE OF A REFRIGERATOR CRISPER.
YOU WILL HAVE NO DIRECT REPORTS AND YOUR JOB TITLE WILL BE "DIRECTOR OF UNNECESSARY AND SPECIAL PROJECTS."
CAN I EVER BE MAXI-MIZED?
MAYBE IF SOME OTHER MANAGER JUMPS OFF THE ROOF.
YOU'RE RIGHT — THE VIEW UP HERE IS SPECTACULAR!

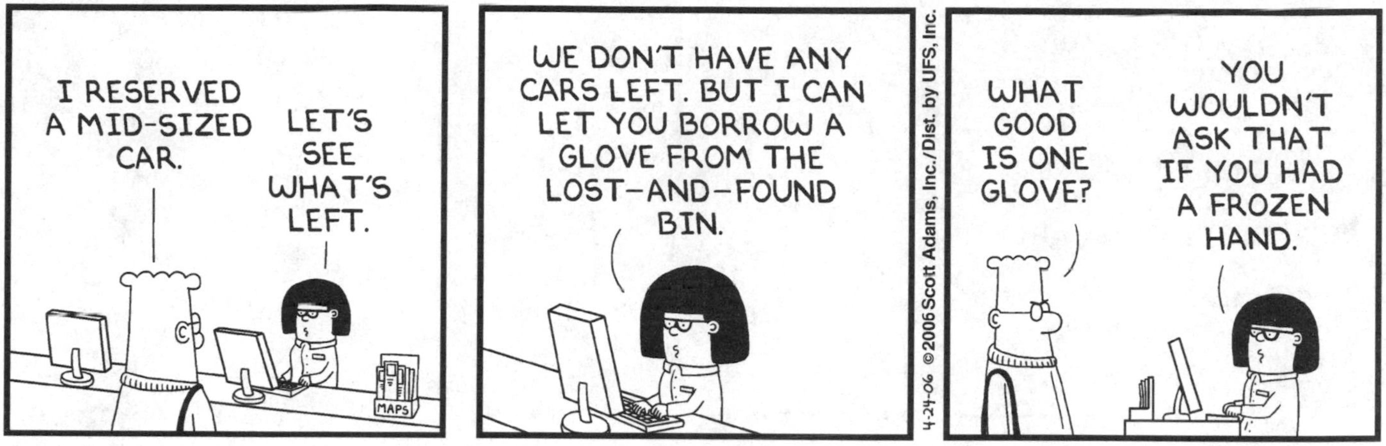
I RESERVED A MID-SIZED CAR.
LET'S SEE WHAT'S LEFT.
MAPS
WE DON'T HAVE ANY CARS LEFT. BUT I CAN LET YOU BORROW A GLOVE FROM THE LOST-AND-FOUND BIN.
4-24-06 © 2006 Scott Adams, Inc./Dist. by UFS, Inc.
WHAT GOOD IS ONE GLOVE?
YOU WOULDN'T ASK THAT IF YOU HAD A FROZEN HAND.

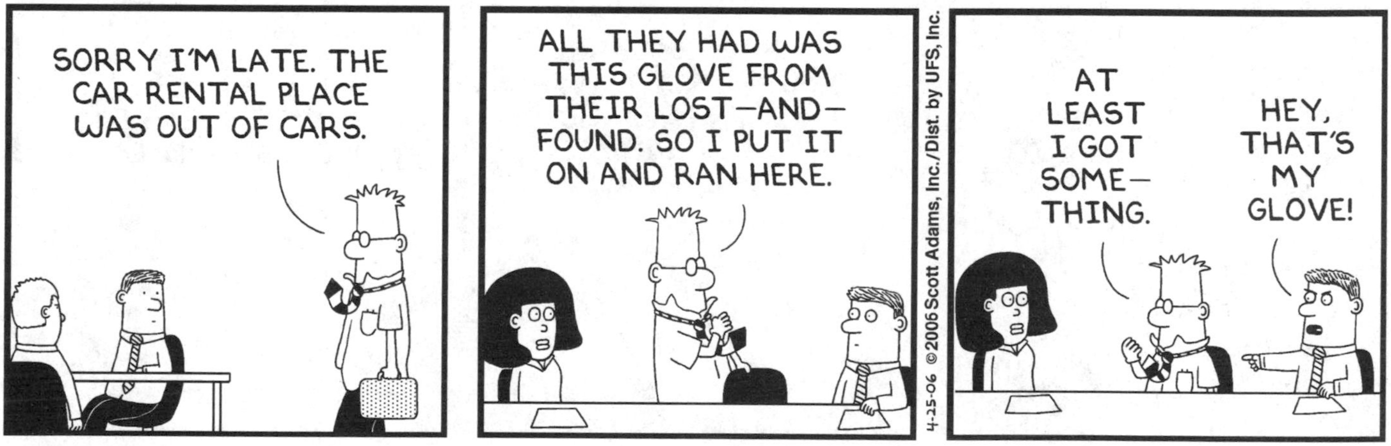
SORRY I'M LATE. THE CAR RENTAL PLACE WAS OUT OF CARS.
ALL THEY HAD WAS THIS GLOVE FROM THEIR LOST-AND-FOUND. SO I PUT IT ON AND RAN HERE.
4-25-06 © 2006 Scott Adams, Inc./Dist. by UFS, Inc.
AT LEAST I GOT SOME-THING.
HEY, THAT'S MY GLOVE!

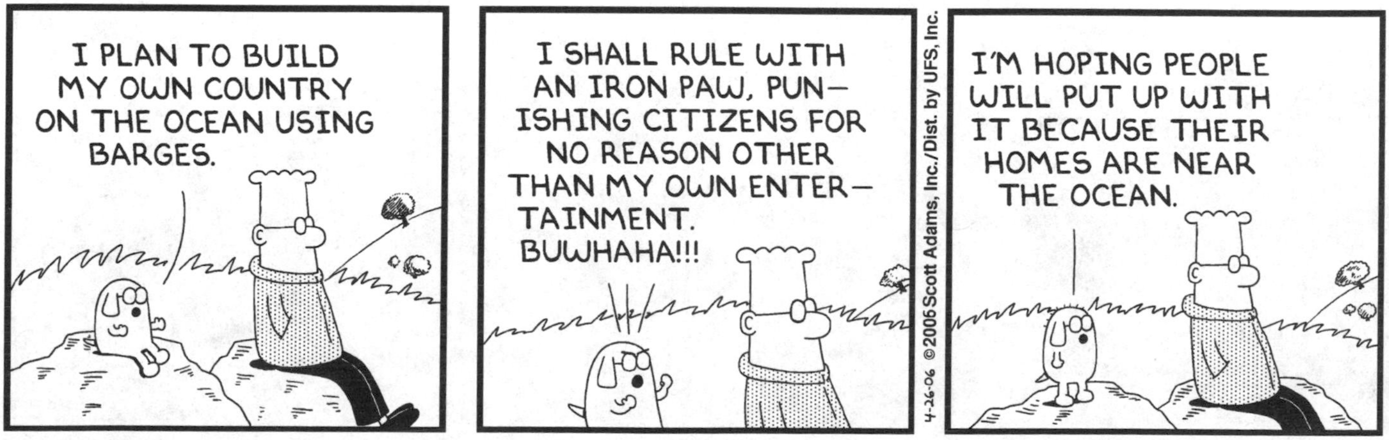
I PLAN TO BUILD MY OWN COUNTRY ON THE OCEAN USING BARGES.
I SHALL RULE WITH AN IRON PAW, PUN-ISHING CITIZENS FOR NO REASON OTHER THAN MY OWN ENTER-TAINMENT. BUWHAHA!!!
4-26-06 © 2006 Scott Adams, Inc./Dist. by UFS, Inc.
I'M HOPING PEOPLE WILL PUT UP WITH IT BECAUSE THEIR HOMES ARE NEAR THE OCEAN.

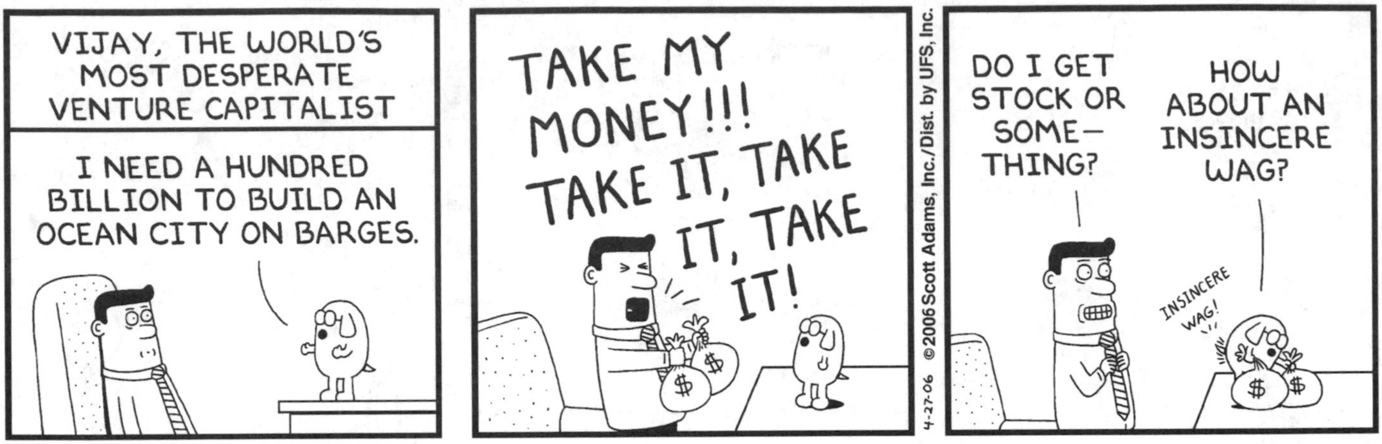
VIJAY, THE WORLD'S MOST DESPERATE VENTURE CAPITALIST
I NEED A HUNDRED BILLION TO BUILD AN OCEAN CITY ON BARGES.
TAKE MY MONEY!!! TAKE IT, TAKE IT, TAKE IT!
4-27-06 ©2006 Scott Adams, Inc./Dist. by UFS, Inc.
DO I GET STOCK OR SOME–THING?
HOW ABOUT AN INSINCERE WAG?
INSINCERE WAG!

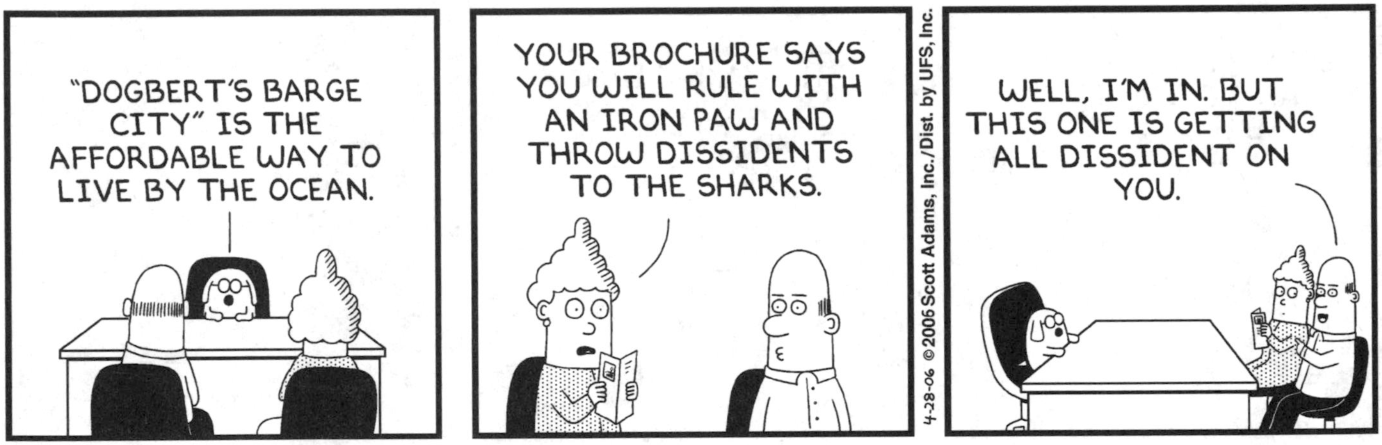
"DOGBERT'S BARGE CITY" IS THE AFFORDABLE WAY TO LIVE BY THE OCEAN.
YOUR BROCHURE SAYS YOU WILL RULE WITH AN IRON PAW AND THROW DISSIDENTS TO THE SHARKS.
4-28-06 ©2006 Scott Adams, Inc./Dist. by UFS, Inc.
WELL, I'M IN. BUT THIS ONE IS GETTING ALL DISSIDENT ON YOU.

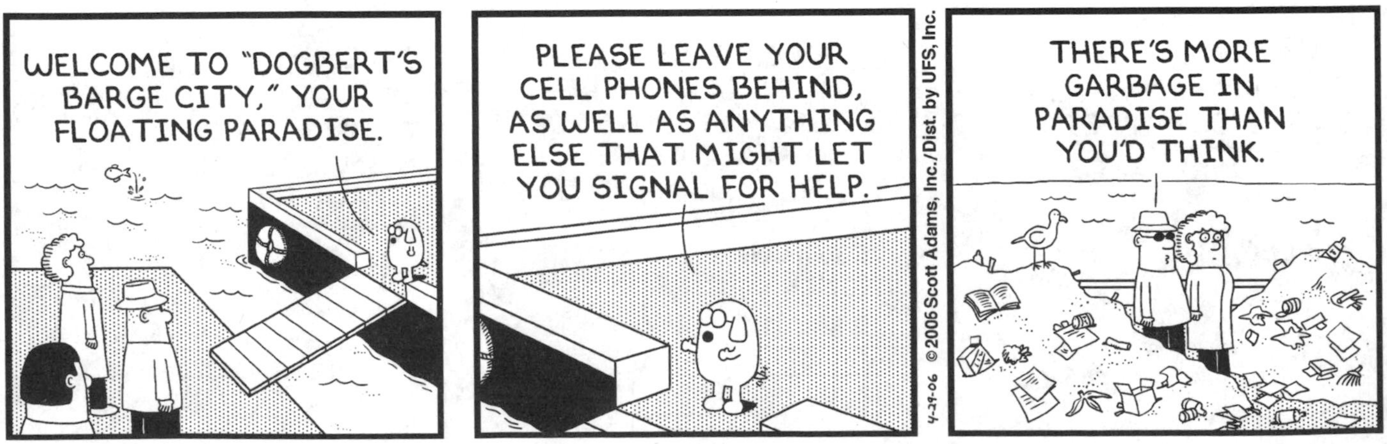
WELCOME TO "DOGBERT'S BARGE CITY," YOUR FLOATING PARADISE.
PLEASE LEAVE YOUR CELL PHONES BEHIND, AS WELL AS ANYTHING ELSE THAT MIGHT LET YOU SIGNAL FOR HELP.
4-29-06 ©2006 Scott Adams, Inc./Dist. by UFS, Inc.
THERE'S MORE GARBAGE IN PARADISE THAN YOU'D THINK.

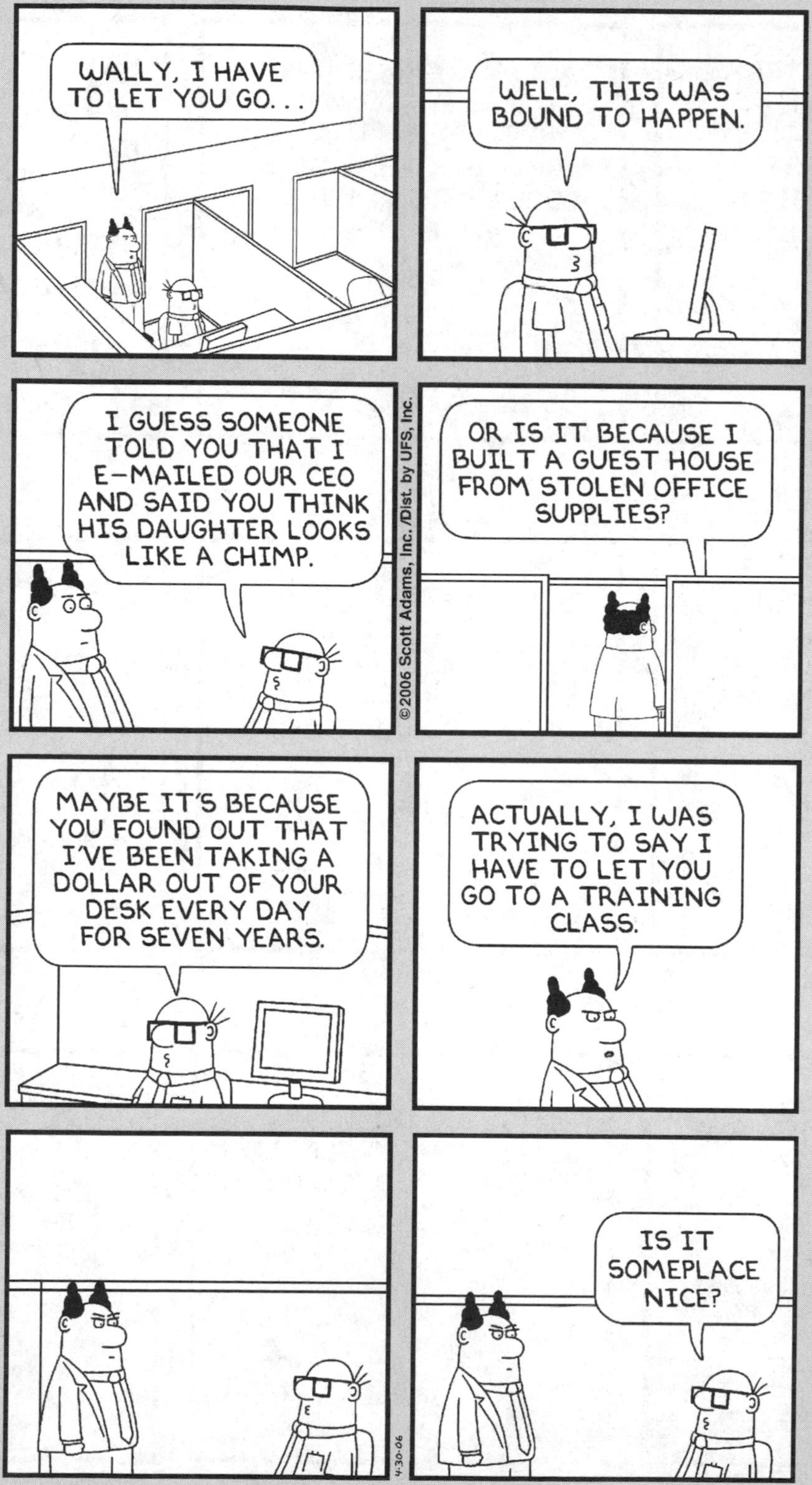
WALLY, I HAVE TO LET YOU GO. . .
WELL, THIS WAS BOUND TO HAPPEN.
I GUESS SOMEONE TOLD YOU THAT I E-MAILED OUR CEO AND SAID YOU THINK HIS DAUGHTER LOOKS LIKE A CHIMP.
©2006 Scott Adams, Inc./Dist. by UFS, Inc.
OR IS IT BECAUSE I BUILT A GUEST HOUSE FROM STOLEN OFFICE SUPPLIES?
MAYBE IT'S BECAUSE YOU FOUND OUT THAT I'VE BEEN TAKING A DOLLAR OUT OF YOUR DESK EVERY DAY FOR SEVEN YEARS.
ACTUALLY, I WAS TRYING TO SAY I HAVE TO LET YOU GO TO A TRAINING CLASS.
4-30-06
IS IT SOMEPLACE NICE?

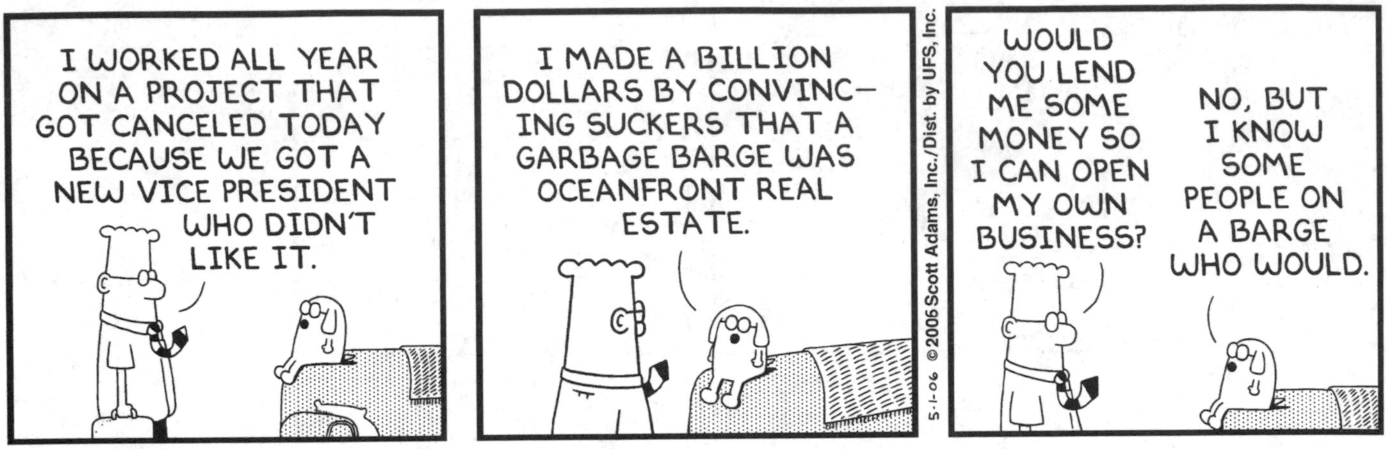
I WORKED ALL YEAR ON A PROJECT THAT GOT CANCELED TODAY BECAUSE WE GOT A NEW VICE PRESIDENT WHO DIDN'T LIKE IT.
I MADE A BILLION DOLLARS BY CONVINCING SUCKERS THAT A GARBAGE BARGE WAS OCEANFRONT REAL ESTATE.
5-1-06 ©2006 Scott Adams, Inc./Dist. by UFS, Inc.
WOULD YOU LEND ME SOME MONEY SO I CAN OPEN MY OWN BUSINESS?
NO, BUT I KNOW SOME PEOPLE ON A BARGE WHO WOULD.

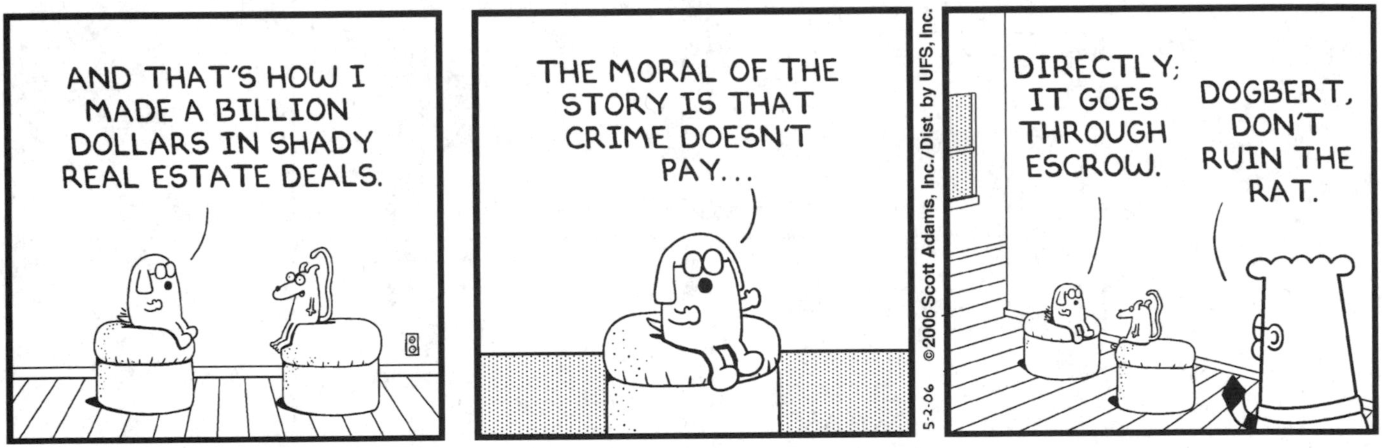
AND THAT'S HOW I MADE A BILLION DOLLARS IN SHADY REAL ESTATE DEALS.
THE MORAL OF THE STORY IS THAT CRIME DOESN'T PAY...
5-2-06 ©2006 Scott Adams, Inc./Dist. by UFS, Inc.
DIRECTLY; IT GOES THROUGH ESCROW.
DOGBERT, DON'T RUIN THE RAT.

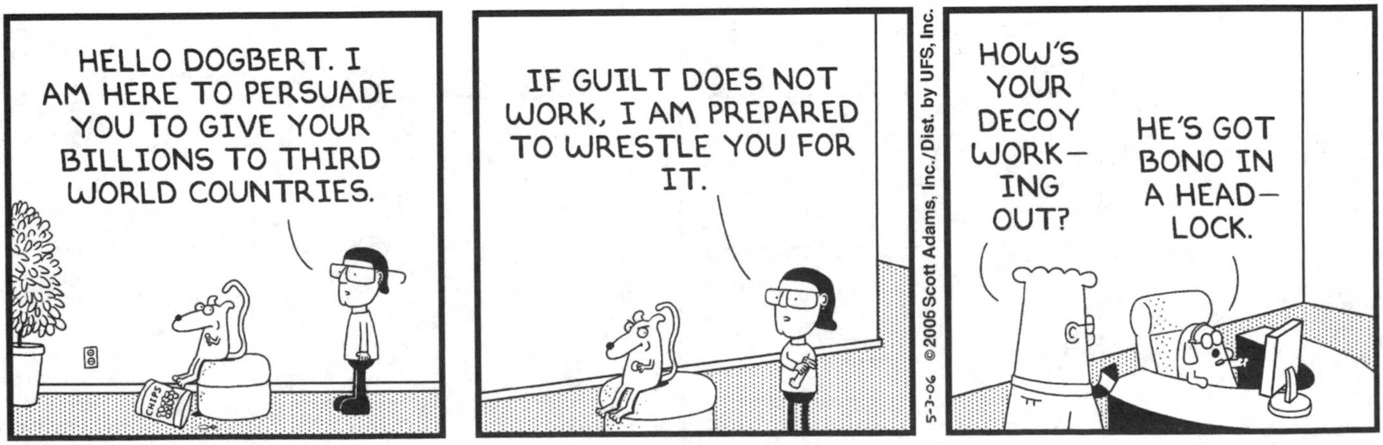
HELLO DOGBERT. I AM HERE TO PERSUADE YOU TO GIVE YOUR BILLIONS TO THIRD WORLD COUNTRIES.
CHIPS
IF GUILT DOES NOT WORK, I AM PREPARED TO WRESTLE YOU FOR IT.
5-3-06 ©2006 Scott Adams, Inc./Dist. by UFS, Inc.
HOW'S YOUR DECOY WORKING OUT?
HE'S GOT BONO IN A HEADLOCK.

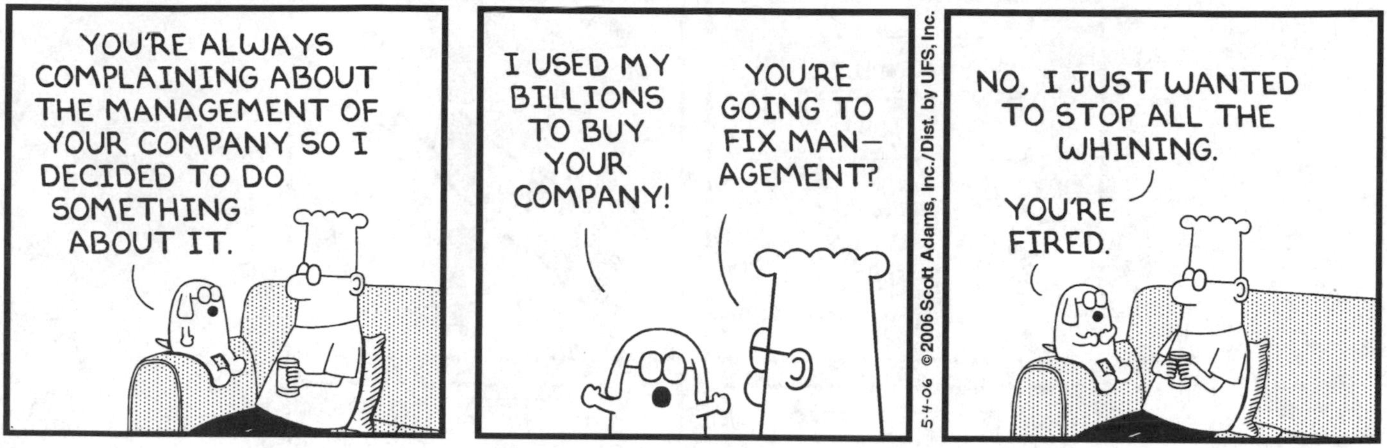
YOU'RE ALWAYS COMPLAINING ABOUT THE MANAGEMENT OF YOUR COMPANY SO I DECIDED TO DO SOMETHING ABOUT IT.
I USED MY BILLIONS TO BUY YOUR COMPANY!
YOU'RE GOING TO FIX MAN-AGEMENT?
NO, I JUST WANTED TO STOP ALL THE WHINING.
YOU'RE FIRED.
5-4-06 © 2006 Scott Adams, Inc./Dist. by UFS, Inc.

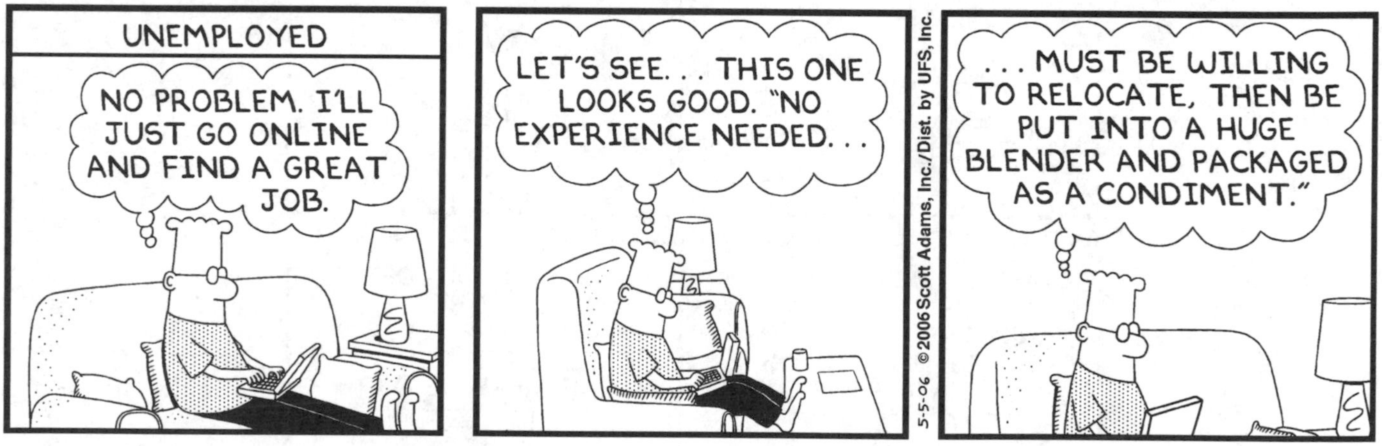
UNEMPLOYED
NO PROBLEM. I'LL JUST GO ONLINE AND FIND A GREAT JOB.
LET'S SEE... THIS ONE LOOKS GOOD. "NO EXPERIENCE NEEDED...
...MUST BE WILLING TO RELOCATE, THEN BE PUT INTO A HUGE BLENDER AND PACKAGED AS A CONDIMENT."
5-5-06 © 2006 Scott Adams, Inc./Dist. by UFS, Inc.

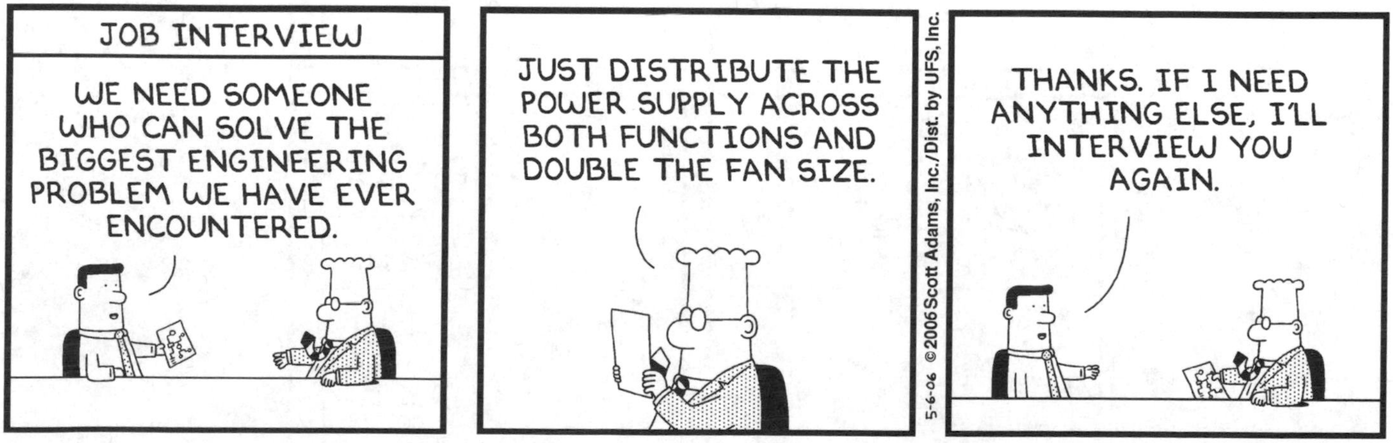
JOB INTERVIEW
WE NEED SOMEONE WHO CAN SOLVE THE BIGGEST ENGINEERING PROBLEM WE HAVE EVER ENCOUNTERED.
JUST DISTRIBUTE THE POWER SUPPLY ACROSS BOTH FUNCTIONS AND DOUBLE THE FAN SIZE.
THANKS. IF I NEED ANYTHING ELSE, I'LL INTERVIEW YOU AGAIN.
5-6-06 © 2006 Scott Adams, Inc./Dist. by UFS, Inc.

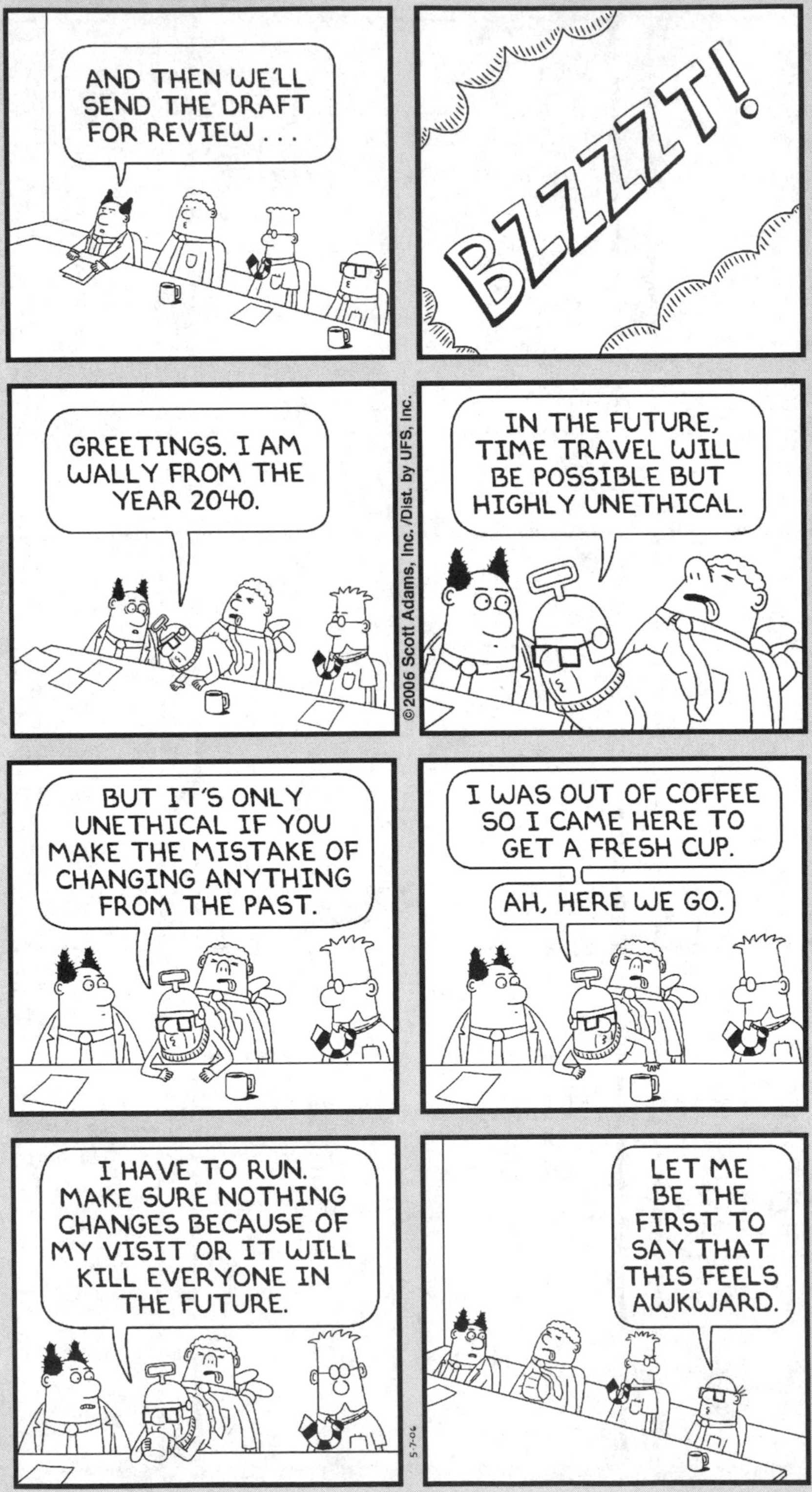
AND THEN WE'LL SEND THE DRAFT FOR REVIEW . . .
BZZZZZT!
GREETINGS. I AM WALLY FROM THE YEAR 2040.
IN THE FUTURE, TIME TRAVEL WILL BE POSSIBLE BUT HIGHLY UNETHICAL.
BUT IT'S ONLY UNETHICAL IF YOU MAKE THE MISTAKE OF CHANGING ANYTHING FROM THE PAST.
I WAS OUT OF COFFEE SO I CAME HERE TO GET A FRESH CUP.
AH, HERE WE GO.
I HAVE TO RUN. MAKE SURE NOTHING CHANGES BECAUSE OF MY VISIT OR IT WILL KILL EVERYONE IN THE FUTURE.
LET ME BE THE FIRST TO SAY THAT THIS FEELS AWKWARD.

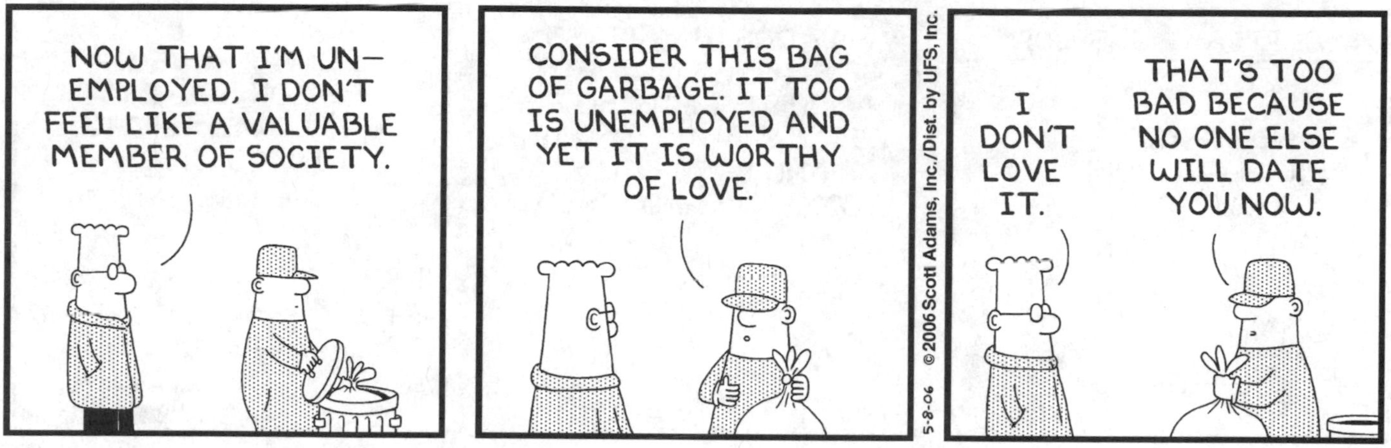
NOW THAT I'M UN-EMPLOYED, I DON'T FEEL LIKE A VALUABLE MEMBER OF SOCIETY.
CONSIDER THIS BAG OF GARBAGE. IT TOO IS UNEMPLOYED AND YET IT IS WORTHY OF LOVE.
5-8-06 © 2006 Scott Adams, Inc./Dist. by UFS, Inc.
I DON'T LOVE IT.
THAT'S TOO BAD BECAUSE NO ONE ELSE WILL DATE YOU NOW.

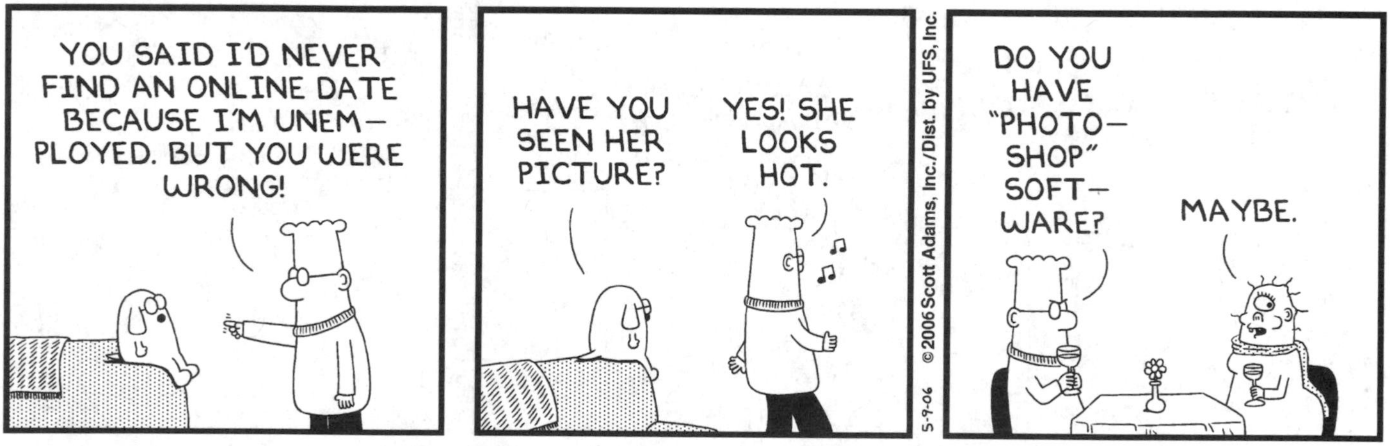
YOU SAID I'D NEVER FIND AN ONLINE DATE BECAUSE I'M UNEM-PLOYED. BUT YOU WERE WRONG!
HAVE YOU SEEN HER PICTURE?
YES! SHE LOOKS HOT.
5-9-06 © 2006 Scott Adams, Inc./Dist. by UFS, Inc.
DO YOU HAVE "PHOTO-SHOP" SOFT-WARE?
MAYBE.

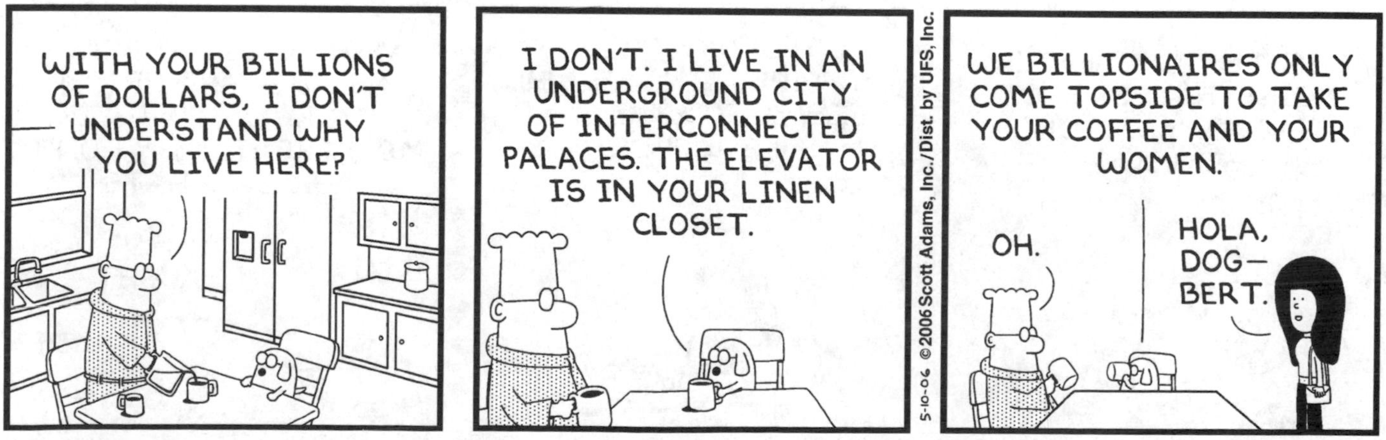
WITH YOUR BILLIONS OF DOLLARS, I DON'T UNDERSTAND WHY YOU LIVE HERE?
I DON'T. I LIVE IN AN UNDERGROUND CITY OF INTERCONNECTED PALACES. THE ELEVATOR IS IN YOUR LINEN CLOSET.
5-10-06 © 2006 Scott Adams, Inc./Dist. by UFS, Inc.
WE BILLIONAIRES ONLY COME TOPSIDE TO TAKE YOUR COFFEE AND YOUR WOMEN.
OH.
HOLA, DOG-BERT.

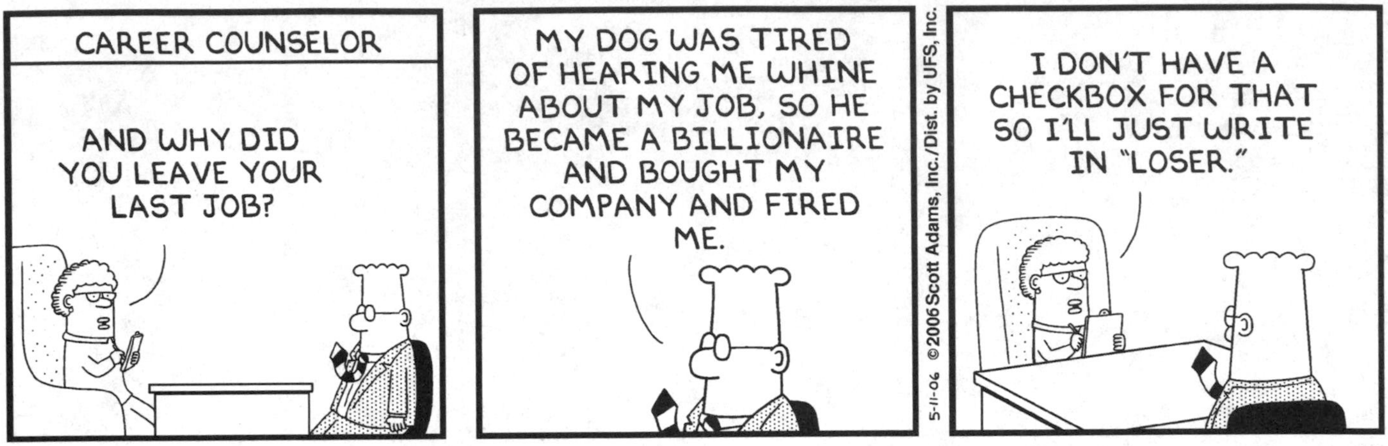
CAREER COUNSELOR
AND WHY DID YOU LEAVE YOUR LAST JOB?
MY DOG WAS TIRED OF HEARING ME WHINE ABOUT MY JOB, SO HE BECAME A BILLIONAIRE AND BOUGHT MY COMPANY AND FIRED ME.
5-11-06 ©2006 Scott Adams, Inc./Dist. by UFS, Inc.
I DON'T HAVE A CHECKBOX FOR THAT SO I'LL JUST WRITE IN "LOSER."

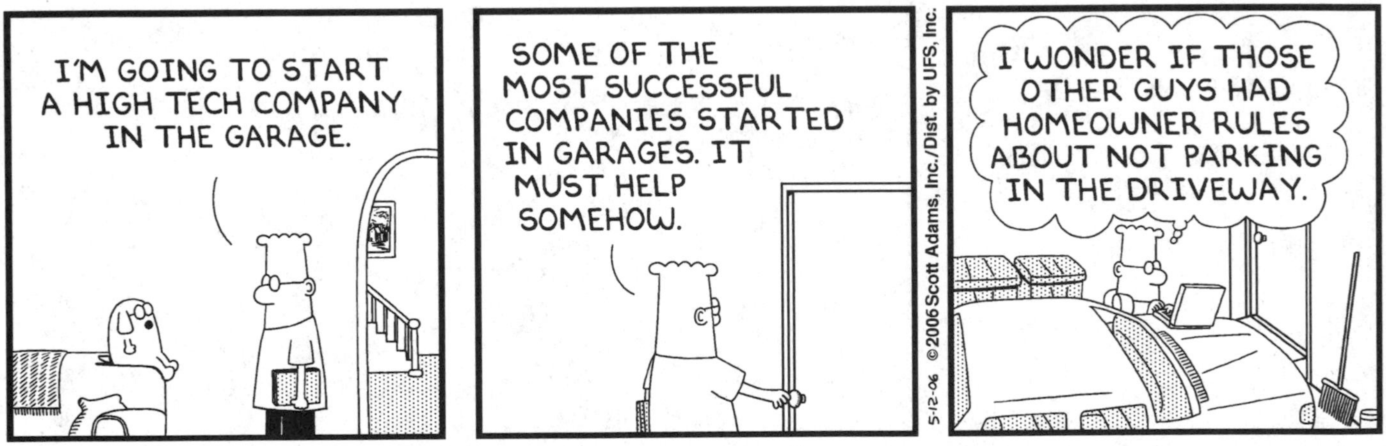
I'M GOING TO START A HIGH TECH COMPANY IN THE GARAGE.
SOME OF THE MOST SUCCESSFUL COMPANIES STARTED IN GARAGES. IT MUST HELP SOMEHOW.
5-12-06 ©2006 Scott Adams, Inc./Dist. by UFS, Inc.
I WONDER IF THOSE OTHER GUYS HAD HOMEOWNER RULES ABOUT NOT PARKING IN THE DRIVEWAY.

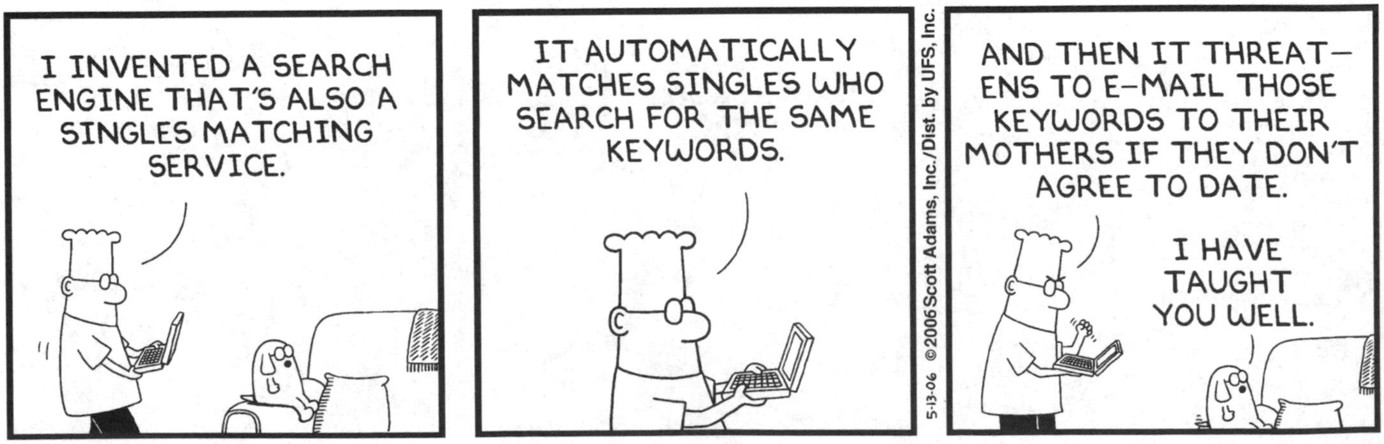
I INVENTED A SEARCH ENGINE THAT'S ALSO A SINGLES MATCHING SERVICE.
IT AUTOMATICALLY MATCHES SINGLES WHO SEARCH FOR THE SAME KEYWORDS.
5-13-06 ©2006 Scott Adams, Inc./Dist. by UFS, Inc.
AND THEN IT THREAT-ENS TO E-MAIL THOSE KEYWORDS TO THEIR MOTHERS IF THEY DON'T AGREE TO DATE.
I HAVE TAUGHT YOU WELL.

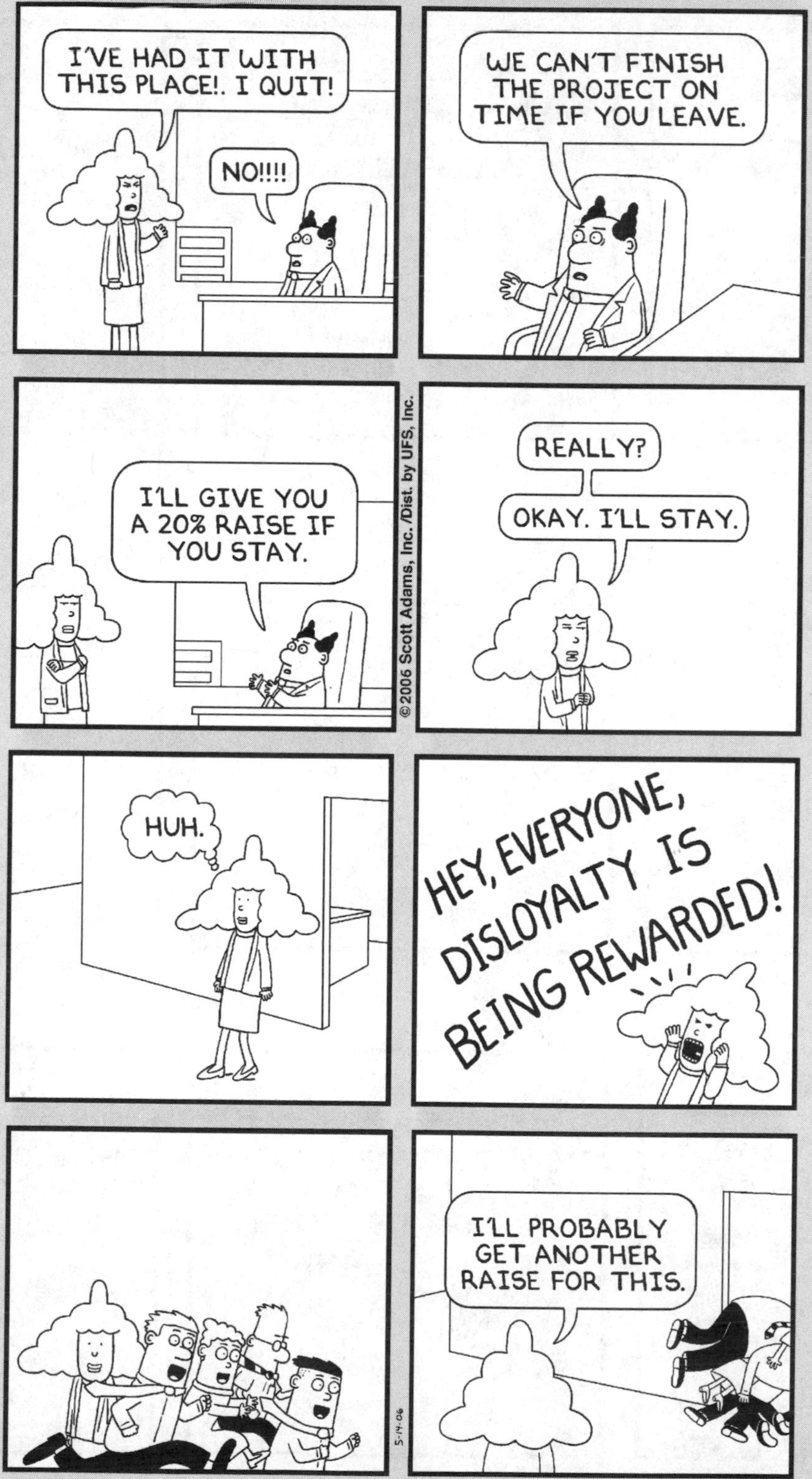
I'VE HAD IT WITH THIS PLACE!. I QUIT!
NO!!!!
WE CAN'T FINISH THE PROJECT ON TIME IF YOU LEAVE.
I'LL GIVE YOU A 20% RAISE IF YOU STAY.
REALLY?
OKAY. I'LL STAY.
HUH.
HEY, EVERYONE, DISLOYALTY IS BEING REWARDED!
I'LL PROBABLY GET ANOTHER RAISE FOR THIS.
©2006 Scott Adams, Inc./Dist. by UFS, Inc.
5-14-06

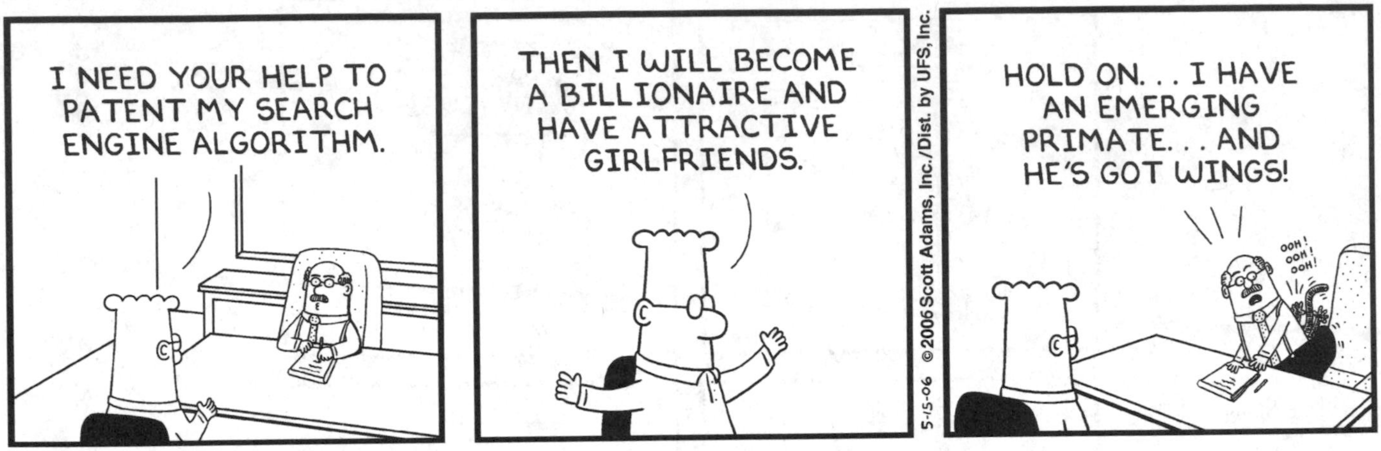
I NEED YOUR HELP TO PATENT MY SEARCH ENGINE ALGORITHM.
THEN I WILL BECOME A BILLIONAIRE AND HAVE ATTRACTIVE GIRLFRIENDS.
5-15-06 ©2006 Scott Adams, Inc./Dist. by UFS, Inc.
HOLD ON. . . I HAVE AN EMERGING PRIMATE. . . AND HE'S GOT WINGS!
OOH! OOH! OOH!

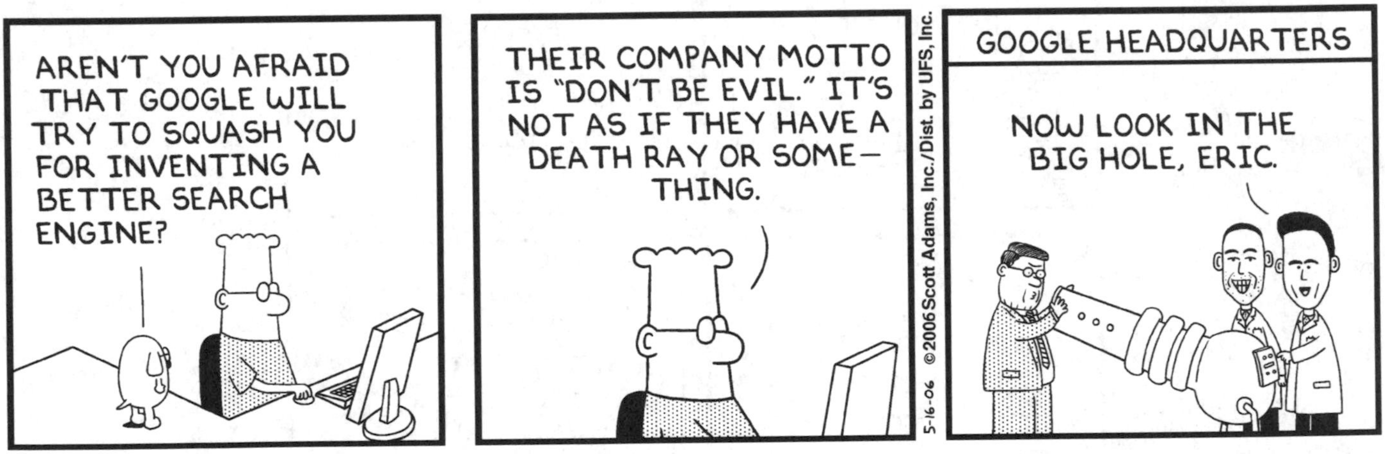
AREN'T YOU AFRAID THAT GOOGLE WILL TRY TO SQUASH YOU FOR INVENTING A BETTER SEARCH ENGINE?
THEIR COMPANY MOTTO IS "DON'T BE EVIL." IT'S NOT AS IF THEY HAVE A DEATH RAY OR SOME-THING.
5-16-06 ©2006 Scott Adams, Inc./Dist. by UFS, Inc.
GOOGLE HEADQUARTERS
NOW LOOK IN THE BIG HOLE, ERIC.

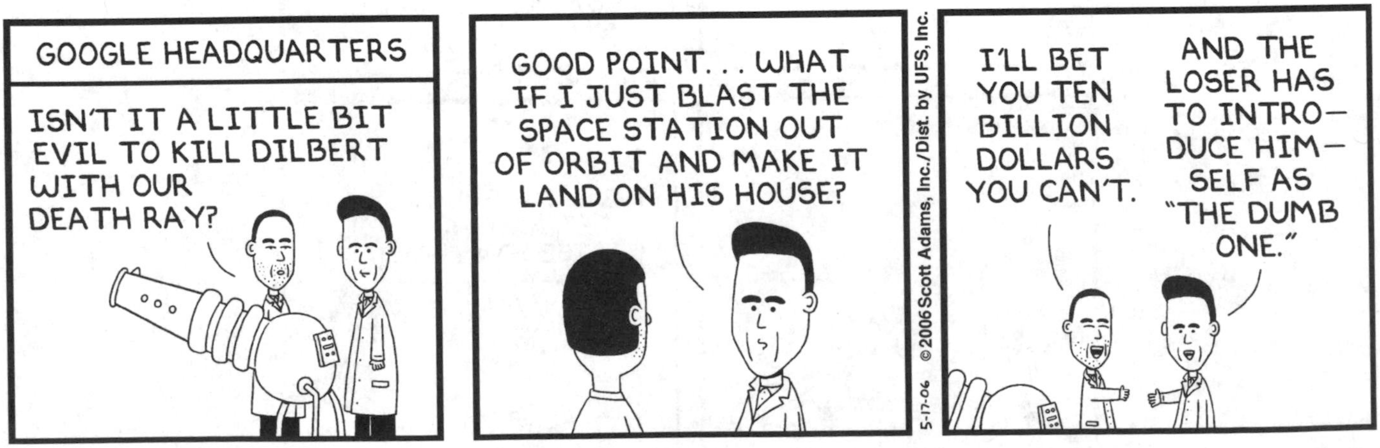
GOOGLE HEADQUARTERS
ISN'T IT A LITTLE BIT EVIL TO KILL DILBERT WITH OUR DEATH RAY?
GOOD POINT. . . WHAT IF I JUST BLAST THE SPACE STATION OUT OF ORBIT AND MAKE IT LAND ON HIS HOUSE?
5-17-06 ©2006 Scott Adams, Inc./Dist. by UFS, Inc.
I'LL BET YOU TEN BILLION DOLLARS YOU CAN'T.
AND THE LOSER HAS TO INTRO-DUCE HIM-SELF AS "THE DUMB ONE."

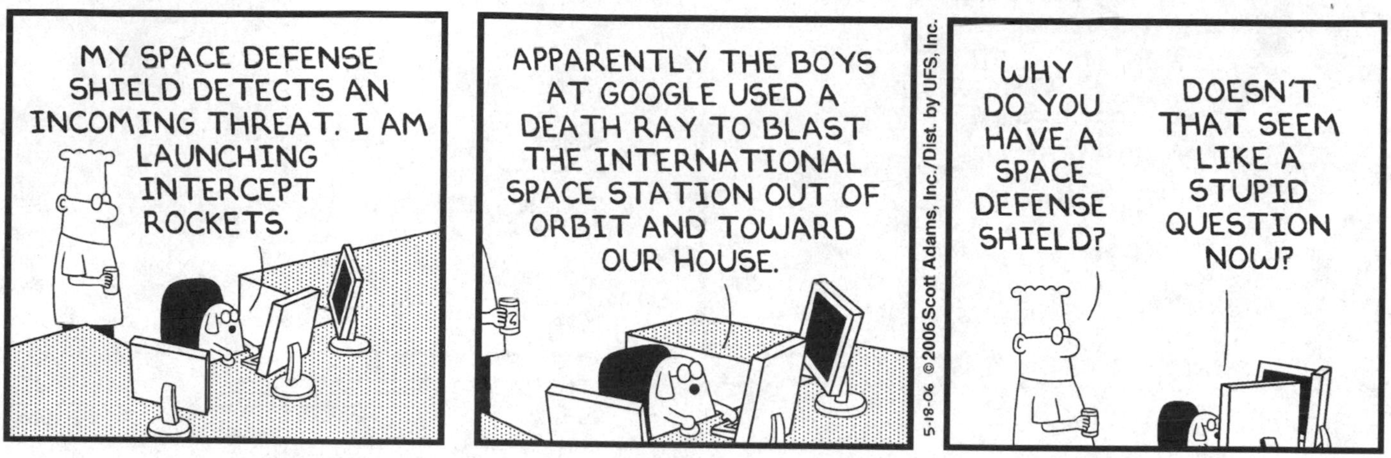
MY SPACE DEFENSE SHIELD DETECTS AN INCOMING THREAT. I AM LAUNCHING INTERCEPT ROCKETS.
APPARENTLY THE BOYS AT GOOGLE USED A DEATH RAY TO BLAST THE INTERNATIONAL SPACE STATION OUT OF ORBIT AND TOWARD OUR HOUSE.
5-18-06 © 2006 Scott Adams, Inc./Dist. by UFS, Inc.
WHY DO YOU HAVE A SPACE DEFENSE SHIELD?
DOESN'T THAT SEEM LIKE A STUPID QUESTION NOW?

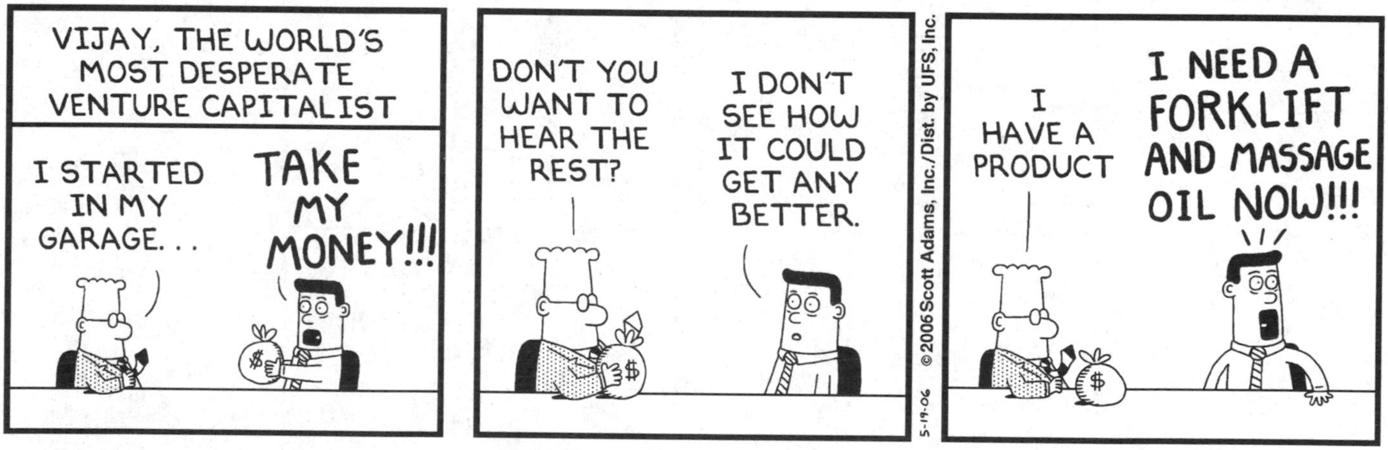
VIJAY, THE WORLD'S MOST DESPERATE VENTURE CAPITALIST
I STARTED IN MY GARAGE. . .
TAKE MY MONEY!!!
DON'T YOU WANT TO HEAR THE REST?
I DON'T SEE HOW IT COULD GET ANY BETTER.
5-19-06 © 2006 Scott Adams, Inc./Dist. by UFS, Inc.
I HAVE A PRODUCT
I NEED A FORKLIFT AND MASSAGE OIL NOW!!!

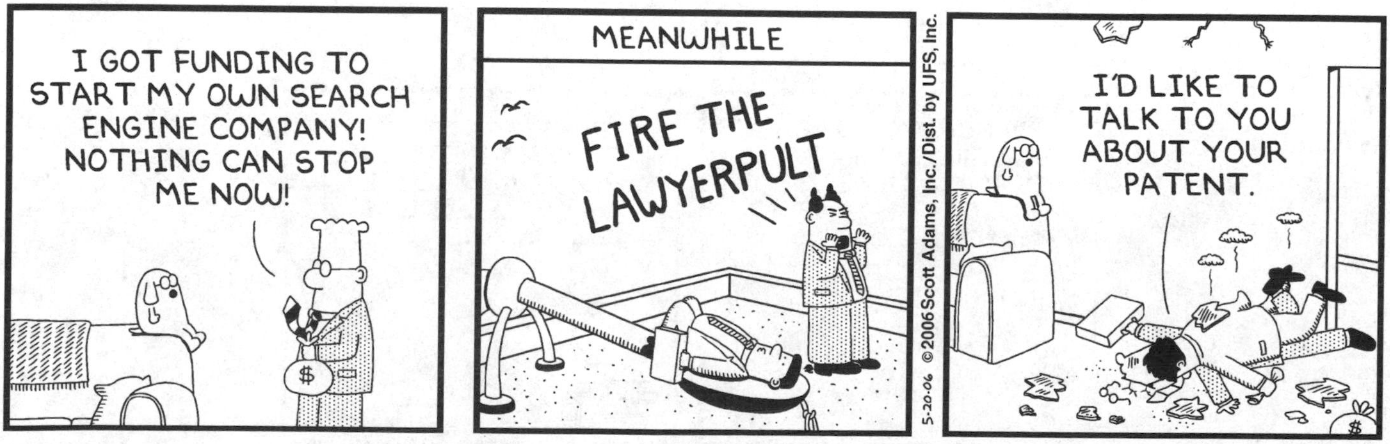
I GOT FUNDING TO START MY OWN SEARCH ENGINE COMPANY! NOTHING CAN STOP ME NOW!
MEANWHILE
FIRE THE LAWYERPULT
5-20-06 © 2006 Scott Adams, Inc./Dist. by UFS, Inc.
I'D LIKE TO TALK TO YOU ABOUT YOUR PATENT.

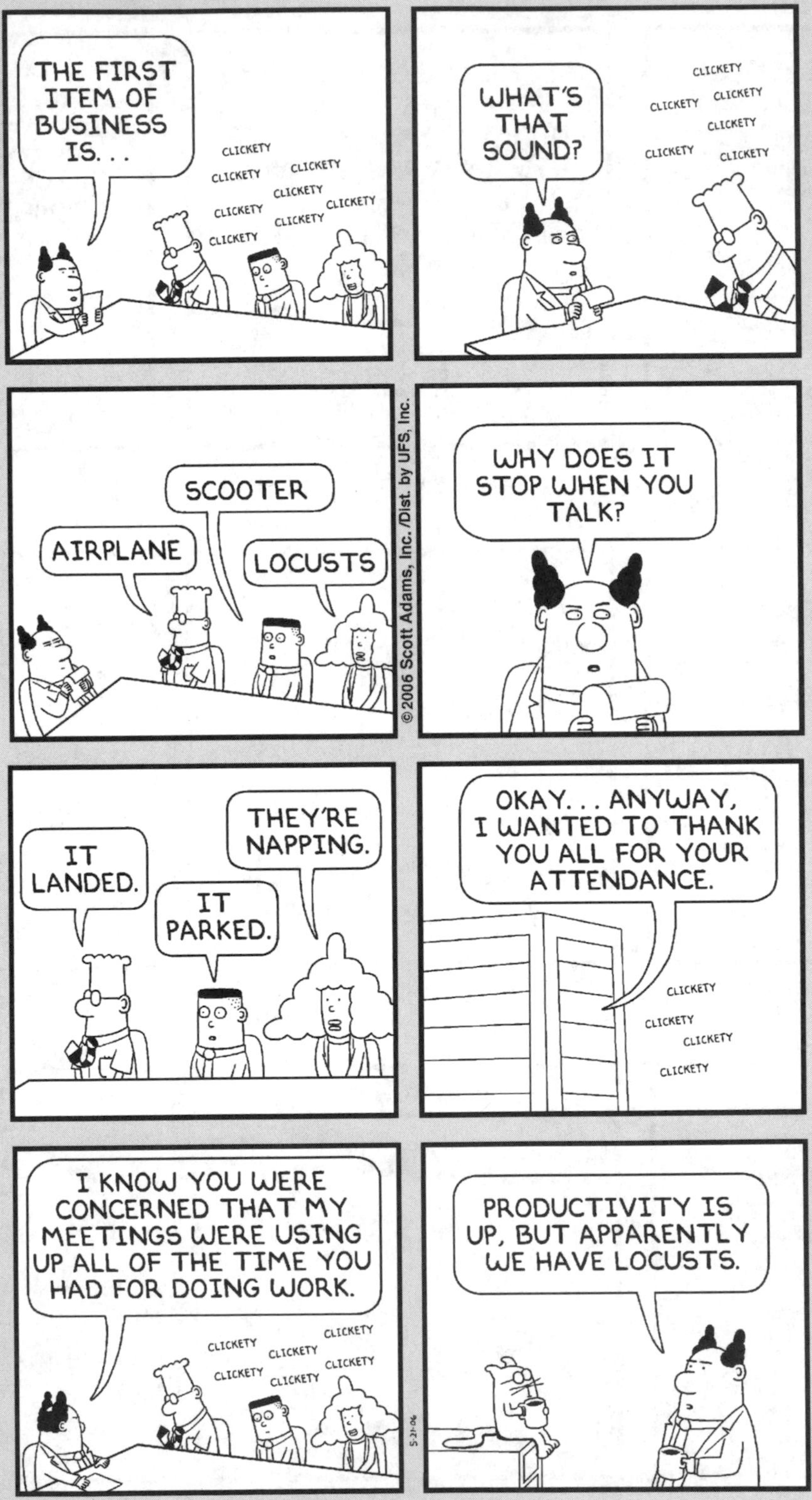
THE FIRST ITEM OF BUSINESS IS. . .
CLICKETY CLICKETY CLICKETY CLICKETY CLICKETY CLICKETY CLICKETY CLICKETY
WHAT'S THAT SOUND?
CLICKETY CLICKETY CLICKETY CLICKETY CLICKETY CLICKETY
AIRPLANE
SCOOTER
LOCUSTS
©2006 Scott Adams, Inc./Dist. by UFS, Inc.
WHY DOES IT STOP WHEN YOU TALK?
IT LANDED.
IT PARKED.
THEY'RE NAPPING.
OKAY. . . ANYWAY, I WANTED TO THANK YOU ALL FOR YOUR ATTENDANCE.
CLICKETY CLICKETY CLICKETY CLICKETY
I KNOW YOU WERE CONCERNED THAT MY MEETINGS WERE USING UP ALL OF THE TIME YOU HAD FOR DOING WORK.
CLICKETY CLICKETY CLICKETY CLICKETY CLICKETY CLICKETY
PRODUCTIVITY IS UP, BUT APPARENTLY WE HAVE LOCUSTS.

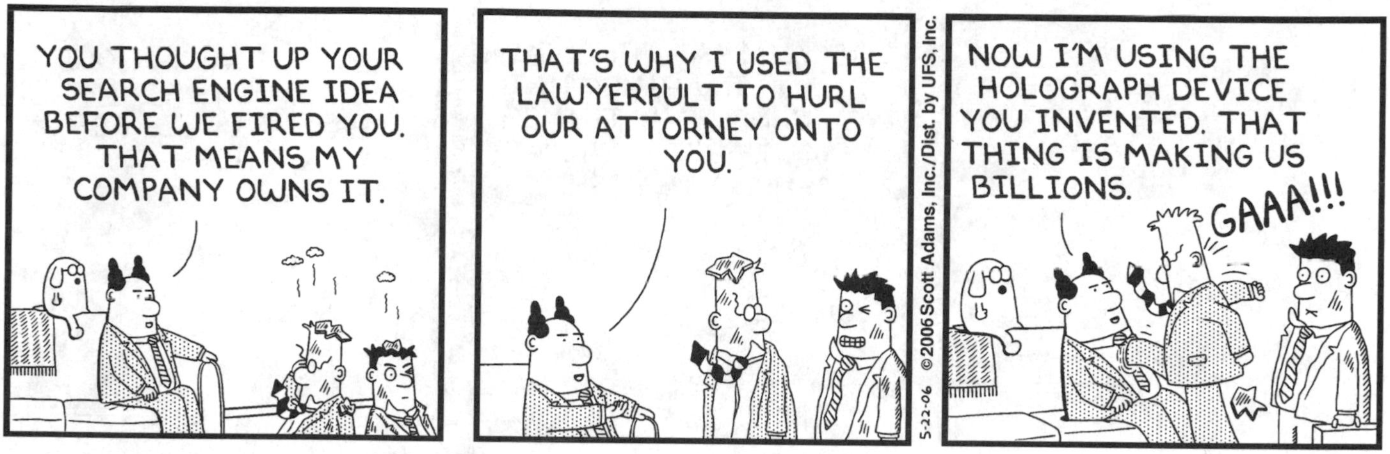
YOU THOUGHT UP YOUR SEARCH ENGINE IDEA BEFORE WE FIRED YOU. THAT MEANS MY COMPANY OWNS IT.
THAT'S WHY I USED THE LAWYERPULT TO HURL OUR ATTORNEY ONTO YOU.
5-22-06 © 2006 Scott Adams, Inc./Dist. by UFS, Inc.
NOW I'M USING THE HOLOGRAPH DEVICE YOU INVENTED. THAT THING IS MAKING US BILLIONS.
GAAA!!!

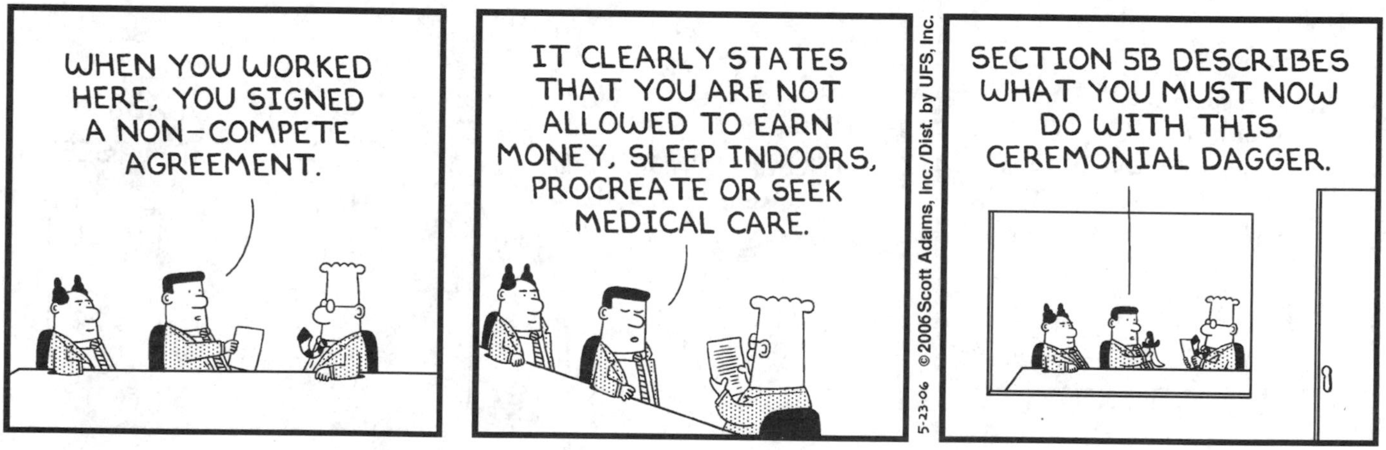
WHEN YOU WORKED HERE, YOU SIGNED A NON-COMPETE AGREEMENT.
IT CLEARLY STATES THAT YOU ARE NOT ALLOWED TO EARN MONEY, SLEEP INDOORS, PROCREATE OR SEEK MEDICAL CARE.
5-23-06 © 2006 Scott Adams, Inc./Dist. by UFS, Inc.
SECTION 5B DESCRIBES WHAT YOU MUST NOW DO WITH THIS CEREMONIAL DAGGER.

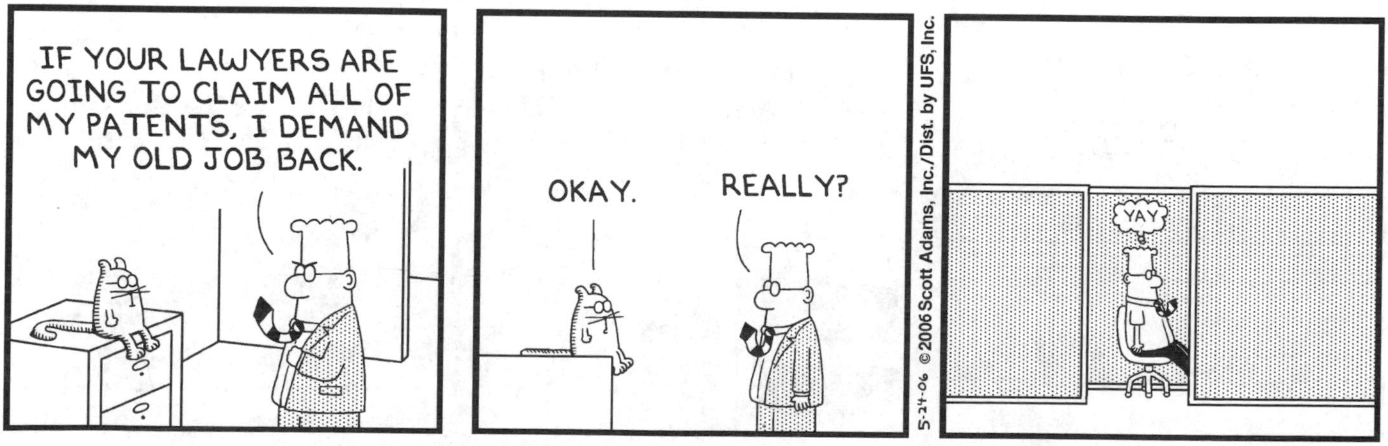
IF YOUR LAWYERS ARE GOING TO CLAIM ALL OF MY PATENTS, I DEMAND MY OLD JOB BACK.
OKAY.
REALLY?
5-24-06 © 2006 Scott Adams, Inc./Dist. by UFS, Inc.
YAY

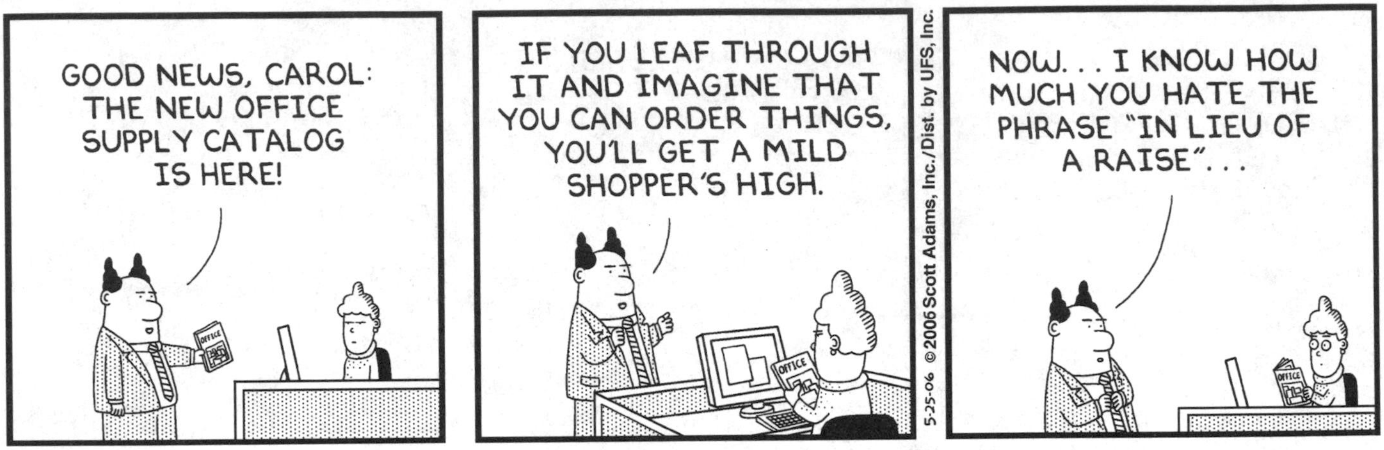
GOOD NEWS, CAROL: THE NEW OFFICE SUPPLY CATALOG IS HERE!
OFFICE
IF YOU LEAF THROUGH IT AND IMAGINE THAT YOU CAN ORDER THINGS, YOU'LL GET A MILD SHOPPER'S HIGH.
OFFICE
5-25-06 ©2006 Scott Adams, Inc./Dist. by UFS, Inc.
NOW. . . I KNOW HOW MUCH YOU HATE THE PHRASE "IN LIEU OF A RAISE". . .
OFFICE

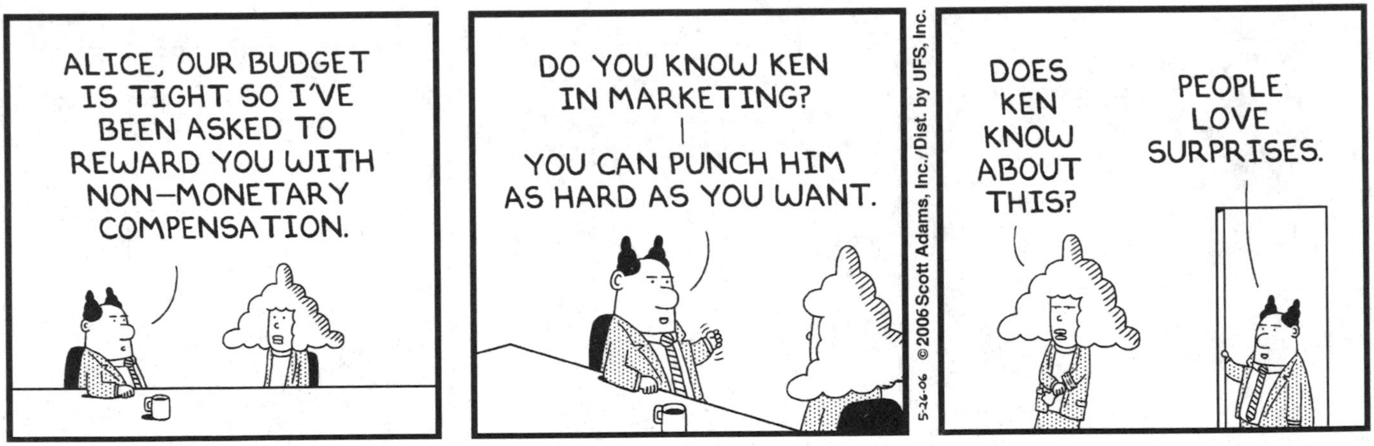
ALICE, OUR BUDGET IS TIGHT SO I'VE BEEN ASKED TO REWARD YOU WITH NON-MONETARY COMPENSATION.
DO YOU KNOW KEN IN MARKETING?
YOU CAN PUNCH HIM AS HARD AS YOU WANT.
5-26-06 ©2006 Scott Adams, Inc./Dist. by UFS, Inc.
DOES KEN KNOW ABOUT THIS?
PEOPLE LOVE SURPRISES.

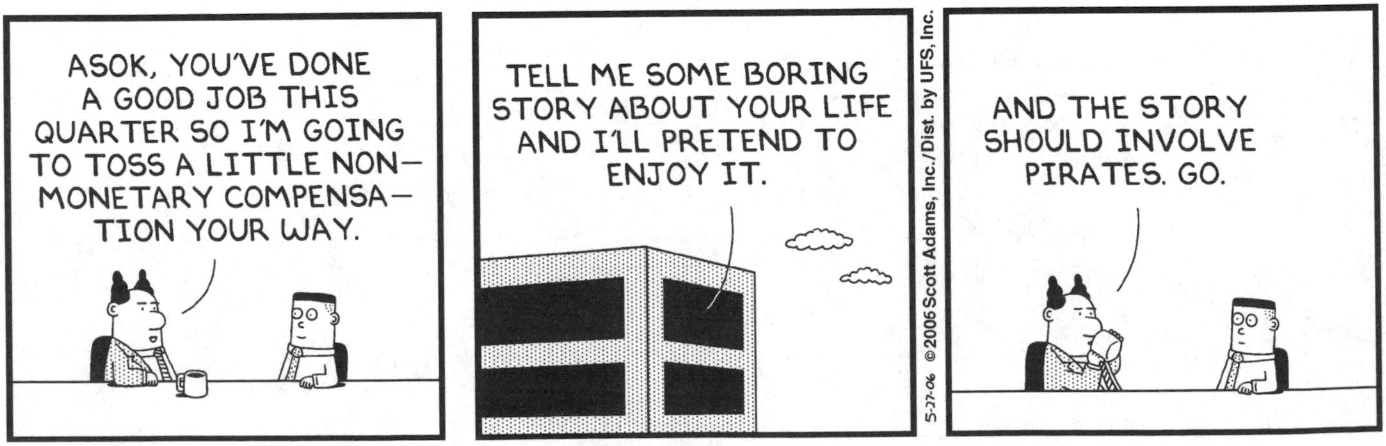
ASOK, YOU'VE DONE A GOOD JOB THIS QUARTER SO I'M GOING TO TOSS A LITTLE NON-MONETARY COMPENSATION YOUR WAY.
TELL ME SOME BORING STORY ABOUT YOUR LIFE AND I'LL PRETEND TO ENJOY IT.
5-27-06 ©2006 Scott Adams, Inc./Dist. by UFS, Inc.
AND THE STORY SHOULD INVOLVE PIRATES. GO.

HERE'S A GAME CARD THAT GIVES YOU A CHANCE TO WIN GROCERIES.
NO THANKS. JUST TAKE A PENNY OFF OF MY BILL AND WE'LL CALL IT EVEN.
UM. . . I CAN'T DO THAT.
WHY NOT? ISN'T THAT GAME CARD WORTH A PENNY?
©2006 Scott Adams, Inc./Dist. by UFS, Inc.
WE DON'T HAVE A PROCEDURE.
HOW'S THAT MY PROBLEM?
LOOK, MAYBE YOU COULD EAT SOMETHING THAT'S WORTH A PENNY AND I'LL LOOK THE OTHER WAY.
HOW ABOUT A GRAPE? I LIKE GRAPES.
IT WOULD HAVE TO BE ONE THAT'S BEEN ON THE FLOOR.
5-28-06
IT TASTED LIKE VICTORY.

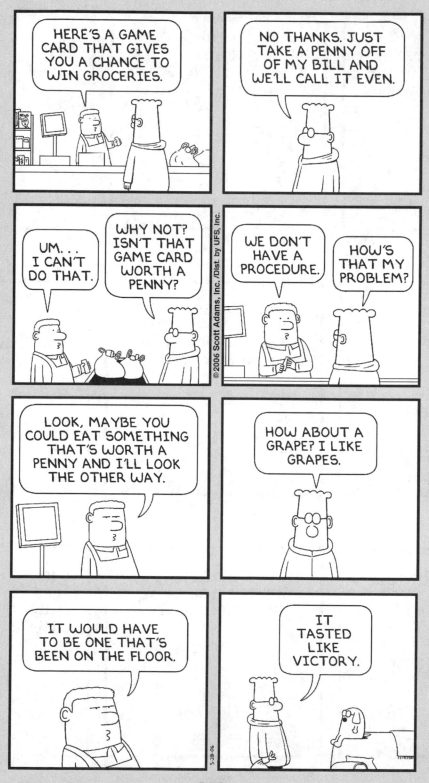

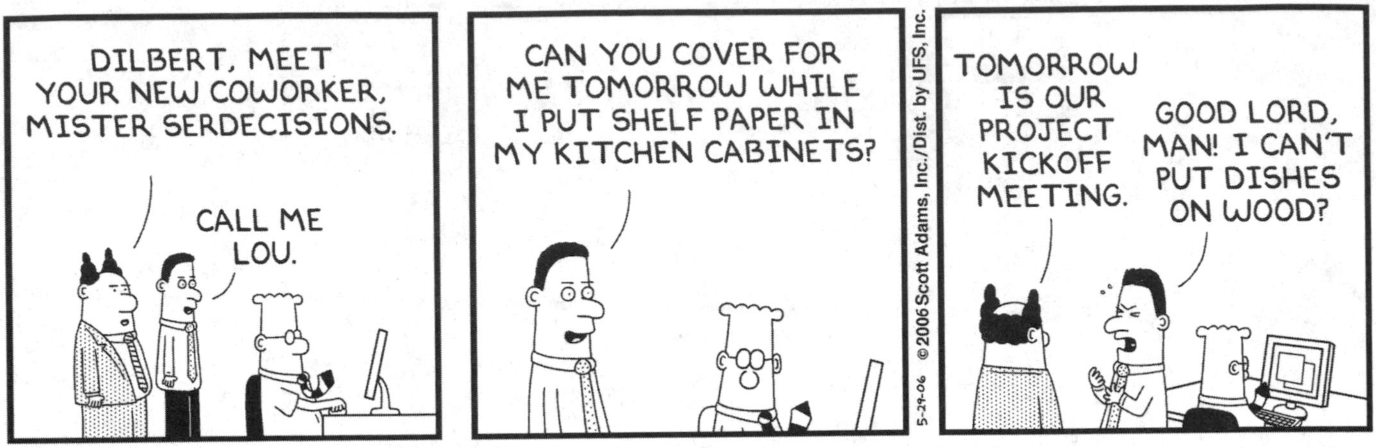
DILBERT, MEET YOUR NEW COWORKER, MISTER SERDECISIONS.
CALL ME LOU.
CAN YOU COVER FOR ME TOMORROW WHILE I PUT SHELF PAPER IN MY KITCHEN CABINETS?
5-29-06 © 2006 Scott Adams, Inc./Dist. by UFS, Inc.
TOMORROW IS OUR PROJECT KICKOFF MEETING.
GOOD LORD, MAN! I CAN'T PUT DISHES ON WOOD?

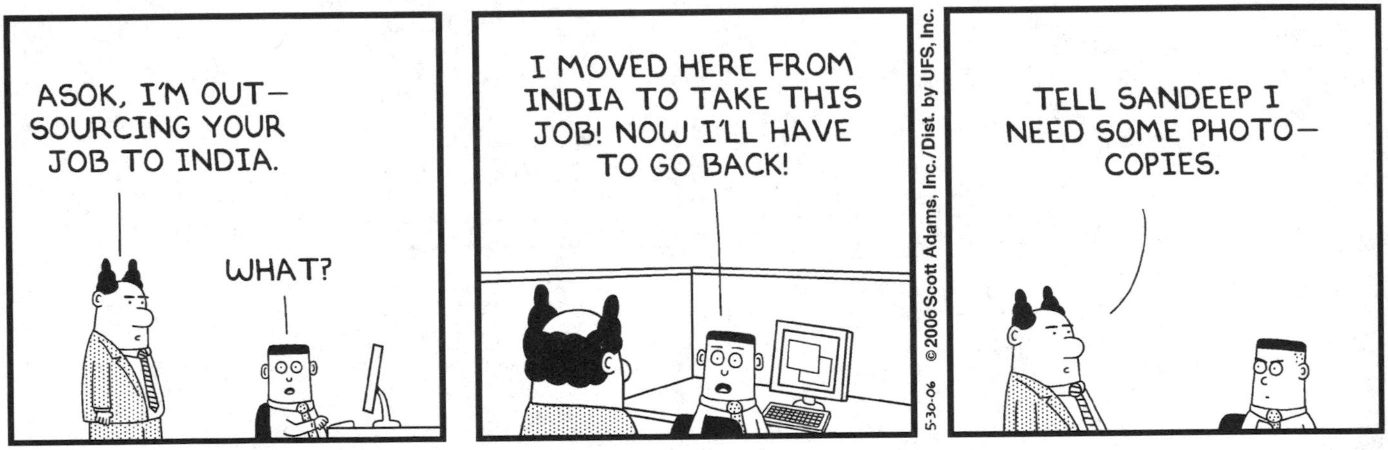
ASOK, I'M OUT-SOURCING YOUR JOB TO INDIA.
WHAT?
I MOVED HERE FROM INDIA TO TAKE THIS JOB! NOW I'LL HAVE TO GO BACK!
5-30-06 © 2006 Scott Adams, Inc./Dist. by UFS, Inc.
TELL SANDEEP I NEED SOME PHOTO-COPIES.

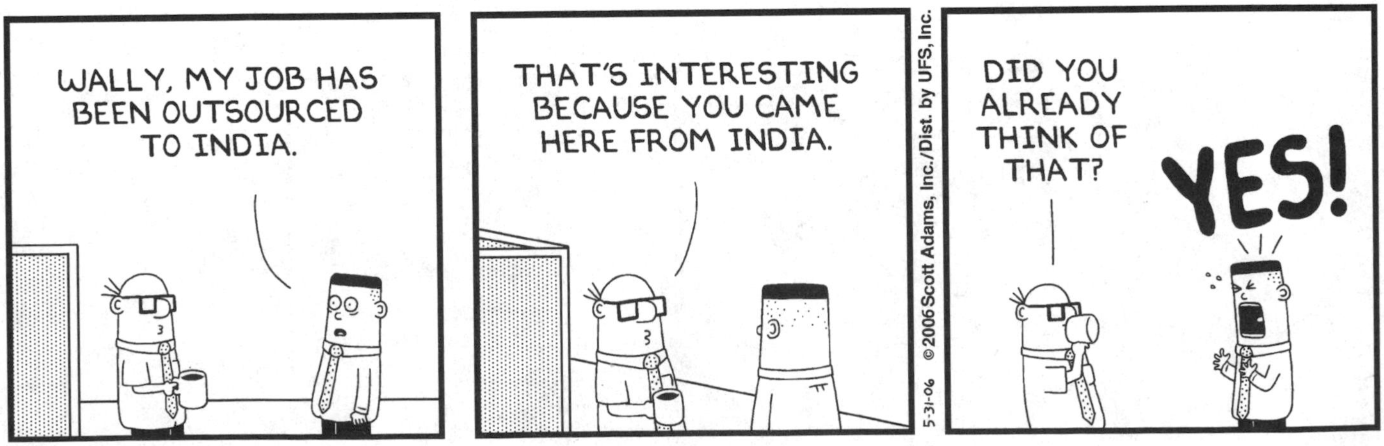
WALLY, MY JOB HAS BEEN OUTSOURCED TO INDIA.
THAT'S INTERESTING BECAUSE YOU CAME HERE FROM INDIA.
5-31-06 © 2006 Scott Adams, Inc./Dist. by UFS, Inc.
DID YOU ALREADY THINK OF THAT?
YES!

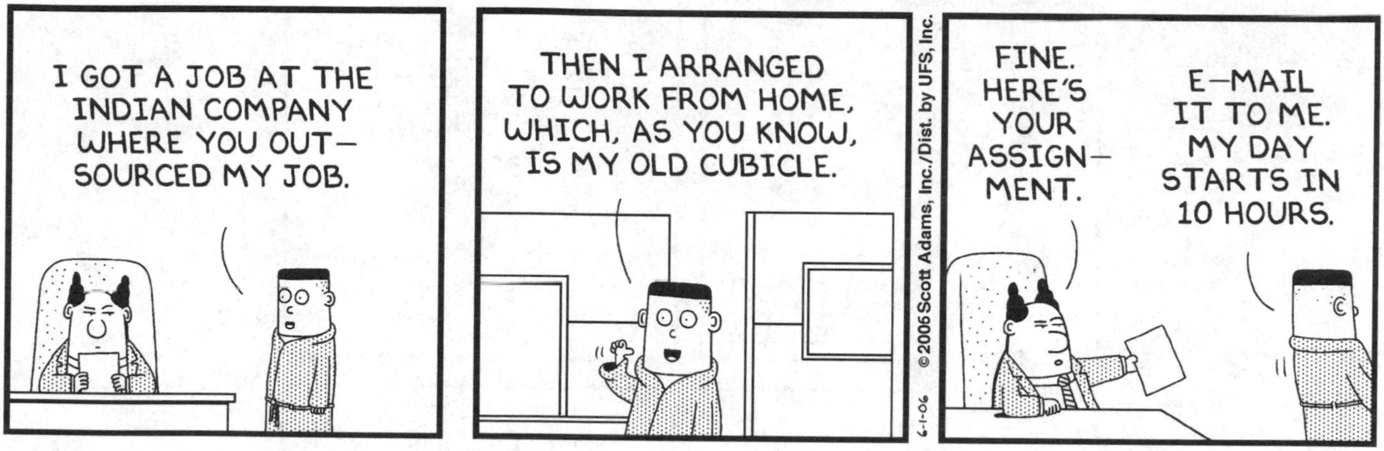
I GOT A JOB AT THE INDIAN COMPANY WHERE YOU OUT-SOURCED MY JOB.
THEN I ARRANGED TO WORK FROM HOME, WHICH, AS YOU KNOW, IS MY OLD CUBICLE.
FINE. HERE'S YOUR ASSIGN-MENT.
E-MAIL IT TO ME. MY DAY STARTS IN 10 HOURS.
6-1-06 ©2006 Scott Adams, Inc./Dist. by UFS, Inc.

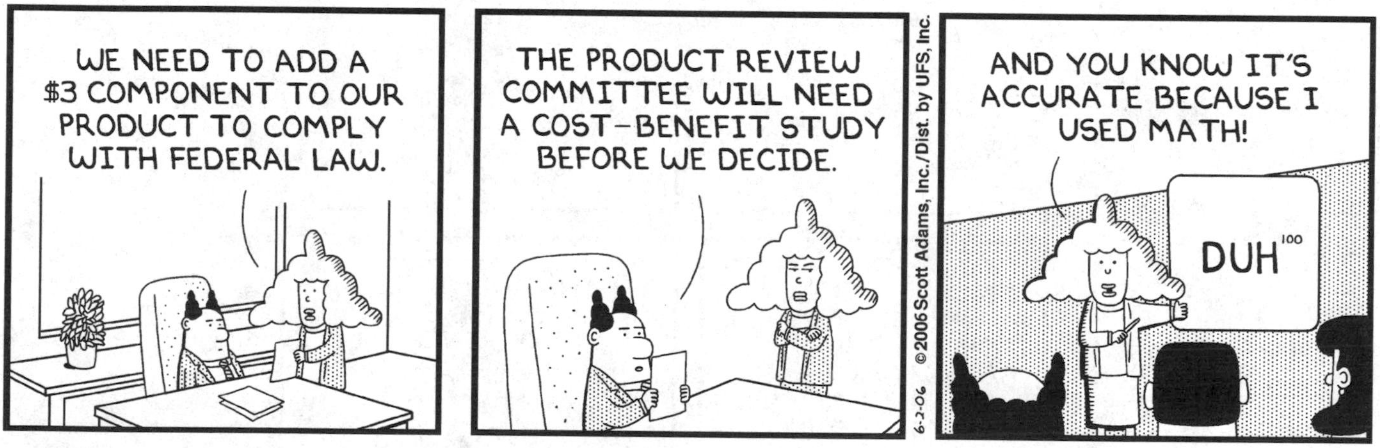
WE NEED TO ADD A $3 COMPONENT TO OUR PRODUCT TO COMPLY WITH FEDERAL LAW.
THE PRODUCT REVIEW COMMITTEE WILL NEED A COST-BENEFIT STUDY BEFORE WE DECIDE.
AND YOU KNOW IT'S ACCURATE BECAUSE I USED MATH!
DUH 100
6-2-06 ©2006 Scott Adams, Inc./Dist. by UFS, Inc.

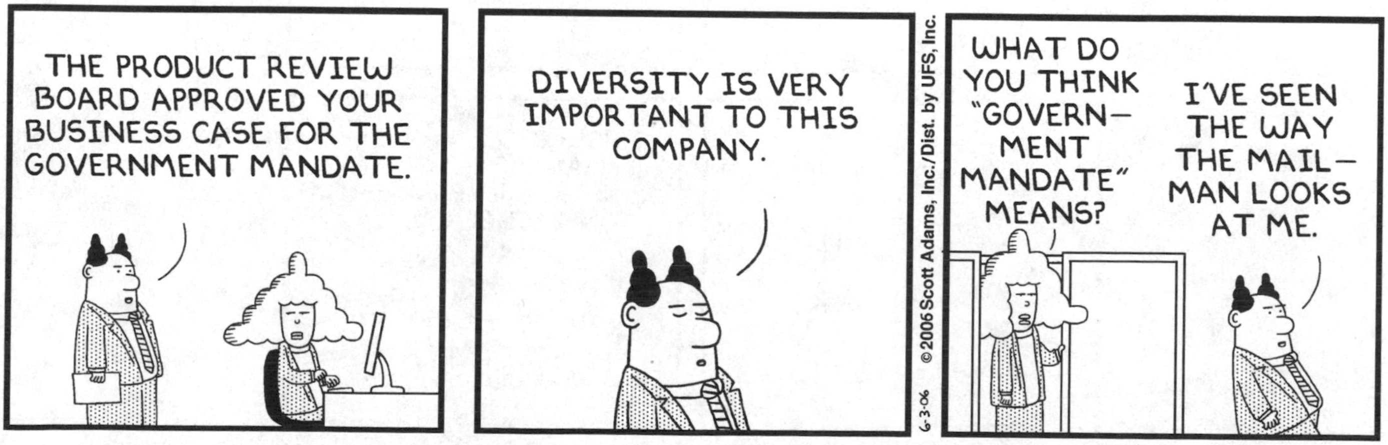
THE PRODUCT REVIEW BOARD APPROVED YOUR BUSINESS CASE FOR THE GOVERNMENT MANDATE.
DIVERSITY IS VERY IMPORTANT TO THIS COMPANY.
WHAT DO YOU THINK "GOVERN-MENT MANDATE" MEANS?
I'VE SEEN THE WAY THE MAIL-MAN LOOKS AT ME.
6-3-06 ©2006 Scott Adams, Inc./Dist. by UFS, Inc.

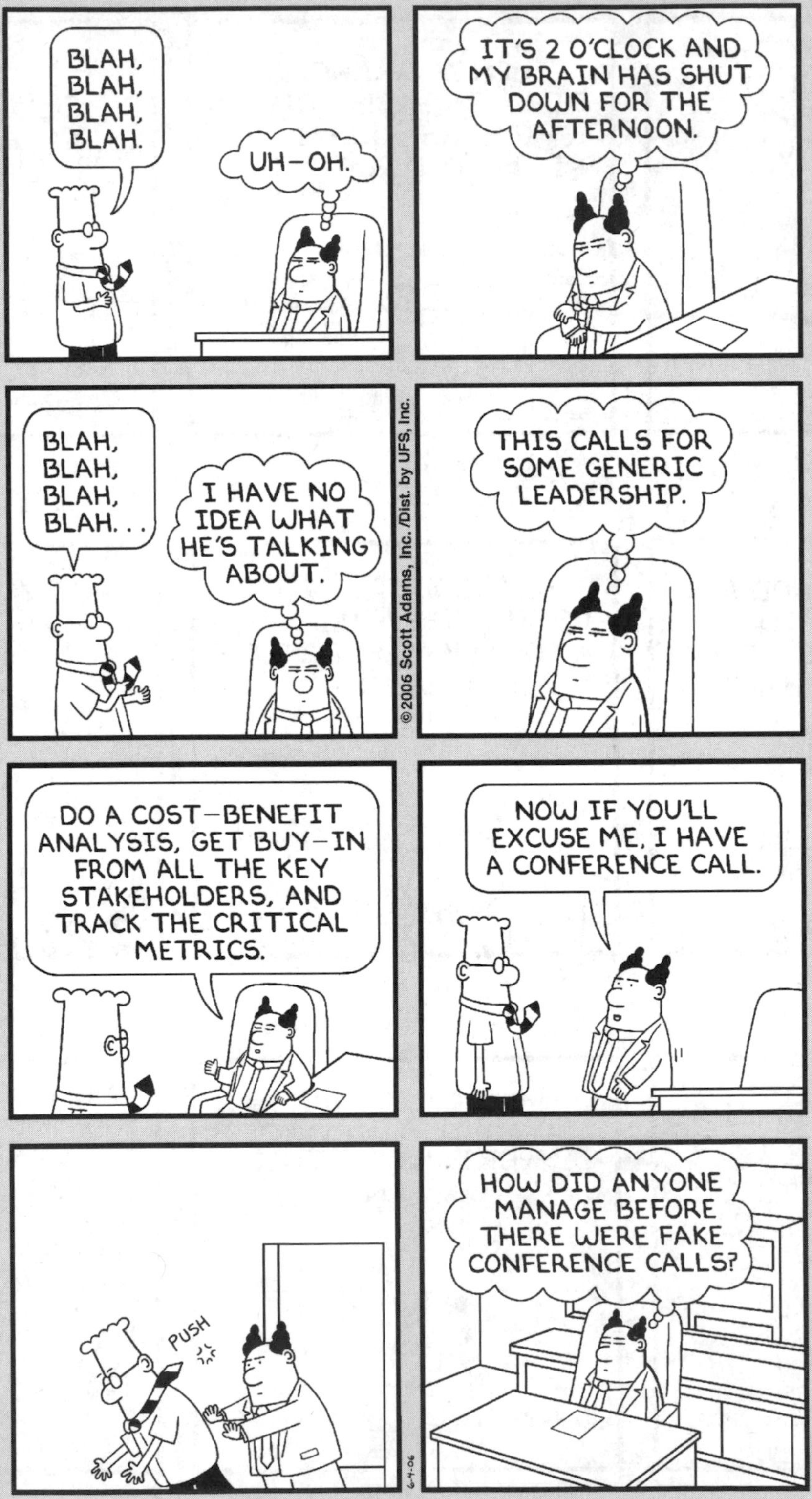

BLAH, BLAH, BLAH, BLAH.
UH-OH.
IT'S 2 O'CLOCK AND MY BRAIN HAS SHUT DOWN FOR THE AFTERNOON.
BLAH, BLAH, BLAH, BLAH. . .
I HAVE NO IDEA WHAT HE'S TALKING ABOUT.
© 2006 Scott Adams, Inc./Dist. by UFS, Inc.
THIS CALLS FOR SOME GENERIC LEADERSHIP.
DO A COST-BENEFIT ANALYSIS, GET BUY-IN FROM ALL THE KEY STAKEHOLDERS, AND TRACK THE CRITICAL METRICS.
NOW IF YOU'LL EXCUSE ME, I HAVE A CONFERENCE CALL.
PUSH
6-4-06
HOW DID ANYONE MANAGE BEFORE THERE WERE FAKE CONFERENCE CALLS?

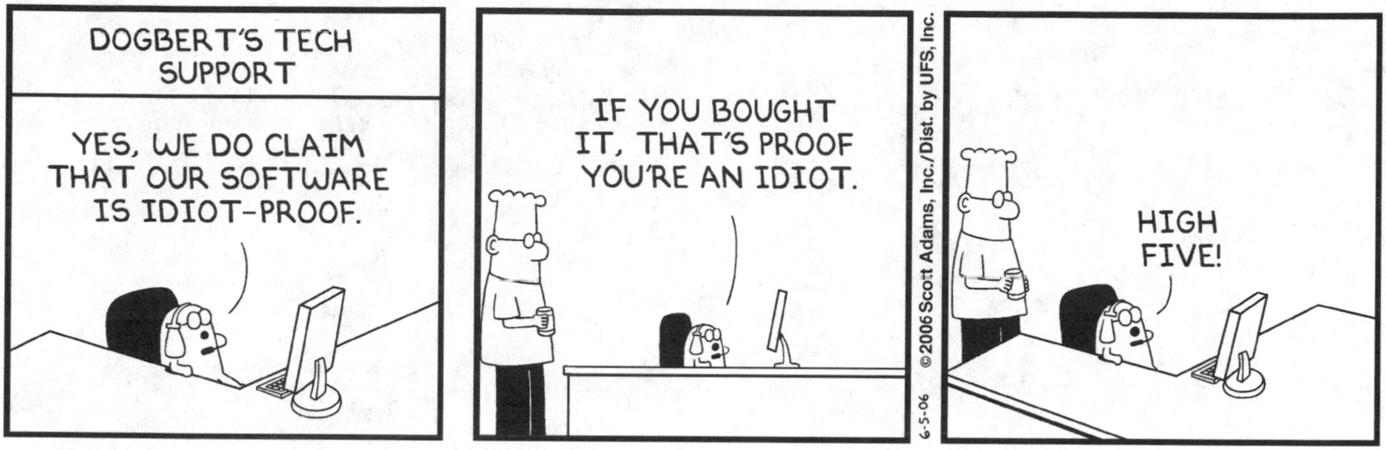
DOGBERT'S TECH SUPPORT
YES, WE DO CLAIM THAT OUR SOFTWARE IS IDIOT-PROOF.
IF YOU BOUGHT IT, THAT'S PROOF YOU'RE AN IDIOT.
HIGH FIVE!
6-5-06 © 2006 Scott Adams, Inc./Dist. by UFS, Inc.

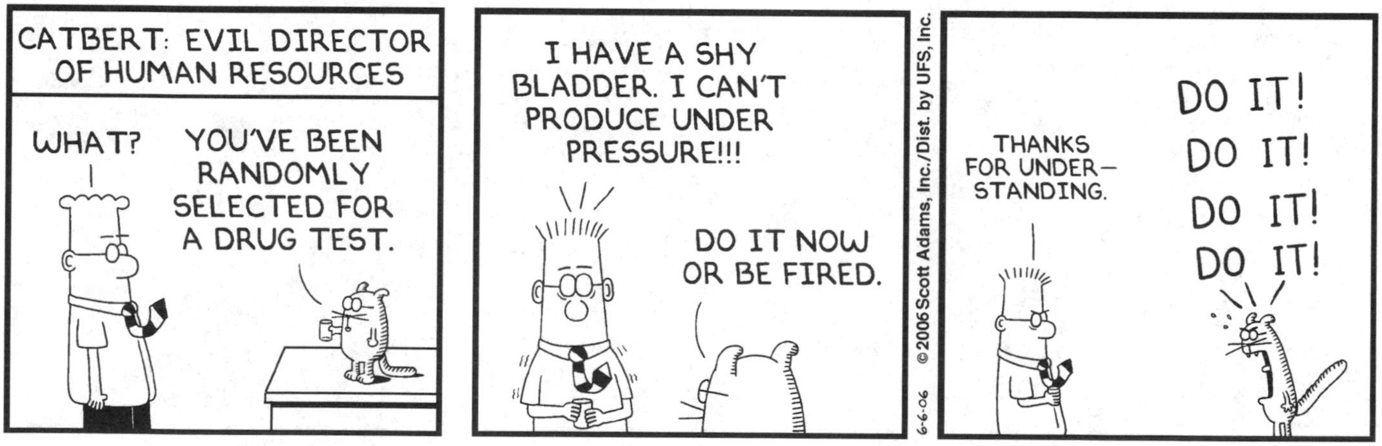
CATBERT: EVIL DIRECTOR OF HUMAN RESOURCES
WHAT?
YOU'VE BEEN RANDOMLY SELECTED FOR A DRUG TEST.
I HAVE A SHY BLADDER. I CAN'T PRODUCE UNDER PRESSURE!!!
DO IT NOW OR BE FIRED.
THANKS FOR UNDER-STANDING.
DO IT! DO IT! DO IT! DO IT!
6-6-06 © 2006 Scott Adams, Inc./Dist. by UFS, Inc.

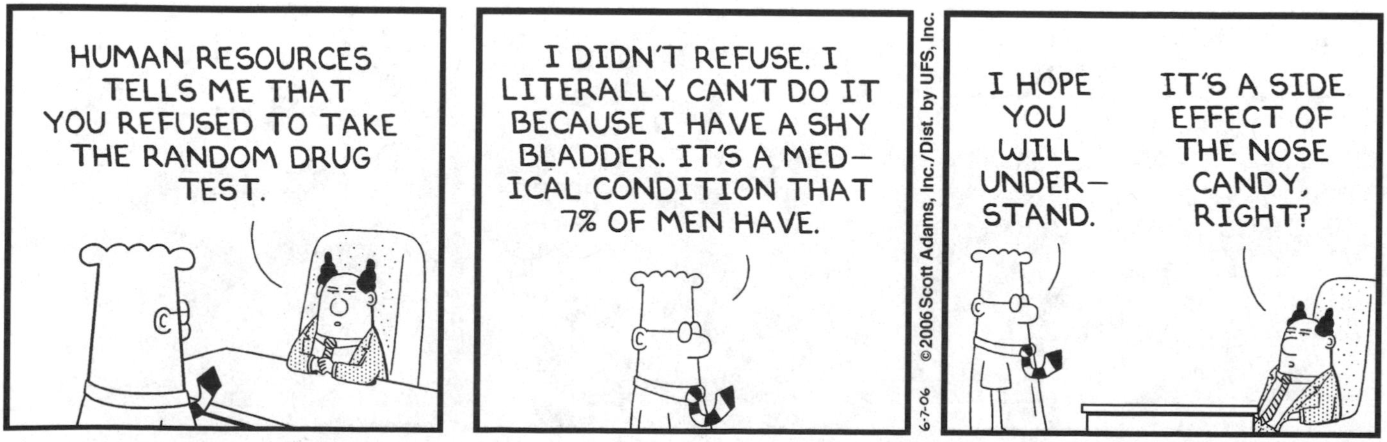
HUMAN RESOURCES TELLS ME THAT YOU REFUSED TO TAKE THE RANDOM DRUG TEST.
I DIDN'T REFUSE. I LITERALLY CAN'T DO IT BECAUSE I HAVE A SHY BLADDER. IT'S A MED-ICAL CONDITION THAT 7% OF MEN HAVE.
I HOPE YOU WILL UNDER-STAND.
IT'S A SIDE EFFECT OF THE NOSE CANDY, RIGHT?
6-7-06 © 2006 Scott Adams, Inc./Dist. by UFS, Inc.

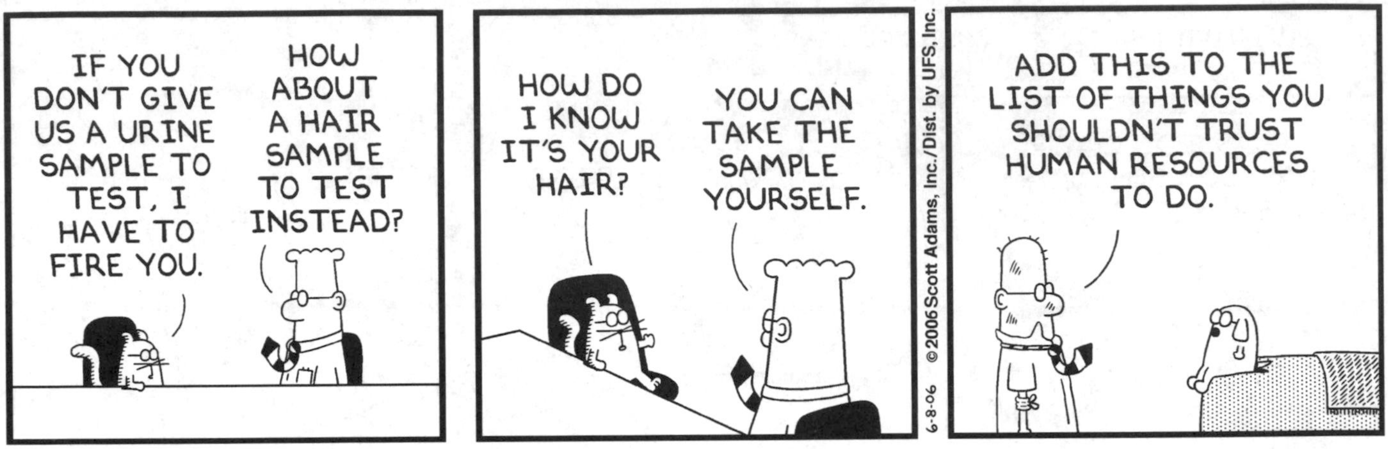
IF YOU DON'T GIVE US A URINE SAMPLE TO TEST, I HAVE TO FIRE YOU.
HOW ABOUT A HAIR SAMPLE TO TEST INSTEAD?
HOW DO I KNOW IT'S YOUR HAIR?
YOU CAN TAKE THE SAMPLE YOURSELF.
6-8-06 © 2006 Scott Adams, Inc./Dist. by UFS, Inc.
ADD THIS TO THE LIST OF THINGS YOU SHOULDN'T TRUST HUMAN RESOURCES TO DO.

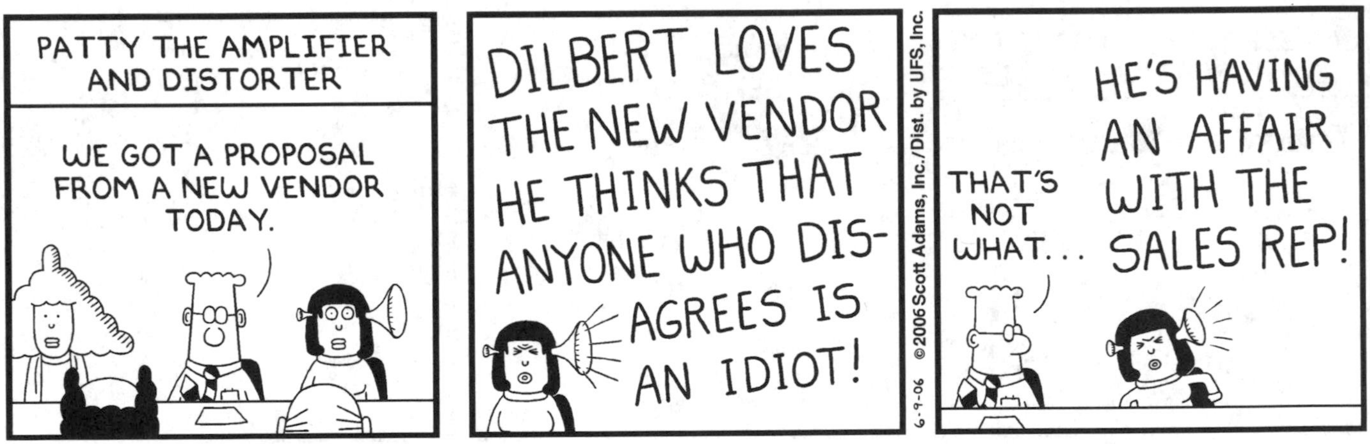
PATTY THE AMPLIFIER AND DISTORTER
WE GOT A PROPOSAL FROM A NEW VENDOR TODAY.
DILBERT LOVES THE NEW VENDOR HE THINKS THAT ANYONE WHO DIS-AGREES IS AN IDIOT!
6-9-06 © 2006 Scott Adams, Inc./Dist. by UFS, Inc.
THAT'S NOT WHAT...
HE'S HAVING AN AFFAIR WITH THE SALES REP!

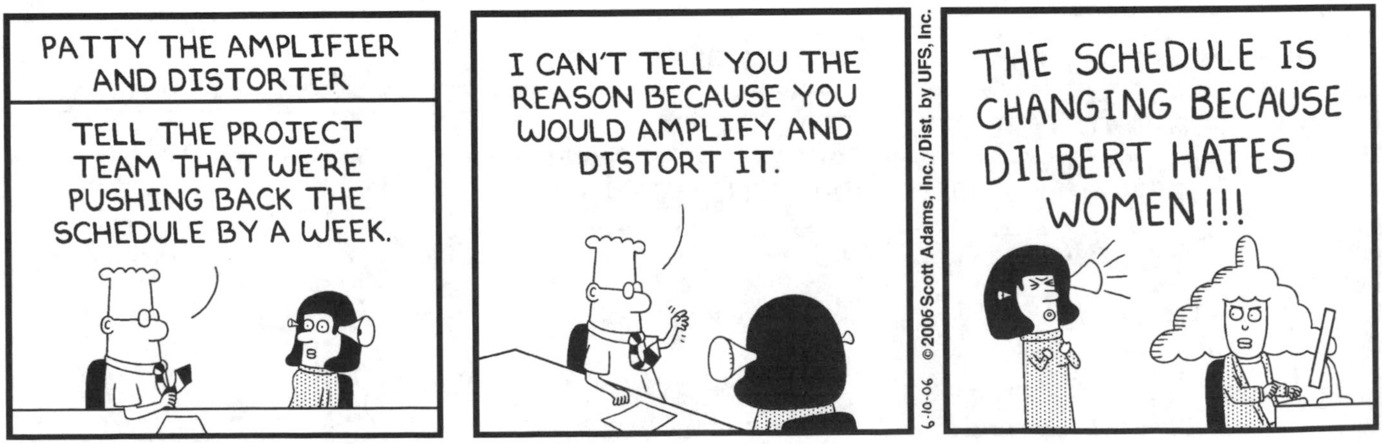
PATTY THE AMPLIFIER AND DISTORTER
TELL THE PROJECT TEAM THAT WE'RE PUSHING BACK THE SCHEDULE BY A WEEK.
I CAN'T TELL YOU THE REASON BECAUSE YOU WOULD AMPLIFY AND DISTORT IT.
6-10-06 © 2006 Scott Adams, Inc./Dist. by UFS, Inc.
THE SCHEDULE IS CHANGING BECAUSE DILBERT HATES WOMEN!!!

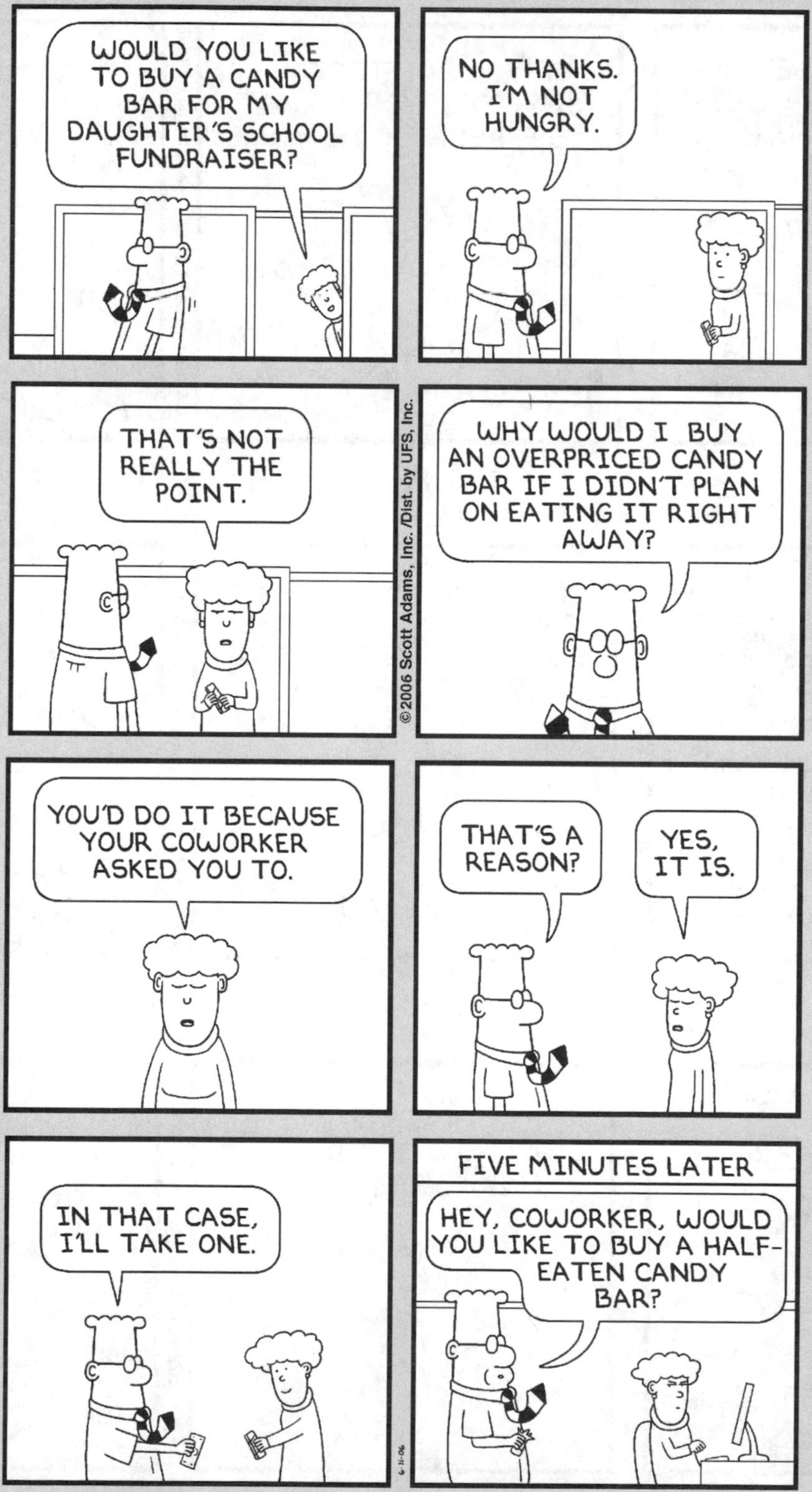
WOULD YOU LIKE TO BUY A CANDY BAR FOR MY DAUGHTER'S SCHOOL FUNDRAISER?
NO THANKS. I'M NOT HUNGRY.
THAT'S NOT REALLY THE POINT.
WHY WOULD I BUY AN OVERPRICED CANDY BAR IF I DIDN'T PLAN ON EATING IT RIGHT AWAY?
YOU'D DO IT BECAUSE YOUR COWORKER ASKED YOU TO.
THAT'S A REASON?
YES, IT IS.
IN THAT CASE, I'LL TAKE ONE.
FIVE MINUTES LATER
HEY, COWORKER, WOULD YOU LIKE TO BUY A HALF-EATEN CANDY BAR?
©2006 Scott Adams, Inc./Dist. by UFS, Inc.

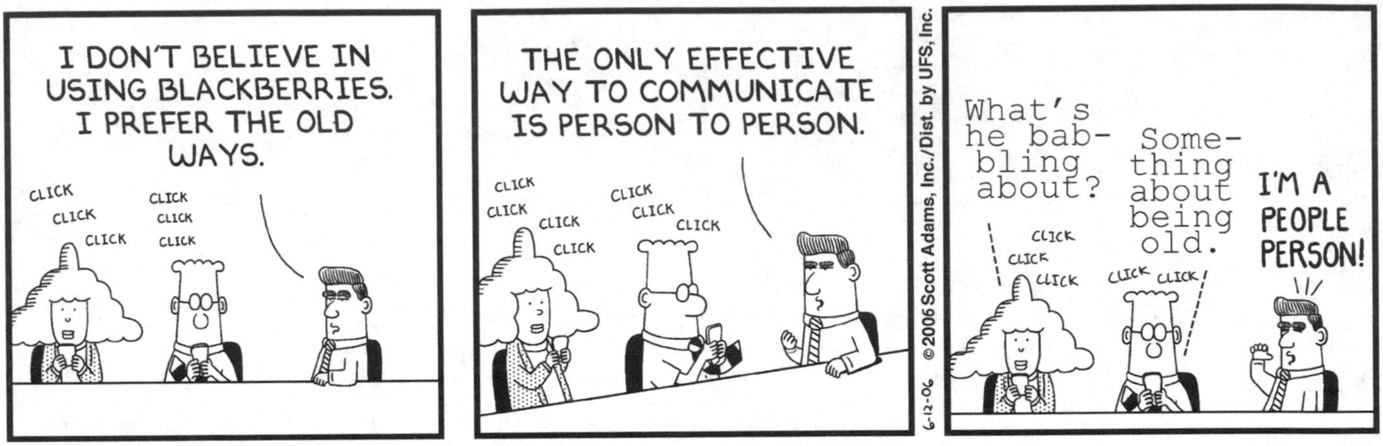
I DON'T BELIEVE IN USING BLACKBERRIES. I PREFER THE OLD WAYS.
CLICK CLICK CLICK
CLICK CLICK CLICK
THE ONLY EFFECTIVE WAY TO COMMUNICATE IS PERSON TO PERSON.
CLICK CLICK CLICK CLICK
CLICK CLICK CLICK
6-12-06 ©2006 Scott Adams, Inc./Dist. by UFS, Inc.
What's he babbling about?
Something about being old.
I'M A PEOPLE PERSON!
CLICK CLICK CLICK
CLICK CLICK

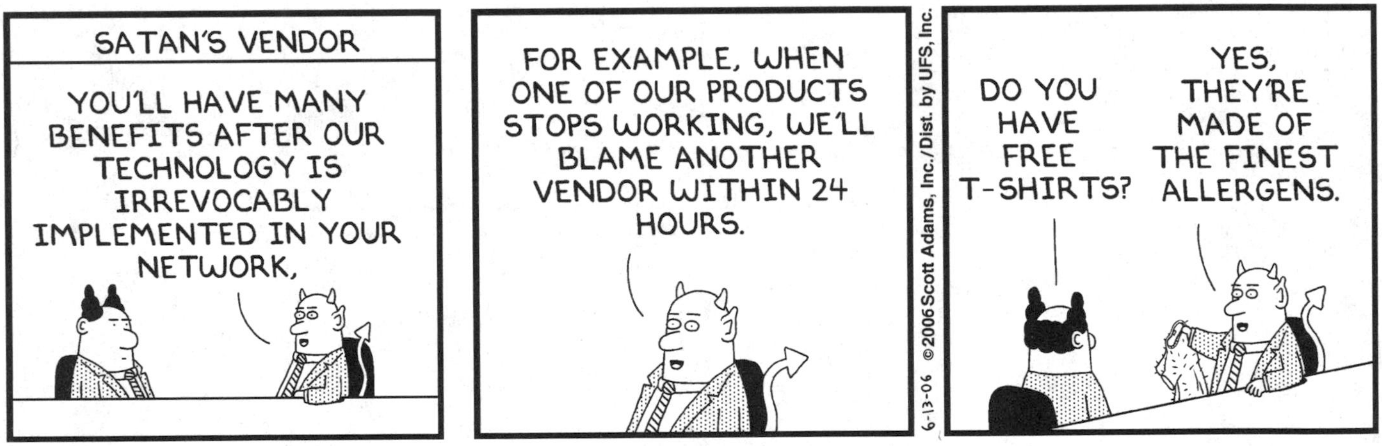
SATAN'S VENDOR
YOU'LL HAVE MANY BENEFITS AFTER OUR TECHNOLOGY IS IRREVOCABLY IMPLEMENTED IN YOUR NETWORK,
FOR EXAMPLE, WHEN ONE OF OUR PRODUCTS STOPS WORKING, WE'LL BLAME ANOTHER VENDOR WITHIN 24 HOURS.
6-13-06 ©2006 Scott Adams, Inc./Dist. by UFS, Inc.
DO YOU HAVE FREE T-SHIRTS?
YES, THEY'RE MADE OF THE FINEST ALLERGENS.

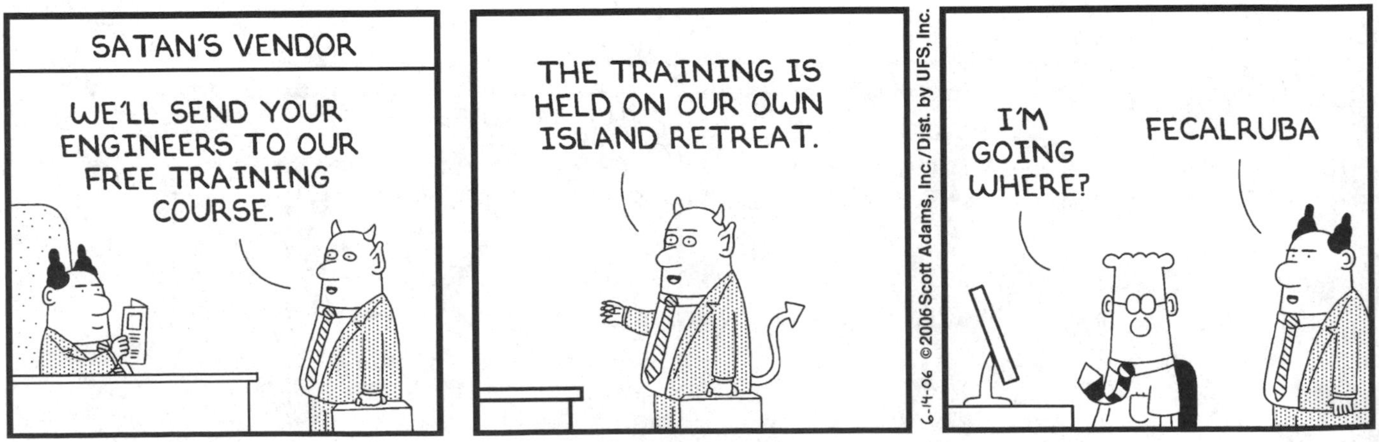
SATAN'S VENDOR
WE'LL SEND YOUR ENGINEERS TO OUR FREE TRAINING COURSE.
THE TRAINING IS HELD ON OUR OWN ISLAND RETREAT.
6-14-06 ©2006 Scott Adams, Inc./Dist. by UFS, Inc.
I'M GOING WHERE?
FECALRUBA

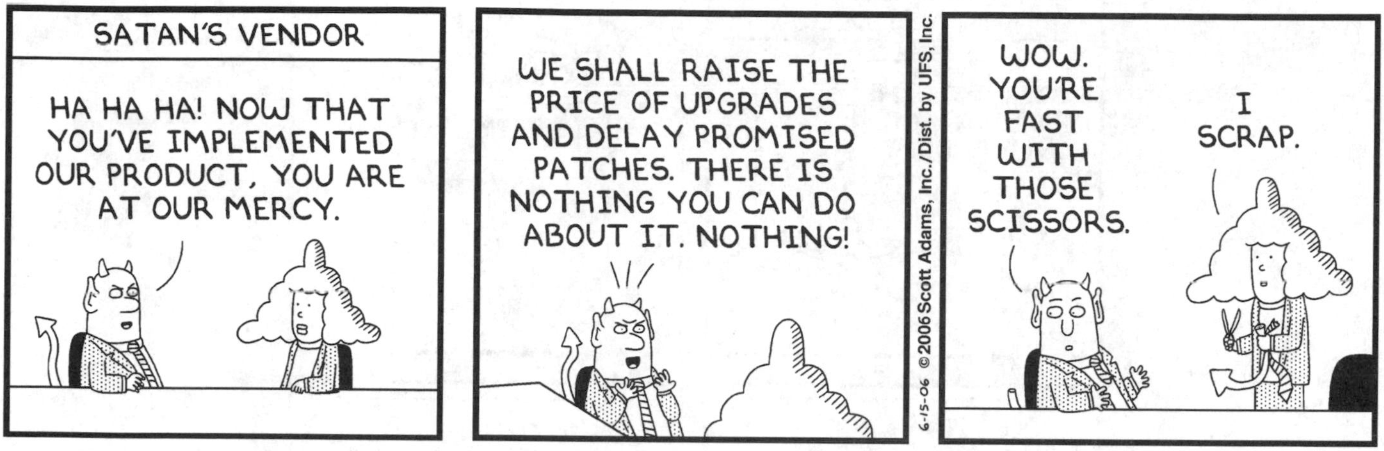
SATAN'S VENDOR
HA HA HA! NOW THAT YOU'VE IMPLEMENTED OUR PRODUCT, YOU ARE AT OUR MERCY.
WE SHALL RAISE THE PRICE OF UPGRADES AND DELAY PROMISED PATCHES. THERE IS NOTHING YOU CAN DO ABOUT IT. NOTHING!
6-15-06 © 2006 Scott Adams, Inc./Dist. by UFS, Inc.
WOW. YOU'RE FAST WITH THOSE SCISSORS.
I SCRAP.

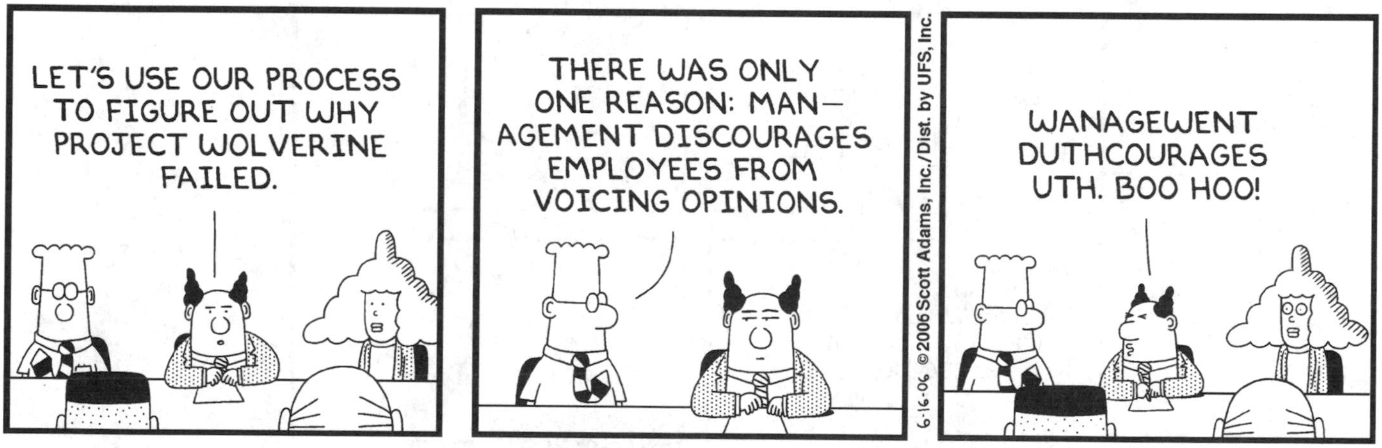
LET'S USE OUR PROCESS TO FIGURE OUT WHY PROJECT WOLVERINE FAILED.
THERE WAS ONLY ONE REASON: MAN-AGEMENT DISCOURAGES EMPLOYEES FROM VOICING OPINIONS.
6-16-06 © 2006 Scott Adams, Inc./Dist. by UFS, Inc.
WANAGEWENT DUTHCOURAGES UTH. BOO HOO!

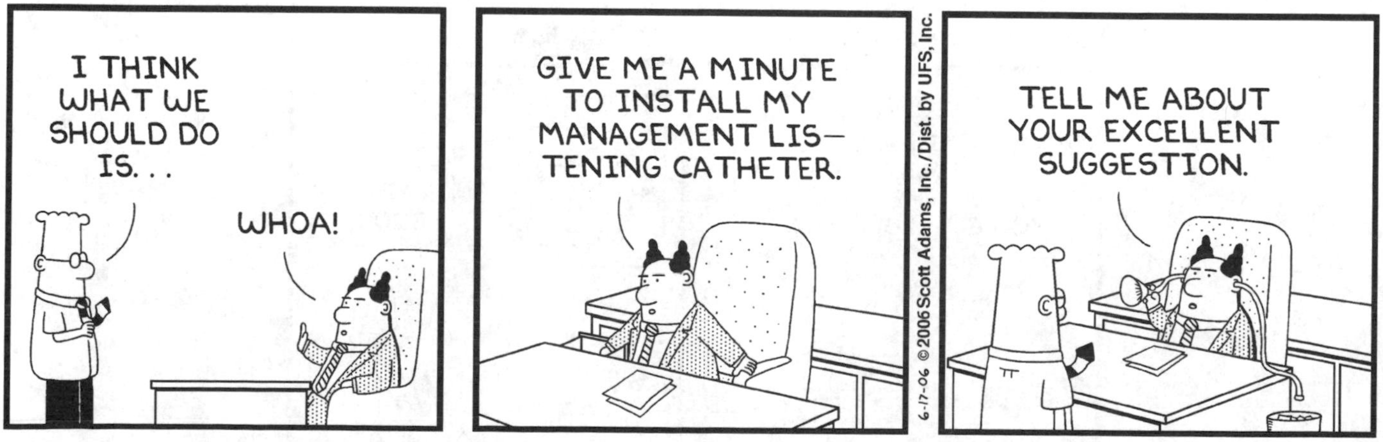
I THINK WHAT WE SHOULD DO IS. . .
WHOA!
GIVE ME A MINUTE TO INSTALL MY MANAGEMENT LIS-TENING CATHETER.
6-17-06 © 2006 Scott Adams, Inc./Dist. by UFS, Inc.
TELL ME ABOUT YOUR EXCELLENT SUGGESTION.

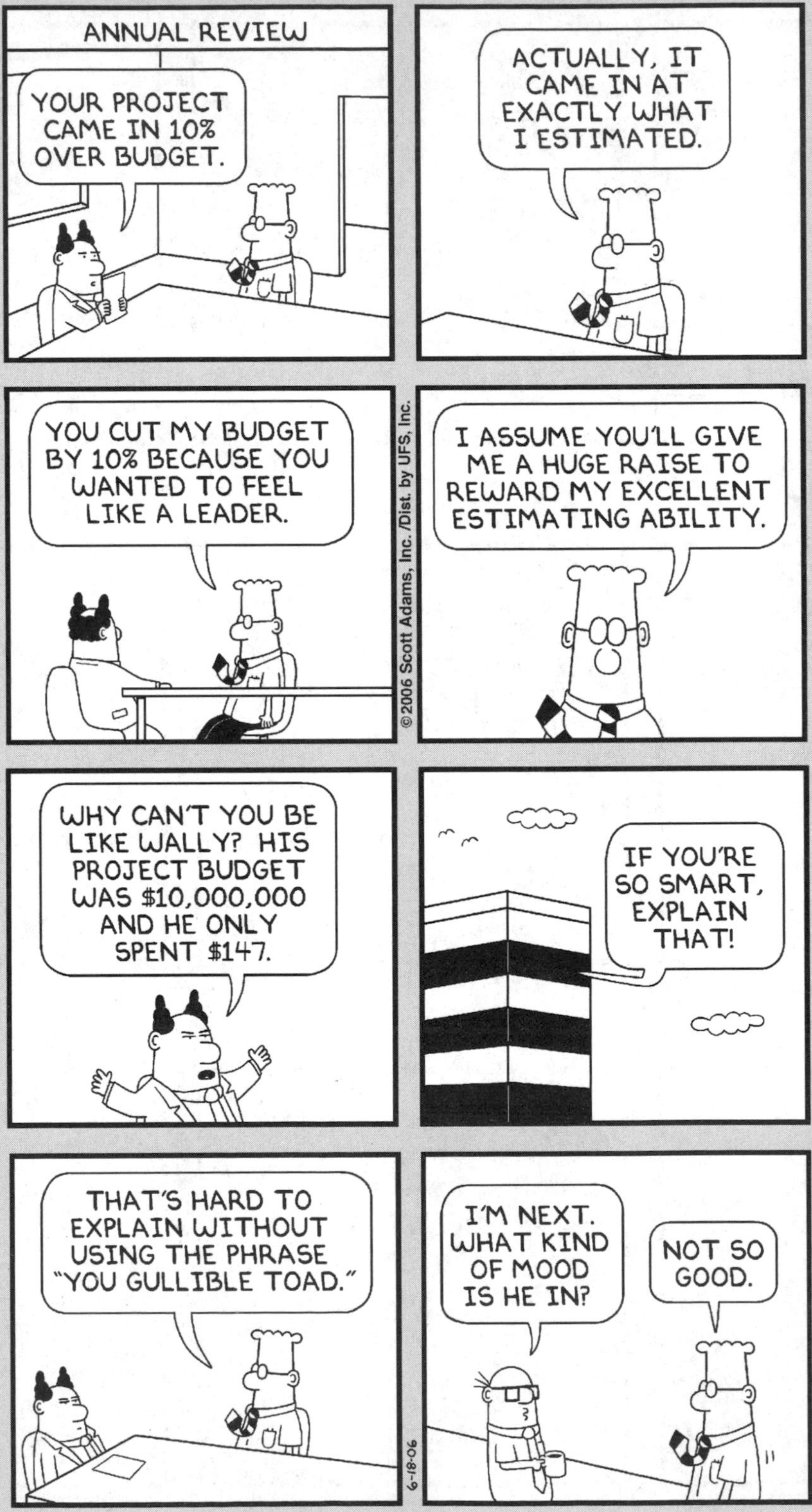
ANNUAL REVIEW
YOUR PROJECT CAME IN 10% OVER BUDGET.
ACTUALLY, IT CAME IN AT EXACTLY WHAT I ESTIMATED.
YOU CUT MY BUDGET BY 10% BECAUSE YOU WANTED TO FEEL LIKE A LEADER.
I ASSUME YOU'LL GIVE ME A HUGE RAISE TO REWARD MY EXCELLENT ESTIMATING ABILITY.
WHY CAN'T YOU BE LIKE WALLY? HIS PROJECT BUDGET WAS $10,000,000 AND HE ONLY SPENT $147.
IF YOU'RE SO SMART, EXPLAIN THAT!
THAT'S HARD TO EXPLAIN WITHOUT USING THE PHRASE "YOU GULLIBLE TOAD."
I'M NEXT. WHAT KIND OF MOOD IS HE IN?
NOT SO GOOD.
6-18-06

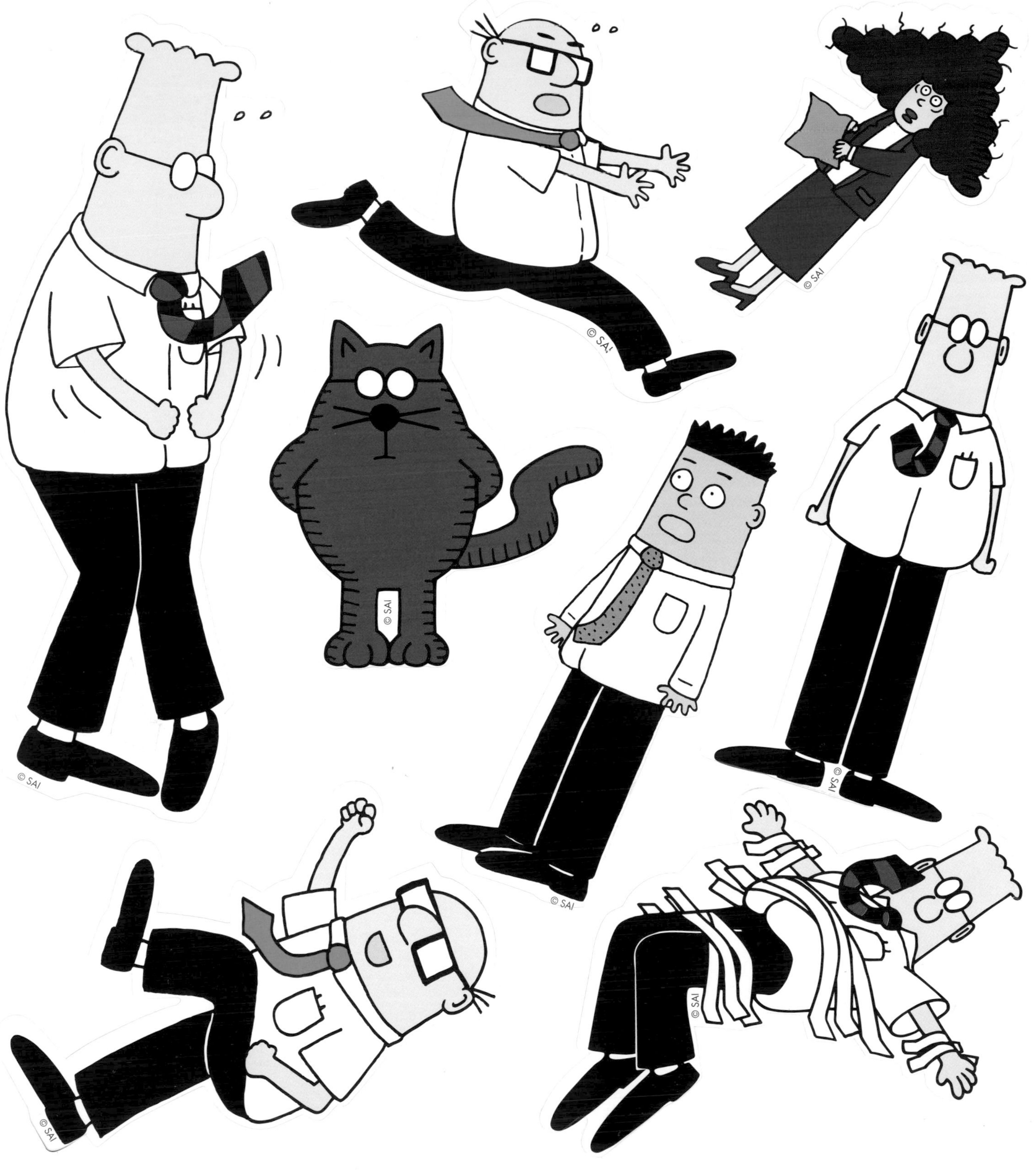
© SAI
© SAI
© SAI
© SAI
© SAI
© SAI
© SAI
© SAI
© SAI